Asian Voices in a Postcolonial Age

This innovative study of intellectuals and their cosmopolitan life trajectories is based on anthropological and historical research in Vietnam and India, two great Asian societies with contrasting experiences of empire, decolonisation and the rise and fall of the twentieth-century socialist world system. Building on the author's long-standing research experience in India and on remarkable family narratives collected in the course of fieldwork in northern Vietnam, the book deals with epic events and complex social transformations from a perspective that emphasises the personal, the intimate and the familial. Its central theme is the extraordinary mobility of intelligentsia lives; the author worked with women as well as men whose critical career experiences have included development work and study sojourns in a host of overseas lands including the former Soviet Union and many former French colonies in north and sub-Saharan Africa. The role of the intellectual in the economic, social and cultural tranformation of the postcolonial world has been widely acknowledged but rarely explored through in-depth ethnographic fieldwork methods. In identifying both parallels and contrasts between Hanoi's 'socialist moderns' and the family and career experiences of their Indian counterparts, the book makes a distinctive contribution to the study of colonial, socialist and post-socialist Asia.

SUSAN BAYLY is Reader in Historical Anthropology in the Department of Social Anthropology, Cambridge University, and a Fellow of Christ's College, Cambridge. From 2001 to 2004 she was Editor of the *Journal of the Royal Anthropological Institute* (formerly *Man*). Her previous publications include *Saints, Goddesses and Kings: Muslims and Christians in South Indian Society 1700–1900* (1989) and *Caste, Society and Politics in India from the Eighteenth Century to the Modern Age* (1999).

Asian Voices
in a Postcolonial Age
Vietnam, India and Beyond

Susan Bayly

CAMBRIDGE
UNIVERSITY PRESS

CAMBRIDGE UNIVERSITY PRESS
Cambridge, New York, Melbourne, Madrid, Cape Town, Singapore,
São Paulo, Delhi

Cambridge University Press
The Edinburgh Building, Cambridge CB2 8RU, UK

Published in the United States of America by Cambridge University Press,
New York

www.cambridge.org
Information on this title: www.cambridge.org/9780521868853

First published 2007

Printed in the United Kingdom at the University Press, Cambridge

A catalogue record for this publication is available from the British Library

ISBN 978-0-521-86885-3 hardback
ISBN 978-0-521-68894-9 paperback

Contents

Maps

Illustrations

All photographs are by the author unless otherwise noted.

Acknowledgements

I am conscious of the many debts of gratitude I have incurred in the writing of this book. First and foremost, I have benefited immensely from the friendship and support I have experienced as a member of the Cambridge University Department of Social Anthropology. Our department's commitment to anthropology's rich intellectual diversity is distinctive in numerous ways, not least in its openness to engagement with other disciplines. Having started my life as a social and cultural historian, I have found this receptive approach an especially rewarding feature of departmental life, and a consistent stimulus in my attempts to develop the comparative and interdisciplinary dimensions of my work.

Many individuals have generously found the time to read preliminary versions of my text, though of course I alone am responsible for its remaining deficiencies. For their invaluable suggestions and the wealth of anthropological insight they have shared with me, I am particularly grateful to Caroline Humphrey, James Laidlaw, Alan Macfarlane, Nikolai Ssorin-Chaikov and Marilyn Strathern. I also warmly thank Hildegard Diemberger, Harri Englund, Leo Howe, Magnus Marsden, Yael Navaro-Yashin, David Sneath, and Sian Lazar for their penetrating comments. I have profited too from many stimulating conversations with past and current Cambridge students, especially Jacob Copeman, Mark Maclean, Markus Schlecker, Soumhya Venkatesan and Maya Warrier, and from the constructive comments of graduate seminar audiences at Harvard, LSE, SOAS, Cambridge and the National University of Singapore, as well as those of three anonymous readers for Cambridge University Press.

Historians both within and beyond Cambridge have also contributed much to the shaping of this project. My thanks go especially to Sugata Bose, and also to Sunil Amrith, Christopher Goscha, Gordon Johnson, Tim Harper, Agathe Larcher-Goscha, Julie Pham, Peter Reeves and Anthony Reid. I also warmly thank my Hanoi-based friends and colleagues Kirsten Endres, Andrew Hardy, Natasha Pairaudeau and William Smith.

x   Acknowledgements

As a Fellow of Christ's College I have long benefited from interactions with lively scholars from many fields, among whom I must particularly mention my senior colleague Lucjan Lewitter. I am very appreciative too of all that David Reynolds has done in the role of sympathetic sounding board over many years. I thank Margaret Rigaud-Drayton for her patient help with my French and Mr Le Viet Hai and the college's other students from Hanoi for their tireless efforts to improve my Vietnamese. I am also grateful to the senior members of my department, together with the Master and Fellows of Christ's and also Professor Ludmilla Jordanova and the Cambridge University Centre for Research in the Arts, Social Sciences and Humanities for the hospitality they provided during visits to Cambridge by my friends and colleagues from the Hanoi social science community in 2004 and 2005. I also thank Peter Kornicki and Francesca Orsini for their help and support. My warm thanks too to Dr Katherine Prior; to Marigold Acland and Helen Waterhouse of Cambridge University Press; and to Su Ford, Jules Vines and Miranda Stock of my department for their highly professional research and technical support.

I gratefully acknowledge generous research and travel awards provided by the Cambridge University Evans Fund, the Cambridge University Travelling Expenses Fund, and the managers of the Christ's College George Kingsley Roth Fund and College Research Fund. A significant portion of this work draws on my research in India dating as far back as the 1970s. Space does not permit detailed acknowledgement of the many people who helped and supported me over all those years, but many of their names appear in my earlier writings and I retain an abiding sense of gratitude to them all.

As far as this book is concerned, my greatest debts are to the multitude of friends, scholars and officials in Vietnam whose many kindnesses made my Hanoi fieldwork both fruitful and unfailingly pleasurable. I warmly thank Dr Ha Huy Thanh and the Institute of Economics, National Centre for Social and Human Sciences of Vietnam, for assistance in securing my visas and for the privilege of affiliation to the Institute during my stays in Hanoi. I also greatly value my enduring association with the Department of Anthropology of the University of Social Sciences and Humanities, Vietnam National University; I warmly thank its Rector, staff and students for their enthusiasm for our shared goal of fostering links between our two academic communities.

I am deeply grateful to all the Hanoi people who welcomed me into their homes and generously shared their childhood and adult memories with me in the convivial company of their families, friends, students and co-workers. I can only hope that they find something of what they sought to convey to me reflected in this work. Among individuals whose help made a critical difference to my research I particularly wish to express my affectionate esteem and most sincere thanks to Dr Truong Huyen Chi, together with Professor Nguyen Van Huy and the staff of the Vietnam Museum of Ethnology, and also Ms Vu Hai Ha and the many other Hanoi scholars who have been generous supporters of this project. I also warmly thank the following distinguished artists for permitting me to reproduce their works: Mrs Vu Giang Huong, Mr Van Tho and Mr Le Minh Chau. I also thank the British Museum, London, and Dr Pham Quoc Quan, Director of the National Museum of Vietnamese History.

As always, my husband Christopher Bayly has sharpened my thinking, enlivened my spirits and sustained my morale at every stage; without his unflagging support and inspiring scholarly example, this work would never have been brought to fruition.

Among my Vietnamese friends, one in particular merits special mention. I am far from alone in my admiration for the boundless energy and matchless erudition of Professor Dang Phong of the Institute of Economics, Academy of Social Sciences of Vietnam. Without his generosity, advice and enthusiasm, my attempts to learn about the past and present lives of Hanoi intellectuals would have come to nothing. It is to him with the utmost respect and gratitude that I dedicate this book.

1 Introduction

Themes and approaches

This book deals with the tumultuous life experiences of Asians whose lives were shaped by the death throes of the great European-ruled colonial systems, and by the making and unmaking of socialism in its various distinctive Asian forms. Its central focus is Vietnam, a country in which the legacies of colonialism and socialism have played out in ways that challenge many current understandings of postcoloniality and the moral and social ambiguities of 'late' or post-socialist societies.

A great deal of this current scholarship uses the Indian subcontinent as the central point of reference in discussions of the psychic and social afterlife of empire, especially in the case of the many educated Asians who identified themselves with nationalist as well as socialist forms of emancipatory modernism. But while the book builds in part on my past research on pre- and post-independence India, its main concern is with lives that offer comparisons and contrasts with those of India's colonial and socialist moderns. In focusing on Vietnam, and more specifically on the distinctively cosmopolitan world of Hanoi's intelligentsia families, its concerns reflect my continuing interest in the comparative study of colonialism and its legacies both within and beyond French- and British-ruled Asia.

As an anthropologist originally trained in history, I have combined the approaches of both fields in this study. Its textual sources include a diverse array of documentary and pictorial materials. Among them are personal letters and photographs belonging to the families with whom I have done fieldwork, as well as propaganda posters and other official texts, and such items as schoolchildren's drawings and lesson books dating back to the days of Vietnam's liberation wars against France and the USA. I also build on previous work using materials such as official records and newspapers from a variety of archival collections in Vietnam, India, Britain and France.

At the book's core, however, is the ethnographic fieldwork I have been conducting over the last five years in Vietnam, working primarily with multilingual men and women who have negotiated a remarkable array of divergent socialist and postcolonial modernities over the past forty to fifty years. My first stay in Hanoi was in the winter of 2000, though I had previously spent time visiting historical and religious sites in Ho Chi Minh City (former Saigon) and the Mekong Delta. Even in that early visit to the south, I found in Vietnam a host of compelling and sometimes perplexing parallels and contrasts with the regions of India in which I had previously worked. Arriving in Ho Chi Minh City for the first time on Christmas Eve 1998, I had a foretaste of the exuberant conviviality and eclectically 'globalised' consumer tastes which also mark present-day urban life in north Vietnam. In the city centre, the streets were thronged with young people on motorbikes shouting 'Merry Christmas' to everyone in sight. Virtually everyone – teenagers as well as parents and their small children – sported a tasselled Father Christmas (Santa Claus) hat. Many women wore these with the tunic and trouser outfit known as the *ao dai*, in past decades a dress style condemned by the Communist authorities as decadent and unproletarian, but very much in fashion in the new age of so-called 'market socialism'.

Over the next few weeks I visited such places as Ho Chi Minh City's Revolution Museum, which was situated next door to a newly opened Toyota car dealership, and a short walk away from the city's recently renovated colonial hotels and elegant shopping boulevards. Some of these were once again being referred to by the French names used in the days of empire. A case in point was the former Rue Catinat, named in memory of the French warship that initiated the colonial occupation of Indochina by bombarding the port of Danang in 1856. Once hailed as Saigon's Champs Elysée, Rue Catinat was renamed Tu Do ('Liberty') after independence in 1954, and Dong Khoi ('Uprising') following reunification with the Communist north in 1976. At the time of my visit it was once again a street of cafés and smart shops with names like Catinat Fashion selling international brand-name goods, together with silk *ao dais* and other luxury items designed for the city's growing mass tourism and expatriate business community markets.

It was striking too that there was active worship honouring ancient heroes, sages and family ancestors in the pagodas and spirit temples. There were also public rites at Tay Ninh, the Holy See of the Cao Dai religion, with its exaltation of the prophetic spirits of Joan of Arc and Victor Hugo. Cao Daiists also honour the classical sage Confucius, together with a sixteenth-century poet now revered as an early prophet of Vietnamese nationhood, and the Chinese nationalist leader Sun Yat Sen (1866–1925) (Bayly 2004b). As I explored these sites, I found myself wondering just how many pasts local people felt they were living with in present-day Vietnam. I wondered too how far their definitions of past and present epochs resembled or contrasted with those shaping Indians' diverse and often hotly contested perceptions of their personal and national histories.

Contrasting intelligentsia worlds: Vietnam and India

Of course anyone doing research in India over the past thirty years will have strong memories of the many ways in which the phenomenon of ethnocommunitarian discord has pervaded public life. This has given rise to contending visions of 'communalism' in the form of Hindu–Muslim conflict as the dominant historical narrative of Indian life and history over many centuries. But during and since that first stay in Vietnam, what I recalled just as vividly from my earliest Indian fieldwork in the 1970s was the ferocity of public debate about the rise of regionally based peasant populist movements. Their prevailing vision was of an India long dominated by 'feudal' elites, and their key rallying cry the call for radical new forms of redistributive justice for the rural 'masses' and other non-elite and deprived groups. These movements were widely characterised as a serious challenge to the high-minded developmental modernism which had long been associated with the still dominant political legacy of Jawaharlal Nehru, one of the leaders of the Indian National Congress which had spearheaded India's anti-colonial 'freedom struggle'.[1]

From the vantage point of the 1970s, Vietnam and India were 'friends' at the diplomatic level and spoke a common language of global anti-imperialism and solidarity with other 'progressive' states including the USSR. As Prime Minister from 1966 to 1977, Nehru's daughter Indira Gandhi had pledged support for socialist North Vietnam's war against the USA and its client regime to the south, the RVN (Republic of Vietnam).[2] Yet in other crucial ways, the two countries appeared to be

---

[1] For an overview of the literature on these topics, see Rudolph and Rudolph 1987; Brass 1990; Brass 1995; Bose and Jalal 1998.

[2] Here, too, the naming of public spaces told a fascinating story. When I first went to Hanoi in 2000, one of the landscaped public garden spaces facing the city-centre lake and ancient island pagoda, which are the capital's most famous landmarks, was known as Indira Gandhi Park, a name honouring the former Indian Prime Minister as an anti-imperialist 'friend' of Vietnam (Logan 1995: 453). In 2005, the garden received a lavish facelift and was reopened under a new name, that of the eleventh-century Vietnamese ruler Ly Thai To, whose giant statue now adorns the park (see Plates 1 and 2). This semi-legendary dynast is now revered as a protonationalist visionary who chose the riverine site of modern Hanoi as his royal capital, thereby paving the way for the commercial take-off which launched the nation on its path to prosperity and 'development'. Among key works on *doi moi* (partial marketisation, usually translated as 'renovation' or 'renewal') in

worlds apart. North Vietnam (the Democratic Republic of Vietnam, or DRV) was a one-party Communist state. Its leaders had fought a revolutionary war against Indochina's former colonial rulers, and then established their authority over the entire country through military victory against the USA and the RVN in 1975. India was a much larger and richer 'non-aligned' power which, despite its warm diplomatic ties to the Soviet Union and other COMECON states, was still committed to multi-party electoral democracy and was soon to embrace liberalising reforms of its 'soft socialist' economic regimen.[3]

So at first glance, these were two postcolonial countries which had taken dramatically divergent paths in the aftermath of empire and in the processes of political partitioning which each had undergone so traumatically. Yet there was a common thread, that of the socialist ideals espoused officially by Vietnam, and also long championed by a high proportion of India's modernist intellectuals. These included the anglophone academics, scientists, development planners and other educated individuals whom I had come to know in the course of my research in the subcontinent from the 1970s to the 1990s.

Such people were precisely those whose leftist cosmopolitanism and patrician lifestyles had come to be widely reviled as élitist and un-Indian by those peasant populists of the 1970s, and latterly by their many successors. The most notable of these more recent anti-'Nehruvians' were the champions of so-called Hindutva or 'Hinduness' who came to prominence in the 1980s and are still a critical force in contemporary Indian life. The Hindutva ideologues have propounded visions of Indian nationhood that are apparently much at odds with the secular Nehru tradition, always strongly associated with opposition to the 'passions' and destructive 'irrationalities' of so-called communalism in its many different forms and manifestations.[4] Although there are many divergent strands in the Hindutva cause, most versions of the 'Hinduness' ideal represent India's past as an enduring struggle between the forces of native faith-based culture and its supposed enemies, Muslim as well as 'secular'.

Everyone I knew in India, including the people with whom I did my fieldwork, and the academics and other university-trained individuals

---

Vietnam see de Vylder and Fforde 1996. On planning and building schemes in Hanoi, see Logan 2000; Thomas 2001; 2003; Waibel 2004.

[3] The Soviet-dominated economic community known as COMECON (the Council for Mutual Economic Assistance) was founded in 1949 as an association of Eastern Europe's Communist states. Mongolia became a member in 1962, Cuba in 1972 and Vietnam in 1978; the organisation was disbanded in 1991.

[4] Madan 1987; Jaffrelot 1998; Hansen 2001.

who befriended me in the course of my research trips, had much to say about these debates over the meaning of the nation's history, and the lessons that should be taught and learned from its ancient and modern pasts. There was one thing about people's engagement with this rethinking of national narratives that I found particularly striking if not altogether surprising. This was that many of the educated people I came to know over a period of twenty years or more had come to question or actively repudiate the Nehruvian 'idea of India' (Khilnani 1997) which had once been so central to their understanding of the lives that they and their forebears had led in the pre- and post-independence periods.

There was a strong personal dimension to this rethinking. By the late 1980s and 90s, what many of my educated Indian friends said they wanted for their children in such matters as marriage, education and career choice no longer had much in common with the ethos of public service and austere secular modernism that I recalled from their professed views and values of the 1970s. I knew people who had once been proudly 'secular' expressing passionate regret that a son or daughter had married a spouse of 'alien' faith. Other friends had discouraged their children from following their paths into public service employment. Some said aloud things that would have been unsayable in 'enlightened' company fifteen or twenty years earlier: the nation's history was full of wrong turnings and opportunities wasted; university careers were futile and unrewarding because 'redistributive justice' policies, once hailed as a righting of historic wrongs suffered by the disadvantaged, especially the ex-'untouchables' or Dalits, gave promotions and plum appointments to the 'unworthy' and unqualified.

Socialism in the 'postcolony'

This shift to very different narrative accounts of personal and public pasts was much in my mind as I began my work in Vietnam. And what I was beginning to learn as far back as 1998 was that Vietnam is also a country in which contending historical narratives have become a prominent and sometimes painful feature of national life. In ways that are strikingly reminiscent of India's encounters with multiple accounts of its national history, Vietnam's people are now dealing with at least three distinct though interacting pasts: that of its colonial experience; that of its revolutionary socialist life in the years of its two resistance wars and their turbulent aftermath; and that of its more recent past of reformist 'market socialism'.

This certainly invites comparison with what I recalled about the multiple pasts with which my educated Indian friends have been contending since the 1970s. Again, what came to mind particularly were the intellectuals I had originally known as champions of Nehruvian 'soft socialism'. These were the people who had rethought their views of the Indian past as a triumphal progress towards national unity, with a common goal of achieving enlightened modernity in the form of equality for all citizens, and a state-regulated market with global capitalism held at bay. As I have already suggested, by the early 1990s many of the educated Indians I knew had embraced new narratives in which a muted but still actively anti-market ethos no longer held pride of place.

As a child of the Cold War, I had been brought up in an environment in which Europe's non-revolutionary forms of socialism were both admired and vilified, while its Chinese, Soviet and other Communist variants were routinely demonised as embodiments of state terror and gulag-based totalitarianism. So I was initially startled when I first met Indian intellectuals for whom the Soviet Union was a 'friend' and role model, much admired in the 1970s as a bastion of staunch Third Worldism and progressive social ideals at home and abroad. What I soon came to realise was that a high proportion of the educated Indians I knew valued the Western-style constitutionalism which made their country very different from the USSR and other Communist states. Yet they also clearly valued the fact that through the language of socialism, with its diverse but distinctive idioms and moral claims, they could speak so readily and on such a strong basis of professed equality with their counterparts in a host of other lands.[5]

As fellow users of those idioms and reference points, either they themselves, or the politicians and statesmen who represented their nation abroad, could present themselves to their fellow Asians, and to Africans, Russians and other COMECON citizens as well as leftists from the capitalist West, as co-participants in a world of common aims and virtues. In this study I use the term socialist ecumene to describe this arena of personal and official contacts, interactions and 'imaginings'. It is a usage which I take more from the work of the Sanskritist Sheldon Pollock on the 'vernacularised cosmopolitanism' of ancient south and south-east Asia than from the ideas of a strictly 'late capitalist' worldwide ecumene proposed by contemporary globalisation theorists (Pollock 1998; see also Humphrey 2004).

---

[5] Khilnani 1997; Zachariah 2005. On past and current interpretations of the Indian national past, see Bose 2003.

These are issues which I discuss in more detail below, building on the perspectives of scholars such as Frederick Cooper, whose studies of 'imperial state-making and un-making' (2005: 154) point insightfully to the many forms of mobility and interaction – pilgrimage circuits, trade routes, migrant labour networks, supralocal and transcontinental information flows, professional career trajectories and merchant diasporas – both defining and constraining political and cultural life in a host of rigorously contextualised sites and settings for which loosely teleological notions of globalisation lack precision and purchase. My thinking in this area has also been shaped by Sugata Bose's nuanced account of the Indian Ocean as a cultural ecumene of 'multiple and competing universalisms' (2006: 270). My particular concern is with the distinctively mobile lives led by students, scientists, medics and other 'moderns' from Asia's so-called postcolonies. I see such people's often very testing experiences of cosmopolitan family and career life as central to the processes which sustained and represented much of what I have in mind in my use of the term socialist ecumene.

The forms of circulation and displacement experienced by large numbers of these educated Asians involved children as well as adults. I hope to demonstrate that the emotional and intellectual lives of the young require particular emphasis in any account that seeks to engage in depth with the world of 'socialist moderns' under colonial rule and in postcolonial settings. And what I want to suggest about the Indian intellectuals I knew in the 1970s and 80s is that as they travelled or projected themselves imaginatively within that worldwide socialist ecumene, they found the use of socialism's idioms and reference points both gratifying and instrumentally valuable. In deploying them, they were able to represent themselves to the people of more 'backward' lands, as well as those of apparently more 'advanced' societies, as 'friends' and fellow anti-imperialists. They could thereby claim to be on an equal footing with all other participants in the great moral projects of socialist life and thought, and thus resist being seen as the relatively advantaged citizens of a still poor or 'developing' ex-colony.[6] I was to find something very similar in the course of my Vietnam fieldwork, when Hanoi people told me about the pleasure they had taken in having been able to forge personal friendships with the Russians, Poles and other

---

[6] Compare Dirlik 1994: 339–40. For an account of the mobile lives led by Muslim intelligentsia world travellers from the French-ruled colonial societies of north Africa, see Bayly 2002.

foreign scientists and 'development' experts they had worked with in such settings as Algeria, Madagascar and Mozambique.

I do recognise that Asia's educated 'moderns' have engaged with a whole host of divergent socialisms rather than a single homogeneous tradition or power structure, and that they have done so as critics as well as admirers of those systems and ideals. Indeed one of the book's key concerns is to show that in that world of harmonious and fraught interactions which I refer to as the socialist ecumene, what these transnational travellers encountered was actually a very broad spectrum of political and cultural modes ranging from those of the two big revolutionary superpowers and their regional neighbours to the vernacularised developmentalisms of Nyerere's Tanzania, Nehru's India and Sukarno's Indonesia.

None of these were self-contained isolates; all interacted, and all presented contrasting visions of socialism's traditions and neo-traditions, thereby offering significant numbers of people the possibility of both actual and imaginative movement across a terrain comprising many more points of reference than those of a single 'postcolony' and its former metropole. Thus for the younger Indians I knew twenty or thirty years ago, professing admiration for the peasant-based radicalism represented by Mao's China and India's rural Naxalite insurgents entailed a repudiation of the 'soft' Nehruvian socialism of their elders. And, of course, even in the 1970s and early 80s there were many educated south Asians for whom all variants of socialism were anathema. Vietnam too has engaged with radically different socialist traditions before and since independence.[7] As I explain in later chapters, steering a difficult middle course between Vietnam's Soviet and Chinese 'friends' was a process that bore very directly on the personal and professional experiences of the Hanoi intellectuals with whom I worked. For some, even the legacy of France's non-Marxist socialist thinkers and activists left distinctive traces in the views they brought to bear on the great changes taking place in their personal lives, and that of the nation.

Furthermore, within as well as beyond the former Asian 'postcolonies', socialism has been much more than an evocative and empowering language, though its discursive qualities have certainly been one of its most enduring and significant features. And for all its diversity, as well as the many challenges to socialist ideas and values emanating from many sources, some inside the officially socialist nation-states,

---

[7] Among key works on this topic see Turner 1975; Pike 1978; Marr 1981; Hue Tam Ho Tai 1992; Duiker 1996; Giebel 2004.

there have been real commonalities at the level of 'imagining' and historic experience for an extremely large number of people around the world. This is why I feel it is legitimate to refer to socialism as a body of shared, supralocal reference points and distinctive claims about the world, made and referred to not only by officials and politicians, but by ordinary citizens. And I see the often strongly articulated language of affect in which socialist ideals have been so consistently expressed as a striking and significant feature of the world in which such citizens led their lives, both at home and further afield.

This notion of socialism as a set of broadly inclusive moral, emotional and even aesthetic dispositions is central to the perspective I adopt in this book. I see it as crucial to my exploration of the lives led by people of intelligentsia background, particularly when they travelled either literally or imaginatively beyond their homelands. I emphasise yet again the importance of their experiences of actual and imagined movement through spaces made productive and morally meaningful in their eyes through these acts of purposeful circulation and sojourning among the near and distant sites and settings of the socialist ecumene. What I seek to show in later chapters is that this is something which has interacted in complex and far-reaching ways with the divergent legacies of colonialism. These legacies are too often treated as the only important force at work in the shaping of intelligentsia minds and epistemes in former colonial societies, and one of the key aims of this book is to call attention to the limitations of such assumptions.[8]

I am certainly not suggesting that the educated Hanoi people I know possess an uncritical allegiance to any of the many variants of Marxist analytical or political thought. Nor am I suggesting that they would all call themselves socialists today, rather than patriots, 'moderns' and/or thoughtful and ideologically uncommitted makers of a new, post-modern world. But what I am proposing is that there is a host of moral and emotional as well as intellectual dispositions which have defined and animated the very broad sphere of operations which I am calling the worldwide socialist ecumene. Its contours have been eroded but not expunged by the demise of official state socialism in the USSR and Eastern Europe, together with the embrace of 'market socialism' in China and Vietnam, and the 'liberalisation' of economic life in much of Africa and South America as well as India. It is certainly alive in the

---

[8] Aijaz Ahmad (1995) and Arif Dirlik (1994) have been powerful contributors to debate on these issues.

memories and personal narratives of the people with whom I have worked in Vietnam.

As I show in later chapters, many key traditions and 'neo-traditions' of the socialist ecumene have recently been given new life in official accounts of Vietnam's long-standing moral legacy as a high-minded participant in worthwhile international exchanges of knowledge and modernising expertise.[9] I also seek to show that it greatly enhances our understanding of past and contemporary life and thought in the sub-continent to recognise the extent to which India's intelligentsia world has been shaped by the moral and cultural interactions of that same global socialist ecumene.

What I found in the course of my fieldwork is that within that supralocal arena of diplomatic, personal and intellectual contacts, socialism has existed as something animating and also transcending the meanings that have been attached to the term for the peoples who have lived within the terrain of any one individual socialist state. I have in mind here the meanings given to the word socialism by its admirers and vilifiers during and since the Cold War. I do recognise that for many people around the world, socialism registers above all as a fearful project to regulate, coerce or override individual will and identity, nourished by a determination to expunge cherished traditions of faith, community and nationhood in the name of progress and people's justice. Yet it is important and illuminating to see socialism as something which many self-avowed Asian 'moderns' have regarded as more than – or not only – the problematic cultural initiatives, planning regimens and allocation arrangements which have been studied as critical features of life within individual socialist states.[10]

---

[9] For the notion of socialist tradition and neo-tradition I am indebted to Harry West: my use of the term focuses on the exaltation of revolutionary ideals and other key elements of socialist life and thought as a distinctive moral tradition still relevant to contemporary 'late socialist' or even 'post-socialist' conditions, rather than the idea of pre-socialist values or reference points enduring within or beneath the officially defined modernities of the socialist states and societies. See Chapters 8 and 9, below.

[10] Fitzpatrick 1992; Verdery 1996. This is not meant as a criticism of those who have done so much to document and theorise socialist life within individual countries. On the contrary: I am greatly indebted to the works of leading figures in the study of socialism, notably C. Humphrey, K. Verdery, S. Fitzpatrick, R. Mandel, C. Hann, D. Kandiyoti, S. Smith, R. Mitter, E. Perry and N. Ssorin-Chaikov. I have also been much influenced by ethnographers of socialist life in non-European societies, especially Donald Donham (1999) whose use of interdisciplinary methods to explore Ethiopians' engagement with the experience and aftermath of socialist revolution has been of great importance to my work. I have also learned much from the writings of Vietnam specialists including Hue Tam Ho Tai, Dang Phong, K. Taylor, P. Taylor, H. Kwon, D. Hémery, P. Brocheux, M. Beresford, D. Marr, C. Thayer, Hy Van Luong,

Turning again to the academics and other educated people who befriended me in my early years in India, socialism was widely spoken of as an inspiring moral project harmonising with and yet transcending the specificities of national identity. For some, this meant above all a cultural and political orientation against what were often spoken of as American views and values. This played out in practice as a widely shared assumption that US geopolitical strategies were immoral and 'imperialist'. It also entailed something I recall very vividly from my first stays in India: a taste for certain forms of distinctly puritanical austerity. This rather uneasily combined a taste for the 'modern' with a pronounced aversion to a wide range of things, ideas and pursuits that could be simultaneously labelled vulgar, un-Indian and American in character or inspiration.

For the academics and other intellectuals I knew in India's major metropolitan centres, that is in Calcutta, Madras, Bombay and Delhi, and also to some degree in the smaller regional centres where I did my research including Bangalore, Trivandrum and Tuticorin, obtaining a first-rate 'modern' education for one's children was a universal goal. This included the expectation that they would be confidently anglophone. Their schools were also expected to confer mastery of the humanist disciplines and the natural sciences, with great attention being paid to the teaching of the nation's history, beginning with the achievements of Asoka the law-giver, and culminating in the triumphs of the freedom struggle and the great deeds of its leading figures – Gandhi and Nehru above all. Equally central to these schools' curricula was the study of the homeland's cultural landmarks in the form of the *Bhagavad Gita* and other classics from the Sanskrit and regional vernacular canons: Tagore in Calcutta; the Tamil epic known as the *Cilappatikaram* in Madras.[11]

Yet I also remember hearing Calcutta families I knew in the early 1970s disparaging one of India's most celebrated (and expensive) educational institutions, the Doon School in the former colonial resort town or 'hill station' of Dehra Dun (see Srivastava 1998). This is nowadays

A. Woodside, S. Malarney, P. Zinoman, C. Goscha, A. Fforde and C. Giebel. My aim is to add further dimensions to their accounts by exploring the ways in which socialism has worked as a set of supralocal reference points in the imaginative life of such people as the Indian intellectuals whom I knew in past decades, and the Hanoi intellectuals with whom I have been working more recently.

[11] On recent battles over the contents of school textbooks in both India and Pakistan, see Jalal 1995: 77–89 and Bose 2003: 143–5. On debates about the relative merits of vernacular and English-medium schooling in contemporary India, see Benei 2005; Donner 2005.

widely referred to as India's Eton. To my friends, including some of the young people as well as their parents, it was a dubious place, tainted by newspaper accounts of the allegedly brattish behaviour of Doon School pupils from famous Indian families, notably one of the sons of the then Prime Minister, Indira Gandhi.

Far from being regarded as a tautly disciplined imitation of Eton or any of the other elite English boarding schools, the Doon School was widely referred to as 'hippyish' and 'American' in tone and ethos. Those who said these things made it clear that this meant a place where children learned to value what they scornfully referred to as 'self-expression' and 'personal fulfilment', rather than self-discipline and dedication to the common good. 'Too much playing guitars', I remember someone saying to me. 'It's the place where foreign wives always want their children to go', said another friend's teenage son.

This was one of the many Calcutta households I knew in which children were encouraged to read P.G. Wodehouse and the Billy Bunter stories. Their parents thought these middlebrow English staples both unobjectionably entertaining and instructively well written. The chaste British mass-market romances known as Mills and Boons were frowned on, but still widely read by girls and older women. At the same time, in all the educated urban households I knew, parents expected their children to appreciate and if possible to sing or play the music of the Indian classical traditions. US comic books were banned, the wearing of jeans reluctantly tolerated by some parents and hotly resisted by others. The schools such parents favoured were the urban day schools run by Jesuits and other Roman Catholic teaching orders. These were renowned for their high academic standards, and praised for their determination to impart strong lessons in character and morality through intolerance of poor posture, sloppy speech and other forms of indecorum.

Such concerns might appear to be no more than a postcolonial variant of the practices observed in studies of class-based 'distinction' in the West, or its classlike equivalents in socialist contexts (Szelenyi 1982; Bourdieu 1984).[12] But as I explain in later chapters, I see these views and activities as something more dynamic and far-reaching than a case of élite parents doing whatever they could to endow their children with a stock of personally empowering cultural capital. What deserves greater emphasis than is common in accounts of the social power of 'élites', both under socialism and in colonial and postcolonial settings, is that the accruing of cultural capital is often anything but empowering.

---

[12] And see Kraus 1981 and Watson 1984.

Indeed its effects can be highly problematic for those who seek to possess or deploy it.

I also believe that it obscures far more than it illuminates to refer to either the Vietnamese individuals and families with whom I worked, or their Indian counterparts, as members of a social or cultural 'élite'. What I learned in the course of my fieldwork is that intelligentsia life can be privileged yet precarious. It is often as perilous as it is rewarding to equip oneself and one's children with the markers of refined aesthetic competence, and in India as well as Vietnam those possessing the recognised hallmarks of 'élite' cultural competence know that it can be hard to predict whether they will be applauded or reviled for the uses to which they put their own or their families' stock of cultural capital. They also know that particular forms of their hard-won cultural capital can go in and out of fashion, with such things as command of the ex-coloniser's language unpredictably losing their value and convertability. This is one of the many reasons why a language of socialist high-mindedness and virtuous affect so often pervades the claims made by individuals and state authorities about the nature and values of educated minds and cultivated sensibilities in a progressive society. Yet it is important not to reduce these concerns to a simple story of instrumental aims and ends concealed by a hypocritical deployment of socialist vocabulary.

Socialism as a selective moral language

In India, what made those views about schooling, reading and dress styles consistent with a recognisably socialist orientation and ethos was the strong suggestion being made through all these judgements that a patriotic modern Indian should be able to tell the difference between good and bad versions of the wider world's modern skills and values. It was neither straightforwardly 'colonial', nor a mark of 'Westernised' values and mentalities, to read Wodehouse, enjoy cricket and educate one's children in a school teaching science and Shakespeare.

Of course everyone knew that these were cultural practices which would not have been embraced in India without the legacy of British rule, or at least not in the forms known in India in those early post-independence decades. Nevertheless, they were widely spoken of as tastes and pursuits which had come to transcend the legacy of colonial intellectual and social interactions. And they were not simply 'Western'. It was important for the people I knew to proclaim a knowing sense of differentiation between things 'American' and other things both material and intangible which could be represented as virtuously modern and scientific, in keeping with distinctively Indian traditions of value and moral worth, and consistent with the principles of progressive global internationalism. These principles included such things as a professed commitment to the goal of first-rate education for women as well as men, and a commitment to the notion of the state as an engine of social justice and distributor of social goods.

Of course these attitudes contained strong elements of ambivalence. In the educated households I knew, US 'imperialism' was invariably condemned; US military action in Vietnam was passionately opposed, and many individuals shared the views expressed in the Indian press and national Parliament about the dangers posed to India's sovereignty and security by the machinations of what was known as the 'foreign hand'. This usually meant either the USA or India's regional neighbour Pakistan, widely represented in the Indian press as a threateningly hostile client of the CIA and other US government agencies. Older Indian friends and also British colleagues who worked in India in the 1960s have told me that in those years, more recent memories of the Suez Crisis as well as the great dramas of independence and partition made attitudes to Britain significantly more mixed. The Vietnam War clearly helped to shift the balance in these attitudes: by the 1970s, there was clearly a widespread view among educated Indians that it was the USA rather than Britain which was the more dangerous global power with unwelcome geopolitical designs on Asia.

Yet the strongly articulated hostility to pursuits, tastes and cultural influences which were thought of as 'American' was never altogether unmixed. Even before the embrace of US-style neoliberal business language, I knew people who expressed a sneaking admiration for certain American products, mentalities and cultural icons. The Soviets and other COMECON states were 'friends', but the high-profile development projects which they financed often fell short of expectations. I remember visiting a south Indian 'friendship' deal power plant built with Czech aid money, and hearing from one of the senior staff about its faulty design and equipment problems. He spoke yearningly of American technology, and asked me what I knew about securing admission to US engineering courses.

Yet the over-used cliché 'craze for foreign' must be employed with care. As far back as my first trips to India, this was a much-quoted expression, often employed in acerbic journalistic accounts of the ways and mores of India's rapidly growing urban middle class. It was supposedly a phrase used in everyday anglophone or 'Hinglish' speech with its much-caricatured idiosyncracies ('I am craze for foreign!'). Its use by cultural commentators signalled a view of this growing urban middle class – especially its women – as aspiring consumers, all too readily seduced by the lure of trashy, international brand-name commercialism (Varma 1998). But as in France in the late 1940s and 50s as documented by Kuisel (1993), the attitudes of the educated Indians I knew seemed far more nuanced than the phrase suggests. Many disparaged the tastes of those they thought of as spendthrift and vulgar, pointing to such things as the display of nouveau riche wealth at the international luxury hotels which were a relatively new feature of big-city Indian life in the early 1970s. But academics and other members of the regional intelligentsias were inclined to insist on fine discriminations between things they thought of as American in source or inspiration – the tacky new hotels, for example – and other things of foreign origin which could be legitimately esteemed for their aesthetic, moral or practical value (see Orlove 1997: 1–30). As I recall them, some of these value judgements seem very close to the attitudes I encountered in Hanoi. Others reflect very different assumptions about taste and value, and in the chapters that follow I explore the parallels as well as the distinctions, bearing in mind that both the nature of the intelligentsias themselves and the form of socialist system under which they lived differed in many important ways.

First encounters in Hanoi

My first Hanoi trip in 2000 was planned as the launch of a new project for which I intended once again to use anthropological as well as historical perspectives. My aim was to explore some of the personal and intimate dimensions of Vietnam's engagement with modernity in its colonial and socialist forms. I thought it would be fruitful and feasible to begin this new venture by building on my knowledge of French, while moving as rapidly as I could towards competence in Vietnamese. The Vietnam specialists I consulted were encouraging about this and suggested a variety of ways to make contact with families whose elder members had been educated in French-medium educational institutions in the pre-independence period.

So from the beginning, I intended to focus on issues of language and educational choice. This clearly offered a means to understand at least something of what it had been to experience Vietnam's transition from colonial to post-independence visions of a multiply modern world presenting both dilemmas and empowerment to those engaging with its tools and everyday embodied practices. Among these I had in mind particularly the new ways of speaking, dressing and acting which constituted the novel 'habituations' of that modern world.

My plan was to work with members of Hanoi families with comparable experiences to those of other educated 'socialist moderns' from the former colonial world. This would of course include the cosmopolitan anglophones who feature so prominently in key critical writings on India's secular, modern-minded 'Nehruvians' and their present-day descendants. In India and elsewhere, it is of such people that the derisive phrase 'colonised minds' has been much deployed. It has been employed not only by scholars and public intellectuals of the stature of Ashis Nandy and Ngugi wa Thiong'o, but far more broadly, in much media output and political polemic in which colonialism of the mind is widely held to be an affliction pervading 'élite' life and thought in ways deforming, corrupting or delegitimating the true linguistic and cultural heritage of particular 'postcolonies'.

In contemporary academic debate, there have of course been many attempts to refine and nuance the view of colonised people with knowledge of foreign languages and the modern scientific learning which made socialism attractive to many anti-colonial intellectuals, as having experienced the so-called Enlightenment project as a form of 'epistemic violence' (Spivak 1988) suppressing creativity and deadening self-worth and moral agency.[13] These views raise many contentious questions about the capacity of colonial subjects and their descendants to live as dynamic, self-aware moral agents with the ability to receive, appropriate and act in a world of mutually constructed colonial and postcolonial interactions.

In my past work on India I addressed some of these issues, arguing that the caste system and also Indians' experiences of conversion to 'foreign' religions – Islam and Christianity – entailed continually negotiated appropriations and 'vernacularisations', rather than a one-way process of imposed hegemonies or coloniser's fabrications.[14] I found similar interactions and exchanges in attempts by pre-independence Calcutta intellectuals to propound visionary new concepts of Indian nationhood by appropriating European Orientalist ideas about the

[13] Of course there is much diversity in this vast and ever-expanding field of study, including work that is richly informed by an understanding of the complexities of colonial intellectual and cultural engagements and their legacy for those grappling with the challenges of intelligentsia life in contemporary 'postcolonies': see e.g. Dipesh Chakrabarty's (2002) discussion of the divergent ways in which Indian intellectuals have engaged with the inheritance of European Enlightenment rationalism. For an eloquent challenge to those applying 'colonised minds' arguments to India, see Nanda (2003). And see Attwell's (1999) challenge to the writing off of the work of anglophone poets in colonial south Africa as the products of 'colonised minds'; also Zachernuk 2000; Larson 1997:970; and Sharp 2002 on the legacy of the key francophone theorists of colonialism's pathological psychic effects, notably Mannoni (1950); Memmi (1957); Fanon 1992[1952], and Césaire (1970).
[14] Compare Peel 1995; Larson 1997; Cooper 2005.

achievements of ancient Indians as 'cultural colonisers' and 'civilisers' within the vast translocal spaces of a so-called Greater India (Bayly 2004c). So in moving to a different and much less familiar intelligentsia setting, that of the Vietnamese who played a key role in the forging of anti-colonialism and post-independence socialist modernities both at home and in a host of disparate overseas locations, I hoped to contribute something new and distinctive to these key areas of current debate.

During that first Hanoi stay in 2000, I spent several convivial evenings visiting the homes of senior academics from some of the city's universities and research institutes. Those visits played a critical role in the gestation of the project. Many of the people I met became friends whose enthusiasm and support contributed immeasurably towards the completion of this study.

Even at that very early stage in my research, my hosts were warmly welcoming and expressed keen interest in my project. They shared delicious food with me, introduced me to other family members and showed me their household ancestor altars and photograph albums. All spoke with animation about the educational achievements of male and female family members dating back over three generations or more. Some had kin who had studied in France before and also after independence. And in most families there were individuals with scientific or technological training in China, the USSR or other ex-COMECON states. Among the adults, most of the men had served in the military during Vietnam's epic conflicts with France and the USA, or in the brief but bloody wars with Cambodia and China in 1977 to 1978 and 1979. I also met female veterans: a retired doctor who had run battle-zone hospitals for front-line troops during the US–Vietnam War, and several women who had served as teachers, administrators or health workers with the Vietnamese occupation administration in Cambodia. And even at that early stage, one or two people pricked my interest by mentioning extended work sojourns in countries with leftist revolutionary traditions in north and sub-Saharan Africa.

Three things rapidly became clear from these initial encounters. The first was the centrality of family identity as a critical point of reference in almost everything I heard and observed during those visits, and in particular a strongly articulated sense of family tradition focusing on educational attainment and intellectual distinction. This began to raise in my mind a whole series of questions about the relationship between an individual's apparently compelling sense of family ties and obligations, and the many other kinds of connections which he or she would have forged through an involvement in the networks and relations which further defined the life of a 'socialist modern' in the course of Vietnam's turbulent history of war and nation-building.

The second of those early observations followed on from this. This was that the families I had visited clearly did not live in a world of narrowly defined two-way former colonial interactions, or even in one defined solely by the broader networks that I refer to in subsequent chapters as the worldwide socialist ecumene. And so, fleeting though they were, those initial glimpses of Hanoi academics' domestic environments and family lives began to generate the concerns that came to be central to this volume. Among these is my interest in the processes of memory and narrative, both personal and public, and in particular in the ways in which the operation of memory at the level of the intimate and the familial may closely connect yet also contend with the work of official, event-centred forms of remembering and representation. These concerns also include the book's focus on childhood, emotion and family experience, and its exploration of the challenging educational and career choices of older and younger people – especially women – in times of war and revolution, and the more recent upheavals of the present-day 'marketisation' era.

The third of the things I found striking about the Hanoi people I met in 2000 was the remarkable degree of movement, displacement and change which they and their families had experienced, within and beyond Vietnam. I had not yet made significant progress in Vietnamese. But the bilingual friends who introduced us translated between English and Vietnamese for the benefit of family members whose second and sometimes third languages turned out to be Russian or Chinese, and in some cases German, Czech, Romanian or Polish. Some also knew Portuguese, the language of intelligentsia life in socialist Mozambique and Angola.

Of course I found too that most households contained younger people who were willing and indeed eager to converse in English. This was unsurprising: in this respect Vietnam resembles the many other countries in which the peoples of 'late socialist' states are engaging with the products and employment opportunities of globalised consumer and media culture (see Fforde 2003; compare Ong 1990; Liechty 2003). Even a first-time visitor to Hanoi soon finds that the city's young people are avid seekers of English-language conversation practice. Those serving in shops and cafés generally have a language study aid to hand, and questions about points of grammar and vocabulary to pose to any reasonably friendly foreigner.

When I rather hesitantly mentioned that I knew French during those first encounters with Hanoi academics and their families, I found that quite a number of people knew it too, and had no apparent hesitation about conversing with me in what I then thought of as the coloniser's language. It was not until my fieldwork began in earnest that I discovered how many members of these families had been involved in the state schemes which had equipped thousands of educated Vietnamese with the necessary language skills to earn remittances for the national exchequer as providers of technical aid and development expertise to Africa's former French- and Portuguese-ruled 'postcolonies'. So far as I know, these remarkable ventures which gave Vietnam a whole new life in a world of far-flung socialist 'friendships' and international exchange relations have never before been documented ethnographically.

My Hanoi informants' personal and family narratives of these experiences are a central element of the book, as are their recollections of wartime childhoods in the remote sites to which they relocated with their families during the 1946–54 anti-French resistance war. Some also had much to say about their experiences as evacuees when their universities or research institutes were relocated to rural areas during the US bombing campaigns of the 1960s and 70s. These narratives made me aware that the idea of life as a continued experience of rupture and separation – an idea which I explored in my earlier work on con- ceptualisations of Asian polity and nationhood – was of equal importance for understanding the lived experiences of the 'socialist moderns' who are the focus of this study.[15]

Like other Hanoi people in comparable occupations, the academics I visited lived in houses of modest size, rather than Soviet-style apartment blocks. My hosts spoke with evident feeling and intensity about the objects in them, and the houses themselves. What they said conveyed a striking sense of lives lived as repeated and protracted journeys, separations and overseas sojourns, and of families sometimes willingly yet painfully divided by career moves and official service demands, as well as war and other episodes of turmoil and danger.

The descendants of one deceased scholar showed me the painstaking work they had done to preserve and catalogue the research notes and book collection which the family had managed to keep intact during the years they had spent in the remote rural areas under the control of the Communist-led Viet Minh movement during the 1946–54 anti-French liberation war. Other people showed me novels, sheet music, souvenir postcards and a wide variety of domestic goods purchased by family members during study tours and work sojourns in places as far afield as

---

[15] See Bayly 2000; compare Stafford 2000.

Moscow, Bucharest, Luanda and Algiers. And people spoke of other small treasures: a wooden comb carved for one young woman's mother while her soldier father did his military service during the anti-US War, or books and other items acquired in the heady days of Vietnam's reunification in 1976.

None of my hosts lived in family houses that had been handed down to them as the descendants of owners or occupants dating back to the colonial or pre-conquest periods. Indeed almost everyone had an acquisition story to tell. Many were tales of achievement, as in the case of relatively new houses built with the proceeds of money earned in the course of gruelling overseas work sojourns. Some were painful. Houses assigned by the state to new occupants after independence in 1954 were often known to have been seized from Vietnamese owners with problematic political or class backgrounds, or to have been 'donated' to the state as demonstrations of loyalty to the new revolutionary order. As a result, even many years later, there were sometimes wistful or bitter encounters with their former occupants (compare Papin 2001: 334–5). These, like so many other narratives recounted to me in Hanoi, were stories of strong emotion and the claims of filial attachment, as in the case of an elderly woman who was described as having wept on being admitted by its current residents to the house in which she had lived as a child, so she could stand in reverence before the site once occupied by her family's ancestor altar.

Other stories had a different kind of poignancy, and a strongly moralising message about separation and rupture in other forms and contexts. One such account was of a house built by a rich Hanoi businessman in the 1920s, and then harmoniously shared by two wartime comrades and their families in the early days of the joyful post-independence period. Over the next few years, I was told, there was a gradual cooling of relations until rigidly separated living spaces were created with lockable doors and dividing walls where once there had been free and open access. I felt even then that what were being aired were reflections about the sad decline of revolutionary idealism and its embodiment in particular forms of emotional and moral commitment in an age of commercialisation and self-interested market values.

I was to hear much more about these concerns and their bearing on family life in the course of my subsequent fieldwork. Much of my research time was spent at my friends' homes and workplaces in Hanoi. But my fieldwork has also entailed a varied array of richly informative visits to the sites of my older friends' wartime childhoods. Much of what I have learned about the past and present experiences of Hanoi intelligentsia families derives from these trips with them to see their former schools and the rural houses in which they lived during the anti-French and anti-US resistance wars of 1946–54 and 1961–73.

My aim in the book is to present this material as a source of humanising insight into the personal costs and far-reaching consequences of connections, interactions and 'projects' that have been enacted and embodied by the actions of living, reflective human beings, both in the past and more recently. The world in which my Vietnamese informants have lived and acted has been shaped by colonialism as well as socialism in a wide range of different forms. I document attitudes and perceptions which are both nuanced and ambivalent, and which I see as offering a wide range of insights into issues of active debate among those currently seeking to understand global modernities in many different settings and contexts. I believe too that my attempt to explore comparisons with the experience of Indians of comparable though far from identical background and life experience throws valuable light on the issues with which I am concerned.

Organisation and key concerns

As I have already noted, the book is centrally concerned with the lives of scientists, academics and other educated 'moderns'. In many studies of the socialist world, and also in accounts of so-called postcolonies, such people have been identified as 'cultural producers'. Such phrasing signals their importance as members of a class or social stratum who play a critical role in the creation and dissemination of their homelands' official narratives. These include their narratives of nationhood and other forms of exclusive cultural identity. It also includes those forms of narrative expression and representation which legitimate and empower their states and rulers in significantly different ways, notably those proclaiming their countries' progressive lives of interaction with other states and peoples.

Thus many accounts have seen members of socialist as well as postcolonial intelligentsias above all as people whose cultural work equips state authorities to deploy both overt and more subtle tools of domination in the form of such things as educational curricula (Verdery 1991a). Other tools they are held to place in the hands of these governing authorities include the intelligentsias' own conspicuous exemplarship of progressive, modern and avowedly 'national' values and lifestyles (Fitzpatrick 1992). But it is important to avoid reductionism. The educated moderns must not be thought of as mere automata, puppet-like doers of the cultural work of states and governments. A key concern of this book is to explore the lived experience of these intelligentsia worlds, and to do so in a way that takes account of the personal, the

intimate and the emotional rather than concentrating on tasks performed, or official strategies and categories deployed or contested.

I believe that an exploration of my informants' personal histories and
family narratives reveals a great deal about the legacy of colonial life and
thought as an enduring presence in their lives today. At the same time, I
believe these explorations also illuminate the many areas of rupture and
discontinuity which divide the colonial from the postcolonial. Among the
most important of these discontinuities, and one to which the Asian
intelligentsias have been very central, is that of the transitions experienced in many parts of the world from colonial to socialist systems of
power and knowledge management. This entry into a broad supralocal
world of socialist views and values has been central to the life of many so-
called postcolonies, though its full significance has not been fully or
widely recognised in the literature on postcoloniality.

The educated Asian moderns I have worked with are people who have
much to say about this wider socialist world, as well as the exercise of
colonial and postcolonial power and representation. In many cases they
have been directly involved in those exercises. At the same time, as
people with training in the skills of articulate verbalisation, they also tend
to have the inclination and ability to reflect on the experiences of others
including their fellow non-intelligentsia citizens in the course of those
same transformations. This personalised reportage is of great interest,
though of course one must be cautious about accepting what is said as a
'true' story of those happenings at either a personal level or that of the
society at large. A further concern here is to identify those things which
make the lives of particular intelligentsias distinctive in specific settings
and periods. Hence my focus on Vietnam as a society which has not
featured very prominently in contemporary debates about the worlds of
the Asian and other 'postcolonies', or in those about the socialist and
'late' or post-socialist world as arenas of massive social and cultural
transformation.

The structure of the book is as follows. Following on from the themes
explored in this introductory scene-setting chapter, Chapter 2 explores
issues of historical memory in the lives of my Hanoi informants. It
explains in further detail why the book is centrally concerned with the
lives of Hanoi scientists, academics and other 'cultural producers',
focusing on their narratives of often gruelling separation and leave-taking
(Stafford 2000), and on the centrality of the family and other key units of
affect and allegiance to their experiences of education, provision and
nurture within the world of the socialist ecumene.

Chapter 3 focuses more directly on the ways in which my informants
have constructed and shared their narratives of intelligentsia experience

both within and beyond Hanoi. In Chapter 4, I discuss the often problematic official categorisation of intelligentsia identity in Vietnam and the wider socialist world. Chapter 5 explores the ways in which India's intelligentsia moderns may be compared to their Hanoi counterparts in the pre- and post-independence periods. The focus of Chapter 6 is an array of 'panoptic' moments which formed the context for people's experiences of their home city's transformation into a zone of revolutionary sites and spaces. Chapter 7 deals with Hanoi people's childhoods in the Communist-controlled 'interzones' or *lien khu*, the 'liberated territories' of the 1946–54 anti-French liberation war. Chapter 8 describes their families' post-war returns to Hanoi and explores their accounts of the new socialist world of the 1950s and 60s. This chapter uses anthropological understandings of gift and exchange relations to explore the remarkable activities of Vietnamese who acted as 'socialist civilisers' in Africa's so-called developing countries from the late 1970s onwards. Chapter 9 concludes the volume by returning to the comparative issues which underpin my discussion of both India and Vietnam.

2   The modern intellectual family: separation, provision and nurture

Introduction

Everyone I know in Hanoi has stories to tell about travel, separation and displacement. Many of these stories focus on the high value which they and their families have placed on learning and educational attainment, and the painful separations which they have endured to achieve these goals. They are also stories which build on, yet subtly differ from, the widely known official narratives of national life in both the recent and more distant past.

Through an exploration of these accounts and the conditions of their presentation, this chapter focuses on the forging of Hanoi intelligentsia life through processes of provision, nurture and expressive interaction. Some of these resemble those described in accounts of the practices of family nurturance and schooling through which 'socialised' comportments are acquired in Asian settings.[1] My concern with dispersal and relocation builds on Stafford's compelling account (2000) of the ways in which familial separation and reunion experiences can be seen to structure emotional life in Taiwan and China.

There are some very distinctive features to the experiences which I explore here, including the centrality of the learnedly written and spoken word to my informants' accounts of their familial relations.[2] I found it striking that both conjugal and parental love were recalled in these terms, that is as a process of nurture and attachment enacted through the power of refined speech and writing, and the cultivation of learned knowledge. At the same time, my informants also made much of the tangible forms of care which anthropologists now see as central

---

[1] Notable works in this area include Stafford 1995; Rydstrøm 2003; Yan 2003.

[2] I do not use the word informant to imply one-sided extraction of 'data' from passive subjects – far from it, given that my research entailed fieldwork with knowledge producers, i.e. with people much involved with processes of active reflection on narrative accounts of personal and national experience. On fieldwork involving consultant-style relations with intellectuals in China, see Litzinger 1998.

to the affective processes of family life, the most notable being the provision by mothers of food and other strengthening substances.[3] But this sense of the familial embraces a host of other affective ties and relations. Bonds with teachers and intimate friends are also spoken of as manifestations of affective warmth which may be experienced through verbal and unverbalised forms of cultivated knowledge. For intelligentsia 'moderns' (*nguoi hien dai*), the sharing of refined sensibility thus allows the familial to span kin- and non-kin-based relations and experiences.

These were far from being unproblematic processes. As I show below, all forms of familial provision can be painfully resisted or aborted. Furthermore, I found that while male and female kin were widely associated with different types of nurturing action, much like the complementary spheres of 'reunion commensality' observed by Stafford (2000: 100–26), this was not always the case. While my informants said much about fathers as models of erudition and verbal skill, these were qualities also extolled when paying tribute to the achievements of female kin. Furthermore, it is not only adult men who are looked to as critical agents in the sustaining of a family's public and 'external' face, and women are not invariably recalled as producers of relatedness deploying skills of loving nurture on behalf of far-flung kin (Stafford 2000: 112). In conditions of repeated and prolonged relocation and dispersal, my informants experienced variants of family life which often took very different forms from those depending on a separation between distinctly male and female spheres or functions within a conventionally structured domestic household. Even conventional distinctions between childhood and adult life frequently took on new or unfamiliar features. This was especially so during the prolonged periods when critical areas of family life including food allocation, wartime billetting arrangements and educational choice became intertwined with official rationing regimens and other arenas of the socialist state's austerity-era provisioning operations.

In exploring people's accounts of the imparting of love and nurture within these disparate settings, I am concerned with a variety of affective and knowledge-related processes. These include the cultivation of the verbal skills through which individuals learn to participate in the diverse arenas of the intelligentsia world. This is a milieu in which a well-informed command of both personal and national histories is greatly prized, including histories of lives led across different geographical and

---

[3] See e.g. Malarney 1996b; Carsten 2000; Stafford 2000; Yan 2003.

temporal spaces (compare Barlow 1991: 213). Yet while I focus on collectivities that are family-like as well as specifically familial, the key allegiances here are those to what Hanoi people call the modern intellectual family (*gia dinh tri thuc*).[4]

'Nous les intellectuels' (We intellectuals), my informants say in French, often following this with an explanation of the phrase *tri thuc*, which came into use in the 1930s to denote an educated person who was 'modern' (*hien dai*) in schooling and ethos, and a participant in contemporary print culture in at least one of its two key colonial forms: francophone and *quoc ngu* (romanised Vietnamese) (Marr 1981: 31–2). It was from this self-consciously modern class that Vietnam's twentieth-century revolutionary nationalist organisations drew their first adherents.[5] But while individuals – both male and female – are frequently referred to as modern intellectuals, people also regularly say 'we come from an intellectual family' (*gia dinh tri thuc*). I have also heard people refer to their own or other people's families as possessing an intellectual tradition (*truyen thong tri thuc*). By this they mean

---

[4] The sense of family (*gia dinh*) in Vietnam involves both the temporally unbounded patrilineage (*ho*; or *toc*, the formal Sino-Vietnamese term) with male forebears receiving veneration in the tradition of the Confucian ancestor cult (*huong khoi*), and also temporally bounded identification with bilateral kindred defined though parental and sibling ties (Hy Van Luong 1989). *Ho* also denotes the hearth-sharing household. The married state is by definition a familial one: to ask someone if they are married one says *Em da lap gia dinh chua?* – literally: 'Have you established or formed a family yet?' The unmarried say 'Not yet' (*Em chua*). See also Malarney 2002:16–17. The people I know speak of families (*gia dinh*) in the same terms. All households I know possess an ancestor altar (*ban tho*) and observe ancestral death anniversaries (*ngay gio*: see Malarney 1996b; Kwon 2007). Modestly sized nuclear households interact and share resources with their wider extended kindreds (Hirschman and Vu Manh Loi 1996).

[5] This is the 'emergent intelligentsia' described by Zinoman (2002: 9), i.e. the urban 'new intelligentsia' (*gioi tri thuc moi*) of the 1920s and 30s which Marr (1981: 32) identifies as a range of people – possibly numbering 10,000 or more by the late 1930s – drawn from predominantly 'petit bourgeois' backgrounds. Their occupations ranged from teaching to artisanship and petty trade, and they had in common a pervasive interest in obtaining modern schooling for their children. They tended to be avid readers of *quoc ngu* newspapers, and keen participants in 'thinking, talking, reading and writing about change', with a propensity to form study groups, 'publish prolifically' and to enjoy debate about social issues with like-minded contemporaries (1981: 30–2). Few of my informants descend from families of big landlords, rich entrepreneurs and high officials; most have the modest but literate family backgrounds described as typical of the new twentieth-century colonial intelligentsia with education up to higher primary school, of whom a minority attended francophone *lycées* and even fewer attended a university either in Indochina or France (Kelly 2000; Marr 1984: 26–41 and 2003; Trinh Van Thao 1990; Truong Buu Lam 2000). For a penetrating account of the dilemmas faced by francophone Vietnamese intellectuals who sought to engage with and 'nationalise' key elements of Western cultural modernity in a context of critical reflection on such attempts in Japan and other Asian societies, see Goscha 2004.

educational attainment spanning both the arts and sciences, and definitely not only the pursuits of those more narrowly defined as 'creative intellectuals' (Ninh 2002: 33).[6]

This chapter's key concern is thus with something which can be a complex and sometimes dangerous business in Vietnam: achieving and maintaining the shared identity markers of this one special kind of family, in the face of rapidly changing official attitudes to the pursuit of 'familistic' interests. I deal particularly with the ways in which this sense of family has been forged and represented, and with the dynamic nature of the bonds and sentiments which it entails. I also explore the special role of children, who feature in personal and official narratives as recipients of nurturing love and care (*cham soc*), and as active and sometimes problematic agents in the shaping of family and national life.

Of course a high proportion of Vietnam's families experienced the separations and dislocations of the anti-French and anti-US wars, and the gruelling austerity years that followed. My informants have also had much to say about the common features of family life for all Vietnamese. Yet they are insistent too about the distinctiveness of the intelligentsia world, in part because they feel that it has been structured around forms of dispersal and separation which are unlike those experienced by other Vietnamese, and also because the official media so often treat them as either admirably or problematically set apart from the nation at large.[7]

---

[6] Recently published tribute biographies regularly describe *tri thuc* intellectual families in these terms, as in the case of the pioneering post-independence Hanoi anthropologist Professor Nguyen Duc Tu Chi (1925–95) whose forebears are identified by the editor of a 1996 reissue of one of his key works as a *gia dinh tri thuc yeu nuoc* (patriotic – literally 'loving the country' intellectual family): his father was a 'modern' medical doctor (*bac si*) who joined the anti-French revolutionary movement (Viet Minh) in 1945 and served as Deputy Health Minister in the provisional government established in the 'liberated territories' (Tran Tu 1996: vii). I therefore take issue with Pelley's (2002) decision to treat scientists and technical experts as falling outside the category of 'creative intellectuals' as defined by those participating in debates about the cultural life of the nation. The people I know define science very broadly, as in both France and the former Soviet Union; subjects such as anthropology are 'sciences', and the possession of scientific credentials is as much a mark of cultivation and refinement as qualifications in the humanist disciplines. They also strongly resist the suggestion to be found in memoirs by Chinese intellectuals that people of intelligentsia background who went abroad for specialist technical or scientific training in the high Maoist period were not true cosmopolitans and intellectuals like their predecessors of the early twentieth-century radical nationalist 'May 4th' movement era (see Schwarcz 1986: 589).

[7] See Hardy 2002 and McElwee 2005 on the post-independence Communist government's mass relocations of lowland peasants to upland forest regions, and Meyerhoff 2002 on pre-independence lowland peasant labour migration to the French-ruled Pacific island colonies of Melanesia.

So my attempt to understand what it is to live as a very particular kind of Hanoi family is a central concern of the book. And, given that so many of the experiences recounted to me were of family lives led in circumstances of 'normalised abnormality' (Fitzpatrick 1999: 219–20), these are concerns raising important questions about the understanding of family experience both anthropologically and historically, especially in situations of rapid change in former colonial and socialist or 'post-socialist' societies. I seek to show that the familial, the intimate and the domestic are still fruitful areas of concern for historically informed anthropology. I therefore draw in particular on ethnographic works which pay close attention to the changing moral and emotional textures of family life, especially those like Yan's (2003) which are concerned with transformations and moral contestation both within and about the familial arena. I build too on works exploring the distinctiveness of merchant and other specialist family traditions, and on those documenting the interaction of local practices of inheritance, marriage and childrearing with the reformist projects of modernising states and nationalist movements.[8] I am also concerned with the place of Hanoi intelligentsia families in the overthrow of colonial rule, and in the shaping of the new socialist society which succeeded it. A critical question here is the extent to which Hanoi intellectuals were either advantaged or encumbered by the legacy of colonialism's educational and cultural capital.

In 1953, at the age of eleven, Mrs Hoa and her eight-year-old sister Lan made a dangerous wartime journey to southern China in the company of eighteen other children and a single adult guardian.[9] Their destination, like that of the hundreds of other young Vietnamese who did this same gruelling trek in the 1950s, was one of the special Vietnamese-run schools which had been established under Chinese sponsorship to train the teachers and other specialists whose skills would help to create the new socialist Vietnam. Those attending these schools were the sons and daughters of revolutionary officials, together with others deemed

[8] On merchant families see Marcus and Hall 1992; Oxfeld 1992; Greenhalgh 1994; De Munck 1996; Collier 1997; Falzon 2004; Engseng Ho 2004, 2006; see also Simic 1983 and Hamabata 1991. On reformist projects and family life see especially Malarney 2002; compare Chatterjee 1989; Kelly 1989; Ong 1990; Riley 1994; Malarney 2002; Stoler 2004, and see Béteille 1991; Cheal 1991; Diamant 2000. For an account of familial gifting in the context of empire, see Finn's discussion (2006) of gift relations in the forging of extended family networks among expatriates in British India.

[9] I use pseudonyms for all informants, and I follow Vietnamese convention by using given names to identify individuals; one does not normally say 'Mr and Mrs Nguyen' to indicate a married couple.

suitable for this much sought-after opportunity by virtue of their parents' contribution to the anti-colonial cause.[10] The story of these institutions is widely known in Hanoi; I often heard about them in the course of my fieldwork and have worked with several of their other former students. The best known is the school at Que Lam (Guilin) in south-west China, in what is now the Guangxi Zhuang Autonomous Region; many former Que Lam students went on to high-flying careers in public life.[11]

Like most of the other people who shared their stories with me, Mrs Hoa situated her account quite explicitly against the background of these official and quasi-official narratives of national achievement. The people I worked with invariably sought out materials such as commemorative articles in the Hanoi newspapers as well as personal memorabilia to point up their narratives. They expressed approval for my research precisely because they saw its concerns as historical, seeing my interest in exploring the living presence of the past in contemporary Hanoi life as something close in spirit to their own sense of history (compare Taylor 2001: 167–89; Kwon 2006).

Most of my older informants have had careers as academics or public servants; some are retired, others still in post. Those like Mrs Hoa who are now in their sixties and early seventies were young adults in the early years of state socialism in the new Democratic Republic of Vietnam (DRV) which was established when the country was partitioned following independence in 1954.[12] Many either studied or worked in the

[10] Dang Phong 2002: 428–9. These schools were modelled on those founded for Chinese cadres' children and attacked as élitist during the Cultural Revolution. See Hong Yung Lee 1975: 676. To be recognised as a 'revolutionary family' (*gia dinh cach mang*) by virtue of a close kinsman's war service still confers entitlements to reduced school fees and other benefits. There is also an official category of heroic or martyr family (*gia dinh liet si*); this is for close kin of those with serious wartime disabilities. With the coming of 'market socialism' (*doi moi* or 'renovation'), the term 'business family' (*gia dinh thuong gia*) has returned to widespread use in Hanoi and is no longer a mark of 'bad class' origins. On the complexity of contemporary attitudes towards entrepreneurship and family-based wealth accumulation in contemporary Vietnam, see Hy Van Luong 1998 and Malarney 1998.

[11] As did their former teachers, e.g. Mong Lan, composer of some of Vietnam's most popular children's music as well as patriotic favourites such as 'Young Age of a Heroic Country' and 'I Am Living in Glorious Days'. This region of rural Guangxi is where Litzinger (2000) has conducted fieldwork among Yao 'ethnic minority' intellectuals. It was a zone of particular turbulence in the peak years of the Cultural Revolution (1967–8) See Sutton 1995: 137. A commemorative volume about the Que Lam students was published in 2003.

[12] I am aware that the 1954 Geneva accord dividing Vietnam at the 17th Parallel was not intended as a permanent partition comparable to that of the two Germanies or the two Koreas. I am equally aware that the Cold War fiction of 'two Vietnams' became a pretext for the US military intervention of the 1960s (Ruane 1998: 34–9). But as I show in

USSR or other COMECON countries, and all have direct experience of those other critical events of Vietnam's turbulent twentieth-century history: the 1961–73 'anti-US War' (*Chien tranh chong My*), and the brief but costly wars with China (1979), and Cambodia (1977–8). In addition to serving in the military in one or more of these conflicts, many also lived as rural evacuees when their universities or research institutes were relocated from Hanoi during the US bombing campaigns of the 1960s and 70s.

Many though not all of my informants come from families with a long-standing tradition of literacy. Most have a family history of 'modern' education (*tan hoc*) dating back to the 1920s or 1930s, and in some cases a tradition of classical Sino-Vietnamese learning (*Han hoc*) and scholar-official state service. Linguistic facility is thus another key tradition among the people I know, one of the shared family memories often pointed to in our discussions being the point at which one's educated forebears made the move from one literacy mode to another. Before independence, this meant a move from Chinese to *nom* (Vietnamese in Chinese script), thence for some to French and/or *quoc ngu* (romanised Vietnamese). In 1952 the DRV ordered its schools to teach only *quoc ngu*, together with Chinese and Russian as the key languages of the wider socialist ecumene. These became the critical languages of intelligentsia career life until *doi moi* ('renovation', the partial though far-reaching marketisation measures implemented initially in 1986).[13]

I have also worked with relative newcomers to the intelligentsia world. A case in point is one of the academics I know whose parents were distress migrants to Hanoi during the 1944–5 Tonkin famine (Nguyen The Anh 1998). Neither was literate; his father became a street-corner cycle repairman. As an outstanding secondary school student, Professor Nhat was selected for a one-year training course in English and French at the national university. This changed his official class designation from 'worker' to 'intellectual' (*nha tri thuc*); he believes that this, and uncertainty about whether his parents were of 'rich peasant' or even 'bourgeois' background, debarred him from Party membership and promotion to officer rank during his six-year army stint. But he fared better than many, completing a degree course after the anti-US war and marrying a senior professor's daughter. He became an established figure

Chapter 8, the experience of Vietnam's division is widely remembered as an experience inviting comparison with those other deeply felt twentieth-century political separations, most notably the 1947 partition of India.

[13] On education policy in Vietnam, see Woodside 1983; Ninh 2002.

in the *tri thuc* world; his children are graduates, and he socialises within an extensive network of established intelligentsia families.

Many of the Hanoi people I know are trained in scientific and technical fields. Others are social scientists and humanists, some with posts in museums and other cultural institutions. All make it clear that they regard the creation and consumption of historical narrative as meritorious and gratifying, however contentious and even hazardous for those charged with framing such accounts. Most take an eager interest in such events as the large-scale public exhibition in 2004 of finds excavated from the city's former imperial citadel precinct.[14] This display, which attracted very large crowds, was held at one of Hanoi's premier public spaces, the Van Mieu or Temple of Literature, an eleventh-century complex with steles honouring successful candidates in the imperial mandarinate examinations (See Plate 6). Far from being condemned as a relic of 'feudalism' (*che do phong kien*), the Van Mieu is extolled as a monument to the nation's tradition of nurturing meritorious 'persons of talent' (*nhan tai*). This Sino-Confucian term identifying those who place their erudition at the service of state and people is still current in Vietnam, familiar to children from its use by the nation's founding father Ho Chi Minh in one of the wartime patriotic aphorisms they learn at school, calling on the young to study hard as a filial and patriotic duty.[15]

Mrs Hoa said that she and her contemporaries who went to China were aware that they were being educated to perform a mission, not for personal advantage or gratification. Their courses were short and

---

[14] The objects were to be cherished, said the official accounts, as a means of enriching the nation's knowledge of the city's 1000-year history of cultural achievement and wise dynastic rule. On history-making in socialist contexts, compare Verdery 1991a. And see Pelley's discussion (2002: 61) of debates between Vietnamese historians about the relating of national history to evolutionist Marxist theories positing generalised developmental models such as the Asiatic Mode of Production schema. Her argument is that this has involved a process of cultural and cognitive decolonisation, its focus being the shifting of Vietnam from a category of backward or evolving 'Third World' society to one situated in a world community of fellow socialist moderns engaged in shared scientific and intellectual enterprise. Compare Barlow's account of Chinese intellectuals as specialists in the 'strategic' construction and vilification of 'multiple pasts' (1991: 212–13). On divergence, contestation and plurality in official narratives of revolutionary political transformations, see Dirlik 1997; Donham 1999; and for Vietnam, Abuza 2001; Giebel 2004.

[15] See Cooke 1995; Malarney 1997; Woodside 1998: 20–1. On Ho Chi Minh's appropriation of concepts of filial indebtedness in the formulation of a revolutionary service morality, see Jellema 2005; on the ethos of duty and service as a sense of active moral agency exercised by knowing actors in relation to the fatherland, see McElwee 2005.

intensive so they could take their place in fields such as teaching and medicine at ages as young as seventeen. This was also the case for the secondary-school students who left home to join the Communist-led insurgent movement, the Viet Minh.[16] I know an energetic couple in their seventies who did precisely that. Both became lifelong Party members. Having joined the Viet Minh as a seventeen-year old *lycéen* in 1945, Mr Binh was sent to take charge of Party work in a populous northern province, having been kitted out with the two items he said everyone recognised as the marks of a Viet Minh cadre: a harmonica and a revolver. During his three months of preparatory training in the remote headquarters area known as the Viet Bac (Northern Region), he recalls learning both to shoot and to play the resistance songs that were an important tool of insurgency propaganda. His future wife was also recruited straight from her own *lycée*, training as a combat nurse while still in her teens.[17]

These are among the few cases I know of young people joining the Viet Minh without their parents' knowledge, and thus without the formalities of leave-taking and sending-off which are as important in Hanoi life as they are in the Chinese settings described by Stafford (2000). Yet for Mr Binh and his future wife, there was no question of a permanent family rupture, or of a life lived without the intimacies of household and family ties (compare N. Taylor 2004: 49–50). I met the couple in the company of their student granddaughter, who whispered to me that she had heard their stories many times. But she radiated warmth and enthusiastic attention as they recounted their experiences, cheerfully describing the ingenious strategy they devised to organise their wartime wedding. Party people were supposed to set an example by eschewing traditional feasting at marriages and funerals (Malarney 2002).Their solution was to commandeer a senior cadre's leaving party.This was an official function, hence inoffensive to the puritanical comrades who would have objected to the frivolity of a purely personal celebration.

---

[16] The full name of the Viet Minh was *Viet Nam Doc Lap Dong Minh Hoi*, League for the Independence of Vietnam, established in 1941 as a Communist-led coalition of anti-colonial resistance organisations. See Fall 1960; Moïse 1983; Dang Phong 2002; Nguyen The Anh 2004.

[17] Compare Hy Van Luong 1992: 154. A comparable account of a wartime marriage between two young Viet Minh intelligentsia recruits is provided in the battlefield memoir of Le Cao Dai, the surgeon husband of the distinguished Hanoi artist Vu Giang Huong, to whom I am much indebted for permission to use her 'Self-Portrait' as the cover illustration for this book. Dr Dai's vivid evocation of military life in the two resistance wars was published in 2005 as *Tay Nguyen Ngay Ay* (That Day at Tay Nguyen) and in subsequent French and English translations in 2006 (Le Cao Dai 2006: 16–19; see also Luong Xuan Doan 2006).

Commenting on her marriage, Mr Binh's wife said, "Il est beau. Tout le monde chante." She did not remember how to construct the past tense in French, but said it again in Vietnamese: "He looked handsome. Everyone sang." Unlike the Hanoi people who revived their childhood French to take up aid and development posts in Africa, Mrs Binh said she had not spoken French since her *lycée* days. But she clearly enjoyed the attempt to do so with me; no-one I know has said they found it demeaning or 'colonial' to reveal a knowledge of French. On the contrary: it was evident that people found it pleasurable and gratifying to summon up their childhood language skills, even though many had long since mastered other languages, especially those of the wider socialist world.

It was common for younger people to speak with pride of their elders' linguistic accomplishments. Older people also liked to show off their students' and younger relations' various proficiencies, often urging them to demonstrate their English and other languages for me. As I noted above, possessing language skills is widely recognised as a Hanoi intelligentsia attribute. So is knowing and valuing the city's historic sites and beauty spots, and being in the know about events such as exhibitions and memorial meetings for noted public figures. Like other Hanoi monuments, the Temple of Literature is now a venue for a wide range of commercial and cultural events. It is also an active ritual space, its altar shrines to the Confucian sages much frequented by family groups making offerings for their children's exam success. In addition, it has become a site for commemorations honouring francophone intellectuals who, despite their patriotic resistance war credentials, have only recently returned to prominence in the national narrative. A notable early instance was a celebration marking the first Vietnamese translation from the original French of a landmark 1944 treatise on national culture by one of the most distinguished of these scholar-patriots, colonial Indochina's first French-trained anthropologist Professor Nguyen Van Huyen (1908–75).[18]

Also popular are public launches of family memorial volumes paying tribute to distinguished savants of that same patriotic resistance war era. Such publications are an instance of something I found to be an important characteristic of Hanoi intelligentsia life. This is the projection of a family's collective identity and cultural capital through processes of oral and written archiving which I discuss in more detail below. The production of these family tribute volumes reflects the new opportunities

---

[18] For a sensitive and insightful account of 'ritual revival' and memorial practices in contemporary Vietnam, see Kwon 2006.

available to Vietnamese intellectuals since *doi moi* ('renovation'). There has been a general loosening of controls on scholarship and literary activity, with the publication of academic works and personal memoirs that go well beyond the perspectives of the patriotic histories and bio-graphies of national heroes which dominated Vietnamese historical writing until the 1990s.[19] Accompanying *doi moi*'s liberalised economic and intellectual policies has been an official exaltation of the family (*gia dinh*) as a locus for economic enterprise. This of course is a significant shift from more conventional views of the domestic unit as a site for the 'socialisation' of modern socialist citizens, with an emphasis on the obligations of wives and mothers to maintain their kinfolk's health and harmony.[20]

So far as I know, the first of these family tribute biographies to be produced in Hanoi was an account of the life and achievements of Professor Nguyen Van Huyen. Professor Huyen is among the eminent francophone scholars referred to in official biographical accounts as a 'revolutionary intellectual' (*nha tri thuc cach mang*), a term used for both scientists and humanists. In Vietnam both are deemed essential to the nation's needs, and the 'revolutionary intellectual' should therefore be confidently conversant with both. The term thus refers to an educated individual combining a modern revolutionary's progressive knowledge and social consciousness, with the old-style Sino-Confucian intellec-tual's dedication to scholarship and virtue.[21]

Although never a Party member, Professor Huyen embraced the Viet Minh cause at the beginning of the 1946–54 anti-French liberation war.

[19] See e.g. the memoir of 'Sister Ba Dinh' (Nguyen Thi Dinh 1976), a celebrated peasant war heroine's account of privation, family separation and heroic resistance exploits, orginally published in 1966. Marr 2000; Malarney 2002: 2; Bradley 2004: 31–6. On exemplary heroic biography in China, see Barlow 1991: 213; Mitter 2004: 90–3.

[20] Malarney 1998 and 2002. On China's legitimation of the family as a key production unit under 'market socialism', see Bruun 1993; Farquhar 1996.

[21] Woodside 1998. Huyen achieved a literature degree (*licencié ès* lettres in 1929) and another in law in 1931; his 1934 Sorbonne *thèse de doctorat* was the first produced by a Vietnamese. His doctoral works on rural alternating-song contests (*Les chants alternés des garcons et des filles en Annam*) and South-east Asian stilt houses (*L'habitat sur pilotis en Asie du Sud-Est*) were published in 1934. He lectured at the Paris Ecole Nationale des Langues orientales vivantes, returning to Vietnam in 1935 to teach at Hanoi's Lycée du Protectorat as well as its university; in 1940 he became a full member (*membre permanent*) of France's most prestigious Asian scholarly establishment, the Ecole Française d'Extrême-Orient (French School of the Far East), serving briefly as director of its successor institution after the 1945 August Revolution (*Cach Mang Thang Tam*) when Ho Chi Minh proclaimed independence for Vietnam and assumed the presidency of its provisional government (Nguyen Kim Nu Hanh 2003; on the Ecole Française d'Extrême-Orient, see Trinh Van Thao 1995).

Accompanied by his wife and children and other close kin, he relocated
to the Viet Bac, accepting appointment as Education Minister in Ho Chi
Minh's provisional government and retaining this post until his death in
1975. Like other Hanoi intellectuals, Professor Huyen's background was
that of a literate urban family of modest means. His father had been a
practitioner of traditional medicine with a pharmaceuticals shop in
Hanoi's commercial 'Old Quarter'.[22] His mother was also active in
small-scale trade, amassing sufficient funds to contribute to the running
costs of a school for girls that had been founded in response to the early
nationalist hero Phan Boi Chau's call for national self-strengthening
through progressive education. Both strongly encouraged their talented
children to progress through the dauntingly competitive francophone
educational system.

Very few people in the pre-independence Hanoi intelligentsia world
came from Indochina's tiny commercial and landed élites. Career
opportunities for literate individuals were extremely limited under
French rule, significantly more so than in Britain's Asian colonies.[23] It is
true that in pre-independence India, impecunious schoolmasters and
clerical workers vastly outnumbered the anglophone professional people
who pursued high-profile careers as lawyers, university-based academics
and civil servants, as well as taking a leading role in nationalist political
life. Yet even allowing for its much smaller size and population, Indochina's educational system was far more modest in scale than colonial
India's. Vietnam's equivalents of the educated Indian 'moderns' with
their degrees and white-collar careers were rarely able to secure comparable employment. Indeed it was extremely rare for Vietnamese to
obtain advanced degrees or qualifications on a par with those of colonial
India's professional and scholarly élites; the '*retours de France*' ('France-
returned') were too few and anomalous to be readily assimilated or
normalised, especially in Hanoi which was a far less cosmopolitan
colonial capital than the big Indian metropolitan centres.[24]

---

[22] So too were the family of the eminent wartime photo-journalist Nguyen Duy Kien
(1911–79), another celebrated habitué of the pre-independence Hanoi intelligentsia
world (Duong Trung Quoc 2006: 6–9).

[23] Woodside's account (1971a: 49–50) of the membership of a major pre-independence
Hanoi-based mutual aid society comprising 'mechanics, shop-keepers and peddlers;
hospital attendants, cashiers, teachers…accountants at enterprises like the Nam Dinh
distilleries…draughtsmen [and interpreters] for French firms…' (49) nicely captures
the mix of small-scale enterprise and service occupations characterising most of those
participating in the urban intelligentsia world in this period.

[24] Woodside 1971a: 43–9; Smith 1972: 465; McConnell 1989; Papin 2001; Tran Thi Lien
2002: 290–9.

Professor Huyen's schooling was financed by a combination of state bursaries and contributions from his parents and other kin, including his elder sister, who taught maths at Hanoi's Lycée du Protectorat. This was a rare achievement for a Hanoi woman in the 1930s. Typical male employment for those recognising one another as *tri thuc* was in teaching, clerical work, and reporting, printing or copy-editing. Translation work was also central to intelligentsia life. As Goscha (2004b: 13–15) shows, the lively pre-war Hanoi press with its *quoc ngu* translations of Victor Hugo and other heroes of French modernism was profoundly influential in shaping the modernity-consciousness of the twentieth-century *tri thuc* world. The pervasive view of this was that such translations constituted a Vietnamising or vernacularising of modernity wholly compatible with an exaltation of Vietnameseness, particularly as it went hand in hand with *quoc ngu* translation of classic Vietnamese works.[25] Medicine and the arts and theatre world were also points of entry. I know several people whose forebears were 'traditional' medical practitioners; others were 'modern' pharmacists (Thompson 2003; Monnais and Tousignant 2006). The grandfather of one friend with Viet Minh parents wrote scripts for the Hanoi *cai luong* 'reform theatre'. Another had a grandfather trained at Hanoi's prestigious Ecole des Beaux Arts who became a revolutionary propaganda artist; an enthusiasm for the work of the city's pre-independence painters, graphic artists and patriotic composers is also a hallmark of the *tri thuc* world.[26]

Intellectuals and families

People old enough to recall their parents' accounts of Hanoi life in the 1930s and early 40s have told me that before the anti-French war, city-dwellers in circumstances like those of Mr Binh's and Mrs Hoa's parents could afford newspapers and illustrated reviews, as well as occasional cinema attendance. They saw plays and frequented the urban concert halls where patriotic music was performed under bland titles which misled the censors into thinking that the lyrics were those of harmless popular love songs. The more prosperous could even aspire to modest luxuries such as locally printed books, French cigarettes and other Western-style consumer products, and visits with their children to the young people's amusement park in the city centre with its pony rides and

[25] Notably the *Tale of Kieu*, discussed in Chapter 4. See also Bauman and Briggs 2003; McHale 2004.
[26] Smith 1972; Marr 1981: 166–7; Hy Van Luong 1992: 92, 102; Taylor 1997, 2004; Kelly 2000.

exhibition pavilions: my older friends recall natural history displays with animal skeletons and pictorial tableaux showing the circulation of blood and the classes and *phyla* of the animal kingdom. And everyone mentions the lakeside cafés where as students and young adults, they or their parents debated politics and poetry with their *lycée*-educated friends.[27]

All these pursuits and consumption patterns were hallmarks of the Hanoi intelligentsia world. Its key sites of modernity were certainly contested arenas which were strongly marked by the coloniser's power. In the expensive shopping area near the Opera House, 'the streets even smelled French', said one of my friends, a Hanoi schoolboy in the early 1940s. But these are also recalled as sites of exhilarating intellectual and emotional life in which there was much more to experience than the pleasures and pains of penetrating or subverting the coloniser's hegemonic 'norms and forms' (Rabinow 1989). It was also a milieu with decidedly open-ended boundaries. At the *lycée* one's friends might be from well-off rural or urban families, as well as those of far more modest origins. Attendance was free to those who could secure entry by means of the notoriously arbitrary admissions exams (Kelly 2000). Those without means could compete for subsistence awards, always eked out with contributions from one's kin. The fear of having one's state bursary revoked hung over those taking part in 'seditious' activities such as the school strikes which are now recalled as important episodes of patriotic resistance. 'Every day was political', said an ex-pupil of the Buoi ('grapefruit') school, the nickname patriots used to avoid its official name, the Lycée du Protectorat. Its pupils joined martial arts circles and exchanged secret resistance salutes learned from their patriotic teachers. On the streets, he said, they stoned the 'collaborators' from the other state *lycée*, the Albert Sarraut, attended by whites and rich *'indigènes'*, including members of Indochina's client royal dynasties.[28]

It is still relatively novel for Party dailies such as *Nhan Dan* (The People) and *Tuoi Tre* (Youth) to carry items in praise of intellectuals

---

[27] On pre-independence intellectual life in Indochina, see Taylor 1998; Marr 1971; 1981; Hue Tam Ho Tai 1992; Bradley 2004; McHale 2004; Wilcox 2006. On street life and urban spaces in Vietnamese contexts, see Drummond 2000; Papin 2001; Schlecker 2005; and compare Lee's penetrating account (2000) of print- and commodity-mediated modernity in pre-revolutionary Shanghai.

[28] Ninh 2002; Trinh Van Thao 2002: 261; Larcher-Goscha 2003; Raffin 2005. Published biographies of famous ex-*lycéens* bear out what informants have told me about the mixed social background of their fellow Buoi School pupils. One ex-Buoi pupil often mentioned is the celebrated Paris-trained artist To Ngoc Van (1906–54), an early recruit to the Viet Minh who came from a family of landless labourers and petty traders based in Hanoi's Old Quarter (To Ngoc Thanh 2004: 3–8; 2006: 3–4).

and 'intellectual families' (*gia dinh tri thuc*) whose members' pre-independence *lycée* educations are pointed to as honourable preludes to a life of patriotic achievement. In these accounts, the family unit in question tends to be defined very broadly to include a key individual's agnates and other 'blood' relations, and also their affines, especially the kin of a wife or husband, but also the bilateral kindred and affines of a child's wife or husband.[29]

Such families are also shown to be recognisably modern and moral by stressing that their bonds of affect and attachment are not confined to the classic Confucian family unit, defined as an enduring patriline. On the contrary, 'family' bonds embrace those of the nurturing natal household constructed by co-equal partners in a companionate 'modern' marriage. The specific variant of this edifyingly modern family – the intellectual family – has thus come to be represented as existing through time as an exemplary moral unit, embodying the nation's special stock of intellectual and cultural distinction, and deploying their share of these attainments and assets for the common good. They do so out of a spirit of dedication to both family and nation which derives its intellectual discipline from the exemplary legacy of the patriline (and sometimes also the matriline), and its will to love and sacrifice from the equally powerful influence of the nurturing natal household.[30]

So I found in recent textual sources as well as the comments of my informants a widely expressed view that to be historically aware is to experience something that unites the filial and the patriotic, since such awareness is by definition a knowledge of the national narratives of liberation and progressive cultural and material development. It also generates strong emotion. References to key moments of national history are often expressed in terms emphasising affective kinship ties, particularly those focusing on emotionally charged turning points such as the triumph of the country's long-awaited 1976 reunification (*Thong Nhat*).[31]

---

[29] Hy Van Luong 1989; Malarney 2002: 16–17; on the pre-independence press and pre- and post-*doi moi* media world, see Marr 2003. The other key novelty is official media reportage celebrating the launching of successful business ventures by Vietnamese entrepreneurs both at home and abroad. These are activities extolled both as fulfilments of socialist 'neo-tradition' and as patriotic contributions in the spirit of the post-*doi moi* marketisation ideology of 'rich people, strong land' (*dan giau nuoc manh*) (Turner and Nguyen 2005). See Chapter 8, below.

[30] Compare Macfarlane 1986: 154; Oxfeld 1992; Parry 2001. For Vietnam, see Hy Van Luong 1989: 749–51; compare Stafford 2000; for Soviet contexts, Thurston 1991: 559.

[31] Official narrativisations of Vietnam's national and regional histories have changed significantly in the pre- and post-independence periods: see Taylor 1998 and P. Taylor 2001; compare Duara 1995. And see Stafford 2000 on China's narrativisation of revanchist goals in relation to Taiwan.

This is an event officially symbolised by one of the country's most famous pictorial images, a celebrated Vietnamese photo-journalist's picture of an aged mother embracing the soldier son from whom she had been separated since the country's division in 1954 (see Plate 20). My informants are familiar with a whole range of propaganda posters using representations of the maternal bond to convey patriotic messages about the nation's strength and valour. One produced during the anti-US war provides a dramatic contrast to the 1976 reunification picture. Its caption is *'San sang lam nghia vu quan su bao ve to quoc!'* ([All are] ready/ willing to do their military service to protect the nation). It shows a young soldier in a village setting with his mother and a younger girl – presumably his sister – in a Soviet-style red youth movement scarf (*khan do*); behind them is a young woman, evidently his wife or sweetheart, and in the distance a troop of marching soldiers. The mother is sending the young man off to join them, not clasping him to her breast as in the reunification poster, but with her hand palm outward against his chest, stoically repudiating any thought of holding him back from his patriotic duty.[32]

Reunification is one of the experiences of national life that people often mention in relation to their own lives, speaking of this and other landmarks in the country's long history of ruptures and dislocations as moments when their yearnings for home and absent kinfolk were either briefly or more enduringly assuaged. It is also by means of historical awareness that self-consciously modern and cultivated people can live up to the standards set by their parents and other elders. For families with a tradition of intellectual attainment, there are powerful obligations to maintain an ancestral heritage of knowledge and accomplishment selflessly placed at the service of family, community and nation.

When I listened to Mrs Hoa and other members of her family, I did not feel that they were recapitulating a predigested or straightforwardly 'sanctioned' national narrative deploying familial images and emotions for crudely instrumental ends (Stoler and Strassler 2000: 12). Nor were they merely attempting to resist or repudiate a dominant cultural model, although they were certainly well informed about a wide range of official narratives, especially those taking a moralistic stance about the place of intellectuals in Vietnamese life. Our encounters therefore seemed to me to be part of a process that was both emotionally intense and sharply

---

[32] On the figure of the heroic mother as a 'cultural vector of grief and memory', see Hue Tam Ho Tai 2001: 177. Compare Stafford 1992; see also Pettus's exploration (2003) of changing official images of Vietnamese women as selfless and self-sacrificing mothers, wives and daughters.

analytical. I see it as an exercise in shared reflective thought for which the term critical memory seems most apt, and certainly not as a passive reception or inhabiting of events recalled or responded to.[33]

Epic journeys

Mrs Hoa's journey to China took three weeks, she told me. The children walked all the way, travelling at night for fear of French aircraft. The terrain was rough; there were frightening bamboo suspension bridges, which Mrs Hoa crossed carrying her sister on her back. On at least one occasion they ran for their lives, caught in the open with French spotter planes overhead, the younger girl clinging on, her feet pushed into Hoa's jacket pockets to steady herself.

Mrs Hoa said that it was four years before she and Lan were reunited with their parents and elder sister, then aged thirteen, whom they had left behind in one of the Viet Minh base areas. The family had already relocated several times within what were known as the interzones or *lien khu*. This is the Chinese-derived term for the largest units in the Viet Minh command structure. By the early 1950s, the six interzones comprising the insurgency's 'liberated territories' had become the provinces of a nascent DRV revolutionary state, with the Viet Minh leader, Ho Chi Minh, as its long-serving President. Mrs Hoa's father was a DRV official and held important posts in the administration both during and after the war years.

The sisters had all been born in Hanoi; her father and mother were both *lycée*-educated. Among my informants, one of the most frequently mentioned features of *tri thuc* identity is the presence of educated women in the family, in some cases dating back to the 1920s or 30s when a small but significant number of women achieved entry to the key institutions of Franco-Vietnamese education: the regional secondary schools and urban *lycée*s, and also the pedagogical colleges, most notably Indochina's premier teacher training institution, the Hanoi Ecole Normale.[34]

---

[33] I say more about these issues in Chapter 3, building on Passerini 1992; Tonkin 1992; Watson 1994; Lambek 1996; Stoler and Strassler 2000; Cole 2001.

[34] As in China, the official definition of a Vietnamese 'intellectual family' would be one with an educated household head, or one engaged in 'cultural work' (Kwong 1994: 263, n.1), but my informants all stressed the centrality of female education and career achievement to their understanding of what defines and animates the modern intellectual family. The idea of French as a male preserve and of French books as reading for men rather than women is something I have not encountered among my informants. See McHale 2004.

The notion of intellectual life as a family calling shared actively if not equally by men and women is a very pervasive one among my informants. The people I worked with made the bilateral kinship unit a central point of reference in almost everything they said, though they also gave emphasis to other affective ties including those of school and military cohortship. I have therefore made the making and unmaking of family and marital bonds, and the experience of friendship and educational cohortship, a critical focus, both in my treatment of children's and older people's experiences during the anti-French resistance war, and in its turbulent aftermath.

As I explain below, I am also concerned with the dynamics of narrative in forms involving multiple voices and shared participation on the part of kin and other intimates, rather than as the voicings of a single male or female narrator.[35] This too is a product of the way in which my fieldwork took shape and, I believe, provides important insights into the forging of both personal and official understandings of the recent and more distant past in former colonial as well as 'late' or post-socialist settings.

Of course this concern with family and other collective units of identity should not be thought of as an orientalist stereotype representing traditional 'Vietnamese minds' as thinking only in collective or relational terms. In fact, from the early twentieth century, Vietnam's educated 'moderns' both embraced and contested visions of the self involving first-person perspectives and individual points of view, not all of which were greatly at odds with those they knew from older Buddhist, Confucian and other discursive genres.[36] My informants were very willing to describe their own experiences and those of individual kin, friends and contemporaries, commenting on such things as specific people's motivations and emotional experiences. Such reflections were often focused on parents or other close relations, though people also speak at length about themselves. They also speak of such things as people's decisions to join the Viet Minh or pursue a new career as decisive episodes in family life, though with a strong emphasis on the initiatives and choices of individuals at such times. What the people I worked with clearly found both appropriate and gratifying was the idea of telling me about the

---

[35] Compare Werbner 1991 and Caplan 1997.
[36] Marr 2000; Nguyen The Anh 2002a; see also P. Taylor's exploration (2001: 99–101) of regional academic literature characterising pre-colonial southern Vietnam as the site of a distinctively individualist sense of identity; in some writings this has been represented as a key factor in the region's much-debated role as a contributor to post-1986 *doi moi* 'marketisation' initiatives.

Hanoi intelligentsia world from the perspective of their family (*gia dinh*) as the key affective unit in their lives.

The account I heard from Mrs Hoa and her relations about the moves they made at the start of the 1946–54 anti-French liberation war is very much a case in point. Having discussed the matter at length with their kin and the group of former *lycée* contemporaries to whom they were particularly close, Mrs Hoa's parents abandoned their modestly comfortable home in Hanoi for the Viet Bac, settling there with their three daughters. People like Mrs Hoa's father, a francophone scholar who had held a teaching post at one of the Hanoi secondary schools, were much sought after as Viet Minh recruits in the early years of the insurgency.[37] Like other educated Hanoi people, they had been active in recruiting those of similar background into the movement. They were soon joined in their interzone relocation site by other close kin, as well as several friends from their school days.

Those who 'went to the forest' (*vao rung*, a phrase often used for relocation from Hanoi to the interzones) usually did so in the company of wives, husbands and children. For many, I was told, this was the first time they and their kin had ever lived in a conjugal nuclear household rather than a multigenerational residence, or one in close proximity to those of parents and other kin with whom they interacted on a regular basis (Hirschman and Vu Manh Loi 1996; compare Bernstein 2005). The necessity of leaving elderly parents or other vulnerable relations behind, either in Hanoi or in a natal town or village without the possibility of regular visits or letters, is widely recalled as one of the painful aspects of these relocations.

A striking feature of these accounts is that the people I know speak of both their parents as providers of care and nurture in forms which are more usually thought of as emanating from the uniqueness of maternal love.[38] Clearly this had much to do with the special circumstances of my informants' wartime and post-war childhoods, with their many separations and displacements requiring habituation to continual movement, and the need to sustain affective ties even with very young children and siblings by means of letters and remittances, rather than the intimacies of face-to-face interaction.

For reasons I explain below, in the post-war years of the 1970s and 80s it was often a father who was left to tend the home and see to his

[37] On recruitment of intellectuals to the revolutionary cause, see Nguyen The Anh 2002b: 62–3; Ninh 2002: 48–9.
[38] Rydstrøm 2003; compare Stafford 1995: 69–78.

children's food, health and schooling, and a mother who was away for long periods on overseas training or work sojourns. Not surprisingly, then, some of my friends' most evocative accounts of wartime family life are to do with moments of exquisite sentiment occasioned by a father's gift of food, or a poignant gesture made when a child had been frightened or endangered. Something more specific to intelligentsia life is that both parents are widely spoken of as verbal providers. The people I know value the ability to write and speak well, and to convey delicate nuances of attachment and concern in everyday interaction. An ability to speak expressively of feelings that are deep and heartfelt (*chan tinh*) is a desirable mark of refinement and intelligence. In this context too I heard much about the actions of both fathers and mothers. Thus in parallel with the inevitable stories of being ardently exhorted to excel at school, I was struck by the many occasions when an account of wartime home life focused on a father's warmth and feeling, often manifested in such things as an enthusiasm for intimate evenings spent in wordplay, poetry recitations and verbal nonsense games.

I say more below about this issue of modern intellectual life as a family tradition of revolutionary and learned achievement. I also discuss the extent to which Hanoi's *tri thuc* intellectuals can be identified as members of an intelligentsia corresponding to either pre-revolutionary or socialist understandings of the term, most notably in Russia and China. Of particular importance is the question of how it is possible to sustain a collective identity as modern intellectuals, given that individual family members often pursued very divergent educational and career paths, with Mrs Hoa and her relations again being a case in point.

There were many other epic journeys in the course of the sisters' eventful lives. When I first met Mrs Hoa she had just retired from a forty-year career as an engineer. When the anti-French war ended in 1954, both sisters continued their schooling in China, then rejoined their parents in Hanoi. The younger, Lan, entered the capital's newly reopened medical college. By this time their elder sister was in the Soviet Union, studying at a Moscow secondary school from which she went on to a Russian university and subsequently became a university teacher in Hanoi. When Lan completed her medical training, she joined the national army's medical corps and found that Vietnam's overseas socialist 'friends' were beginning to bring undreamt of modern marvels within her reach. As I was proudly told by one of her younger relations, a woman academic in her early thirties, Dr Lan was one of the first women in Vietnam to receive pilot training, having eagerly taken up the offer of flight instruction when she learned that there were places available on a training scheme run by a unit of Czech military advisers posted near Hanoi.

Dr Lan was already married and a mother at the beginning of the 1961–73 US–Vietnam War; her husband was a Hanoi academic. Much of her wartime service involved long periods away from home, running army hospitals in forward areas, travelling for long distances along the famous network of covert supply routes known as the Ho Chi Minh Trail. Until the final weeks of her second pregnancy, she served in one of the most heavily bombed areas of the war zone. This was Vinh Linh, the site of one of Vietnam's celebrated military tunnel complexes, located just north of the 17th Parallel dividing the DRV from the US-backed Republic of (South) Vietnam or RVN. Dr Lan was permitted to make the difficult journey to Hanoi for the baby's birth, going into labour at the height of the US air offensive known as the 1972 Christmas bombing.

Both the ways in which these stories were recounted, and their compelling contents, connect directly with this study's central concerns. One issue is that of the intellectual family as a shared project involving initiatives and productive activities which might at first appear to be at odds with the inheritance and reproduction of *tri thuc* (modern intellectual) identity. Yet like many of the individuals I met or heard about, particularly educated women, Dr Lan spoke about herself as an active sharer in this identity. She was also spoken of with pride by others, especially her younger kin, as an active and important contributor to their life as an intelligentsia family, both by her own example of career achievement, and in her support for the education of other family members. This involved both emotional support, and the contributions she made from her army salary towards their schooling costs.

My informants spoke of both brothers and husbands as recipients of such women's support, as well as that of their own or other family members' children – girls as well as boys. I have also met women who went into the armed forces in order to free a brother or husband from his compulsory military service, thus allowing him to carry on with his studies. And in the 1970s and 80s, when the export of factory labour to other COMECON countries became a critical source of state revenues, an educated woman could also free a brother or husband from his conscription obligations by taking up a post as supervisor of Vietnamese workers recruited for factory employment in the USSR or Eastern Europe. This too would enable the man to establish himself in an academic career.

These are the kinds of gendered occupational distinctions that have been characterised in a wide variety of south-east Asian contexts as relegating women to a lowlier sphere of money-making and entrepreneurial activity, thus freeing male kin for a more exalted life: in past centuries that of a mandarin examination candidate, in more recent times a 'modern' man of learning.[39] This is not a view expressed by any of the women I know. Younger women in particular speak admiringly of the achievements of female elders who had spent their adult lives as army officers or in overseas 'expert' or factory management work. This was neither a sacrifice made at the behest of patriarchal elders, nor a sign of a woman's inherent lack of intellectual worth and refinement, but a choice made actively and willingly by educated women in the interest of all those with whom they shared ties of nurture and feeling (*chan tinh*).

As I show in Chapter 8, which explores the lives of female 'experts' who took up overseas work postings in Africa, such women represent themselves as direct participants in intelligentsia life, and indeed as active embodiments of the intellectual tradition which they and their kin had struggled to maintain in the face of many challenges and difficulties. Indeed the claim made by both the women themselves and their younger kin is that those who undertook these testing tasks are not to be seen as self-effacing nurturers who spent their lives fulfilling quintessentially female roles, i.e. the 'maintaining [of] kin and neighbourly relations' (Ong 1990: 261) and the provision of financial and emotional support for their children's educations.

Of course these accounts do bear on the much-discussed issue of whether new employment opportunities and recent changes in the dynamics of gender relations in private life have advantaged or dis-advantaged Asian women.[40] But my concern here and in later chapters is not primarily to do with issues of familial power relations. My main concern is with my informants' representations of familial feeling as an energising principle in the lives they have sought to lead as socialist world citizens and nation-builders, as well as contributors to their families' stock of cultural and moral capital. A modern intellectual should be by definition a person who finds pleasure and gratification in such things as aesthetic appreciation, a love of books, and warm-hearted relations with both friends and kin; both nation and family are enhanced and sustained

---

[39] See Hy Van Luong 1998: 300–5; compare Papanek and Schwede 1988; Brenner 1998; Rato 2004: 326.

[40] See, e.g., Yan 2003.

by such sensibilities. This is what came across with particular force when my friends sought to establish, both for me and for others taking part in our discussions, that women like Dr Lan derived personal gratification, as well as a sense of familial and public obligation fulfilled, from their efforts to transmit and exemplify the hallmarks of intelligentsia refinement both within the home, and in the course of their overseas work and training sojourns.

Worldwide friendships

A further issue, and one which also comes to the fore in later chapters, is that of socialist Vietnam's tricky relations of tutelage and fraternal 'friendship' with its far larger and richer allies and aid providers, especially China and the Soviet Union, the countries to which tens of thousands of Vietnamese were sent for scientific and specialist technical training in the post-independence years (Marr 2003: 274).[41] These powerful but often problematic interactions bore very directly on the lives of my informants and their families through a host of moral and practical experiences ranging from education and career moves to personal tastes and consumption choices. As I explained in Chapter 1, I am using the term worldwide socialist ecumene to refer to that set of visions which were once so widely shared both within and beyond Vietnam. Today these ideas are still regularly evoked though also subtly challenged and reformulated by many of the individuals I know, and in the country's official media. And on this issue as on others discussed by my informants, public narratives as well as individuals' more intimate accounts are often couched in an idiom of deep emotion, with much emphasis being placed on sentiments of loving warmth and true feeling (*chan tinh*) as an indispensable marker of virtue and worth, both in relations with kin and friends, and in interactions with those encountered both within and beyond the socialist ecumene.[42]

---

[41] According to Marr (2003: 273–5), the USSR trained 70,000 Vietnamese specialists between 1955 and 1985; another 30,000 went to eastern Europe's socialist states and an equal number to China. On Vietnam's relations with China, see Thayer 1994b.

[42] The socialist ecumene is not the same as other transnational or supralocal imagined zones of interaction, i.e. not the same as those linking old colonial metropoles and their former colonies, or fascist powers, or 'modernity' in general (Cooper 2005). It had the formal institutional arrangements of economic union and strategic alliances through COMECON and other official Soviet-centred networks. Yet at the same time, it entailed a much more widely shared set of political ideas, and also a host of symbolic reference points. These include ideals of redistributive justice and pantheons of revolutionary heroes and heroic attainments, thereby creating a real if open-ended sense of commonality uniting formally Communist countries with 'soft-socialist' states like

Long central to official and personal imaginings of this worldwide ecumene are conceptions of interactive fraternal community forged by both states and individuals on the basis of enduring revolutionary solidarities and 'friendships'. The term used in Vietnamese for such friendship ties is *quan he huu nghi*. In Vietnam, these ideas of global socialist modernity have interacted in complex and often surprising ways with the cultural and moral legacies of French colonial rule. It has been intellectuals, including many members of formerly francophone families, who became critically important to the forging of these nation-to-nation friendships. A key element in this process was the deployment of Vietnam's educated people as agents of developmental modernity in former African colonies. For these individuals, many of whom had Hanoi *tri thuc* backgrounds, it was in large part thanks to their francophone (or Franco-Vietnamese) education and linguistic facility that they were able to play the role which both they and the state authorities defined as that of socialist civilisers. As I show in Chapter 8, which explores Hanoi people's narratives of dispensing and acquiring both cultural and economic capital in 'friendly' African states, they and their families derived significant benefits from these overseas sojourns, though often at considerable cost. To be used as 'experts' (*chuyen gia*) in foreign lands threw doubt on their credentials as authentic intellectuals, even though much was said officially about the fact that their skills and knowledge were being deployed as a means of doing good for 'needy' Africans, as well as bringing in much-needed remittances to the national exchequer.

Following Chapter 4's account of the ways in which Vietnam's intelligentsia families have experienced the praise and denigration directed at them in official discourse, I turn in Chapter 5 to the issue of comparisons between their world and that of the Indian 'socialist moderns' whose experiences are both like and unlike those of the Hanoi people with whom I have worked. First, however, there are further points to make about the nature of my fieldwork and the conditions under which my informants delivered their personal narratives. These are the concerns of Chapter 3, below.

India into a world of progressive achievement rather than 'Third World' development 'problems'.

3 Narrating family lives in present-day Hanoi

Urban contexts

Having focused in the previous chapter on the importance of family and family-like relations to my informants' narratives, I turn now to the contexts in which I heard these accounts. My concern here is with the things I believe my informants were seeking to achieve through narrative, and with narration itself as a way of creating and enacting these affective attachments. I comment too on what informants conveyed about my own role in this process.

Mrs Hoa was among the many Hanoi people who usually spoke to me in the presence of other members of her household and extended family. My fieldwork has involved many such narrative occasions: congenial and often boisterous gatherings in which family members came together, generally in the presence of students and younger family friends. For those in their late fifties and above like Mrs Hoa, these were occasions to acquaint me, the visiting foreign researcher, and the young people who joined us, with matters they felt should be known and shared with others.

Of course I have also had many one-to-one encounters, both in informants' homes and in the course of enjoyable walks around the city. While my friends point to their *que* (ancestral village) as a place of special meaning for them, they also express warm affection for Hanoi's sights and spaces. They have made a point of showing me the city's lakeside beauty spots, and the cafés which are still spoken of as sites of typically Hanoian conviviality. The pleasures of café life were much missed, they say, during the years of post-war austerity which I describe in later chapters.

For older people, these visits have also been opportunities to hark back to the cultivated pleasures they recall from their years as students or 'experts' in the wider socialist world. Sitting over coffee with me, a former 'expert' who taught at a pedagogical college in Madagascar in the 1980s said, 'I was surprised that there were cafés. I read newspapers and

met people there, like in Hanoi, and Moscow when I was a student.'
The speaker was male; women said such things of Poznan and Moscow,
but not of African cities and especially not of those in Algeria, where
public spaces were spoken of as unwelcoming or dangerous for women.
For younger people, these images of cosmopolitanism are strongly
associated with childhood and their yearnings for absent 'expert' parents. Taking me home to meet her father, an academic who had worked
in Mozambique in the same period, a woman in her thirties said, 'He
wrote to us and said the city had a park with beautiful trees. He fell ill.
We were very worried, but he said he had friends and they went to the
café together.'

For the people I know, it is important and pleasurable to display this
sense of appreciation for sociable urban pastimes. This is something
conveyed through two distinct strands of cityscape narrative. One
entails a celebratory recounting of the sights and scenes of Hanoi life,
with much emphasis on the pleasures of achieving knowledge of good
places to drink coffee, buy books and appreciate fine views of its lakes
and architecture. These displays of proficiency in urban ways and
practices often hark back to their parents' Viet Minh experiences, much
as in published memoirs of the anti-French war such as *Au Coeur de la
Ville Captive* (*Giua Thanh Pho Bi Chiem*: In the Heart of the Captive
City, 2004). The book's author, Nguyen Bac, describes himself as a
first-generation Hanoi *lycéen* from a modest rural background who
spent the war years posing as a respectable francophone bourgeois
while recruiting in secret for the Viet Minh among the city's *lycéens* and
tri thuc modern intellectuals. The implication of the book's title is that
for francophone patriots of his generation, Hanoi was a quintessentially
Vietnamese home, its landmarks recalled with love and yearning by
former *lycéens* when called to serve in rural areas.[1] The city had been
made 'captive' by the foreign occupiers but not truly colonised. Despite
all the French had done to remap its streets and transform its vistas
with monumental building schemes, it had not been robbed of life and
meaning for those who had come into their own in its cherished spaces.
Like my friends, the author celebrates the city as a space possessed and
mastered in youth, partly by his efforts and those of the comrades with
whom he shared the city's pleasures, and partly through the sustaining
care of the kin who provided for them during their schooling and war
years.

---

[1] See Papin 2001: 295–301. On Asian and African cities as colonised space, see Mitchell
1988; Rabinow 1989; Wright 1991; Perera 2002.

So these are not accounts of first-generation incomers abashed and dispirited amid the anonymising 'hybridities' of a colonial metropole, like the Calcutta newcomers lampooned by Bengal's nineteenth-century *Kalighat* satirists (Guha-Thakurta 1992). And while grim things could happen to young patriots in wartime Hanoi, what these narratives recall about its public spaces is that they are the sites where the clever and daring could subvert the coloniser's gaze. On this theme the Nguyen Bac narrative has striking similarities to the things my informants have recounted about their Viet Minh parents' covert lives in the city, cultivating innocuous respectability in their French-style garments, exchanging secret hand signals with fellow patriots, painting slogans on public buildings under cover of darkness. 'We were there and they never saw us', one man said. He was another first-generation city-dweller; he too had the view that his generation's acquired knowledge of its streets and sophisticated ways equipped them to make their city a site of resistance, even in the years when some Hanoians – perhaps even a majority – were shamefully lacking in patriotic spirit (see Papin 2001: 306–7).

The other key strand in my friends' urban narratives is that of the cosmopolitanism they attained beyond Hanoi, in 'postcolonies' as well as COMECON states. This too is mastery achieved through warmth of feeling, as well as the deployment of cultivated knowledge. People often mention occasions when acquaintances in other lands embraced them as socialist 'friends', as when the man who had worked in Antananarivo told me about finding a city-centre square named after President Ho Chi Minh, and his gratifying encounters with Madagascans who praised Vietnam for its resistance war triumphs. At such moments, discerning world travellers can connect their homeland to a wider world of fellow 'socialist moderns' with their own histories of personal and national modernity forged (and of course contested) in urban settings.[2]

My friends do speak of darker memories of the colonial past, pointing out urban sites which they associate with acts of subjugation at the hands of the French, the Japanese or even Russians and other socialist 'friends' in the years after independence. I return in later chapters to this particular form of indignity, very painful for those who set such store by their identity as full participants in the cultural and intellectual exchanges of the socialist ecumene. My informants also speak of themselves and their forebears as bringing to Vietnam experiences and insights from far beyond the horizons of the colonial world, as in the case of the knowledge they acquired of such faraway

---

[2] On socialist and other forms of cosmopolitanism, see Chan 2002; Humphrey 2004.

places as Japan, Soviet Russia and even the USA. It is this double or treble layering of cosmopolitanisms that enables them to narrativise their lives and those of their families in ways that transcend exclusively colonial 'enframings'.

Much as they value these occasions when they can represent themselves as urbane café-goers and newspaper readers, it is not only sites of cultivation and conviviality which people speak of in these terms. Many identify sites of scientific modernity dating from both before and after independence as affective landmarks for them. My friends are enthusiastic about showing me their old schools, and such places as the laboratory complexes attached to the national university, and the big public hospital and medical school founded by the pioneering bacteriologist Alexandre Yersin (1863–1943) who famously isolated the plague bacillus in 1894 (Thompson 2003: 129).

Sharing family narratives

I have generally heard about experiences like Mrs Hoa's war service on more than one occasion, sometimes from the individual concerned, but often from younger family members. Sometimes these accounts have included recollections of other times when a particular story had first been heard, either from other relations, or from the person herself. This was usually followed by gatherings at which one or more individuals spoke at length about matters in which I was known to have an interest: education and school life; career decisions and employment experiences both at home and abroad; the learning and teaching of foreign languages. Of course other families were spoken of as well; the Hanoi *tri thuc* world is intimate and gossipy, its cross-cutting networks of intermarriage and educational cohortship generating a dense but open-ended web of friendships, rivalries and enmities.

Family members liked to consult one another before sharing their narratives with me, often conferring at length before deciding whether to air sensitive matters in my presence, and then following up with additional thoughts and details after further discussion among themselves. I found it instructive to receive multiple accounts of individual events or experiences.[3] It was enlightening too to see their communication networks in action. As recently as the early 1990s, the sharing of news within the intelligentsia world was done almost exclusively by word of mouth. It often fell to children to circulate information about everything

---

[3] Compare Werbner 1991 and Peel's (1995) account of 'doubleness' in narrative.

from births and deaths to the availability of new money-making ventures in the cash-strapped post-reunification period. One woman I know recalls doing these duties in the early 1980s, riding her household's single shared bicycle from house to house to tell kin and friends about matters for which there were no other reliable sources. This included important news such as the death of a much-loved senior academic who had taught her parents and many of their contemporaries. At each house, she said, she heard some small but memorable detail about the great man and his family, and the loving relations sustained between him and his former students throughout their adult lives.

These contacts played a key role in maintaining the ties of knowledge and affect that nourished and sustained the *tri thuc* or 'modern intellectual' world. My friend said that even at twelve, she felt herself an active agent in these exchanges, both contributing to and learning from the things said and shared between the households in her family's network of city-based kin and friends. While modes of communication have changed immensely now that even the modestly prosperous have telephones and email access, the importance of acquiring and sharing information is still central to *tri thuc* life within and beyond the family.

I was continually struck by the detailed knowledge which even very young people had of their own ramifying kin networks, as well as those of their elders' friends and teachers. Of course when a teenaged student from a distinguished revolutionary family rattled off the birth, marriage, colonial incarceration and death dates of all four grandparents, together with those of all their siblings and most of their spouses, I knew she had probably done a fair amount of advance preparation. Yet no-one thought there was anything unusual about such command of family history. The people I know like to give detailed accounts of the educational attainments of their parents and other elders, including their attendance at colonial Franco-Vietnamese schools. Some in their sixties and above also recall their parents' families as having equipped their sons and sometimes their daughters with a grounding in traditional Sino-Vietnamese learning, which meant having them taught the rudiments of Chinese and *nom* (or *chu nom*, the ideographic Chinese-derived script in which Vietnamese was written before the adoption of romanised *quoc ngu*). 'My father was in the *service cartographique*. He knew many Chinese characters; he attended the *lycée* and spoke good French', I was told by a former Viet Minh draughtsman and map-maker. My friends are also well informed about the big personalities of the Hanoi intellectual world, including individuals not personally known to them or their families. And as I explain in Chapter 4, they thought of their own families as having lived under a permanent public spotlight, with their doings much discussed by those both within and beyond their own networks of kin, friends and teachers.[4]

As far as my own fieldwork was concerned, I was also reassured by the consultative aspect of this process. It is not all that long ago that unmonitored interactions with foreigners were suspect if not impossible for most Vietnamese. Naturally I had official approval for my research and was often told that my interest in the country's educational achievements and the careers of its intellectuals was both creditable and gratifying. But I was still glad that those with whom I spoke could take ample time to consider how much they wished to share with me. The people I have worked with are articulate verbalisers with experience of many biographical and autobiographical narrative processes. These include the conventions of funeral oratory and memorial tribute occasions, as well as the many contexts including newspaper and school textbook accounts in which exemplary individuals are held up as models of national virtue.[5] Everyone I know has also experienced the official narrativisation processes by which details of a person's family background, education and career landmarks take shape as a permanent record of their merits or demerits as socialist citizens. The presence or absence of black marks in a personal dossier (*ly lich*) can still determine eligibility for Party membership, university admission and coveted opportunities for overseas work and training. The people I have worked with are also familiar with the presentation of formal public accounts of themselves at the periodic official assemblies or *mit-tinh*s (from the English 'meeting') which are still a set-piece feature of Party and workplace life. In the past, such occasions often involved the demanding conventions of self-criticism, an obligatory schoolroom practice in the Democratic Republic (DRV) in the post-independence period. Though rarely taken to the extremes once common in China, its regimens were also a key experience for the children who studied in the Chinese People's Republic (PRC). Mrs Hoa's family have kept a treasure trove of family letters including those exchanged between the three sisters in the

---

[4] On the preservation of knowledge about illustrious ancestors in China, see Cong Cao 1999: 1001.
[5] The 'People' section of the official Party daily *Nhan Dan* is a fascinating source of such tribute writings. On modes of narrative see James 1997; among the many important works on memory as an active moral and emotional process, see Zur 1999. Some Vietnamese lineages maintain written histories containing genealogical details and other important information about family events and achievements (Rydstrøm 2003: 7); the urban people I know say these registers (*gia pha*) are maintained by their rural kin and kept in their ancestral villages.

1950s. Those from the two studying in China mix affectionate greetings to their elder sibling with the painfully confessional phraseology of self-criticism.[6]

Like other anthropologists researching personal memory, I was much struck by the significance which the presentation of life-history narrative held for my informants. I too see the recounting of individual and family experience as an act of moral agency, as well as a source of gratification and a means of achieving a variety of instrumental ends. Thus while there was much light-hearted banter and teasing in the course of our gatherings, and a general fondness for wordplay and poetic quotation, much of what I heard was recounted in a strongly emotional register. At certain times almost everyone spoke of matters that both speakers and listeners referred to as moving, heartening or saddening. There were occasions when those present shed tears and spoke forcefully and at length about the sensations of regret, indignation or joy evoked by a particular account or memory.[7]

In all this there are parallels with the narrative situations documented by ethnographers working in a host of post-socialist and postcolonial settings. It is clear why Skultans and others dealing with memories of mass deportations and other traumatic experiences have found it illuminating to theorise the processes they document through models of cathartic public testimony and medical case-history narrative. But the narrative occasions I experienced in Hanoi differed in important ways from those documented in these and other accounts of painfully retrieved recollection in the aftermath of massive state repression. My own informants clearly had a number of aims in mind when they shared their accounts with me, including the sharing and stockpiling of knowledge, and the fostering of a sense of both individual and family achievement on the part of younger kin and other important participants including their students and colleagues. And for these occasions, I believe a rather different model is appropriate, the one I suggest being a model of nurture and provisioning.

As noted earlier, these are actively reflective as well as affective processes for which I use the term critical memory. But I also see them as involving something akin to the provisioning acts by which people attain and impart necessities to close kin. Thus through these exercises of shared critical memory, I believe that my informants collectively pool,

---

[6] See Ninh 2002: 105–6, 113–17. On the use of 'self-examination' (*jiancha*) language in Chinese schools and workplaces, see Yang 1988.

[7] Lambek 1996; Ries 1997; Skultans 1997; and see Stoler and Strassler's account of memory as 'interpretive labour' (2000: 9).

transmit and deploy the factual and emotional content of their narratives, experiencing them as a stock of resources to be accessed and used in a variety of ways, stockpiling and exchanging them, and exploring them in a range of intimate and more public settings. This is often done for gratification, but it also serves practical and instrumental ends. Paramount among these is the sustaining of families as affective moral units whose members share valued knowledge of their kinfolk's achievements and thus acquire an ability to interact through knowledge exchange with other families, especially those of the Hanoi intelligentsia world.[8]

What then of my own presence among them? In writing of those who took an understandably proprietary attitude towards her research with former residents of her Algerian ancestral home, the anthropologist J. Bahloul uses the phrase 'ethnography as dictation' (1996: 6). I too found that both younger and older people took a distinctly proprietary interest in my work, taking pains to make our encounters both convivial and distinctly didactic in form and tone. My presence at workplace and family gatherings seemed to be welcomed for a variety of reasons, one being that it was an opportunity for the more senior people to operate in a quasi-classroom mode, taking note of my progress in Vietnamese, and commenting authoritatively on such matters as word derivations and the use of Chinese-derived neologisms in modern Vietnamese. They frequently arranged for students and junior colleagues to listen to our exchanges, enjoying my mild embarrassment when they held me up as a

---

[8] This is, of course, a highly selective process: on the importance of the suppression of tragic and divisive family memories relating to the separations and dislocations of war and its aftermath in Vietnam, see Hue Tam Ho Tai 2001: 189–92. See also Humphrey 1994; Schwarcz 1994; Lambek 1996; Tarlo 2003; Passerini 2005. These are the reference points which Skultans (1997) and others have discerned when their informants have described their memories of traumatic events such as Stalin's mass deportations in the Baltic (Kleinman and Kleinman 1994; contrast Watson 1994). And see Cole 2001. Stoler and Strassler (2000: 7) note that theories of memory focusing on ideas of perception, construction and representation are now favoured over quantitative 'storehouse' and stock retrieval models (Koriat and Goldsmith 1996). What I am proposing for the distinctive context of shared family memories is a modified combination of the two: for Hanoi intellectual families there do seem to be forms of shared knowledge that are important to store, archive and retrieve, and the quantitative side of this process is as important to those involved as its affective or qualitative dimensions. Compare Rabinow's (1996) account of ethnographic encounters with scientists whom he found to be more like interactive colleagues than conventional 'informants'; also Carsten's (2000) account of fieldwork in which she was more 'witness' than interviewer, with informants delivering long, emotionally intense narratives, especially her emphasis on the role of 'the ethnographer who listens' as a key figure in the process of forging identity (in this case of intellectuals and of intellectual families) through the recounting of narrative (2000: 698). See also Leshkowich 2006.

hyper-conscientious role model: 'Suzanne takes her notes so carefully! You must do the same. She is so serious – she notes down everything!'

Being both female and younger than many of my key informants, I have been treated by many people much as they treat their younger kin and close colleagues, speaking to me warmly and banteringly when we are alone or with other close friends and kin, instructing me in proper comportment before important activities like visits to officials, and embracing me affectionately when we meet and part. On initial acquaintance, most addressed me formally as *chi* (older sister), the relational pronoun appropriate for female colleagues in a workplace situation. But older people subsequently adopted the much less formal *em*. Many of my friends are deans or heads of their departments or research institutes and have the title *giao su*, professor. People took pains to establish that my own title is 'doctor' (*tien si*), and that for most of my time in the field my academic post was that of lecturer (*giang vien*). These were matters of which both older and younger people took careful note: when I was promoted to a readership in 2005, my friends tried hard to work out a Vietnamese equivalent.

It is also significant that I belong to a university which Hanoi people regularly refer to as 'famous' (*noi tieng*: celebrated or renowned), a word carrying much weight in Vietnam, as does *lon*, big or famous, used to identify people of great distinction: this has been used in recent newspaper items about 'revolutionary intellectuals' like Nguyen Van Huyen. Both may be used out of politeness, or to ingratiate. But those who show knowledge of 'famous' people and institutions are also signalling something about themselves, demonstrating that they are educated and 'cultivated' (*co hoc thuc*).

What people said about my own university – apart from that knowing comment 'ah, *rat noi tieng*!' ('very famous!') – was that as a Cambridge academic, I come from a country that is 'innocent' (*vo toi*) in its past dealings with Vietnam, unlike France and the USA. And it was important that I was comparatively new to research in Vietnam. This, and the fact that as someone younger than many of my informants I was a relational junior in Vietnamese terms, reinforced the quasi-didactic aspect of our exchanges. I could thus be treated both as a fellow researcher and devotee of 'science' (*khoa hoc*) – i.e. an intellectual among fellow intellectuals – and at the same time, as a kind of junior colleague receiving the expert tutelage which only they were qualified to impart.[9]

---

[9] Compare Boyer and Lomnitz 2004: 105, citing Bauman 1987: 8.

Most were aware that I had spent many years doing research in India, but this has been of little interest. The key issue was that I was someone to share information and feeling with in ways appropriate for intelligentsia cosmopolitans, and above all someone to teach about Vietnam. This is an enterprise relished by all, and one that older people said was reminiscent of the forging of affectionate friendships with foreigners from the COMECON states in their years of overseas study and 'expert' work.

It has been clear that some people have aired memories in my presence that they have not previously discussed with outsiders. What this meant in particular were recollections of painful times when they felt that they and their families were fighting a losing battle to retain their identity as educated moderns. This sense of the emotional and practical struggles involved in remaining in the world of the *tri thuc* intellectuals was central to the narrative logic of their accounts and is an issue to which I return below. The point to stress here is that for many, the telling of their stories was itself a means of giving substance to their families' shared intelligentsia identity. I was therefore conscious of reticences, evasions and silences, and of the fact that certain people were willing to speak of things avoided by others, including the delicate subject of trading for profit which I discuss in later chapters. Like Stoler and Strassler, I recognise that the exploration of such matters entails working at 'the fault lines of memory, the places of discomfort and disinterest as well as those of safety and concern' (2000: 11). But I had to accept that there were topics too dangerous or otherwise impossible to touch on in relation to people's own families, though sometimes hinted at in comments about others: family members who made problematic marriages with foreigners or 'class enemies'; kin who 'went south' or fled the country for France or even the USA, or underwent imprisonment or Chinese-style 'rustication' (compulsory rural labour) in the 1950s and 60s. My concern had to be with what people considered appropriate to present as a matter of shared critical memory, not to demand entry to terrain they considered improper for us to traverse together.[10]

---

[10] See Beatty 2005 on the complexities involved in accurately documenting 'feeling' and emotional practices in fieldwork; and Malarney 1997. While I heard much about both the ideal and the practice of loving intimacy in familial relations, like Oxfeld (1992), whose fieldwork focused on narratives of familial life among Calcutta's Chinese immigrant entrepreneurs, I also encountered elements of tension and ambivalence in people's accounts of filial experience, as I show in later chapters. See also Malarney 1998: 282–3.

Narrators, selves, collectivities

Although I have spent much time in people's homes and workplaces, much of my fieldwork has taken the form of trips with older friends to the sites of their far-flung wartime childhoods. These were arranged at their initiative and included stays in such places as Thanh Hoa province, 100 miles south of Hanoi. During the 1946–54 liberation war, Thanh Hoa was one of Interzone IV's key production zones. Renowned for its high concentration of intellectual recruits to the Viet Minh, this region contained a celebrated university preparatory school, the Du Bi Dai Hoc or 'Pre-university'. Some of my informants taught or studied there. Others are the sons and daughters of intellectuals with skills and knowledge equipping them for service in its printing, map-making and technical design operations.[11]

Everyone agreed that until I had seen their childhood homes in the interzones and such places as their relocation sites during the anti-US War, I would not truly grasp what they wished me to understand about their lives. Older people liked me to meet pivotal figures from their childhoods, especially their schoolmates and former teachers, but also villagers who had befriended them during their evacuation sojourns. My friends took pains to convey the feel and affective significance of those remembered experiences. As we strolled along a sunny riverbank near the ruins of a French blockhouse dating from the liberation war, Dr Tran, a distinguished academic in his mid-sixties, suddenly hurled himself to the ground, distorting his face into a painful grimace, a finger in each ear and his thumbs forced under his lips to hold his mouth agape. This, he said, was the way the Viet Minh fighters he knew in childhood had shown him the technique of protecting their ears and inner organs when they mounted grenade attacks on French observation posts like the ones he was showing me. By forcing their mouths open, he said, they reduced the risk of internal injury when the blast forced all the air from their lungs.

This grim little demonstration was for my benefit and that of the students travelling with us, and punctuated a series of stories about the village families with whom he had lived in his interzone relocation sites. Later that week, we met one of the families with whom he was still in regular contact; he had been billetted with them in the late 1960s when his Hanoi-based research unit was relocated to their village during the anti-US war. We subsequently attended a wedding at their home. The

---

[11] Vasavakul 1995; Dang Phong 2002: 42–9; Ninh 2002: 86–8; Marr 2003: 266–7. Thanh Hoa was a mandarinal examination site until the early nineteenth century (Cooke 1995).

groom's father had lost a leg in an American bombing raid. With encouragement from Dr Tran, and the accompaniment of ribald commentary from his kin and friends, Mr An showed us how he had learned to ride a motorbike while wearing his prosthesis. 'So I could work again', he said, explaining that from then on he provided for his family as a local produce trader.

Thus it was in the course of these visits that I learned most about people's consciousness of belonging to that wide array of both smaller and larger family and family-like moral units which I discussed in the preceding chapter. On the road and in the countryside, and especially as we walked the lanes of their wartime relocation villages, my friends had much to say about both the forging of these attachments, and the affective awarenesses that underpinned and sustained them. Once again, I learned a great deal from the ways in which my informants helped to shape the methods and logistics of my fieldwork. It became clear as we travelled and discussed the lives they had led during the two resistance wars that their experiences of family rupture and separation were often painful and perilous. Yet these were also recalled as separations which they and their kin had embarked on willingly and purposefully, using them as opportunities for the creation of new affective relations which often spanned very wide geographical and temporal spaces. Those recalling these experiences made it clear that they wanted me to move with them as they relived this forging of new, quasi-familial networks which, in theory at least, both complemented and enhanced those of their more conventional kin and marital ties.

So the 'family' as a moral, ritual and affective unit has long been a highly variable entity for the people with whom I worked. As I show in Chapter 8, in the economic crisis years that followed reunification in 1976, almost everyone I know developed survival strategies which relied on the pooling of information and scarce material resources amassed through networks of both natal and marital kin. This activation of family ties involved both relations living within the city and also people's all-important bonds with their rural kindred. In many cases, this meant a revival of arrangements remembered from the pre-independence period, when a son or sometimes a daughter studying far from home in a market town secondary school or Hanoi lycée relied on rural kin to supply them with food and other necessities. Of course this was above all a means of stretching their tiny student bursaries. But these acts of provisioning were also a key means of maintaining ties of warmth and feeling with a natal household and 'home place', as well as the individual's wider kin network. This is still an important part of Hanoi student life. Anyone visiting the countryside is expected to be a willing carrier of local delicacies and such things as locally produced medicinal and cosmetic products as tokens of loving nurture for sons and daughters attending universities in Hanoi, as well as those studying abroad.

There is an instructive parallel here with Stafford's account of the close connection between food and medicinal substances in Chinese villages, and also the link between both the family's – and especially mothers' – key role of nurturing their kin through feeding, and the many other acts of bodily sustenance and provision which are regularly performed in these Chinese contexts (Stafford 2000). Whether performed in wartime or in the post-war scarcity years before 'renovation', the provisioning activities recalled by my informants are also understood as acts of nurture based on principles of mutuality and feeling. They are not conceptualised as instrumental acts of exchange, but as an activation of the forms of mutual aid and feeling which have defined both the 'traditional' and 'modern' socialist family in Vietnam. Yet what is specific to the Vietnamese context, and in particular to the lives of Hanoi intelligentsia families (though perhaps also to be found in China), are the very long distances and time spans across which these nurturing ties have been experienced, with the result that Hanoi people often speak of a distinctive and strongly enhanced quality of affect pervading both the items themselves, and the relations which they embody. I return later to these issues of family gift and provisioning practices, focusing on the high value placed on the letters and gift items brought or sent back by loving friends and parents from their faraway work and study sites in the wider socialist ecumene.

My informants also made much of the family-like bonds forged between army friends during the war years.[12] They recall these groupings as collectives united like a household around a single shared cooking pot. 'I'll show you how to eat like the Viet Minh!' said Mr Duy, as we sat together at an outdoor supper among friends and family members at a famous mountain beauty spot. We had been eating in familial mode, the younger people attending to everyone's rice bowls, their elders occasionally placing a special morsel in a junior's dish. With his chopsticks and the soup ladle, Mr Duy demonstrated the technique of pooling the evening's rations, playing the part of the group's 'elder brother'. In this context too there had to be an elder to nurture the juniors, this comrade's

---

[12] Compare Malarney 2002: 181. Shared imprisonment in the brutal 'colonial Bastilles' is also widely represented as an experience engendering powerful quasi-fraternal bonds between political prisoners of intelligentsia background (see Zinoman 2001a: 116). On the forging of sibling-like bonds between revolutionary activists, see also Giebel 2004: 23–4; N. Taylor 2004: 49–50.

task thus being to share out the food with great precision, ensuring that everyone's portion contained an exactly equal amount of fat, bone and gristle, with any precious fragments of lean meat distributed fairly among them all.

But it was invariably the 'real' family (*gia dinh*) to which my informants gave the greatest emphasis, both as a source of sustenance and a focus of enduring emotion. My interest in families was an unfailing door-opener, and my wish to hear about what a distinguished forebear had done as a scholar or scientist invariably met with approval. It was something which showed proper feeling (*chan tinh*) on my part, as well as providing their kin, friends or students an opportunity to manifest their own filial feelings by sharing their recollections with me.

While my friends had much to say about the formally structured side of filial relations, including such matters as age deference and junior–senior linguistic usages (*xung ho*), their sense of the family unit (*gia dinh*) as a focus of personal identity was both fluid and open-ended. Of course the significance of the patriline (*ho*) is very apparent. It is recognised through the rituals of household ancestor altar worship and annual Lunar New Year (*Tet*) visits to the tombs of paternal ancestors. Yet in conversation and everyday interactions, the bilateral nature of familial attachment is very apparent. Those whom individuals identify as 'family members' and whose attainments merit pride and praise include the kin and forebears of both parents, and also marital kindred (Hy Van Luong 1989 and 1992: 70–9).

Even though many of the families I know still live in allocated or official housing, kin often find ways to live in close proximity to one another, though often not on a conventional pattern of patrilocality and agnatic connection. In the early *doi moi* ('renovation') period when private house ownership became permissable, one family I know used their earnings from overseas work sojourns to build three modestly sized houses on adjoining residential plots. These were on the site of a colonial villa allocated in the early days of the DRV to an eminent Hanoi intellectual and his *lycée*-educated wife; both died in the 1970s. Two of the three married siblings are the deceased scholar's daughters; the third is their younger brother (compare Papin 2001: 334–5 and 368, n. 2).

This then was much like the urban familial networks observed by Bernstein in Japan (2005: 296–7). I too was told that it was not unusual for closely interacting urban kin to be connected through wives and sisters rather than a husband and his male kin. In this family, each of the three siblings lives with his or her spouse and unmarried student-age children. The deceased scholar's collection of books and papers, together with other items including striking watercolours painted by their mother, is lodged in the younger daughter's household. This was the house to which I was usually invited to hear about the family's educational and career experiences. The lives of the three siblings' parents were generally at the forefront of our discussions, but when we spoke there was a continual to-ing and fro-ing between the houses as both older and younger people dropped in to listen and contribute anecdotes about themselves and their own cross-cutting networks of natal and marital kin. Thus, as in official media stories about exemplary intellectuals, when people say 'we come from an intellectual family' (*gia dinh tri thuc*), they clearly have in mind a broadly inclusive unit embracing affines as well as 'blood' kin. This is also the way they speak of the taking of critical decisions such as relocation to the interzones through the consultative processes described above.

My friends also discussed the making of 'modern' marriages in much the same way, that is as decisions in which individual inclination played a large part. Yet they also speak of these choices as being made through kin and quasi-kin, even among revolutionaries. Mr Binh and his wife, whose wartime marriage I described above, told me that it was he who first caught sight of his future bride at the military hospital where she worked. But it was his youthful comrades who pronounced her a suitable partner for him, encouraging him to pursue the relationship even though they knew it would be months or even years before they could marry. I was also told that in the years before the anti-French war, individuals with 'modern' views and educations were content for their 'blood' kin to arrange their marriages. Dang Van Ngu (1910–67), one of the DRV's leading 'modern' medical practitioners, wrote in his autobiography that he left it to his parents to select his bride. They ensured that she had a 'modern' education as befitted the spouse of a *tri thuc* 'modern'. But they also made the match in the way a traditional mandarin's parents would have done; the couple thus met for the first time six years later, in 1937, after he had completed his studies and immediately before the wedding.[13]

I never came across stories of marriages made on Party orders, though the sociologist Pham Van Bich documents the vetting of Party members' marriage choices (1999: 133–4). What people did say was that in relation to marriage and other personal matters, the forging of soldiers' friendships and other quasi-familial ties both enhanced and interpenetrated with those animating their marital and natal bonds. In the chapters that follow, I explore my informants' engagements at all these levels of

[13] See www.vietnamnews.vnagency.com.vn/08SUN181205.

affective life. I include those collectivities officially sanctioned by the state, most notably those of the progressive 'new culture' family (Malarney 2002; Schlecker 2002). I do not mean to overlook the comparatively impersonal ties that all citizens are called on to forge through occupational and professional unions, workplace committees, military unit associations and so on (Schlecker 2005: 521). But my central concern is still the claims and commitments of family in its varied forms and manifestations interacting – both harmoniously and problematically – with other key allegiances, especially those forged and experienced within the wider socialist ecumene.

Maintaining family and learning

The sending of children to distant lands is not spoken of by my informants as a denial of the family, or a sign that the country's leaders expected filial claims and bonds to be expunged by those of nation and revolution. There was of course an extensive pre-independence literature on the 'problem' of the patriarchal 'Annamite' family. And, after independence, the DRV launched a series of campaigns to reform those aspects of family life allegedly perpetuating 'feudal' or 'backward' values.[14] Indeed in contrast to Chatterjee's idea of the family and household as redoubts against colonialism (1993), both pre- and post-independence reformist messages stressed the need to take Vietnamese youth out of the home and into healthy external spaces including brightly lit modern schools, youth organisations and even overseas locales and learning environments. Without this enlargement of experience, it was said, the arena of the family could indeed be asocial, confined and backward-looking. Such an environment would be inward turning, productive of weedy Confucian proto-scholars, rather than healthy, modern patriots and socialist world citizens.[15]

It is also true that as in China, one of the grim features of the 1953–6 anti-landlord purges known as Land Reform (*cai cach ruong dat*) was the enforced repudiation of kin condemned as 'class enemies' (Watson 1994: 65–6; Malarney 2002: 23–51; compare Feuchtwang 2006). But family consciousness per se was not systematically attacked in Vietnam.

---

[14] Turley 1972; Marr 1981: 131–3, 333–5; Malarney 1996b and 2002; compare Yan 2003: 47–57; and Xin Liu 2000: 331–51.

[15] See Bayly 2004a; compare Stafford 1995: 3–30, 56–68; and Fitzpatrick 1992: 102–3. On Vietnamese mothers as protectors of their family's educational attainments, see Phan Dai Doan and Nguyen Quang Nuoc 2002. And see Hy Van Luong 1992; Malarney 2002: 55; N. Taylor 2004: 24.

Family altars and household ancestor veneration were not proscribed after independence. This was in contrast to the policy regarding one of the key institutions of rural life, the communal village hall or *dinh* housing the altar of the village's guardian deity, and serving as a focus for the community's collective ritual life. DRV reformers condemned the *dinh*s as sites of 'superstition' and 'hierarchy'.[16] But all families should honour their ancestors. Modern individuals should feel impelled by a sense of filial obligation. One should not think of this as Confucian or neo-Confucian 'traditionalism'. To defer to the claims of filial piety, said Ho Chi Minh, to feel bound in duty and gratitude to virtuous exemplary forebears, was in keeping with the values of a modern patriot selflessly serving party, state and nation, exalting youth and progress, and looking fearlessly to the future.[17] So the sense of one's family as possessing a distinguished tradition of intellectual attainment places powerful obligation on individuals to live up to this model of parents and forebears who selflessly placed their accomplishments at the service of community and nation. This can be both painful and exalting, as I show below.

There is a long tradition in Vietnam of families pooling resources to finance at least one kinsman's schooling (Malarney 1998: 276), and of such children being placed with others to further their educations. In past centuries, this often meant a family of modest means arranging for a talented son to reside in a richer household with the means to educate him. The case of the national hero Marshal Vo Nguyen Giap (b. 1912) is regularly referred to as a modern instance, as is the fact that he conformed to another element of this tradition by marrying one of the daughters of this household, that of the francophone Viet Minh cultural supremo Professor Dang Thai Mai.[18]

Under the French, schools teaching the modern Franco-Vietnamese curriculum were few in number; many of those enrolled had to lodge far from home in order to attend. Boys were inevitably in the majority at the regional secondary schools and urban *lycées*, though in the 1930s and 40s there were significant numbers of girl *lycéens*. In a number of published

---

[16] See Nguyen Van Huyen 1994: 96–106, 202; Endres 2001; compare Kwon 2007.

[17] Launching the mass literacy drive in 1946, Ho Chi Minh identified the household unit as a key site for its achievement: 'The husband will teach his wife, the elder brother…his brothers and sisters, children will teach their parents, the master in the house will teach those who live under his roof' (Vu Can 1971: 87) See also Cao Thi Nhu-Quynh and Schafer 1988: 772n.

[18] Ninh 2002: 74–87; see Chapter 6 below. Giap is renowned as the architect of Vietnam's military victories against both the French and the USA. Compare Bernal 1981: 159 on Dang Chinh Ky, leader of the Nghe Tinh insurgency of 1930, who was the early revolutionary Phan Boi Chau's secretary and tutor to his sons.

autobiographical accounts, narrators pay tribute to the kin who provided for them during their school days. My informants too have paid tribute to the acts of filial nurture that sustained them through their schooling both close to home and further afield. 'Paris-returned' sons and daughters were even fewer in number, of course, and a focus of intense interest, much discussed by other intellectual families and often referred to in the press.

The reabsorption of such individuals could be problematic, even for a family of Hanoi 'moderns'. And while the sending of children to China during the anti-French war is still much hailed as a valued opportunity for those involved and a boon to the whole nation, it too is spoken of as a challenging matter for the young people and their families. Some returned with ideas that were found to be greatly at odds with those of their parents and other kin, even in households where one or both parents were Party members. Thus even in households like these, whose elder members had given much thought to the balancing of kin ties and a sense of distinctive family tradition against the claims of workplace, nation and party, it was a shock to be told by a child newly returned from China that their reverence for universities and academic qualifications was 'bourgeois'.

When people referred to these experiences, they sometimes mentioned anxieties surrounding another group of young people whose special circumstances they said were much discussed both during and after the anti-US war. These are the children whose parents served as covert DRV agents in the south, working against the American-backed RVN (Republic of Vietnam) regime during the anti-US war. Having been relocated for safety to the DRV, their children too were placed in special schools, remaining out of touch with their parents and other kin for years at a time. I was told that 'on their own' – i.e. having been perilously unmoored from family care and nurture (*cham soc*), and unable to receive letters, gift items or any other tokens of love and sustenance, such children were thought of as problematic. The phrase people used was 'uncared for' (*nhung dua tre khong nguoi cham soc*), and the consequences thought of as a tendency to behavioural problems and academic underachievement.

These views clearly overlapped with anxieties recalled from the early years of reunification about the difficulties arising from the union of the country's two long-divided populations, with their radically different experiences of the post-1954 partition years. This too is an issue to which I return in later chapters: children are precious assets, yet are not to be thought of merely as passive recipients of love and nurture, to be shaped and guided as their elders determine. On the contrary, even the very young are active agents in the moral life of both family and nation and thus possess the capacity to think and act in ways which can both enrich and endanger the viability of that moral life.

Intelligentsia children can be particularly problematic in this respect. This is because of their high visibility, and their comparatively privileged lives and opportunities, a matter which can attract dangerous resentments and suspicions in a socialist society. It is also because of the many expectations visited upon them. These expectations emanate from their kin, for whom they carry forward the hopes and cherished traditions of their families. They also emanate from the state and Party for whom they are key embodiments of the nation's future. This is a future to be understood as one of participating in the great projects of socialist modernity both at home, and in the country's interactions within the wider socialist ecumene, where its young people's performance and conduct will be under worrying international scrutiny.

In my discussions with two brothers who are now in their sixties, I learned a great deal about these concerns regarding the education and provisioning of revolutionaries' children. The elder, Mr Nam, is a retired secondary-school teacher; his brother is a Hanoi professor. They spoke to me together, in the presence of family members and several former students. Like Mrs Hoa, Mr Nam had made the difficult trek to the Que Lam school for cadres' children in south China. There were thirty children in his group; their journey took nearly five weeks. They too walked all the way, carrying little more than their rice sacks and a change of clothes. At sixteen, Mr Nam was the eldest, so it was his task to carry their single cooking pot. They travelled by night; it was December, a cold month in the north; Mr Nam said he tried to keep warm by wearing his two shirts and two pairs of trousers one on top of the other.

At this time the brothers were living with their parents in a village near Thanh Hoa in Interzone IV. Their father and mother were francophone; they too had both attended Hanoi *lycées*. Both parents were Viet Minh officials. Like Mrs Hoa's parents, they had lived in modest comfort before relocating to the interzones. Neither had travelled abroad before the anti-French war, though both subsequently experienced brief periods of training and Party delegation work in China. Like Mr Binh's family, Mr Nam's parents had respectable rather than grand rural ancestry. Their forebears included practitioners of Vietnamese traditional medicine but no Confucian degree holders.

Mr Nam and his brother have a collection of evocative family photographs from the pre-war period and their interzone days. All were taken by itinerant photographers, touting from house to house; only the rich owned costly items like cameras and radios. There is a striking image of their mother in the small garden of their Hanoi house in about 1941. She is reading a newspaper, very much the informed modern Hanoi woman, and she is dressed in a decorously cut *ao dai*. This distinctive tunic and trouser outfit is now sometimes referred to as 'traditional' Vietnamese attire but was in fact popularised as modern national dress in the 1930s.[19] Mr Nam said his mother always wore an *ao dai* and the elegantly upswept hair that younger people immediately recognise as characteristic of genteel urban women in the 1930s and 40s. As I have seen in other friends' photos, it was younger unmarried girls who had their hair cut Western-style and adopted sporty open-necked shirts and skirts when they went to the interzones. Most families I know have photographs from their interzone years, all looking banally domestic until one remembers that the young people in the pictures are Viet Minh officers' and cadres' children. In one group, the little boy perched on a pony – not a pet but a service pack animal, I was told – was being given a farewell treat before setting off on the trek to China (see Plate 16).

Mr Nam's father had secured comparatively well paid white-collar employment in the period immediately before the 1945 August Revolution. The family had led a typical Hanoi 'petit bourgeois' life, said his brother, employing both the French term and its Vietnamese equivalent, *tieu tu san*. Yet while the family had eventually attained the trappings of a modestly comfortable *tieu tu san* existence by the early 1940s, their earlier married years had also been truly deprived, he said. Only a few years previously, at the time of the elder brother's birth, the couple's means had been so straitened that the baby had been born weak and sickly. Their elder relations had wanted them to give up the child to a Catholic foundling hospital. They had refused to comply, the clash involving two conflicting visions of nurture and provision: the elders' harsher view was that the family should not lavish scarce resources on such a frail child. And while the brothers said their parents had felt entitled to make their own decision on the matter, they did not represent the older generation's attitude as heartless or unfeeling (*vo tinh*).

They then recounted another story which they said their parents had told them. It too pointed up the couple's lingering anxiety about the elder boy's small stature and fragile physique. Their parents had waited until the younger child was a toddler before taking both boys to the municipal offices to register their births. What they stressed about this

[19] Leshkowich 2003; compare Finnane 1996 and Goscha 2004a: 21–2. For a critical account of pre-independence literary representations of the educated modern urban woman as an idealised embodiment of the Vietnamese nation, see Wilcox 2006.

was not the act of registering as a manifestation of the colonial state's regulatory and surveillance powers, but a far more intimate aspect of the situation. This was the fact that the younger boy was so well grown that he was able to walk at his mother's side to the registrar's office, while the elder was still being carried in her arms. To their distress, he looked younger than his brother to the official who processed them.

For the brothers, this was a story about colonialism. They connected it with their parents' fierce resentment at the injustices of colonial rule, recounting it as an evocation of a colonised world in which both peasants and educated city-dwellers were denied the means to provide for their cherished young. In this it calls to mind the eugenicist themes invoked by the many pre-independence Asian polemicists who denounced their colonisers for impoverishing their homelands, thus denying them health and sustenance and so systematically weakening their 'race'.[20] In India particularly the 'drain of wealth' was a long-standing anti-colonial theme, and the influence of eugenicist race science was apparent in many nationalist writings about the degeneration of land and people under British rule. It is striking though that Vietnam's polemics about the degenerative effects of colonial rule stressed the horrors of penal deportation and represented colonialism as a force driving overtaxed and immiserated people to seek new livelihoods in upland forests and other 'unhealthy' environments (Hardy 2002). In both cases, the damage done to race and nation was portrayed as a product of separations which ruptured families and condemned those affected to live in settings where health and strength were unsustainable (Luong 1992).[21]

Of course as Stafford shows so well for China and Taiwan (2000), all life entails separations, their effects continually dealt with through the acts of protective care and nurture which are central to family life.[22] Yet the really testing paradox for Vietnam was that to resist the nation's enemies and then to advance and flourish in the wider socialist world, Vietnamese would have to continue enduring painful and dangerous forms of dislocation and familial rupture. These experiences are still commented on as both physically and morally problematic for nation and people.

---

[20] Phrasing used in Ho Chi Minh's August 1945 Declaration of Independence address (see Nguyen The Anh 2002b: 71); compare Hy Van Luong 1992: 129–30.

[21] For India see Alter 2004: 519, 526; Watt 2005: 143–51, and compare Dikötter 1998; on Vietnamese understandings of bodily health and function, see Craig 2002.

[22] Hence the continual enactment of affective and ritual reunion processes described by Stafford (2000).

When Mr Nam and his brother told me about the household dis-cussions which preceded Mr Nam's departure for China, questions of separation and provision loomed very large. The first issue to be decided was whether one or both boys should go. There was no question of compulsion, they said. People described the sending of children to China as both a patriotic duty and an act of care and nurture. The schools were thought to be in safe territory, well away from the war zones, as well as being regarded as places where the deserving young would receive a superior education combining revolutionary ideals with high-quality modern teaching.

Individual choice was also a factor, they said. Mr Nam was eager to go; his brother less so: 'I liked Beethoven and Mozart, like my father', he said, his point being that these were the tastes of people who were well equipped for a modern revolutionary's life, yet still unlikely to feel at home in the PRC.[23] In any case, their parents were unwilling to risk both boys on the perilous overland journey. Then there was the question of provision. The household had a single item of value, a gold ring, and debated whether they should sew it into Nam's jacket for use as emer-gency currency. Yet once in China, 'everything would be provided', Mr Nam said.

So as the brothers now tell the story, a process of debate and reflection ensued. I was struck by the fact that they said 'our parents finally deci-ded', not 'my father decided', or 'my mother agreed', or 'this was my mother's province and she decided'. What they described thus sounded much like the process of debate, consultation and eventual consensus which my informants said was normal practice within their families, both in the past and today, as when seeking to reach decisions on such matters as relocation to the interzones, or in more recent times, whether a son or daughter should make a major career shift – especially one involving a move from the public to the private sector – or indeed whether to share sensitive family memories with me. What Mr Nam and his brother told me about the ring was that their parents were torn, concerned to do all they could for the son from whom they were soon to be separated. But to give him the ring might imply a lack of confidence in the care he would receive in China. Also, there was the possibility that with their elder son under the care of the Party and the DRV's Chinese 'friends', they and the younger boy might find themselves in far greater need. In the end, they gave the ring to Mr Nam; he never had to use it, though he recalls selling

---

[23] In later life he too spent time in the Soviet Union and is still an avid consumer of Russian novels and symphonic music.

the mosquito net his parents gave him and using the proceeds to buy a yearned-for meal of noodle soup (*pho*).

Mr Nam said he missed his family, but that his time in China was happy and fruitful. His brother too felt the separation keenly and recalled the thrill he felt on the day the family received a postcard from his brother. It had taken months to arrive by way of the covert postal network linking China with the interzones, and he remembers being fascinated by the Chinese script picked out on it in gold. Mr Nam too became a lifelong Party member; he praised his Vietnamese teachers at Que Lam and represented the school as a centre to which the world's modern knowledge was brought as a great flow of resources assembled and imparted for their benefit, with the young people being trained to recognise those elements of the wider world's scientific and intellectual resources which they could put to productive use in Vietnam. In later chapters, I return to this notion of education as a process enabling enlightened, discerning Vietnamese – children as well as adults – to act as recipients as well as providers of the tangible and intangible forms of aid and expertise flowing between Vietnam and its other socialist 'friends'. Both within and beyond Vietnam, this notion of friendship was widely conceived of as an ideal of familiality involving active if often problematic participation in the great flows and exchanges of a worldwide socialist gift economy.

Conclusion

The focus of Chapters 2 and 3 has been the question of what it is that has given life and purpose to the world of Hanoi's pre- and post-independence intellectuals. What I have learned from my informants, and from the official media to which many have been contributors, is that the intelligentsia world is often represented both publicly and privately in ways that focus on the special qualities of the modern intellectual family (*gia dinh tri thuc*). Such families are widely conceptualised as moral and affective units with a strong sense of purpose, and a history-conscious way of life which my informants made continuing efforts to enact and display for me. They did so in particular through the processes of both individual and shared narrative for which I am using the term critical memory. My key concern in this chapter has been with the ways in which my Hanoi friends have sought to make me an active part of the conversational occasions through which they regularly exchange and pool the affective and practical knowledge that serves as a critical resource of *tri thuc* family life. Doing this is regarded as valuable and gratifying, and also serves a variety of instrumental ends, including the enfolding of younger kin into the open-ended familial networks which may also embrace such people as friends, students and even visiting foreign researchers, as well as marital and natal kin.

As I show in Chapter 4, while official attitudes to them have been ambivalent or even hostile, intellectuals and their families do loom large in contemporary Vietnamese thought. The Hanoi intelligentsia world has been particularly prominent in these representations. It is often educated Hanoi people who are pointed to as sharers in this very particular kind of family tradition involving the leading of both affective and productive lives across extremely wide geographical spaces and time spans. Even compared with the landed and commercial families whose distinctive histories and lifestyles have been documented in other Asian contexts, this element of dispersal is very striking.[24]

In this respect, Hanoi's *tri thuc* families invite comparison with the diasporic Sindhi trading families described by Falzon (2005). Engseng Ho's account of Hadrami Muslims pursuing the life of scholar-merchants across the expansive Indian Ocean trading world offers an equally striking parallel (2002; 2004). Like Hanoi intellectuals, the Hadramis whom he calls 'local cosmopolitans' have been amassers of credentials in the form of Islamic teaching certificates (*ijaza*s) that had value wherever they travelled. And their vision of themselves as 'active creators of a universal world' structured around the transregional ideals and texts of their faith, together with their use of genealogical knowledge as a 'language of cosmopolitanism' (Ho 2004: 217) calls to mind some of the key hallmarks of Hanoi intelligentsia life.[25] Even while very young, people from the Hanoi *tri thuc* world have had to be highly mobile to garner the forms of social and cultural capital which have been their stock in trade. And they too have had to travel both literally and imaginatively, adapting to a wide range of intellectual and occupational arenas and knowledge traditions and making strenuous efforts to maintain contact with kin, teachers and schoolmates (compare Ho 2002: 220).

As will be seen in later chapters, this way of life could prove both painful and insecure. Yet in the socialist era, the undertaking of these particular tasks within the socialist ecumene equipped intelligentsia families to endure and even flourish in ways that Vietnam's richer commercial and landed families could not. Thus even though they might look 'élitist' in the eyes of other socialist moderns, theirs was still a form

---

[24] Compare e.g. Rudolph, Rudolph, and Singh 2000; Bayly 1983; White 1991; Ho 2004.
[25] Though, of course, there are obvious differences between the universalising mission of twentieth-century socialism and the prophetic 'transregional space' (Ho 2004: 220) defined by the expansive scholar-traders of pre-modern Islam.

of family life that could be represented as an honourable model for the nation to emulate. This protected them yet was often problematic, since the work that their members were called on to do as providers of specialised skill and expertise was not easy to reconcile with older and newer ideals of the intellectual family as an embodiment of cultivation and refinement.

Of course in past centuries, young male Vietnamese carried the hopes of their families and wider communities to faraway places when they left their homes to be educated and examined in the great sites of Confucian learning. In more recent times, Hanoi intellectuals have had to be even more amenable to the partings and separations involved in the quest for scientific training and other modern forms of credentialised learning. At the time of the anti-French war and its challenging aftermath, parents had to accept that both their sons and their daughters might take their own initiatives in this respect. They also had to learn the skills of provisioning and equipping their young for dangerous journeys to distant lands.

Under French rule, educational opportunities within Indochina were so limited that those seeking distinguished credentials had to travel far from home, if possible to the distant colonial capital or even to France itself, and on occasion much further afield, as in the case of those who pursued scientific and technical training in Japan during the 1930s and 40s. And among the intellectual families who embraced the Viet Minh cause during the anti-French resistance war, travel to China and other 'friendly' socialist lands became an increasingly important option, especially for the children and adolescents who were exalted under the DRV as critical contributors to the nation's imminent revolutionary transformation, and as embodiments of the bonds of solidarity and tutelage linking Vietnam with its larger and richer socialist allies and supporters.

Both my informants and the official accounts with which they engage represent the business of education as a nurturing act involving the purposeful exercise of both will and affect. Those representing the imparting of love, care and teaching in these terms include those who recall their effects from childhood, as well as from experiences as adult experts and aid providers in a wide range of settings both at home and abroad. As I show below, with the onset of 'marketisation' at the time of doi moi ('renovation') the official media now point approvingly to the achievements and defining virtues of certain other kinds of families, especially those hailed as deployers of commercial skill and acumen for the nation's benefit. The key point of this chapter has been that the narrative life of intellectual families has taken shape around something apparently much safer as a claim about family tradition in a socialist society: the mustering of credentialised knowledge and learning as productive forms of provision for the benefit of both kin and nation.

These, of course, are processes which are represented as existing through long periods of remembered and historic time. This strong time sense is yet another distinctive feature of the Hanoi intelligentsia world, arguably even more so than in the case of the dispersed merchant, scholar and service families to be found in other parts of Asia, though in these other cases too a consistent mustering of documented or recalled family history can be a significant asset in the advancing of individual and collective interests. In the case of the Hanoi intellectuals with whom I have worked, this sense of belonging to a dispersed but highly productive kin group engaging in meritorious personal and public initiatives across extensive temporal spaces emerges very powerfully from my informants' narratives. Yet as in other parts of the formally socialist world, Vietnamese intelligentsia life can be highly insecure. This has also been the case in India and other so-called postcolonies where intellectuals have found themselves under fire for embracing as well as rejecting the modernist aims and values of the socialist ecumene. Chapter 4 describes the ways in which my informants have experienced and negotiated those insecurities, pointing forward to Chapter 5's exploration of aspects of modern Indian life which relate to my concerns with the forging of intelligentsia identities through the provision of care, the imparting of education and nurture, and the intimacies of parent–child and conjugal relations.

4   The pains and perils of intelligentsia life

Introduction: deflecting the 'exhibitionary gaze'

Like their counterparts both within and beyond the Asian socialist world, Hanoi's *tri thuc* scientists and 'cultural producers' have had to recognise that it can be problematic and even dangerous to possess the hallmarks of a credentialised intelligentsia in a socialist society.[1] The people I know have experienced much of what the literature on colonial, socialist and Western intelligentsias has sought to illuminate, especially the painful ambiguities of living as intellectuals in societies where both the governed and the governing demand contradictory things of scholars and other knowledge producers. My informants' narratives call to mind many of this literature's key concerns. This includes the many writings on the hybridities, transculturations and other destabilising cultural processes that are said to be central to the experience of empire.[2]

My informants do not identify colonialism as the main point of reference in their lives, despite their eagerness to discuss their elders' achievements in the resistance years. Yet I have heard accounts of the 'exhibitionary gaze' which they or their elders experienced under French

---

[1] I have not encountered in Hanoi anything comparable to what the historical sociologist Perry Anderson has documented in contemporary Russia, this being the pervasive discrediting of the term *intelligent* (member of the intelligentsia) among people who would once have taken pride in its use as a marker of achievement and cultivated antecedents. Far from signifying association with a rejected revolutionary or collectivised past, the term *tri thuc* is still much used among the people I know and does not seem to be falling into disuse in favour of something like the Russian neologism *intellektual*, which Anderson says is being used now to signal a 'new independent-minded individual' making an American-style career choice. (See Anderson's essay 'Russia's managed democracy', *London Review of Books* (pp. 3–12), 25 January 2007, p. 9.)

[2] Key works on intellectuals under socialism include Judd 1985; Goldman 1987, 1999; Barlow 1991; Watson 1994; Fitzpatrick 1999; Gu 1999; Kim 2002; Riegel 2002; and for Vietnam see Ninh 2002; Pelley 2002. On transculturation, a term coined in the 1940s by the Cuban anthropologist Fernando Ortiz to describe the reciprocities and dynamic interactions entailed in the processes of colonial culture contact, see Spitta 1995 and Young 2001: 201–3.

rule. A case in point is a story about the childhood of a francophone luminary, Le Van Hien, still referred to as *'nha tri thuc cach mang'* (revolutionary intellectual).[3] Hien was Minister of Finance under Ho Chi Minh and the architect of the 1945 Gold Week (*Tuan Le Vang*) campaigns (Smith 1978: 589). These initiatives dramatised the unseating of 'feudal' and 'bourgeois' class privilege through spectacles in which young women in the white dress of students – emblematic of the nation's new life of progressive gender and class solidarities – ushered forward the wives of the rich to 'donate' their jewellery to the revolution.

I heard a version of the Hien anecdote at a memorial meeting commemorating his life and work.[4] The speaker who recounted it was himself a *tri thuc* 'modern' in his sixties, who said he heard it from Hien himself as an account of his key moment of adolescent radicalisation in the early 1930s. The setting was the annual awards ceremony for his home region's Franco-Vietnamese schools. Hien was the top student of his year. The speaker said that when Hien went forward to receive his award, the official making the presentations struck him in the face with his prize book, calling him a beggar in a torn shirt (*nhu mot thang an may*), his tattered clothes an insult to the colonial state which had nurtured and educated him. In fact, the memorialist said, Hien came from a poor family and had no other garments. He also said the book was that key text of French linguistic authority, the *Dictionnaire Larousse*, making the episode all the more suitable for representation as an act of colonialism's 'epistemic violence' (Spivak 1985).

In private, people do express doubt about whether stories like this were anything more than devices proclaiming the proletarian credentials of a 'big man'. Indeed, my friends acknowledge their significance in communicating something of great importance in the intelligentsia world: that the linguistic and intellectual capital attained under colonialism did not bespeak willing or even unconscious collaboration in the cultural projects of the coloniser. Whether literally true or not, there are many autobiographical works containing similar accounts.[5] Yet my informants have also had much to say about forms of scrutiny which were equally painful and demeaning, but which involved experiences of the

[3] Hy Van Luong 1992: 144; Zinoman 2001b: 21; Nguyen Bac 2004: 15.
[4] On funerary commemoration see Marr 1981: 21–2; Hue Tam Ho Tai 2001; Malarney 2001; compare Cooke 1995 on the conventions of pre-modern imperial tribute biographies.
[5] Ninh 2002: 50–1; Trinh Van Thao 2002: 261. During school strikes in the 1920s and 1930s, militant students often used petitions claiming racial abuse by teachers as a means of communicating anti-colonial messages (Lessard 2003). But there are also warmly reminiscent memoirs of *lycée* life: see Huu Ngoc 2002; Dang Phong 2002: 4.

post-independence period rather than during French rule. As socialist citizens they have been very conscious of being people in the public gaze as members of a class or social 'stratum' (Szelenyi 1982) which officialdom – and sometimes even their own children – have defined in terms both extolling and demonising them for being 'cultured' (*van hoa*), hence markedly unproletarian in manners and lifestyle.

In Vietnam as elsewhere, élitists and élitism are offensive to socialist morality, bespeaking unmerited privilege and 'bad class' antecedents. As in the USSR under Stalin (see Fitzpatrick 1992),Vietnam's leaders have been scourges as well as champions of their country's learned people, frequently articulating fears that 'undisciplined' (*khong vao khuon phep*) intellectuals who misuse their gifts and privileges might derail the revolution. At the same time, it was proclaimed from the early days of the revolution that as a progressive socialist 'postcolony', the DRV (Democratic Republic of Vietnam) had to nurture 'persons of talent', deploying the skills of science and learning for the benefit of all. Indeed the people I know are accustomed to the words for élite and élitism (*phan tinh tuy*; *chu nghia tinh tuy*) being used in a positive sense to mean outstanding excellence, as in the case of someone's academic merit. Thus from this vision of a society which values intellect, even in times of war and deprivation committing scarce resources to schooling and cultural life, has come the ability to proclaim that one's homeland is not out of step with the great processes of modernising transformation that have mattered to the world.

Donald Donham has shown how powerfully this universalising master narrative acted in the 1970s and 80s as goad and stimulus to Ethiopia's revolutionary 'Marxist moderns' (1999). In Vietnam too, the presentation of the world's history as a triumphal march of progress led by enlightened nations and cultures has been widely embraced as a narrative in which Vietnam has had an exceptionally significant place. As I explain below, official versions of this narrative have given much emphasis to Vietnam's role as a revolutionary hero nation and selfless bringer of modernity to the disadvantaged of other lands.

It is this enduring concern with Vietnam's credentials as a modern society in a world where nations and individuals are continually scrutinised for signs of backwardness that has made the country's intellectuals both valued and vulnerable. While there are many socialist contexts in which the 'rootless' cosmopolitan may be reviled as a racial alien and class enemy (Humphrey 2004), in a socialist 'postcolony' there are good grounds to fear being thought of as backward and insular if one's citizenry are visibly lacking in knowledge of the wider world. Thus in Vietnam, the official media have found many ways to represent the nation as a confident sharer in the narrative of global modernity. Prominent among these is reportage pointing to the achievements of learned Vietnamese who seized opportunities to train and inform themselves in faraway places, subsequently returning to serve the motherland during the two resistance wars.

Such individuals are not to be confused with so-called dissidents and other unworthy 'gone abroads'. The good 'France returneds' of the pre-independence years are represented as pure-hearted patriots thinking always of the fatherland while acquiring the skills and knowledge required to meet its needs.[6] Much is also made of those who interacted with the intellectuals of other distant lands, taking part in learned endeavours in Japan, China or the USSR, then sacrificing comfort and career advantage to commit their talents to the nation. A case in point is Professor Dang Van Ngu, the hero of revolutionary science whose marriage I described in Chapter 3. In 1948 Ngu returned to Vietnam after a five-year stay in Japan working with scientists attempting to create a fungus-derived equivalent of the West's new 'wonder drugs'. The official tributes hail him for his efforts to create a pro-DRV expatriates' association under the noses of post-war Japan's US occupiers, and for his epic trek to join the Viet Minh, travelling undercover with nothing but his 'ardent heart' and a vial of maize fungus with which to pursue his attempt to produce a battlefield penicillin substitute.[7]

Other figures extolled in official accounts are the francophone intellectuals who spearheaded the country's mass literacy campaigns during the 1940s and 50s. The massive rise in male and female literacy in the post-independence period is widely hailed as a key achievement of the DRV, clear evidence that Vietnam was the architect of its own modernity, beholden neither to France nor its socialist superpower allies for this key measure of national attainment (Woodside 1983). As I show in subsequent chapters, these themes are now being recapitulated

---

[6] Nguyen Van Ky 1995: 279–80; Ninh 2002: 19; Trinh Van Tao 2002: 265–7.

[7] Online *Nhan Dan* at www.nhandan.org.vn/20001014 at www.//vietnamnews.vnagency. com.vn/08SUN181205; see also the report of an interview with his sister-in-law, herself a former Viet Minh medic, Dr Nguyen Thi Ngoc Toan: www.vietnamnews.vnagency. com.vn/04SUN161005. And see Craig 2002: 54–5. Another key case is that of the Paris-trained philosopher Tran Duc Thao (1917–93), also recently extolled in a *Nhan Dan* article, who was active in the circles frequented by Sartre and other major figures of the Left Bank intellectual world in the late 1940s. Thao gave up a Sorbonne post to join the Viet Minh education service; he became chair of History at Vietnam's new National University in Hanoi after the liberation war but was subjected to public self-criticism during the 1958 purge of those who had spoken out during the DRV's short-lived period of pre-*doi moi* political and literary liberalisation. This had begun in 1956 and was a close counterpart of China's Hundred Flowers campaign. See Papin 2001: 307–11; McHale 2002; Ninh 2002: 143; Herrick 2005; Cheng 2004.

in official accounts of Vietnam's relations with a host of African 'postcolonies'. In both north and sub-Saharan Africa, Vietnam's aid and development schemes are celebrated as gifts of enlightened tutelage bestowed on needy lands through the dedicated work of its educators and technical experts.

As I noted above, the people I have worked with are very knowledgeable about these narratives, connecting their families' stories of education and career life with official representations of the country's achievements as a revolutionary exemplar and aid bringer to the wider world. A key part of the intellectual's role in a socialist 'postcolony' is to know and disseminate such accounts, drawing knowledgeable parallels with narratives of other countries' key moments of revolutionary transformation (compare Donham 1999). In addition, as in the colonial period, the educated people of a 'postcolony' will inevitably be well versed in the demeaning narratives representing their homeland as a backward place in need of tutelage. Those claiming this right to uplift and instruct included the colonial powers' self-professed modernisers and civilisers, and also the richer and more powerful providers from the socialist world when former colonies became recipients of their aid and 'friendship'.

At a later point I explore the ways in which Vietnamese intellectuals found themselves having to handle the implications of these problematic socialist gift relations. The point to make here is that in Vietnam as in other former colonial societies, intellectuals have had the task of articulating the counter-narratives that challenge these debasing accounts. They have also been called on to embody the life of progressive, informed modernity that proves the point. The key problem is that there is a subtle but important difference between being an intellectual who makes honourable sacrifices for the nation's needs by becoming a remittance-earning 'expert' or mass literacy worker, and one who risks bringing discredit on self, kin and nation by failing to maintain a true intellectual's commitment to the learned and cultivated life.

There is, of course, an even darker set of narratives from the wider world that has played the role of counterpoint or subtext to such accounts. These are the stories of intellectuals reviled and persecuted as class enemies and counter-revolutionaries in other socialist countries. Many Hanoi intellectuals had their first overseas 'expert' postings in Cambodia, working as reconstruction officials in the occupation administration which ran the country for nearly ten years after its defeat in the 1977–8 Vietnam–Cambodia war; French was their medium of interaction with those educated Cambodians who had survived the Pol Pot years.

My friends have said little about the Khmer Rouge era and the Chinese Cultural Revolution. Some have pointed obliquely to the horror they felt as direct or indirect observers of these events, evoking a widely shared vision of Ho Chi Minh as a francophone lover of learning whose great achievement was to maintain the country's all-important alliances with its difficult socialist superpower 'friends', while protecting Vietnam and its intellectuals from the full rigours of Maoist or Cambodian-style 'excesses'.[8] They speak too of the Soviet Union and the European COMECON states as socialist powers with attitudes to learning and high culture that were much more compatible with Vietnam's reverence for modern and 'traditional' art and scholarship.

Yet older people mention the COMECON states' 1950s show trials, and the banning of books by Russian poets and novelists, as grim reminders of what could happen to a socialist state's intellectuals. Some have also spoken about Vietnam's own campaigns of ultra-radicalism in the 1950s, both the 1953–6 Land Reform campaigns and the attacks on urban 'bourgeois elements' that succeeded them. Fearful as these were, they never took the form of wholesale attacks on intellectuals on anything like the scale of the Bolshevik purges of the 1920s, still less the 'social rectifications' of Cambodia and China (the PRC) under Mao. Of course as I have already noted, class did matter in the DRV. Throughout the long period of austerity-era planning and allocation which lasted well beyond the anti-French and anti-US wars, and the equally difficult period following reunification in 1976 and the subsequent wars with China and Cambodia, a household's official class designation determined the size of its monthly ration from the state provisioning outlets, with significantly higher entitlements for workers and peasants than for families of 'brain workers'; those in trade and commerce received least of all.

There was a similar entitlement system for access to higher education. Much as in the allocation of places at the special DRV schools in China, service to the revolution gave one's child special eligibility for a university place. Otherwise, even the child of an intellectual who was not officially 'bad class' but had not served as a soldier, Viet Minh cadre or high-profile 'progressive personality' (Nhu Phong 1962: 54–5) had a lower claim than the son or daughter of a worker, peasant, soldier or 'war martyr'.[9]

---

[8] On intellectuals and the state in the Chinese People's Republic (PRC), see Bonnin and Chevrier 1991; Hua 1994. On Ho Chi Minh's vision of the states and peoples of the Communist world as 'the great Socialist family', see Brocheux 2007: 27.

[9] For China compare Yan 2003: 19. See Malarney 2002; the treatment of household 'hearth units' as the basis on which classing and ration entitlement decisions were made was yet another factor pushing the moral unit of the family into a tighter shape – though without overriding the sense of attachment and identity relating to the wider kin grouping (Hy Van Luong 1992).

Intellectuals and 'culturedness'

These are issues that the Hanoians I know have broached in terms of the refinement of feeling which they value so strongly, both as a hallmark of Vietnameseness in general, and at the same time as definitive of intelligentsia life. This is what was emphasised in a story I was told by a friend in her sixties in the presence of other members of her family. It concerned their father's negotiations of the dilemmas facing intellectuals in comparatively secure situations during the dangerous 'social rectification' years. 'We never knew at the time. But when he died, people wrote to tell us what he had done.' She was referring to the circle of former students and other educated subordinates her father gathered around him at the time of the Land Reform purges, when he held a senior official post. Nothing could be done for kin falling foul of officialdom, she said, describing his distress at his inability to help a close relation's son denied university entry on grounds of his mother's 'bad class' antecedents. The merest suggestion of 'familism' was a damning smear for intelligentsia 'moderns'. The official's children learned years later that their father took daring steps – 'out of feeling' (*chan tinh*: heartfelt sentiment), she said – when a young assistant was summoned to his natal village to appear before the Land Reform cadres. His parents were landowners, so he faced harsh or even lethal treatment in a Chinese-style 'delegitimation' session. What a superior could do in these situations was to plead the nation's need. Her father managed to get the summons repeatedly deferred until the purges ended, maintaining that the aide had special skills and could not be spared from his duties.[10]

A younger Hanoi academic told me a story about an elder kinsman who died shortly after being targetted as a 'class enemy' on grounds that as a traditional healer he had exploited the poor, making undue profit from his treatments. My friend Dr Tuan said that his kinsman's funeral became the occasion for a remarkable enactment of feeling (*chan tinh*) on the part of his fellow villagers. The brutal practices of 'delegitimation' were organised specifically to sever 'class enemies' from the world of human interaction – specifically understood as the sharing

---

[10] On intelligentsia 'familism' in China, see also Davis 1992. On class 'rectification' in Vietnam, see Hy Van Luong 1992: 189–91; Malarney 2002: 23–51; McHale 2004: 134. According to Turley (1972: 798) a man's 'bad' (i.e. bourgeois or landlord) class background could be neutralised by marriage to a woman of 'good' (peasant or worker) origins, but such a woman would lose her right to be classed as a peasant or worker after three years of marriage to someone of élite/bad class origins (compare Hy Van Luong 1992: 187; Malarney 2002: 154–8).

of feeling – by obliterating the relational address forms and other enactments which signal inclusion in the affective ties of kin and community co-residence.[11] This is precisely what the villagers denied, Dr Tuan said, turning out in great numbers to join his kinsman's burial cortège in a way that unmistakably challenged the cadres' verdict. This was a display of emotional connectedness, a public acknowledgement of the healer's generosity in the use of his learned skill. He said his kinsman is still referred to in the village by the honorific *thay*, master or teacher, a term still in use and traditionally employed for knowledge specialists including teachers, monks and astrologers.

Officially, the consequences of a 'bad class' label could prove impossible to expunge, even though the 'excesses' of Land Reform were repudiated in the late 1950s, and many such judgements re-examined and reversed. Dr Tuan achieved a university education, but says he was denied Party membership because of his class background, thus missing out on promotion and other career advantages.[12] And as I show below, Vietnam's 'brain workers' received many unsettling reminders that both collectively and individually, they could all too easily be represented as quasi-bourgeois, their refinement of feeling a deficiency rather than a sign of worth, their skills and knowledge not a stock held in trust and shared out to all as the act of a true provider, but assets amassed for advantage, like a merchant reaping profit from his gains.

When older people have told me about the years after their return to Hanoi from the interzones, they have certainly mentioned the traumas of Land Reform, and the 1958 purge of the small but high-profile group of intellectuals who were involved in the short-lived *Nhan Van/Giai Pham* 'dissident' movement.[13] Yet even those who say they experienced these bad times have also spoken of the years after official decolonisation in 1954 as the time 'when the new books came', a period of cultivated pleasures and achievements when Hanoi people could revel in the new cultural materials beginning to flood into Vietnam from other socialist lands. There were Soviet films in the cinemas, and Tchaikovsky and Borodin performed by visiting artists. Those learning Russian discovered literary treasures that had hitherto been unobtainable in Vietnam. People say they still had French novels and poetry collections at home, even

---

[11] Malarney 2002. In other contexts too, anthropologists have documented the importance attached to the capacity to feel and share emotion as definitive of human as opposed to animal life. See e.g. Ohnuki-Tierney 1994: 238.

[12] Compare Dang Anh Dao 1999: 56.

[13] Boudarel 1991; McHale 2002; and see above, note 6. The term *Nhan Van/Giai Pham* refers to the journals that published participating intellectuals' writings.

though these were no longer part of the school curriculum. But they also recall reading Pushkin and Tolstoy, and Russian translations of 'progressive' (*tien bo*) anglophone works: Jack London, Shakespeare and Walter Scott. By the late 1950s, these and other approved foreign writings were available in Vietnamese translation, published with commentaries on how to apply correct class analysis to them. Scott's swashbuckler *Ivanhoe* was to be read as a story of class oppression under feudalism, though a man who recalled reading it as a 22-year-old said that what thrilled him was the power of the love story, and the vision of young men defeating their enemies through heroic feats of arms.

What he and others say they savoured as students and young academics were precisely the forms of cultivation that Soviet leaders had long exalted as markers of civilised life for their citizens.[14] As Fitzpatrick shows in her exploration of 'culturedness' (*kul'turnost'*) under Stalin (1992, 1999), Soviet definitions of desirable cultural skill focused on the knowledge that persons of advanced education were expected to master so as to equip themselves as role models for the wider society. Since it would take many years for all citizens to become fully 'cultured', it was initially for the culturally advanced, the intelligentsia, to embody what would one day be the norm for all.

In Stalin's Russia, this category of the culturally 'developed' had been reconceptualised to include scientific and managerial specialists, as well as scholars, artists and 'creative' thinkers. According to Fitzpatrick, these were people who were expected to achieve the standards of knowledge and comportment to which every citizen would eventually progress under the guidance of Party and state. Being cultured in this sense entailed the mastery of good grooming and the other forms of civility that revolutionaries had previously condemned as bourgeois, but which in the 1930s were enshrined as key attributes of the well-conducted socialist citizen. It also meant being 'civilised'. This entailed virtually the same cultural mastery which had distinguished Russia's pre-revolutionary intelligentsia: a knowledge of 'world' masterpieces such as the writings of Heine and Shakespeare, though with pride of place given to the great works of the pre-revolutionary Russian canon.[15]

In the DRV too, the attainment of 'civilisation' (*van minh*) was embraced as a key ideal. And although intellectuals were still engaged in

---

[14] On the rejection and subsequent revival of Pushkin in the Soviet literary canon, see Fitzpatrick 1992: 9; on the Soviet civilising mission and its key task of imparting 'culture' in both material and intangible forms, see Fitzpatrick 1999: 67–88; Buchli 2000; Slezkine 2000; Ssorin–Chaikov 2003.

[15] Fitzpatrick 1999: 80. For the contrast with China see Judd 1985; see also Ninh 2002.

debate about which of Vietnam's historic cultural traditions were worthy of preservation or revitalisation, official views of the education required by the new socialist citizen gave prominence to a strongly nationalist canon of artistic works and reference points (Marr 1981; Ninh 2002; Schlecker 2002; Goscha 2004). By this time all privately run educational institutions had been closed or placed under government control. As I noted above, the new school system's paramount concerns were the spreading of literacy, and the teaching of the national language in romanised *quoc ngu* script.[16]

The DRV's decision to make Vietnamese the medium of instruction at all levels, from primary school to university, gave rise to a massive translation initiative, as well as the coining of suitable vocabulary that could act as the country's new voice of modernity. But while the sciences were pre-eminent, there was also much emphasis on the treasures of Vietnamese high culture. All schoolchildren were to study *Truyen Kieu* (The Tale of Kieu), the verse epic still taught in all schools as the supreme achievement of Vietnamese literary culture, with its narrative of injustice, parted lovers, self-sacrificing familial devotion, and the heroic endurance of suffering interpreted through a suitable application of Marxist-Leninist theory.[17] Indeed there was a continuing emphasis on Vietnam's place in the wider socialist world. Learning the languages of that wider world, and becoming conversant with its forms of high culture, were tasks officially prescribed for those people who came to be identified as exemplars of comportment and cultivation (*co van hoa*) to the rest of society. This too meant the intelligentsia.

Deploying the 'moderns'

So who and what were they? And to what extent had Vietnam's 'brain workers' taken on something akin to one of the two key roles for intellectuals before the great twentieth-century revolutions: that of the pre-modern Sino-Confucian mandarins and their Asian counterparts who had acted as conscience and moral critics of their rulers, or that of

---

[16] The term *van minh* was much debated in pre-independence modernist writings. See Marr 1981; Bradley 2004; Goscha 2004b: 9; compare Winichakul (2000) on the notion of *siwilai* (being 'civilised') in nineteenth- and early twentieth-century Siam. On education and the imparting of 'culture' in post-independence Vietnam, see Woodside 1983; Schlecker 2002; Ninh 2002.

[17] Marr 1981: 143, 154–5. Of course every child was also to know the nation's history, taught since the early years of the DRV as an epic account of patriotic popular will inspiring repeated feats of resistance to the forces of foreign invasion and class injustice. See P. Taylor 2001; Pelley 2002; Giebel 2004.

the pre-revolutionary intelligentsias – especially those of China and Russia – who had claimed the right to show a backward society how to attain modernity? Here the figure of Ho Chi Minh's successor Le Duan is instructive. A former railwayman whose Party nickname was *Anh Ba* ('Brother Number Three'), Le Duan was already a leading Politbureau figure when he used the occasion of the 1957 August Revolution commemoration to make a major pronouncement on the subject of Vietnam's intellectuals.[18]

This speech is still widely known. My younger friends can quote from it: it is still a required text in the 'Marx-Lenin philosophy studies' classes (*Triet hoc Mac-Lenin*) in which passing grades must be obtained by all degree candidates.[19] Its ostensible subject was the class basis of the anti-French resistance struggle, but its representation of the national liberation narrative conveyed an unmistakable message about contemporary life in the DRV. The speech was delivered at the time of the brief Hanoi 'dissident' episode, so its passages about the problematic class character of *tri thuc* intellectuals were clearly to be read as a warning to those who thought of intellectuals as licensed critics rather than self-effacing servants of state and Party.

What is signalled very clearly in this part of the speech is that a socialist state can never fully trust its educated citizens because intellectuals do not think and act in the spirit of the true revolutionary classes. Vietnam's authentic revolutionaries were its peasants 'under the leadership of the proletariat'; together they had been the 'vanguard army' of the country's liberation; it had been their struggles against capitalist exploitation and foreign rule that had achieved both freedom from the French and the revolution. This was to be recognised as a self-achieved moment of entry into the progressive mainstream of historic revolutionary time, an idea reminiscent of Donham's account of the view of revolutionaries of other 'postcolonies' that the revolution achieved on home soil is a joining of the wider world's flow of meaningful, progressive time (1999: 1–35, 122–50).

[18] This is Vietnam's Independence Day, celebrated on the anniversary of Ho Chi Minh's 1945 Ba Dinh Square declaration, still the most important date in the public calendar. On Le Duan see Tran Van Dinh 1976; Le Duan 1977; Young 1979: 777–8; Porter 1994: 103–7; Dang Phong and Beresford 1998: 40–2, 61–71; and numerous tribute items in the official press, e.g. at www.nhandan.com.vn/english/news/miennam/leduan.htm (7 May 2005).
[19] At the time of writing, my friends were following with interest a debate about whether these required courses should be slimmed down or abolished to maximise time available for teaching in subjects said to be better suited to contemporary 'development' needs.

So what Vietnam's revolutionary classes had achieved, Le Duan proclaimed, was 'a revolution to emancipate the people and take them to a new road, the road of [the] modern history of mankind'.[20] By way of contrast, his far from flattering portrayal of the patriotic literati of the pre-independence period was very much in the spirit of Kautsky and the other European revolutionaries who had disparaged the intellectuals of their own societies as arrogant individualists for whom workers were pupils rather than comrades, and 'discipline' – i.e. subordination to the collective – dismissed as an obligation for the masses but not themselves (Kautsky 1903: 2).[21] So for Le Duan, Vietnam's pre-independence intellectuals were a petite bourgeoisie (*tieu tu san*) whose patriotic sentiments, though real enough in their way, were never sufficiently strong or selfless to constitute a true revolutionary force. Clearly love of country and service to the anti-colonial cause were not enough to qualify the 'brain worker' to guide the country through the challenging currents of revolutionary time. Intellectuals were needed, but only as tools and agents of the revolution. Thus under socialism they were to embody modernity within the new society, but not to question the Party's decisions about how to achieve it.

What then of the claim that the intellectual is by definition a person of refined speech and feeling whose capacity for 'heartfelt' emotion is the mark of true humanity, thus by definition a socialist virtue? The most notable section of Le Duan's speech is a withering account of the intellectuals of the 1930s and 40s as people who by nature led a 'rich sentimental life' and could therefore 'share very easily the national feeling' so that '[at] times, their patriotism was very boiling. They were enthusiastic when the national-liberation movement reached a high tide, but usually they wavered between the bourgeois road and the proletarian road' (Le Duan 1977: 13), deluding themselves with the thought that

---

[20] Le Duan 1965: 1. Its title is 'Reassessment of the leadership of the Vietnamese proletariat', and it is published in translation in *On the Socialist Revolution in Vietnam* vol. I, pp. 1–17, at www2. cddc.vt.edu/ marxists/reference/archive/le-duan/works/.

[21] A view also expressed by Lenin. Le Duan himself used Kautsky as an example of an intellectual whose bookishness and academic credentials proved to be no substitute for true revolutionary verve and who though 'respected by Lenin as a teacher' was ultimately '[bogged] down in the quagmire of opportunism' (Le Duan 1964: 6 and see Halfin 1997). In another work, entitled *This Nation and Socialism are One*, Le Duan distinguished between the DRV, where socialism engendered a life of high culture and virtuous ideals uncorrupted by the indulgence of individualistic passions and desires, and the degenerate south (the RVN), where city life was especially depraved, its culture 'mongrel' and 'decadent' and, rather than inculcating positive and socially beneficial forms of emotional expression, 'gave stimulation and encouragement to the basest instincts and most vulgar tastes' (quoted in Young 1979: 778).

they were making revolution by engaging in trivial acts of 'bourgeois' creativity. So the 'petty bourgeois intellectuals' deserved only faint praise for what Le Duan called their 'short-lived mettle and audacity'. When these abortive moments of premature insurgency failed, the thinkers revealed their impotence as a social force. The dismissive tone is unmistakeable. 'In the end, these social sections [or strata] carried on their task of "national liberation" by composing some poems, writing a literary work or publishing some novels or newspapers of bourgeois reformist character' (Le Duan 1977: 4–5).

Le Duan is still a giant in Vietnam, his grave among the inner circle of national leaders in Mai Dich national cemetery (see Plate 29). In 2005 the Prime Minister made a widely reported homage visit to his ancestral village and performed a commemorative incense burning at the memorial museum housed in his birthplace. In 2007 large-scale commemorations of the hundredth anniversary of his birth were staged in both Hanoi and Ho Chi Minh City.[22] He is clearly not a person to denigrate in the presence of a foreigner. Yet people have mentioned him obliquely, in relation to such seemingly innocuous things as the name changes and amalgamations of provinces which he oversaw as Party general secretary in the 1970s, suggesting in roundabout ways that there was something lacking in his appreciation of historic matters. They did not say, 'he was wrong to disparage us and our parents', or 'it was painful to have to study that speech as students'. Yet much of what they did say on these occasions was to do with their own implied and explicit narratives and explicit counter-narratives of the ways in which intellectuals have found themselves being held up to scrutiny in relation to national events, both in the past and in the far more positive accounts of the present day.

Intellectuals have certainly had high visibility in socialist Vietnam. Even more so than in Stalin's Russia, the DRV's intelligentsia were people who could be called on to enact modernity for important audiences both at home and abroad. Even before the expulsion of the French in 1954, there were key public moments when as families and individuals, people of known *tri thuc* intellectual background were placed in the limelight as national exemplars and role models. Such moments are

---

[22] These commemorations included publication by the Viet Nam News Service of a memorial essay by his daughter, a Hanoi professor, whose article pays loving tribute to his life of service and describes the many separations the family endured. She too was sent to China as a child and later to Moscow, meeting her father for the first time since her infancy as a fifteen-year-old student when he made a state visit to the Soviet Union with Ho Chi Minh in 1957 (www.vietnamnews.vnagency.com.vn/showarticle.php? num=01SUN080407).

regularly alluded to. A recent item in the 'Socio-Culture' section of the Vietnam News Agency's online daily *VietNam News* paid tribute to the achievements of Professor Le Thi, the septagenarian daughter of a noted francophone *tri thuc* intellectual.[23] As the article explains, at the age of eighteen, Professor Thi was one of two young women entrusted with the honour of hoisting the national flag before the great crowd assembled at the start of the famous public gathering in Hanoi at which President Ho Chi Minh made his Declaration of Independence speech at the climax of the 1945 August Revolution (see Plates 26 and 27). She did so wearing the white *ao dai* (tunic and trouser outfit) that identified her as a woman student, and hence a key embodiment of national enlightenment and social progress.[24]

Young women in white *ao dai*s appeared in many other key rites of revolutionary action, as I have already noted, and also very often in contexts celebrating education as an embodiment of all that is modern and moral in socialist Vietnam. As I show below, even in the austerity years of the late 1970s and 80s, scarce resources were committed to the kitting out of expert (*chuyen gia*) remittance-earners in appropriate modern garb before sending them to represent the nation overseas. Thus as in the USSR, matters of dress and comportment had great significance in the DRV. One of the earliest large-scale 'friendship gifts' to Vietnam from its richer socialist benefactors was the children's activity complex known as the Children's Culture Palace (Cung Van Hoa Thieu Nhi). This is modelled on the young people's cultural centres that were once sites of compelling socialist ultramodernity everywhere from Leningrad to Pyongyang.[25] Hanoi's was built in 1957 on the site of the

---

[23] Her father was Professor Duong Quang Ham, a francophone literary scholar and early Viet Minh recruit; his writings on the history of *chu nom* (the Chinese-derived ideographic script used for literary works including *The Tale of Kieu*: Marr 1981: 141–3) were published in French-language learned journals. He was Rector of the Hanoi Ecole Normale (Pedagogical College) at the time of the 1945 August Revolution and became the first Vietnamese director of Hanoi's celebrated Chu Van An secondary school, the former Lycée du Protectorat.

[24] The report says that Prof. Thi had marched into the square at the head of her National Salvation Association youth troupe. Her co-participant in the flag hoisting was a female 'ethnic minority' guerrilla fighter; together, they symbolised the selfless ardour which Vietnamese revolutionaries defined as the special attributes of emancipated womanhood (Marr 1981: 251). Prof. Thi is quoted as saying that she had hoped to study at the Hanoi Ecole Normale but instead spent the war years as a cadre with responsibility for mobilising women in the northern border regions; she completed her higher studies in post-war Hanoi and became a social scientist specialising in family and women's studies. See www.vietnamnews.vnagency.com.vn 4 Sept. 2005.

[25] See Reid 2002. The term *van hoa* (culture, cultured) is used in Vietnamese in much the same sense as its Russian counterpart *kul'turnost'* i.e. the state of advancement to which

children's amusement park (Au Tri Vien) which my older friends recall visiting in the 1930s. The Culture Palace was still active at the time of my fieldwork, a gated complex in unmistakable Soviet modernist style, its stark concrete structures a conspicuous contrast to the neighbouring art deco colonial villas (see Plate 25).

Those who knew the Culture Palace both in the 1950s and in the more recent pre-'renovation' years describe it as a place where the gifted young could experience remarkable things: ballet classes in a mirror-lined practice room, violin and Russian lessons, encounters with foreign delegations. One thing made clear to them all was that when entrusted with the task of greeting and presenting flowers to these visiting foreigners, they had to perform creditably, speaking their Russian correctly and conducting themselves with confidence and decorum.[26] Here, too, there is a parallel with Fitzpatrick's (1992) account of the ability to speak well at public meetings as yet another of the key socialist cultural skills which Soviet citizens should strive to master. And once again, although in theory these were skills that all Vietnamese would eventually attain under socialism, in the short term it was the country's intelligentsia who were the key people of 'culture' (*van hoa*) in this sense. Like the girls in white *ao dais* at public ceremonies, the younger children at the Culture Palace had the task of embodying bright-eyed, healthy, well-schooled modernity for all to see, with their ability to do so under the gaze of foreigners being of particular importance. Even though the visitors were almost always socialist 'friends' – indeed all the more so because they came from such places as the Soviet Union and the DDR (East Germany) – these keen-eyed observers from the wider socialist world had to be shown that

individuals and citizenries may be brought through education in the arts and sciences, and the mastery of 'civilised' skills and knowledge including knowledge of such things as the works of the great literary and artistic masters of the past (Fitzpatrick 1999; Taylor 2001: 45–6; Ninh 2002). See note 14, above.

[26] This exaltation of the skills by which a 'cultured' socialist citizen produces high standards of refinement in home and workplace is still very visible in Vietnam. It has been widely noted that good grooming and comportment are expected of women (Rydstrøm 2003), but it should also be noted that certain forms of such refinement are specifically thought of as intelligentsia qualities. Again there are parallels with Fitzpatrick's account of items such as lace curtains coming to be hailed as tokens of the Soviet good life: in Hanoi the plying of crochet hooks and knitting needles by fashionably dressed young women with university degrees and 'modern' jobs is a common sight. No-one appears to see such pastimes as old-fashioned or 'bourgeois'. As I show in later chapters, these are the practices even very young people learned in childhood: in the post-reunification austerity years, girls, women and even some men in intelligentsia households helped to make ends meet by practising various forms of needlework, learning to knit, sew and crochet with salvaged remnants of yarn and string.

Vietnam was not a backward or 'undeveloped' land. And it was the well-groomed, well-spoken children successfully acquiring 'culture' at this and other showcase sites who were called on to prove and embody these claims.

A disproportionate number of these key modern sites were in Hanoi, of course. Official representations of the learned and scientific world do pay tribute to people and institutions based in other towns and cities, notably in the former imperial city of Hue. But Hanoi retained its pre-eminence after independence as the nerve centre of the *tri thuc* world, home to the DRV's best schools, as well as the National University, publishing houses, research institutes and other major institutions of intelligentsia life.

With hindsight, my friends say they recognise that until quite recently, few workers' children were in a position to attend classes at the Culture Palace. There were no fees. But in the pre-*doi moi* ('renovation') years, only such people as academics or officials – especially those from former francophone intelligentsia families – were likely not only to value what was on offer, but to be able to manage the basic logistics. In the years when public transport was sparse and only the fortunate possessed bicycles, a worker family would find it far harder to allocate the time to deliver and collect their children, and encourage them to press on with their practising in chess, dance or languages.

Of course polishing one's Russian at the Culture Palace was also a recognised means of improving one's chances of selection for that most desirable of prizes: further study in the USSR or another COMECON country. One friend remembers her mother, a Hanoi scientist, speaking elegiacally about her time in Moscow in the early 1960s, describing the films she had seen and the art museums and concert halls she had frequented, and holding out the same prospect of fulfilment as she encouraged her to work hard at her Russian and ballet lessons at the Culture Palace twenty years later. If there were bad times in Moscow – hostility or coldness from Russians, homesickness or anxiety about kin and friends at home – she never spoke of them. Theirs was a family in which female as well as male achievement had been prized since the 1920s. Her grandmother, who married a celebrated pre-independence scholar-patriot, was yet another woman whose parents had heeded the pre-independence reformist call for right-thinking 'moderns' to educate their daughters as well as sons. Her family was affluent, unlike those of my other informants, and she was driven to her *lycée* in one of Hanoi's few Vietnamese-owned motorcars. In the post-independence period her *alma mater* became Hanoi's highest-ranking co-educational secondary school, admitting pupils with the top scores in the highly competitive state admissions exams. My friend, now a Hanoi social scientist, attended this school in the 1980s, as had her mother in the early post-independence era.

This is the kind of thing that can still be reviled in Vietnam as a sign of 'amoral familism' (Banfield 1958) but with the ethos of asocial clannishness attributed to the petit bourgeois 'brain worker', rather than the peasant or proletarian 'masses'.[27] My friends recall that this was what was often said or hinted at when the child of a well-known 'intellectual family' (*gia dinh tri thuc*) achieved a coveted school or university place, or was selected for overseas training. Thinking back to the days when these concerns were more aggressive and dangerous than they are today, they have told me about the ways in which intelligentsia families could appear to others to be survivors of a pre-revolutionary élite whose advantages came from backstairs connections and accrued cultural capital.

As I show in later chapters, the charge of being bourgeois in taste and manners often threw a spotlight on the sensitive issue of how children from supposedly privileged families were to be raised and nurtured as good socialist citizens. Whether made by one's own children or as a gibe by others, these claims about 'élitist' ways and mores indicated very clearly that filial relations were expected to develop in ways that reflected all the key moral principles of the new Vietnam. While the family unit was to be a fundamental building block of the new revolutionary society, it was also to be an arena of change within which individuals gradually distanced themselves from outmoded 'traditions' and deficient class values.[28] For this reason, both during and after the early years of socialism, the figure of the child was if anything even more important in Vietnam's socialist imaginings than in those of other Communist societies (see Plate 22, a typical representation of Ho Chi Minh as loving elder to the nation, with a child as the other key element in the poster's visual syntax). Both in official representations and in my informants' personal recollections, concerns about the nurturing of children loom very large, with much attention being paid to the moral significance of the bestowing and receiving of nurture, and – in the case of intelligentsia families – to the importance of distinguishing between correct and incorrect ways of imbuing the young with refinement of thought, manners and sentiment.

---

[27] Compare Broaded 1983: 130; Potter and Potter 1990: 158. On the extent to which 'entrepreneurial familism' has contributed to China's economic growth under 'market socialism', see Whyte 1996. On intelligentsia 'familism' in China, see Davis 1992.

[28] Hy Van Luong 1992; Malarney 2002; compare Stafford 1992.

Of these, it is the inculcation of proper sentiment that requires emphasis here. As I have noted, sentiment or feeling (*chan tinh*) is an important category in personal and official representations of moral life. In contemporary Vietnam, many conventions of 'emotional practice' (Beatty 2005) reflect the instrumental aims and demands of state and Party, as when Vietnamese are called upon to be lovingly committed to the family as an affective unit, though one bound at all times to the ordered, co-operative whole that is 'society' (*xa hoi*) (Schlecker 2005: 521). Thus, as both a conjugal household and a wider array of enduring kin ties, the family must be energised and rendered productive by its ties of affect and obligation to that wider web of collective units to which all citizens belong.[29]

A related and equally important demand by the state – made from the early years of the DRV and reaffirmed in the 1980s in the form of the New Culture Family campaign – is for citizens to recognise that the rites of veneration they perform on such occasions as funerals and the paying of respect to ancestors during the Lunar New Year (*Tet*) festival should be understood as enactments of sincere and appropriate emotion, rather than instrumental acts (Malarney 2002: 74–147). A rational and scientific socialist mind can and should experience emotions such as gratitude for those who have worked and provided for the needs of family, society and nation.[30] It is thus entirely proper for enlightened socialist citizens to express feelings of respect and gratitude to the forebears who nurtured them, and to do so with formal enactments on the appropriate calendrical occasions. But no-one should cross the fine line distinguishing grateful remembrance from the 'superstitious' practices (*me tin*) which state and Party condemn, especially the use of ritual spaces such as family altars as sites for communication with the dead, and supplication of their aid and favour. 'Wasteful' display in the form of lavish feasts which enact or recreate 'feudal' status hierarchies are also abjured. These demands have been made clear through decades of propaganda and the strictly supervised example of Party members (Malarney 2002; see also Kwon 2006 and 2007).

In practice, however, this is a line that people clearly do cross. In intelligentsia households, ancestor altars are certainly sites of respectful

---

[29] Beatty 2005. These units include those of the workplace – unions, committees and many other sites of organised citizenry. See Werner 2004; Schlecker 2005.

[30] Indeed in the early 1940s, at a time of fierce debate about whether romanised vietnamese (*quoc ngu*) was a suitable medium for modern thought and writing, a case was made for recognising the language's emotional expressiveness as a matter of national pride and cultural distinctiveness (Ninh 2002: 65).

feeling and commemoration. When I arrived at a friend's house with photocopies of a distinguished forebear's scholarly writings in a French learned journal, these were immediately placed on the altar (*ban tho*) in their main reception room. But in some cases they are clearly more than that. There have been occasions when a deceased parent or other cherished forebear was very much a living presence for those who invited me to their homes to discuss matters of family experience and history with them. Thus the fact that people hear so much from the state and Party in the way of injunctions and official policies about families does not make their sense of the familial any less real or potent for them.

Languages and service

When the Soviet Union acclaimed forms of 'culturedness' such as refinement of manners and the ability to dress and speak well as intelligentsia attributes, Stalin's officials used the term intentionally to evoke the prestige of the old pre-revolutionary intelligentsia, attaching it to bureaucrats as well as 'cultural producers' whose duty was to serve the socialist state as a recognised cultural vanguard.[31] But the position of intellectuals in a socialist 'postcolony' is obviously more complex. Many of my friends have forebears who are known to have attained eminence under French rule. In the past such people might have been acclaimed as productive scholars or proficient men or women of science, but the accolades they had received from French savants would not have been made much of in biographical tributes to them. And as the case of the Le Duan speech illustrates, until recently even the deeds of distinguished kin who had rallied to the Viet Minh cause could be read into the national narrative in decidedly unsympathetic terms.

Indeed with the examples of China and Cambodia so close at hand, it has been even more important in Vietnam than the USSR for intellectuals to establish that their families have lived lives of service, and that the visible fruits of this service did not constitute private gain. Like Russian intellectuals insisting that they were not a propertied élite because their dacha furnishings were spartan and state-allocated (Fitzpatrick 1999: 103–4), the people I know have good reason to stress

---

[31] See Fitzpatrick 1992; and on late Soviet attempts to reinstate intelligentsia usage as the model for correct Russian speech, see Kelly 2001: 336.

that their Hanoi residences were assigned to them by the state in recognition of both need and merit, and were not ancestral homes. The
possessions they contain today – modest collections of books, pianos,
recordings of Rachmaninov and Liszt, the occasional prized piece of
antique 'Annam' porcelain – are emphatically not bourgeois luxuries,
but rather the trappings of a soberly learned life held in trust for the
general good by those with the knowledge to preserve and value them.

Again, their service was that of mastering and deploying skills and
attaining knowledge of such things as foreign languages. They speak of
using these as cultural capital for the nation, and of having obeyed
instruction from Party and state to use them for the benefit of those with
whom the nation chose to share these gifts of enlightenment. People who
have told me about their lives as intellectuals have often directed me to
the sayings and writings of President Ho Chi Minh on the topic of the
value of educated men and women to the national cause, citing celebrated anecdotes and aphorisms in which these sentiments were given
tangible and enduring form.

I say more below about this language of affect pervading personal and
public accounts of President Ho Chi Minh as a paragon of virtues
which are seen as distinctively Vietnamese, yet also universal in their
'heartfelt' morality. For the people I know, certain forms of narrative
centring on Ho Chi Minh provide an implied and sometimes explicit
counter-narrative to those associated with Le Duan and those sharing
his unsympathetic view of Vietnam's intellectuals. Both in speaking of
their own activities, and in paying tribute to their parents and other
elders, my friends frequently point to Ho Chi Minh as an exemplar and
reference point. It is he, they say, who defined the purposes of intelligentsia life for the modern nation, bestowing on them the gift of his
trust as they carried out the tasks he assigned them. Such accounts
often feature anecdotes of Ho Chi Minh personally recruiting them or
their parents to serve the national cause, either in the resistance era or
in the post-independence period, communicating with them either by
letter – with such documents now retained as valued mementos – or in
a cherished moment of face-to-face contact when he confided his will to
a chosen individual. The memory of those direct interactions is much
emphasised; they turn the mundane business of recruitment into the
conferring of a mission.

President Ho Chi Minh sent for my father [in 1946]. He needed him. He knew
he was willing to join the Party. But he told him: no you must not join. There
must be people in the government from outside the Party because we are a united
front.

This was said by a Hanoi intellectual of his father, an academic who became a leading figure in the mass literacy campaign.

Bac Ho called me to his office; he said, 'I am sending you to Guinée'. He told me what he wanted of me. I said, 'Sir: I will go.'

This was recounted by a man who was sent to serve as a cultural attaché in Conakry in 1962: in later chapters I discuss the significance of this still very common use of the familial term *Bac*, 'Uncle', to refer to President Ho Chi Minh as leader and beloved elder kinsman of all the nation.[32]

Thus recruited as warriors against 'word blindness' and civilisers of those hitherto condemned to backwardness and superstition, they were being called to service, often at great personal cost. Many narratives focus on personal sacrifices made and pain willingly endured, as in the account by the man quoted above:

Sir, my son is sick and I will find it hard to leave him. But I know you need me. I will go', I said. *Bac Ho* took my hand. I found it hard, but I knew he needed me to go for him.

The thrust of these stories is clear. Many people have been explicit about their distress at knowing that others see them or their parents as intellectuals who relinquished or even betrayed their calling for personal advantage. Both taking a government post and becoming an 'expert' – i.e. a technical specialist – rather than a scholar or scientific researcher are moves to be defended as acts of service rather than betrayals of one's learned calling. Intellectuals use a variety of means to show that they have not sought undue rewards for their work. Until recently, it was common to publish research-based monographs under a pseudonym (*but danh*). One might thereby avoid censure for saying something novel or daring, and indeed there was a better chance of getting a mildly controversial work published by practising this form of socialist intellectual etiquette.[33] One can also demonstrate the

---

[32] *Nguoi* (individual) with upper case initial letter N is also used in print for Ho Chi Minh; it means something like The Person or The One, and is never used for any other individual. (See Hy Van Luong 1988: 248.)

[33] As in the case of the pioneering anthropologist of the post-independence period Professor Nguyen Duc Tu Chi, warmly recalled by his former students as the man who introduced them to the ideas of the French structuralist anthropologist Claude Lévi-Strauss following his stint as a *chuyen gia* expert in Guinea in the early 1960s. Professor Tu Chi had found Lévi-Strauss's celebrated *Tristes Tropiques* (1955) in the national library at Conakry and generated great excitement when his attempt to apply structuralist analytical techniques to the Vietnamese context led him to posit a transformational connection between the design motifs of the country's most famous

self-effacing virtues of a socialist intellectual by committing time and energy to the translation of foreign-language works. Like teaching, this too is a means of using intellect for purposes of imparting and sharing, recognising and disseminating the work of great individuals, rather than claiming that one's own thought or discoveries should command attention.

Conclusion

In a widely cited critique of the postcolonial studies field, Arif Dirlik concedes a number of merits to its leading authors' attempts to displace 'foundational', Eurocentric and essentialising accounts of global history based on 'centre-periphery binarisms' and other structuring 'meta-narratives' that have been widely seen as inherent to colonial modes of thought. He writes,

There is no denying that postcolonialism expresses not only a crisis in the ideology of linear progress but also a crisis in the modes of comprehending the world associated with such concepts as Third World and the nation-state. Nor is it to be denied that as the global situation has become blurred with the disappearance of socialist states, with the emergence of important differences economically and politically among so-called Third World societies, and with the diasporic motions of populations across national and regional boundaries, fragmentation of the global into the local has emerged into the foreground of historical and national consciousness. Crossing national, cultural, class, gender and ethnic boundaries, moreover, with its promise of a genuine cosmopolitanism, is appealing in its own right. (Dirlik 1994: 347)

With many of the same reservations and qualifications, I too recognise the value of those versions of postcolonial theory deploying deconstructive conceptual tools to identify the processes of blurring, fragmentation and movement which have shaped the 'disjunctions' and 'displacements' of colonialism and its many divergent global afterlives.[34] But Vietnam is a socialist state which has not 'disappeared'. Indeed the tendency of many theorists to equate the so-called postcolonial condition with the supposed failure, collapse or disintegration of global socialism greatly oversimplifies the qualified and dynamic nature of the 'late' and

---

national heritage relics, the Bronze Age artefacts known as the Dong Son drums, and the traditional weavings produced by the 'proto-Viet' Muong people with whom he did fieldwork in the 1970s. (On the Dong Son drums, see Chapter 6, below.)

[34] See e.g. Prakash 1996: 188–9.

post-socialist transformations which ethnographers have explored in a host of regional and supralocal settings.[35]

As in the case of so-called market socialism in China, *doi moi* ('renovation') has not overridden the many moral and cultural reference points which have connected Vietnam's post-independence life to the domestic and supralocal practices of socialism, not least because so many of these reference points have become so strongly embedded within the intimacies of personal and family life. This has been the case even for those whose intellectual lives have entailed appropriations or vernacularisations of a wide range of ideological systems and paradigms, both 'native' and external in origin. I have also sought to show that colonial and socialist state power entailed very different things for intelligentsia 'moderns', not least in relation to the family, a site of affective experience endowed with 'privatised' meanings in colonial settings and with universalising claims and obligations under socialism. I have been arguing too that socialism itself generated important opportunities for the blurring and traversing of national and other boundaries and provincialisms, and that for Vietnam as for other socialist 'post-colonies' it has been the intelligentsia moderns who have been vested with the burdens and privileges of embodying both 'culturedness' and a particular kind of purposeful and patriotic cosmopolitanism for the society at large.

This makes it particularly important to avoid using simplistic and homogenising terminology for the educated professionals, semi-professionals and intellectuals of the former colonial world. The widely used term élite is particularly problematic, bespeaking a tendency towards caricature and reductionism which would surely be unacceptable to those who call for properly nuanced understandings of the lives and 'voices' of colonial and postcolonial 'subalterns'. The case of India has loomed very large in accounts of colonial and postcolonial 'subjectivities' and 'modernities', though all too often without sufficient attention being paid to the singularities of south Asian encounters with the divergent ideologies and developmental projects that interacted both within the subcontinent, and further afield.[36] It certainly cannot be assumed that there was any easy or straightforward transition from colonial to post-colonial intelligentsia life in any of the complex settings where the value

---

[35] Including China and Cuba as well as Vietnam where socialism has been transformed but not displaced. See Feuchtwang 2002; Hann 2002; Hy Van Luong 1989 and 1992. And see Borneman 1995 and Humphrey 2002 on the material and affective processes of post-socialist transformations.

[36] On this point see especially Dirlik 1994; Slezkine 2000; Zachernuk 2000; Cooper 2005.

and convertibility of an intellectual's social and cultural capital have been subject to so many unpredictable alterations and reformulations. I believe that this is an issue inviting cross-cultural comparison, and I address the question of how to compare and contrast my Vietnamese case with that of India's twentieth-century 'socialist moderns' in Chapter 5 below.

5 Comparative modernities: India as a domain of socialist postcoloniality

Introduction: morality and national development

The aim of this chapter is to complement my account of colonial/ postcolonial and socialist/post-socialist contexts in Vietnam by exploring the experiences of India's developmentalist intelligentsias in a number of colonial as well as post-independence contexts. A key concern here is the parallels that would be easy to miss if one were to insist on simplified liberal stereotypes denying comparability between India as an electoral democracy and Vietnam as a one-party Communist state. But of equal interest are the nuances of difference that emerge if one resists homogenising the two countries into an undifferentiated category of 'the postcolony'. Focusing on environments in which Indians embraced and contested the skills and values of intelligentsia 'culturedness', the material presented here draws on my memories of research encounters dating back over the last thirty years or more. I also build on a variety of textual sources to provide context and background. Nevertheless, this discussion does rely very largely on an attempt to use my own memories as an ethnographic resource. I have tried to bear in mind that like those of my informants, the production of my memories has also been shaped by many interacting processes, including the changing intellectual orientations underpinning my past and current research.

Vietnam is far from being the only former colonial society in which those who personify high-profile forms of modern 'culturedness' can find themselves both exalted and vilified. This vulnerability may be especially severe when such people find that their narratives of virtuous familial achievement are contested by counter-narratives emanating from those with a different but equally deployable stock of cultural capital. In India, independence in 1947 brought to power a nationalist political and bureaucratic leadership whose members became increasingly easy to vilify as self-serving technocrats with 'colonised minds',

and a misconceived commitment to reformist 'soft socialism'.[1] Since
the 1960s, India has been home to a diverse array of populist movements whose leaders achieved either fleeting or longer-term political
success as self-proclaimed champions of the 'common man'. These
radical populists gained electoral credibility by contending that they, as
visionaries propounding regionally based goals of peasant entitlement
and/or emancipatory cultural chauvinism, were true socialists or at least
true protectors of the masses, while their 'Nehruvian' rivals were not.
Many of these movements' leaders also represented themselves as
guardians of more worthy forms of modern 'culturedness' than those of
the establishment anglophone cosmopolitans whom they were seeking
to displace.[2]

These contentions anticipated the writings of those theorists of postcoloniality who have portrayed the inclusive secular nationalism of Nehru
and his allies and heirs within the Indian National Congress party as an
ideology of élitists with a wrong-headed commitment to 'Enlightenment'
values and rationalising development goals.[3] As noted in Chapter 4, these
goals and their underlying conceptual principles are nowadays widely
seen as part of the enduring epistemic legacy of colonialism. Indeed, it is
now widely argued that after and in some cases well before the Second
World War, colonial rule in many settings had acquired much of the style
and ideology of these regions' much-maligned postcolonial 'development
regimes' (Ludden 1992). It is thus clear that these were the sources of the
moralising reformist goals and governance tools through which post-
independence rulers in India and other 'postcolonies' subjected their
citizenries to interventionist strategies of discipline, order and 'panoptic'
rationalisation (Ferguson 1990; Worby 2000).

Studies building on these perspectives have identified the family unit
as a critical site of tension for those struggling to embrace or reformulate
the moralities of colonial or neocolonial domestication and citizenship
'projects'.[4] What has not been widely recognised is that revolutionary
states like post-independence Vietnam have also been 'development
regimes' in this sense, though with an even more complex history of

---

[1] This is the modernist political tradition that is often referred to as Nehruvianism, a
reference to Jawaharlal Nehru's powerful and enduring, though today much-contested,
vision of modern Indian nationhood. See Brass 1990; Khilnani 1997; Das 2001; Parry
2003.

[2] See Brass 1995; Khilnani 1997; Varshney 1998; Duncan 1999; Hansen 1999; Jaffrelot
2002.

[3] Madan 1987; Nandy 1988; Mitra 1991; Chatterjee 1994; Baxi and Parekh 1995; Baber
1998; Pantham 1997. Important critiques include Bose 2003 and Sen 1993 and 2005.

[4] Hancock 1995; Stoler 2002; Clancy Smith and Gouda 1998.

engaging with the legacy of modernist morality projects deriving from the planning and reform schemes initiated in the waning days of empire by their former colonial rulers.[5]

Even less widely acknowledged is the extent to which these developmentalist projects' idealisations of domesticated nationalist virtue have been vilified as well as praised and deferred to, with problematic consequences for those subjected to such critiques. My concern here is therefore with a different kind of post-imperial tension, one that has arisen in settings where credentialised 'moderns' have had to recognise that their distinctive kind of family life has been identified by many other citizens as something other than an ideal model of cultivation and national enlightenment. What is particularly notable in the Indian case is that a language of familial provision and nurture has been deployed by those on both sides of these hotly contested internal 'culturedness' wars.

Looking back over thirty years to my earliest stays in India, I recall that the anglophone academics, professionals and upper-level administrators whom I believe compare most closely with my Hanoi intelligentsia informants did not refer to themselves as members of a particular kind of family. Nor did they commonly use terms corresponding to *gia dinh tri thuc* (modern intellectual family) to distinguish themselves from those whose forebears had not entered the world of anglophone education and self-consciously modernising home and career life under colonial rule. Yet then as now, few Indians were unaware of the distinctive educational and occupational traditions marking out such people as the *rentier*-descended upper-caste Bengalis known as *bhadralok* ('genteel folk') and their many regional counterparts.

These include the networks of Smarta Brahmans and other high-caste Hindus whose members attained prominence in public life and the modern professions in the Tamil country under the Raj, passing on through networks of marriage and kin ties a strongly family-based tradition of educational and career achievement. This emphasis on distinctive familial identity rather than a more generally inclusive sense of caste-defined connectedness was characteristic of their Chitpavan and Chitrapur Saraswat Brahman equivalents in western India. It also typified a variety of other loosely integrated regional status groups, including the Nehru family's Kashmiri Brahman 'Pandit' ancestors, and the Kayasthas and Kanyakubja Brahmans who established themselves as proverbially

---

[5] As well as under the influence of the visionary modernism of their 'friends' and role models in the Soviet Union, China and other socialist societies. Compare West 2001; Cooper 2005.

adaptable literate service specialists in the Hindu- and Muslim-ruled realms of north and south India.[6]

In conversation, the anglophone Indian 'moderns' I knew were strikingly family-conscious, often commenting on the remittance obligations they sought to fulfil during their overseas stints as graduate students or while travelling on government or academic business. They followed the school and career achievements of their kin with close attention and took it for granted that they should save part of their bursaries and travel expenses so they could contribute to the education costs of 'blood' kin and affines. The care of elders was another concern, especially for hard-pressed urban career women living in nuclear conjugal households but with an expectation that they would spend much of their time attending to the needs of aged parents and in-laws.[7]

Many of these Indian academics and professionals had forebears who had published in a variety of modern narrative genres. These writings included 'public life' autobiographies by men who had achieved eminence in fields such as law, medicine and public administration both before and after independence.[8] In some of the Indian families I came to know, there had also been notable female autobiographers. Such women's memoirs from the nineteenth and early twentieth centuries have been much explored as sources of insight into the subjectivities of colonial domestic life, especially among educated Bengalis who wrote of urban 'office' experience (*chakri*) under the Raj as oppressive and uncongenial despite its financial rewards (Sarkar 2002), and of the uneasily modernised conjugal home as a privatised refuge in which men found only defective forms of solace.

Companionate marriage and intimate connubiality are often written of as coercive ideals of the 'new patriarchy' with its regimens of 'bourgeois domestication' for wives and daughters, and its exhortations to 'virtuous wives' to remake themselves as self-denying helpmeets in an oppressively 'ordered home'.[9] Yet as Raychaudhuri has shown (2000), there are some Bengali *bhadramahila* ('gentlewoman's) memoirs from the colonial period which employ a language of warm emotion to describe the lives of career officials' wives in the period when upper-level administrative posts were being opened to educated Indian 'competition-*wallahs*'. In particular, Raychaudhuri cites the lyrical idiom in which the married

---

[6] Khare 1971; Gordon 1990; Bayly 1983; Bayly 1999.
[7] Compare Seymour 1999; Prendergast 2005.
[8] This was a much older, freer and more diverse print culture milieu than Vietnam's: see McHale 2004.
[9] Chatterjee 1990; Chandra 1992; Burton 1997; Walsh 1997.

'new woman' recalls her married life and that of her contemporaries. To do so she draws on the regional devotional lore of exalting love and yearning for a lord-like spouse. But this is a modern lord who both cultivates and communicates his tender feelings: a man of sentiment with the skill to convey his conjugal affection in eloquent speech, and also in letters sent during the separations occasioned by his 'out of station' duty tours (Raychaudhuri 2000: 369).[10]

The autobiographical writings of Gandhi and Nehru, both still widely read in India, are didactic 'imaginings' of nationhood which also exalt experiences of conjugal emotion, linking these personal subjectivities to the tasks of enlightened nation-building. Both famously present vignettes of loving but often painful communication and tutelage, often in settings of separation and parting which are reminiscent of those described in Vietnamese intelligentsia memoirs and by my own informants in Hanoi. The case of the Hanoi family's debate about the gold ring which I discussed in Chapter 3 is a case in point, even though this was recounted to me as a story of consensus. Such moments could also take the form of painful conflict about what constituted progressive as opposed to unprogressive acts of provisioning and nurture. As an exemplification of the selflessness and austerity required of Indians in both family and national life, Gandhi's autobiography describes his efforts to convey to his wife why she should renounce the gifts of gold jewellery which his admirers had presented to them during his years of service in South Africa, and on their departure in 1914. Arguing against her husband and sons, she had pleaded to retain these costly items because they had been 'lovingly' given, and also, Gandhi records, on the grounds that a Hindu wife had a duty to possess such objects. This was not a matter of greed or vanity, but need: specifically that of her future daughters-in-law to whom she would one day pass them on.[11]

Companionate conjugality and its conflicting emotional effects also feature in Nehru's writings, and these too sometimes touch on issues of provision and nurture of the kind described to me in Hanoi. Nehru's prison memoir *The Discovery of India*, first published in 1946 and widely used as a school text since independence, propounds an elegiac vision of a democratic, plural, modernist, secular and socialist India which is now

[10] See also Amin 1996; Karlekar 1993; Walsh 1997.

[11] She also claimed a right to keep them, he reports, because she had 'wept bitter tears' through her years of living the life of service he had imposed on her (iii, Ch. 12: 114–15). On the possession and transfer of gold in north Indian Hindu families, see Ward 1998; compare Sarkar (2002: 30) on 'spendthrift' Hindu wives. Socially conscious writings from the colonial period were rich in accounts of home life as a battleground in which such issues were painfully contested between husband and wife and parents and their reformist children: see Chandra 1992: 73.

hotly contested from many quarters, including the left and the Hindu chauvinist right. Yet it is important to recognise that there are still influential versions of the country's narrative which bracket Nehru with Gandhi as idealised mentors to its citizenry. Either alone or in loving partnership with the Mahatma, Nehru has thus been for many Indians, though definitely not all, as much a personification of the national family's virtues and resistance struggle as Ho Chi Minh has been in Vietnam.[12]

In *The Discovery of India*, Nehru prefaces his account of India's glorious 'variety and unity' (1956: 48) by reflecting on the many separations of his marital and parental life. In so doing, he merges the figure of his ailing and often absent wife – his elusive 'Indian girl' – with the idealised Mother India (*Bharat Mata*) whose 'banked fires' he learns to cherish through what he calls his great voyage of discovery (Nehru 1956: 45). By this he meant the speaking tours which took the form of exemplary dialogues of enlightenment with the urban and peasant masses.[13] He mentions a photograph of himself with his wife which he had observed during his speaking tours, displayed in the bazaars as an image of idealised conjugality (Nehru 1956: 30). The other critical figure in this account is Nehru's daughter Indira, India's future Prime Minister (1966–77; 1980–4), in adulthood his official hostess and close intellectual companion. During his prison terms, which lasted for much of her pre-independence childhood, she too was a recipient of loving, exhortatory letters demanding progress reports on her studies and calling on her to read Garibaldi and H.G. Wells.[14] Nehru worried about how to provide her with a fitting, cosmopolitan education, at one point in the 1920s demanding her withdrawal from a convent kindergarten at which she was teased as the only child wearing Congress *khadi* (coarse homespun, a key Indian nationalist symbol). This poignant image of unkind schoolmates deriding a child decked out in the accoutrements of an out-of-place modernity is very similar to an experience recounted to me in Hanoi, which I discuss in Chapter 8.[15]

---

[12] 'Netaji' Subhas Chandra Bose is a very different personification of national (or subnational, specifically Bengali) exemplarship. See Bose and Bose 1997. On Nehru's autobiography, see Arnold 2004. And compare Zinoman 2001b.

[13] The travels are an imparting of tutelage and a journey of personal enlightenment, both contributing to the forging of 'imagined' nationhood. See Nehru 1956: 47–9. Like Ho Chi Minh, India's other key nationalist leader Subhas Chandra Bose professed lifelong bachelorhood. On didactic autobiographies see Khilnani 1997: 7–8; Arnold and Blackburn eds. 2004. And for Vietnam, compare Zinoman 2001b.

[14] The complex emotional textures of their exchanges invite comparison with Stoler's account of the painful father–daughter relations revealed in the letter collections she explored in the Dutch East Indies colonial archive (forthcoming).

[15] See Bayly 1986; Tarlo 1996; Frank 2002: 67.

The academic and professional families I knew in Calcutta, Madras and Delhi in the 1970s and 80s also led lives of high mobility in which the amassing of credentials and the sharing and imparting of sensibility and verbal art were played out against a complex background of contending national narratives. Those years of my early research were well before the moves towards economic liberalisation which brought into being a very different material culture of middle-class consumerism. The strictly controlled output of the state television service had yet to begin broadcasting when I first worked in Madras in the mid-1970s, and even in the early 80s international brand-name goods were still costly rarities among the middle-class people I knew.

Even so, my acquantainces in the Indian academic and civil-service worlds led lives that were far more secure and materially advantaged than those of their Vietnamese counterparts. Most had a far larger and more diverse stock of accrued cultural capital to deploy on their own behalf and that of their kin, coming in many cases from long lines of anglophone achievers and establishment luminaries.[16] Many had parents, grandparents and even great-grandparents who had been prominent in both pre- and post-independence political and cultural life in one or more of India's metropolitan centres. These metropolitan centres were both more numerous than Vietnam's and home to a much larger and more diverse 'modern bourgeois' world than that of Hanoi's far narrower pre-independence *tri thuc* milieu.

Yet what the Vietnamese and Indian 'moderns' had in common is something that I describe more fully in later chapters: the distinctive experiences of family life among the scientific and technical 'experts' who spent much of their post-independence lives moving from posting to posting across the disparate spaces of the worldwide socialist ecumene. There are many intriguing points of comparison here. In India, the people I knew who have led something closely comparable to the peripatetic life of those Vietnamese 'experts' include south Indian and Bengali academics with university posts in cities far from their ancestral 'native places'. They also include government service 'batchmates' with posts in the supremely prestigious Indian Administrative Service (IAS). Then as now, at Mussoorie, the central IAS preparation establishment in the Himalayas, these officials were trained in the great tradition of even-handed developmental modernism that became the hallmark of India's post-independence

---

[16] In contrast to Vietnam's families of 'new moderns' whose entry into a world of *tri thuc* schooling, careers and home life dates back only to the 1920s in most cases, the mid-career academics and officials I knew in India in the 1970s had much longer-standing urban roots.

administrative culture. Having mastered its anglophone linguistic conventions and quasi-socialist ideals of technocratic state power, the men and women officers of the IAS traversed the country as agents and embodiments of what was in effect an expansive inner socialist ecumene.[17]

What I am suggesting is that these administrators' postings and career trajectories can be seen as the mapping out of a distinctive moral and political space. This entailed processes which created within India something resembling the experiences and moral narratives of the worldwide socialist ecumene. Thus I am suggesting that there emerged in India a direct parallel to the ways in which those supra-local interactions were understood by believers in the shared emancipatory projects identified both within and beyond the COMECON states as central to the world's traditions of global revolutionary modernism. From the vantage point of these Indian central government modernisers, the lives they led projected onto the diverse cultural and regional geographies of their homeland a kind of homogenised super-India. This Nehruvian vision of the Indian Union also made emancipatory claims. It too was widely represented as a moral project, with the professed aim of overriding or harmonising particularities of community, region and caste, much as the COMECON vision of a socialist ecumene idealised the overriding or harmonising of the particularities of nationhood and cultural difference in the lands it sought to embrace through the provision of aid, tutelage and 'socialist friendship'.

To fulfil their central projects of development and emancipation, both the Indian and global versions of this ecumene ideal needed educated 'moderns' who could traverse its far-flung spaces and enact its disciplines, selflessly and faithfully bringing the same universalising standards of technocratic skill and progressive social practice to the provincial environments in which they found themselves. Yet as I explain below, even when occasioned by a call to serve the nation and meet its needs, such mobility and the rewards it brings could (and still can) become a focus of mistrust and contestation.

Separation and dislocation in Indian intelligentsia life

Despite their evident prosperity and material advantages in comparison with my Hanoi informants, many of the Indian academics and civil servants I knew in those years had lived through episodes of dislocation

---

[17] I am indebted to James Laidlaw for suggesting this perspective on India's cosmopolitan nation-builders.

and upheaval comparable to those experienced by their Vietnamese counterparts during the anti-French and anti-US wars. I knew Calcutta people who told me grim family stories about their elders' experiences during the 1943 Bengal famine and the Hindu–Muslim massacres known as the 1946 Calcutta killings. I also knew people in both Delhi and Calcutta whose families had experienced the calamitous mass Partition migrations of 1947–8 and had then struggled to create new careers and households in initially unwelcoming urban settings. Although most had become enthusiastic habitués of the big cities in which they came to reside, some told me that they still yearned for the ancestral homes from which they had been displaced in Sind, east Bengal and the cross-border regions of the Punjab and Kashmir. All were well read in the vast literature on those displacements, and several had written on the subject.[18]

Many of the Indian intellectuals I knew came from families with strong traditions of activist allegiance to the Indian National Congress. Several had both male and female forebears who had experienced prolonged separations from their kin during periods of imprisonment in the great mass agitations of the anti-colonial freedom struggle. Some of my Calcutta acquaintances also took pride in family connections with the Axis-sponsored insurgent force created during the Second World War by the revolutionary leader Subhas Chandra Bose, a fierce opponent of Gandhi and Nehru. Like the Viet Minh, Bose's Azad Hind (Free India) movement had a modernising socialist ethos and a radically un-Gandhian strategy of mobilising women as arms-bearing participants in its south-east Asian jungle campaigns. I recall meeting a Calcutta woman who had been a teenage recruit to the famous regiment of female fighters who served with the Azad Hind movement's military wing, the INA (Indian National Army).[19]

These were circles in which young people too were familiar with a whole range of the different socialisms and revolutionary ideologies which have been an active part of India's diverse political landscape. Thus, in addition to those Bengalis for whom the Bose tradition represented a strongly anti-Nehruvian ideal of socialist modernism, I

---

[18] See Rahman and van Schendel 2003; Butalia 1998; Pandey 2002; compare Falzon 2004: 86–101 on Bombay as the diasporic Partition migrant Sindhis' 'heart-home'. On the idea of people's desh/bari (ancestral home) as an affective reference point, which I see as comparable with the Vietnamese concept of que, see Chakrabarty 2002: 120–1.

[19] Gordon 1990; Fay 1993; Bose and Bose 1997; Hills and Silverman 1993. Most INA recruits were Tamil migrant labourers and other members of the Indian diasporas in Burma, Singapore and Malaya, hence part of an earlier prefiguring of the translocalities I am referring to as a worldwide socialist ecumene: see Bayly 2004a.

had near-contemporaries who in their teens and early twenties had been on the fringes of the neo-Maoist Naxalite movement which attracted many middle-class Calcutta student radicals in the early 1970s. When I met them a few years later, they still spoke of Vietnam's revolutionary exemplarship as a key inspiration for their short-lived involvement with the Naxalite cause. And, like the young Hanoi *lycéens* who left home without parental sanction to join the Viet Minh, these were people who subsequently re-embraced conventional household life, returning to their schools and universities and taking up the kinds of academic and professional careers which were characteristic of such families.

As in the case of the Vietnamese intelligentsia families described in previous chapters, the reverence for linguistic skill and other erudite accomplishments that I recall among my Indian intelligentsia friends did not create a clear-cut separation between intellectuals and technical/ managerial specialists. Members of the same household and extended family followed a wide range of career paths. One key distinction between the Indian and Vietnamese intelligentsia families I know is that few if any of the Indian intellectuals had kin in the military. Despite the large size of its armed forces and its long history of professionalised soldiering both before and during colonial rule, post-independence India has not experienced anything like the mass military mobilisations of Vietnam's wartime years.

Thus career soldiering does not interpenetrate with India's intelligentsia worlds to the extent that it does in Hanoi. Among Indian intelligentsia families I did not encounter anyone like the female army doctors and career soldiers whom I know in Hanoi. Those middle-class Bengali women who had soldiered in the 1940s with Bose's revolutionary Azad Hind army, or involved themselves in 1970s Naxalite radicalism, were exceptional: part of movements which were profoundly at odds with what had become the mainstream national narrative of political life. Sentimentalised 'love the army' iconography is now fairly common in India. In my early fieldwork days, apart from a remarkable poster I saw in Calcutta soon after the 1971 Indo-Pakistan War depicting three chubby-cheeked babies in generals' uniforms, I recall little that was comparable to Vietnam's many images of the nation as a family under arms[20] (see Plates 3, 4, 5, and 11). Indian

---

[20] As in the propaganda posters depicting mothers enduring separation from beloved sons for the good of the nation, and President Ho Chi Minh as a war leader in khaki. See Pinney's account of a patriotic Indian oleograph representing the beloved nation as a pair of toddlers garbed as a soldier and a turbaned peasant (1995: 104–5).

intelligentsia families were certainly not experienced in the life of war as a moral arena in which to enact the intimacies of conjugal and parental provision and nurture.

What my Indian and Vietnamese intelligentsia friends do have in common was the experience of having continually forged and reforged the residential sites and domestic regimens of family life in their years of repeated relocation across the spaces of their respective ecumenes. And as in Vietnam, what I believe can be learned from my experiences of Indian officials' households is that here too, the much-deployed model of privatised, inward-looking bourgeois domestication is not well suited to the home lives of these peripatetic 'moderns' (Chatterjee 1990; Chakrabarty 1994). Indeed if anything, for my acquaintances among the Indian intelligentsias, it was the big, mobile, outward-facing world of the wider socialist ecumene that had come to be experienced as something of a refuge or retreat from the problematic form in which domestication had been defined in these families' home localities.

What I am referring to here is the much-discussed idea of Indian nationalist ideologies as premised around defence of a spiritualised home space. This is widely said to have been defined through the exaltation of feminised bourgeois domesticity, often allied to the creation of ethno-linguistic identities as personified in a feminised 'mother tongue'.[21] My experiences in both Vietnam and India suggest that to capture the dynamism and complexity of my informants' experiences, there is a need to pluralise this domesticity model, thereby doing justice to a whole series of complexities and diversities which have involved the pitting of one kind of domestication ideal against the professed moralities of another. In so doing, we can see that the people who have been told by regional cultural nationalists that they are unwelcome aliens within the localised world of 'mother tongue' and ethnolinguistic homeland have had good reason to be responsive when called on to look outward to a different moral world where they can try to forge their own connections between ideals of family and nationhood. For many educated Indians, this other moral world has been defined around the spaces and career trajectories of India's supra-local inner socialist ecumene. This has been a setting in which peripatetic educated 'moderns' – archetypal 'Nehruvians' – have created their own distinctive kind of home, structuring this around distinctive forms of nuclear family life. I discuss my encounters with such families in the remaining sections of this chapter.

---

[21] Chatterjee 1990; Hancock 1995; Ramaswamy 1997.

The intelligentsias vilified

In the course of several periods of ethnographic and archival research in the 1970s and 80s, I became acquainted with a mid-career IAS officer whom I will call Mr Raman. He had the volubly confident and energetic manner that was typical of officials with his background and education. When I first met him, Mr Raman occupied the post of Collector in one of the districts of the south Indian state of Tamil Nadu. Districts are the principal administrative divisions of India's provincial states. Most are extensive; his had a recorded population of nearly 3 million. Each district is under the authority of a single Collector (or District Commissioner in the north) answerable to their state's civil service secretariat, and through it to the elected ministries on whose behalf they act.[22]

Mr Raman was by background a Tamil Smarta Brahman, hence a member of one of those distinctive regional Indian status groups with a strong family-based tradition of distinguished educational and career attainment. Like many IAS officers, he had been posted to serve in his home state, and it was his duty to carry out whatever administrative tasks were assigned to him by the Party politicians in power in the state capital, Madras (now Chennai). Yet as Collector he was a central government official and thus in principle the regionally based eyes and ears of the enlightened and enlightening modern Nehruvian state. The key problem he faced was that like my Hanoi intelligentsia friends, he and his family were inheritors of forms of linguistic and cultural capital which both he and his kinfolk had to try to deploy and defend at a time when such assets were being accorded extremely uncertain valuations within the various moral and political economies in which they were operating.

Then as now, Tamil Nadu state's ruling political party was identified with the militant social justice tradition known in the early twentieth century as non-Brahmanism, and more recently as Dravidianism. This had originated as one of a range of lower-caste self-assertion movements taking shape under British rule as calls to arms on behalf of those of non-élite caste origin. In post-independence Tamil Nadu, Dravidianism's self-styled revolutionary leaders (*puratchi thalaivars*) propounded ideals of people's justice and ethnolinguistic cultural nationalism expressed through vilification of people with precisely Mr Raman's background. The movement's leaders still portray themselves as social

---

[22] The titles Collector and District Commissioner originated in the colonial period, and the posts retain the administrative and policing powers that defined them under British rule.

revolutionaries and loving champions of the poor, though nowadays without anti-capitalist or radical wealth-redistribution policies. They have also rejected the other key strand of their early Marxian orientation as propounded by E. V. Ramaswamy Naicker (1879–1973), the *Periyar* ('Great Sage') whose iconoclastic atheism had been inspired by a stay in the USSR in 1931. By the time of my stays in India, the movement was strongly committed to de-Brahmanised forms of Hindu piety focusing on regional shrines and devotional traditions, dismissing both India's Communists and its Nehruvian 'soft socialist' secularists as unvirtuous materialists.[23]

Central to the Dravidianism cause is the portrayal of Brahmans as descendants of rootless, skill-selling Aryans, a term derived from colonial race theory (Bayly 1999; 2002). Tamil Nadu's Dravidianism revolution claimed the right to displace these alleged aliens on grounds of the unmerited cultural and political predominance they had supposedly maintained through exploitation of the region's 'masses'. Smarta Brahman 'culture brokers' – people like Mr Raman's family of urban lawyers, doctors, civil servants and academics who were well known for their patronage of certain forms of regional high culture, particularly Carnatic music and *Bharatnatyam* classical dance – have been a particular focus of this demonisation.[24]

Both the terms and arguments of these vilifications recall those used by anti-élitist Vietnamese Party commentators to criticise intellectuals in Vietnam.[25] To Mr Raman's outspoken indignation, the distinctive forms of refinement identified with Brahman 'culture brokers' like his forebears were still being condemned in Dravidianist polemics as unhealthy and corrupt, and the region's lines of priestly, scribal and scholarly Brahmans routinely accused of having misused their skills and learning to advantage themselves at the expense of the virtuous 'common man'. The Indian National Congress was the party in power in Tamil Nadu when

---

[23] To the colonial authorities, such movements were welcome counterweights to what in much of India had been the Brahman-dominated leadership of the Indian National Congress. The neologism *puratchi* – revolution – had been coined by an early non-Brahman polemicist to convey to Tamil-speakers the significance of the 1917 Bolshevik Revolution. The movement's leaders portrayed themselves as moral and social revolutionaries, and as superior to Marxists whom they dismissed as unvirtuous materialists. On non-Brahmanism and Dravidianism, see Barnett 1976; O'Hanlon 1985; Pandian 1987; Price 1989; Ramaswamy 1993; Bayly 1999; Harriss 2002; Hodges 2005; Pandian 2007.

[24] These musical forms were embraced by pre-independence nationalists as key embodiments of pan-Indian Hindu/Indic culture.

[25] On the view of intellectuals as 'necessary but dangerous' in socialist societies, see Watson 1994: 68, 69.

the Dravidian movement won its first major electoral victory in the state in 1967. Its former leader Rajagopalachari, one of the grand old men of the anti-colonial freedom struggle and a key figure in the movement to identify Carnatic music as a pan-Indian cultural symbol, was reviled by Dravidian movement leaders as a Brahman who had plotted with Nehru and other 'Aryan' northerners against both the culture and the material interests of 'true' Tamils. The most notable instance of this was the campaign to impose the use of Hindi as a language of 'national integration' in the southern states.[26]

These were all very live issues for Mr Raman. In my conversations with him, he spent much time representing his own and his forebears' achievements as selfless and honourable, their learning amassed not for reasons of self-gratification or material advantage, but to endow the nation and the world at large with the gifts of their civilising virtue. These were views which I heard expressed with great vehemence both then and since. It should be noted that in contrast to Vietnam, Indians have had far greater scope to express opinions which diverge from official state narratives. Even during the period of authoritarian rule known as the Emergency (1975–7) I heard strongly worded criticisms of state and central government policy from friends and acquaintances.[27] And while India's serving officials are expected to execute official policy without comment or criticism, individuals identifying themselves as retired civil servants frequently say things in print and online which their counterparts in Vietnam might only hint at behind closed doors, if at all.

In common with the many other mass movement populists who have come to prominence in the Indian states since the 1960s, Tamil Nadu's spellbinding Dravidian leaders also cultivated a personalised, score-settling style of 'big-man' politics which people like Mr Raman spoke of as repellant and corrupt.[28] A key features of this 'dada-populism' has been the deployment of state power as an engine of largesse. Displays of theatrical emotion have been critical to this kind of vote-seeking. One widely disseminated official photograph of a key Dravidian movement politician, the much-venerated former cinema hero M. G. Ramachandran, showed

---

[26] Hardgrave 1965; Irschick 1996; Ramaswamy 1993; Price 1996.

[27] Compare Tarlo 2003.

[28] Though they had little choice but to try to adapt to it: a much-discussed grievance of people in his position was the use of punitive transfers and repostings as a sanction against civil servants who displeased elected politicians. It was the disruption of children's education that was a particularly feared and resented consequence of such forced moves.

him as Chief Minister tenderly embracing a weeping elderly woman with the dress and fragile physique of the very poor.[29] The goals and leadership style of these regional governments were thus profoundly at odds with the Nehruvian ideal of even-handed, institutionally formalised political life.

Particularly distasteful to people like Mr Raman who were represented as the villains in the Dravidianism story were the means by which its leaders had pursued the movement's long-standing goal of leading those of non-élite caste to the restoration of their home region's ancient glories. These efforts involved the exaltation of a purified (i.e. de-Brahmanised) version of the Tamil country's linguistic and spiritual heritage by unseating those whom the movement portrayed as historic oppressors of the non-Brahman 'masses'. These were Tamil Nadu's Brahmans. Like their north Indian counterparts, families with this background were heirs to caste-specific traditions of priestly and scribal literacy which gave many of them both the means and the incentive to equip their sons (and latterly their daughters) with the training and language skills required for remunerative modern service careers. To displace them from their disproportionate presence in public life in the pre- and post-independence periods, the Dravidian movement's politicians made much of education as the means by which those of non-Brahman caste could attain what many though certainly not all of them had lacked, i.e. what in the wider socialist world would be defined as 'culturedness'. What enraged people like Mr Raman was the score-settling side of these initiatives. These have taken the form of 'reservations', i.e. quota-based compensatory discrimination in public-service employment and university admissions. In practice, these operate as exclusionary anti-Brahman quotas, since those deemed to be entitled to 'reserved' benefits have come to include virtually everyone in the regional populations who could demonstrate that they were not of Brahman birth.[30]

---

[29] See Pandian 2007; Price 1989 and 1996. On '*dada*-populism', see Price 1996: 380, citing its use by Hansen in an unpublished paper (and see Hansen 1999). In addition to the use of images such as the picture of Ramachandran with the weeping woman, there were also public outpourings of emotion including suicides during his many illnesses and at the news of his death. On competitive Brahman and non-Brahman claims to be true lovers of Tamil, see Ramaswamy 1997.

[30] Various attempts have been made to make these schemes work to the advantage of the materially disadvantaged rather than those for whom Indian sociologists coined the term 'creamy layer', i.e. those members of a non-élite caste whose families had achieved modest economic and educational success: in some states there are now online certification forms requiring applicants for so-called backward-class (i.e. non-élite caste) reservations status to provide documentary evidence that they do not belong to the 'creamy layer' of their caste or tribal community.

In the 1970s and early 80s a series of highly charged battles about the proposed expansion of these quota schemes was a major talking point everywhere I went. South India's versions of these schemes had long been more far-reaching than those of other Indian regions. Mr Raman was deeply hostile to the reservation system, reflecting its profound implications for families like his. Since the 1960s, south Indian Brahmans had been migrating to other Indian states and more recently to the USA and other countries where they and their children had better prospects of employment and educational access. People like Mr Raman insisted that there was nothing unearned about what their families had attained. Their claim was that what they had, and had taken pains to pass on to their children, were habits of patient study and mental discipline tempered by the willingness to cultivate a feeling heart and restrain inharmonious desires and passions.[31]

The implicit contrast here was to those who sought what was widely referred to as 'unmerited' access to educational and employment opportunities. For people who expressed these views, the region's politicians were perverting the relations which should prevail between the state and its citizens by dispensing benefits on a tawdry, short-term, immediate-return basis. This made them providers of flashy largesse in return for electoral gain, in contrast to people from families like Mr Raman's who represented themselves as givers of virtuous gifts. The message here was very like the views I had heard expressed in Hanoi, though with an element of affective language drawn from predominantly Hindu devotional sources which was distinctive to the Indian intelligentsia world. In south India, particularly, I remember people conveying to me that what they had attained in the form of education and cultivated knowledge was something widely shared and imparted. Those whom they advantaged were not only their own deserving kin. Indeed the whole nation benefited from what they did with their skills and knowledge which they freely gave to others, not as seekers of credit or undeserved gain, but as doers of loving, dedicated service (*seva*).

These views were also evident in what I recall Mr Raman saying about the lavish, publicly funded cultural projects which the Dravidianism

---

[31] Many of Mr Raman's relations had made new professional careers in other states or overseas, though they had met regional mass-movement chauvinisms elsewhere in India, notably the Shiv Sena's anti-incomer populism in Bombay. On emotional practice in Tamilnadu, see Trawick 1990. Dravidian movement polemicists have long represented Brahmans as the slaves of indecent drives and passions, their own sensibilities being true, refined and 'heartfelt'; throughout India, Muslims are vilified in the same terms by Hindutva ideologues.

politicians sponsored. I was bemused as a research student to find that the staging of what were called World Tamil Congresses and the building in 1973 of a giant themepark-like recreation of the semi-legendary port and temple city celebrated in the ancient *Cilappatikaram* verse epic were successful vote-winning gambits for Dravidian party leaders (Cutler 1983). Mr Raman pointedly distanced himself from these state-supported initiatives with their de-Brahmanised account of the region's heritage. Those like him who were hostile to these Dravidianist cultural narratives had their own set of high-profile arts and culture initiatives to praise and patronise.

Obviously these tensions between the raucous world of party politics and the career administrators' professionalised service ethos created a context which is very unlike that in which my Vietnamese intelligentsia friends have made their careers. What they and their Indian counterparts had in common, however, was this undercurrent of unresolved conflict about whether the conspicuously well-educated people who did the state's business were doers of virtuous service to nation and people, or venal beneficiaries of accrued cultural capital, much of it inherited from colonial sources. In both cases too, these battles were fought out in an emotionally charged idiom of competitive socialist virtue, with each side demonising the other as profiteers making illegitimate gains from the possession and use of tangible and intangible assets deployed at the expense of the 'masses'.

Despite the pressures which Mr Raman faced as a Brahman in Tamil Nadu, for an IAS official the post of Collector was and is a career plum. Mr Raman had extensive powers and heavy responsibilities. In his district he lived very much in the public eye, surrounded by the panoply of office that was then as now a distinctive feature of Collectors' lives. Many of the conventions of that life were colonial in origin, the innumerable 'chits' or forms he dealt in still couched in a Raj-era English vocabulary of 'intimations in triplicate', 'charge-sheeters' and 'undersigneds'. Like his British predecessors, he had badge-wearing orderlies known as *peon*s to run his errands, and deferential subordinates continually at his elbow. Yet he did not speak of these norms as archaic or sclerotic, but as the proprieties of a brisk modern administrator's world, its ethos far superior in his view to the spendthrift personality-cult lordliness of the state's elected officials. In this he resembled the Hanoi people who have delicately hinted to me that they take a dim view of senior Party officials who revel in the trappings of high office that typify many socialist societies. The adult son and daughter of a Hanoi intellectual who became a senior DRV official made a point of telling me that their father was known for his warmth and accessibility to ordinary citizens, and that the villagers from a remote 'ethnic minority' region where he had worked paid tribute to him after his death, recalling a visit he had made when he had shown his warm heart and delicacy of feeling (*chan tinh*) by walking among them during his stay, rather than allowing himself to be driven about in his official car.

Mr Raman can also be compared to those of my Hanoi friends' parents whose task as Viet Minh officials at the time of the anti-French liberation war was to establish the structures of revolutionary administration in the territorial units of the Viet Minh-controlled 'liberated territories' which the DRV called *lien khu* (interzones). As Collector, Mr Raman spoke of his district as a moral space with features much like those of a *lien khu*, its people placed in his care to 'develop' by enlightened, scientific means.

Like Indian districts, the interzones were not thought of as arbitrarily designated administrative units. As I explain in Chapter 6, Interzone IV, where many of my informants lived as children, had a particularly strong identity in these narratives, its distinctive heritage derived from its importance as a site of both modern and traditional intellectual life, as well as its epic history of patriotic local resistance movements. These Vietnamese revolutionary stories of micro-regions and their protonational and national achievements thus gave a prominent place to the locally based old-style intellectual families once honoured with the imperial title *ho dai khoa* ('great scholar families'), that is the village patrilines with strong traditions of grooming boys for success in the imperial service examinations. It is true that both they and the intellectual 'moderns' were not always celebrated in these narratives as patriotic and virtuous, and indeed much of what their detractors say about Tamil Brahmans has been said of them, as in the comments of critics like Le Duan. The key difference, however, is that Vietnam's intellectuals have not been confronted with a fully developed counter-narrative in which the liberation of their regional homeland's creative genius required their displacement and the discrediting of the learned traditions which they have embodied, either individually or as members of families with a known abundance of intellectual and cultural capital.

A voracious and eclectic reader with a formidably retentive memory and sufficient means to indulge in a variety of erudite pastimes, Mr Raman was a top Madras University arts graduate. This colonial foundation had a strong pre- and post-independence reputation for excellence in numerous fields: Mr Raman's intellectual heroes included the university's long line of contributors to Tamil and Sanskrit lexicography and literary studies. He also paid tribute to his father, from whom he said he had acquired his passion for learning. His father too had been a Madras University arts graduate, and it infuriated Mr Raman that the state's 'reservations' regimen was closing its doors to the deserving young from families like his.

Like many of my Hanoi friends, Mr Raman delighted in cultivated conversation and the delivery of epigrammatic pronouncements on the many historical and cultural topics that interested him. Looking back, I believe that he too liked the idea of reaching out in a confident manner to a wider world of international intellectual life by acting as patron and mentor to a researcher from Cambridge, even – indeed particularly – a researcher as junior and inexperienced as I was. Cambridge was 'famous' for him as it is for my Hanoi informants and thus a site within that wider global ecumene with which he too wished to connect in a credible manner. It was therefore all to the good that my Tamil was hesitant and self-conscious; he had a lyrical command of both its literary and everyday colloquial forms. He also clearly revelled in speaking English. As for other south Indians of his career and background, English was the language of his home life, and also that of his interactions with other senior officials. His was eloquent, sonorous and flawlessly grammatical, rich in vocabulary and punctuated by quotations from Shakespeare, Dickens and Macaulay.[32]

Mr Raman had also steeped himself in the published writings of the British scholar-officials who had produced English-language accounts of his district's history and cultural life. Those he particularly mentioned were the nineteenth-century officials who initiated scientific land surveys and irrigation projects in the years after the region had been 'settled' through the imposition of a coercive revenue demand on what had been seen as a region of refractory martial 'tribes' and warlords (known locally as *poligars*) (Ludden 1985: 26–41). He was unembarrassed about his admiration for these nineteenth-century officials; there were other 'Britishers' whom I recall him disparaging as racist, brutal or corrupt. But while he was no apologist for colonial rule in general, it was clear that he felt entitled to exercise critical judgement in deciding which former officials merited his praise for having served his district well by researching its history, 'developing' its material and human assets and

---

[32] Unlike my Hanoi informants, who use Vietnamese in everyday conversation. Compare Benei 2005. As I recall, Mr Raman's Macaulay quotations were from the 1848 *History of England*, which he admired for its sonorous prose and vivid narrative style. He also knew the work that is now so widely cited in postcoloniality literature as a critical text of the colonising process, Macaulay's 1835 'Minute on Education' which calls for the creation of 'brown Englishmen' through English-language education. But like my Hanoi informants, Mr Raman expressed strong views about the difference between indoctrination and the deliberate appropriation of empowering knowledge.

protecting its people from those he regarded as dangerous and predatory. These included the old *poligar* warlords and their descendants. He made no secret of the fact that he regarded the politicians of his own day as direct heirs of the wild-man excesses and rapacity which he associated with the rule of these former regional chiefs. On one occasion he made a point of warning me off visiting the seat of one of his district's former *poligar* chiefdoms, giving me to understand that the heirs to the region's mini-princedoms lived licentious and disorderly lives like their meat-eating, mustachioed forebears.

This was a view expressed by other local 'moderns', including teachers from the district's schools and colleges. Mr Raman made it clear that while in his district I should not stray out of *sircar* ('state') territory, meaning that I should not venture into these shadowy rural realms where he said the writ of the old chiefs still ran, and a young female researcher would be at risk. The implication of this was that even in his own day, all that an honest, zealous official could do was to keep these dark forces at bay. This, he made clear, was what his predecessors had achieved, and what he was seeking to do as an enlightened Nehruvian. In the same vein, he also expressed admiration for the scholar-missionaries who had produced the first published Tamil dictionaries and grammars, although he had no sympathy for their Christianising aims.[33]

The family and the modern nation

Mr Raman liked me to attend the big set-piece occasions of Collectorate life at which he acted as a visible embodiment of the purposeful Nehruvian state in action, notably in his 'mass contact' sessions, receiving delegations of district people with grievances to air and disputes for him to adjudicate. Like other Collectors, he was much in demand to act as a legitimating presence at school prize days and other public events. At home too he led a life of high visibility in which he was both a source and object of scrutiny. His doings received extensive local press coverage, and he was an inveterate deployer of the media, regularly attended by a cameraman from a local photographic studio whose recording of his daily round he monitored attentively. These pictures, like his home life, blurred the boundaries between the public and the familial. They also incorporated me. He regularly made a point

---

[33] Indeed like the former Madras civil servants who now publish critiques of secularism on Hindu cultural chauvinist websites, he and his wife both spoke in praise of the Hindutva (Hinduness) cause.

of including me in his 'mass contact' photos. On one occasion he summoned the studio cameraman to the Collectorate bungalow to take a picture in which he posed in his crisp working-day safari suit, seated next to me with his wife and small daughter on my other side.

Like my Hanoi friends' former Viet Minh parents, Mr Raman and his immediate family lived in government-issue accommodation, and at a considerable distance from their other kin. Some of their elder relations lived in extended-family households in what had long been a predominantly Brahman residential area in Madras. The house assigned to them in the district was the massive official residence which had housed Collectors and their families since the early nineteenth century. As was typical of such structures, this was a dwelling in which public and private spaces adjoined and intersected. Set in its sizeable walled compound, the house was situated well outside the crowded residential and market areas of the town where the main Collectorate offices and other public buildings were located. There were armed police at the gate, and garages and staff housing inside the compound. Its most prominent structure was the sprawling bungalow with its carriage drive, garden and residential quarters for the Collector's family.

In some ways Mr Raman led a life closely resembling that which nineteenth- and early twentieth-century official manuals of conduct and career requirements had prescribed for colonial district officers, accessible at all hours, and using his home space to transact official business, especially when this involved receiving what the manuals had called 'native gentlemen' and district people of the 'better sort'.[34] Mr Raman was on amiable terms with a wide range of such individuals. But while earlier Collectors would have interacted with the 'native gentlemen' on terms defined by the intricacies of regional power relations involving the colonial state's local agents and co-opted 'collaborators', Mr Raman's contacts connected him to a far wider world. In those pre-liberalisation years, India was still doing a great deal of business with the Soviet Union and other COMECON countries. The Collector's web of acquaintances gave him many points of access to these arenas of global socialist 'friendship'. One local man to whom he made a point of introducing me was a businessman with an opulent new house and a well-stocked cattleshed in which he took much pride. A high-profile benefactor of the region's Hindu temples, this doer of dutiful service to 'mother cow' was a big man in the intricate power

---

[34] There are fascinating guidelines of this sort in the 1931 *Indian Civil Service Manual* (*Madras*), pp. 42–7.

politics of the state and district. But he had also established himself in that world of external interactions among fellow socialists which Nehruvians were still championing in those days. When I met him, he was about to visit one of the COMECON states to close a big deal in locally grown 'agri-export' products.

When at home, Mr Raman clearly did not inhabit a feminised zone from which he ventured forth to play a lone part on a narrowly post-colonial public stage. As in the case of my Hanoi friends, what I recall about the Collector's home life was the way in which he and his wife used their allocated residence as a site from which to engage in vigorous moral commentary both within and about the wider world, doing so in ways that incorporated and also transcended the psychic and social afterlife of empire. His wife was an energetic participant in these processes, reading widely, pursuing interests in Carnatic music and *Bharatnatyam* dance and supervising the household's ritual life. This was one of the more striking ways in which they imposed their own regimens of identity and purpose on the house, maintaining a vegetarian kitchen and a *puja* (worship) room attended by a local *purohit* (Brahman ritualist).

Their small daughter was also an active figure in these endeavours. During an early visit to their house, I was shown the little girl's school exercise books. Dressed in a starched Western-style dress of the kind widely worn by small girls and referred to then as now in India as a 'frock' (Tarlo 1996), she sat with us as I was shown her fine penmanship and the good marks she had received from her teachers. She then stood to attention, as Indian children still do on formal classroom occasions, and performed her repertoire of memorised recitations. These were from texts learned both at school and from her parents. The longest, and the one in which both she and they evinced most pride, was a startlingly accurate rendition in English of Nehru's famous 'Freedom at Midnight' speech. This is the celebrated piece of oratory which Nehru delivered as the nation's first Prime Minister on the eve of Indian independence in 1947. To demonstrate the accuracy of her performance, they played a gramophone record of the original speech. I remember that she had indeed captured every intonation and cadence.

While Mr Raman and his wife applauded those elements of the Neh-ruvian 'project' that they associated with science and modernity tempered by respect for progressive forms of Hindu faith and heritage, they did not regard Nehru himself with uncritical adulation. Rather than the great man's *anima*, I think it was the empowering oratorical skill and know-ledge of a landmark national moment that the child had been encouraged to absorb and replicate. Clearly there were subtly subversive mimetic elements in the many acts of citation, quotation and image-making which

Mr Raman displayed to me and to other observers of his life in the public eye. Yet it would be reductionist to regard them all as projections either directly or through his child of a mimetic subversion of the official hierarchies in which they were all enmeshed. Nor were they just complacent showings off of a privileged family's safely accrued cultural capital.

Looking back at the child's recitation, it was evident that all three took pleasure in that show of verbal art effectively imparted and displayed. It was clearly a moment when she had demonstrated on behalf of herself and her parents the key virtues of the modern Indian family as Nehru himself had defined it: not an instrument of controlling power or a model of citizen-subject subordination, but a nurturing unit, lovingly producing both sons and daughters equipped for the progressive life of an advancing nation.[35] This is closely comparable to the progressive modern family as defined in socialist Vietnam, and enthusiastically embodied – though often at great cost – by the people who have told me about the conjugal kin units that they or their elders forged both within and beyond Hanoi, learning to lead an intelligentsia family life in conditions of separation and displacement, and having frequently but not invariably been applauded for doing so.

On that occasion and many others, I recall the Ramans' expressions of concern about the uncertainties that awaited their child as she moved back and forth between their enlightened, nurturing household spaces, and those in which they believed she would meet unjust exclusion from the nation's modern life. They were fiercely resentful that the proponents of ethnicised social justice goals within their home region were defining people like them as rootless outsiders without a rightful place in that common regional homeland. This is precisely what enemies of Nehruvianism as a secular ideology of Indian nationhood have said about Nehru and his own family, that as Kashmir Pandits they too were unanchored people who learned languages instrumentally and used the places where they found service as mere bases of operations, never truly inhabiting them in the way that a real son or daughter of the soil served and valued a familial hearth and homeland. The claim here then is that such people had no cherished home place, no 'passions of the tongue' (Ramaswamy 1997), only spaces used and profited from and skills amassed and sold.[36] It was this which Mr Raman and his wife were seeking to counter, speaking in a language of care and nurture about

---

[35] Compare Parry's account (2001) of the Bhilai steel plant as a site of exemplary modernism with Nehruvian goals, where the making of apparently casteless marriages connects with the developmental modernism of the factory environment.
[36] Ramaswamy 1997; and see Spodek 1974: 450.

everything that their detractors represented as ignobly amassed cultural capital. What this included was their capacity to pass on to their child something which they held to be precious and wonderful both for her and the nation. This was the ability to speak English with the poetic fire and passion which educated people I knew from their generation still spoke of in those days as part of what they cherished about that epiphanic moment of the nation's birth.

Like my Hanoi friends, Mr Raman and the other Indian cosmopolitans I knew who were in much the same situation were far from powerless in relation to the public narratives which disparaged and defamed them. Together with their other forms of cultural knowledge, their own command of narrative and authoritative historical discourse were powerful assets in these encounters. So too was their ability to make much of their continuing ties to that wider world which had provided a significant part of the Nehruvian ideal's moral context. This wider world of socialist aid and 'friendship' relations was also central to the visions of family and national life which featured in my Hanoi informants' accounts of childhood experience in 'liberated' Hanoi and the wartime revolutionary interzones. It is to these that I turn in Chapters 6 and 7.

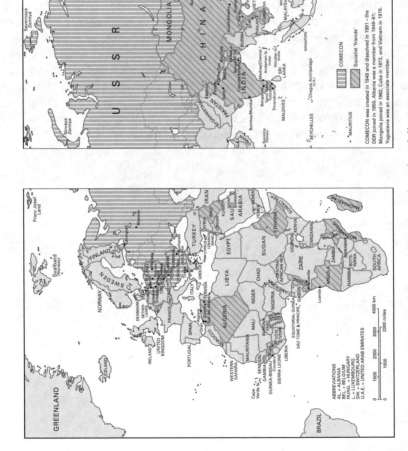

Map 1 Journeys recalled: Vietnam and the remembered socialist ecumene

The map is an approximate rendering of the political situation in 1950

◿◿◿ French 'occupied' territories

⬚⬚⬚ Viet Minh controlled or 'liberated' zones

Map 2 Vietnam's inner frontiers during the 1946–54 anti-French resistance war

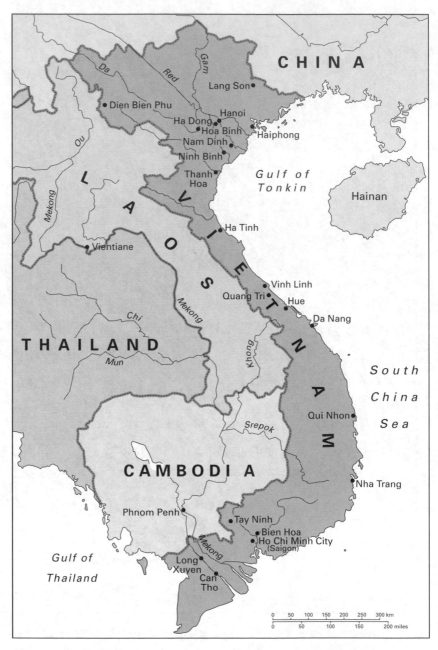

Map 3 Vietnam today

Plate 1 Remembering a pre-
modern hero: the Emperor
Ly Thai To.

Plate 2 Hanoi's famous island pagoda seen from the former Indira
Gandhi park.

Plate 3 Hanoi victory monument, erected on the fiftieth anniversary of the end of the anti-French war.

Plate 4 'Resolved to die for the nation's eternal life'. Poster of Ho Chi Minh inspiring the liberators, marking the sixtieth anniversary of the onset of the anti-French war.

Plate 5 Another sixtieth anniversary poster: the anti-French resistance struggle commemorated in 2006.

Plate 6 Site of intelligentsia family commemorations: the Temple of Literature (Van Mieu).

Plate 7 From a Hanoi intellectual family's photo album: two small boys in imported baby suits *c.* 1937 (Private Collection).

Plate 8 Garments from the Rue Paul Bert 'where even the streets smelled French' (Private Collection).

Plate 9 A *lycée*-educated Hanoi mother in an *ao dai* (Vietnamese 'national dress') with her two small sons, *c.* 1939 (Private Collection).

Plate 10 Taking enlightened possession: Hanoi woman reading a *quoc ngu* (romanised Vietnamese) newspaper, *c.* 1941 (Private Collection).

Plate 11 A pen-holding intellectual and a trader (second from right) with other makers of the socialist nation. From the news-sheet *Viet Nam Doc Lap* (Independent Vietnam), June 1945.

Plate 12 'We're not buying!' Viet Minh poster with a 'buy native – boycott foreign luxuries' message. © The Trustees of the British Museum.

Plate 13 'Wherever you roam, go home for Wounded Serviceman's Day'. Viet Minh poster showing peasant traders taking part in a village commemoration. © The Trustees of the British Museum.

Plate 14 Intelligentsia life in the Viet Minh 'liberated territories'. Young women in khaki, *c.* 1951 (Private Collection).

Plate 15 Western-style dress in the 'liberated territories', *c.* 1951 (Private Collection).

Plate 16 Childhood in the 'liberated territories'. A cadre's son on a Viet Minh pack pony, *c.* 1949 (Private Collection).

Plate 17 Revolutionary youth chorale performing in Interzone IV, *c.* 1949. (Private Collection).

Plate 18 Another wartime musical performance (Private Collection).

Plate 19 An intelligentsia family in post-liberation Hanoi, *c.* 1955 (Private Collection).

Plate 20 Vietnam's most famous image of the nation reunited in 1976. Courtesy of Chinh Tri Quoc Gia Publishing House.

Plate 21 'The Party has brought enlightenment'. A work of revolutionary art by the contemporary painter Le Minh Chau. Courtesy of the artist.

XÂY DỰNG LẠI ĐẤT NƯỚC TA
ĐÀNG HOÀNG HƠN TO ĐẸP HƠN

Plate 22 Beloved kinsman to the national family: President Ho Chi Minh's image on display in Hanoi.

Plate 23 Hero of the socialist ecumene. Hanoi memorial to the Cuban revolutionary José Martí Pérez (1853–95).

Plate 24 Poster celebrating the work of peasants, soldiers and an educated 'modern' in shirt and spectacles.

Plate 25 A socialist 'friendship gift'. The Hanoi Children's Culture Palace.

Plate 26 Witnessing the nation's birth. Detail from Van Tho's panoramic painting of the declaration of national independence on 2 September 1945. Courtesy of the artist and the National Museum of Vietnamese History, Hanoi.

Plate 27 The decorum of the *foule révolutionnaire*. Van Tho's Independence Day painting was commissioned in 1979 for the National Museum of Vietnamese History.

Plate 28 Commemorative poster showing the microphone through which '*Bac Ho*' exchanged utterances with the crowd on Independence Day, 1945.

Plate 29 A national giant entombed. The grave of Ho Chi Minh's successor Le Duan in Mai Dich national cemetery; in the foreground, an incense burner and commemorative offering vessels.

Plate 30 Hanoi's Opera House, completed in 1911. To the right, a *doi moi* landmark: the Hilton hotel, opened in 1999.

6   Cosmopolitan spaces in revolutionary times

Introduction: the liberated city

Having focused in the preceding chapter on intelligentsia life in India's inner socialist ecumene, I return now to my Hanoi informants' familial environments. My concern here is with their accounts of the novel forms of sociality shaping their lives as children during the anti-French resistance war (1946–54) when the new DRV party-state was being forged.[1] In exploring these accounts, I return to my theme of intelligentsia mobility, focusing on visual and verbal images of space and its mastery on the part of those forging these new forms of social life. This chapter also deals with the creation of these new socialities as a process giving rise to a sense of immediacy and tangibility on the part of those seeking to live as 'socialist moderns', and in so doing to visualise a new national future for Vietnam.

The idea of purposeful movement was a key feature of my informants' accounts of wartime family life. It shaped their engagements with official narratives of the liberation process and interacted in complex ways with the sense of active agency pervading their accounts of remembered urban and rural landscapes. They all represent themselves as makers rather than passive objects of revolutionary spectacle and panoptic enactments within these spaces, even when very young. Indeed the tools through which revolutionary geographies are made and known feature strongly in their accounts. The formal mapping of such spaces is something to which they attach strikingly personal meanings: I discuss this below as an affective process for which I employ the term auto-cartography.

My informants' sense of mobility is also manifested in something reminiscent of the thinking of Indian intelligentsia moderns about the forging of the new moral spaces which I am calling an inner socialist

---

[1] The Democratic Republic of Vietnam or DRV was officially brought into being by the Viet Minh leadership under Ho Chi Minh in August 1945 (see Marr 1995a; Goscha and Tréglodé 2004).

ecumene. What I have in mind are their claims that as people of scientific knowledge and refined sensibility, their traversing of liberated urban and rural terrain was a significant contribution to the nation's future. This was an imminent and tangible future, to be lived and visualised in a wider world of cosmopolitan knowledge and empowering socialist 'friendships'. My friends claimed to have taken part in the creation of this impending future in ways that both built on and transformed their families' distinctive linguistic and other cultural capital, much of it deriving from colonial sources, but still amenable to the purposes of the revolution and the securing of that new national life.

All the Hanoi people I have worked with experienced the forging of family and other kin-like ties in the context of what the historian Dang Phong has called Vietnam's 'life of war' (1999). As I explained in Chapter 2, for those who were children or young adults during the anti-French war, this meant the dangerous urban life of the underground infiltrator or patriotic schoolchild exchanging secret signs and slogans with like-minded comrades. Often they were briefly or more enduringly parted from close kin, and sometimes painfully at odds with them. But it has been the sharing of memories of wartime schooling and home life in the revolutionary interzones (*lien khu*) or 'liberated territories' that has been particularly important to my informants from this age group.

In the book's penultimate chapter I return to the separations and relocations which these sixty- to seventy-year-olds experienced in adulthood, focusing on their accounts of crossing and recrossing the cultural spaces of the two great interpenetrating networks which shaped their lives after independence: the former French-ruled colonial empire and the post-1945 socialist world system. But the crossing of boundaries is also central to this chapter. The concern here is the negotiation of wartime frontiers, a process of relocation and dispersal recalled in an idiom of strong emotion often relating to the tangible and intangible possessions, skills and acquisitions associated with parents and other elders.

My friends' reflections on these memories convey something emerging very regularly in their accounts of living as exemplary cultured moderns, this being the recognition that revolutionary states are not only political constructs, but moral spaces created through the enactment of new forms of sociality. Not all of these are prescribed or generated by official authorities. I have already shown that both children and adults can be active agents in this process. I say more below about the ways in which the domestic lives of revolutionaries can constitute a separate arena from that of the reformed or invented socialities experienced through approved organisations such as schools, youth groups, workplace units and military cohorts, sometimes harmonising with their official norms and regimens, and sometimes very much in tension with them.

Most of the people mentioned in this chapter were children of francophone intelligentsia parents who left Hanoi with their families soon after the outbreak of the anti-French resistance war in 1946–7, often relocating several times, and undergoing bombing raids, food shortages and prolonged family separations in the course of their sojourns in the Viet Minh interzones. Some retain vivid memories of negotiating the dangerous but highly permeable frontier separating the 'liberated' and 'occupied' territories, which included all of Vietnam's major cities and their hinterlands.[2] I have already mentioned Dr Tran, the friend who has taken me on extended visits to the sites of his interzone childhood. Now a retired academic in his late sixties, Dr Tran was born in Hanoi. His parents were Viet Minh officials, and he spent all nine years of the anti-French war in the area around Thanh Hoa in the far south of the Red River delta. This core region of Interzone IV was an area in which large numbers of the Viet Minh's intelligentsia recruits were concentrated, some specialising in academic, creative and propaganda work, but many others taking posts in the DRV technical and production services. I deal below with the exalting of such people as bringers of skill and science to the interzones, as in the case of Mr Lanh, the former Hanoi *lycéen* whose father was a draughtsman in the colonial *service cartographique*. He too was skilled in drawing and draftsmanship, serving as a map-maker and producer of technical drawings for the Viet Minh armaments workshops near Thanh Hoa.

A more widely known use of the Viet Minh's intelligentsia adherents was as 'brain workers' assigned to Interzone IV's officially designated literary villages (*lang van*), producing writings and art works for use by the DRV propaganda directorate (Ninh 2002: 87). Many also taught in the region's schools and pre-university, the Du Bi Dai Hoc (university preparatory school). Dr Tran was one of its pupils. He said its students were encouraged to regard themselves as the active, achieving embodiments of a national future that had begun with the 1945 August Revolution and was continuing to take shape within the interzones. That triumphant modern future in the making would be brought to fruition at the point of liberation (*giai phong*), when they, the first generation of brilliant young people being groomed for the life of educated socialist modernity within their liberated homeland, could take their places in a fully fledged national university in the nation's capital. As I was told by

---

[2] Dang Phong 1999a; 2002.

one of his former Du Bi Dai Hoc contemporaries, 'We thought about it. It was why we studied hard. We thought how it would be when we were there in our university.'

Like other things that my informants told me they looked forward to during their interzone years, this was something they say they thought of in highly visual terms. These imaginings do not appear to take the form of the distant and otherworldly 'dream of the future' described by Elisabeth Croll in her account of the remote and disembodied 'rhetorical gaze' to be seen in the imaging of futuristic revolutionary aspirations in China's propaganda posters, with their long-sighted eyes fixed on a brilliantly coloured, heaven-like socialist future far beyond the body and its senses.[3]

One of my friends said that he and his interzone classmates formed their ideas about the post-war future from a far more sober set of pictures. These were images that their teacher had shown them of students in a Soviet university. From then on, he said, when he imagined life after liberation, he saw himself in a concrete and tangible setting: a place with books on shelves, and a lecture hall with raked seats. He knew that no such place yet existed in Vietnam. But it was part of the future that was already taking shape in all that he and his friends and family were doing in the interzones and beyond. This included their elders' efforts to equip the 'liberated territories' with the signs and sites of productive socialist modernity: clinics, schools, manufacturing operations. For the young, it meant the schooling they were receiving in the interzones and further afield in China. When liberation came, their efforts would come to fruition in the lives they would lead in the new national university.[4]

Socialist time and the future

These were all elements of that DRV dream of an achievable socialist future to be inhabited in a domain of proximate, tangible clock time rather than a distant, disembodied millennial future. As I explain below,

---

[3] Croll 1994: 4; Lu 2005. On the more immediate 'present-future' depicted in Soviet propaganda art, see Bonnell 1997. On the life and work of Vietnam's revolutionary artists including those trained at the Ecole des Beaux Arts and combining revolutionary Soviet and French romantic aesthetics, see Vu An Chuong 1994; Papin 2001: 320–3; Harrison-Hall 2002; Ninh 2002; N.A. Taylor 2004. On the complex temporal messages conveyed in popular Indian calendar art, see Pinney 1995.

[4] The drive to equip revolutionary space with modern trappings in the form of bureaucratic practices, official language and such items as desks and typewriters invites comparison with the attempts of other twentieth-century insurgencies to vest remote base areas with these signifiers of sovereign state power. Examples range from Mao Zedong's China in the early years of the revolution to the forest camps of Kenya's Mau Mau insurgents (Esherick 1998; Smith 1998).

both in the past and more recently, Vietnamese 'moderns' have come to know the world as a highly plural array of political orders. Rather than comprising a single defining colonial or socialist point of reference, the world with which they engaged involved a multiplicity of sometimes distinct and sometimes interacting colonialisms and socialisms. This may well be the source of their distinctively tangible sense of socialist temporality.[5]

With regard to my friends' accounts of their pre-independence student years, the key point was that the existing university at Hanoi – Indochina's only higher educational institution under colonial rule – had been maintained at a level far below that of France's metropolitan universities (Kelly 2000). As I noted earlier, this was an intentional strategy. France's aim was to avoid creating anything of the size or standard of India's pre-independence university system, which French officials regarded as a breeding ground for anti-colonial subversion. This is why it was of such importance to the DRV authorities that there were already so many young and older people leading a life of high-level 'culturedness' within the interzones, and why so much effort was made to represent that life as part of the new revolutionary order that was already being enacted within the 'liberated territories'. And, of course, the pre-independence intellectuals who became key recruits to the Viet Minh included a significant number of those colonial intellectuals who had been permitted to study for higher degrees in France. This made it all the more important to represent such people's overseas sojourns as selfless initiatives which bore fruit in their work as bringers of science and learning to the interzones, in anticipation of the post-liberation era when modern learning could be imparted to every citizen.[6]

As in other socialist contexts, visual materials have been a key feature of these attempts to project thought and feeling forward into the nation's life to come. In previous chapters I noted my informants' awareness of the many kinds of images that these efforts have generated, and

[5] For insightful discussion of diverse temporalities in Vietnamese representations of modernity, see P. Taylor 2001. On socialist temporality in the Soviet context, see Ssorin-Chaikov 2006.

[6] Trinh Van Thao 1990; Kelly 2000. There were other elements of that revolutionary order, including government departments and ministries, but much effort was put into the attempt to demonstrate that the *lien khu* (interzones) were units of a rapidly developing proto-state with an active social and cultural life. The pictorial media were crucial to these efforts; from the early stages of the resistance war the Viet Minh propaganda service deployed the work of poster artists and photographers in consciousness-raising among those who had relocated from the 'occupied' territories as well as local people. Harrison-Hall 2002; N.A. Taylor 2004: 42–62; on revolutionary art in China, see Judd 1983; Sullivan 1999.

particularly their familiarity with famous poster representations, notably those featuring President Ho Chi Minh. Such knowledge is very pervasive among Hanoi intellectuals, and both the younger and the older people I know take an enthusiastic interest in viewing and discussing these materials. I have also mentioned my friends' remarkable family photo albums, and the ways in which they have made much of both personal and official images when they have shared their family narratives with me.

I have also mentioned their ideas concerning refined speech and writing as critical elements of intelligentsia sociality. But the visual had a particularly striking presence in my friends' accounts of their interzone childhoods. Powerful as they were as propaganda tools, such items as posters of Ho Chi Minh as '*Bac Ho*' ('Uncle Ho'), beloved kinsman to a united national family, are much more than artefacts of 'panoptic' control (see Plates 4 and 22). Nor is it right to dismiss them as relics of a socialist past that have been made irrelevant in the age of 'late socialist' marketisation.[7] Thus although Hanoi people are now accustomed to a cityscape suffused with images of pop stars and international consumer goods, my friends have conveyed something far more complex than a simple story of old socialist visuality regimens being overridden by those of the new marketised world. What I have heard does not suggest any clear-cut dichotomy between state-generated image-making and the personal iconographies which people speak of as evoking the love and care of their revolutionary parents, and of their own powerful memories of childhood life. This does not mean that they are naively sentimental or uncritically accepting in their attitude to official images and the ideological messages which they encode. But they do tend to invest such representations with strong personal meanings, speaking of these in a composite language of service, sociality and cherished nationhood, and doing so in ways which both interact with and subtly differ from official claims and messages.[8]

When Dr Tran has told me about his memories of 'going to the forest' (*vao rung*), i.e. leaving Hanoi for the 'liberated territories' with his parents and elder brother in 1947, he has begun his accounts by taking me

[7] See e.g. Logan 2000: 253; Thomas 2003: 174. Compare Holm 1991.

[8] Unlike the Indian informants whom Pinney describes as unresponsive both to and about the propaganda images on display in the industrial town where he did fieldwork (1995: 86–7), my friends are enthusiastic commentators on such iconography. They often blur the boundaries between personal images and those emanating from the official propaganda sources: several have amateur or professional artists in their families, and most speak of visiting museums and art galleries as an important feature of *tri thuc* intelligentsia life.

through the family photographs which document their experiences in Hanoi and the interzones. What is captured in the earliest of these pictures is that world of cultivated pastimes and modestly prosperous urban domestic lives which characterised the pre-independence Hanoi *tri thuc* intelligentsia milieu. Both his parents were *lycée*-educated. His father joined the Viet Minh shortly after its foundation in 1941 and found salaried employment in a French-owned commercial firm. This provided cover for his resistance activities during the Japanese occupation, and equipped him with specialist skills which he was able to put to use in his interzone work. He rose to senior rank in the DRV administration during the anti-French war, specialising in production and *stockage* (supply). In the early war years before Mao's victory in 1949, this meant sourcing weaponry and other scarce strategic necessities from areas of southern China that were under the control of the Guomindang nationalists (Goscha 2000). Dr Tran's father also undertook dangerous missions inside the French-controlled 'occupied territories'. Like many of the other intelligentsia women who relocated to the interzones, his mother also held a variety of interzone administrative posts.

Dr Tran speaks with pride and deep emotion of his parents. He is not a Communist Party member, but his father was: 'tu comprends, Suzanne: membre du Parti; un vrai militant!' – a genuine and committed revolutionary (*nguoi cach mang*). Yet his recollections of his parents are steeped in a conviction that camaraderie, human warmth and an appreciation of civilised pleasures and accomplishments were entirely compatible with the ideals of the revolution. From early childhood Tran was expected to master the refinements of speech and manners which are still essential attainments for a well-brought-up Vietnamese child. As I have observed in numerous household settings, from an early age Vietnamese children are taught the proper civilities to be observed at mealtimes, and in the handling of the numerous relational pronouns through which juniors show respect to those senior in age and status. Food on plates or trays should be offered with two hands. Elders must be given due precedence; relations and guests must be called to eat in proper order, and with the correct mode of address. Toddlers learn to say such things as 'Father (or Grandfather, or Senior Aunt, etc.) I invite you to take rice', referring properly to themselves as 'son/daughter' (*con*), 'grandchild' (*chau*) and so on, pairing each self-reference with the correct term for the person being addressed (Rydstrøm 2003: 59–82).

At an early age the young also learn the polite syllable *a* with which a junior ends sentences as a mark of respect for seniors. When old enough, children learn to sit by their mothers and assist with the serving out of rice. There are many other refinements, many of them summed up, I was told, through the various maxims which parents routinely pronounce in the process of imparting good manners. A favourite is 'eat and watch' (*an trong noi; ngoi trong huong*, lit: 'When you eat, look at the pot; when you sit, look out for the direction'), the meaning of which is something like: don't be greedy; keep an eye on people's plates to see if they should be offered more; keep an eye on where you are sitting, never turn your back on other people or the household ancestor altar.[9]

These conventions are not exclusive to the Hanoi *tri thuc* milieu, though I have never encountered anyone who would have considered such proprieties with their emphasis on polite speech and the recognition of elder–junior hierarchies either too 'élitist' or traditional for revolutionaries to pass on to their children. But as Tran and his brother grew up, their father also told them about wine, and about the Sorbonne as the intellectual centre of the world. The French colonisers and French civilisation were not the same thing: 'On peut distinguer', he said (We knew the difference). From their parents and interzone teachers they also learned about the music and writings of the great romantics, both Russian and French. Dr Tran still quotes the verses of Lamartine and de Vigny, citing their evocations of verdant nature, moral worth and human fortitude as 'inspirations pour la formation spirituelle de notre génération' (inspirational for the spiritual formation of our generation). That savouring of names and knowledge should not be seen in simplistic terms as a display of élite tastes and habituations, and certainly not as the bolstering of a fragile sense of self against the traumas and insecurities of a postcolonial existence (Nandy 1988). My Hanoi friends have made it clear that for them there is nothing narrowly colonial about either Paris or those *lycée* curriculum staples, taught since the early days of the Third Republic as a means of transmitting patriotism and good morals to the children of the republic and to those so-called *évolué* subjects in the colonies who were deemed suitable for education as potential citizens.

The French literary classics were still widely taught in the interzones until 1952 when the ban on French was imposed. Yet even those who recall burning their French books and turning eagerly to the study of Chinese and Russian as the proper vehicles for Vietnam's future ties with the socialist world now say that their knowledge of French was a fitting accomplishment for the children of revolutionaries. When learned at home and from one's patriotic interzone teachers, French was a language of power and modernity: 'langue des révolutionnaires, de

---

[9] Hy Van Luong 1988; compare Stafford 1995: 95–111.

modernité' (a language of revolutionaries, of modernity) said Dr Tran's contemporary from the Du Bi Dai Hoc (university preparatory school in Thanh Hoa).

There is no sense in what my informants say on this subject of the plight of the alienated colonial subject who learns the colonisers' language but fears himself despised as a '*babu*', fruitlessly striving to be 'white' but eternally 'not quite' (Bhabha 1994). Dr Tran says that the first time he remembers speaking French to a Frenchman was to echo the words he heard being said to a captured soldier by the Viet Minh fighters who were guarding him: 'haut les mains' – 'hands up!' And he can still sing both the French and Vietnamese versions of the marching songs he learned as an adolescent member of the uniformed scouting movement created under the sponsorship of the wartime pro-Axis Vichy administration. These too were strong men's words, he says, inspiring and thrilling as he marched to their jaunty tunes in his cap and uniform shorts:

> Si nous voulons être fort,
> Si nous voulons marcher droit...
> Muon nen nguoi hung trang doi nay,
> Muon cho duong doi tien len hoai...[10]

In his interzone days, Dr Tran said, his great treasure trove was the *Dictionnaire Larousse*. He said it was a book he read for pleasure, especially the potted biographies of great achievers: Goethe, Edison, Marie Curie. Another friend told me about his excitement as a teenager when he found a reproduction of Picasso's *Guernica* in a French children's encyclopaedia, brought from Hanoi by one of his interzone secondary school teachers. Such knowledge of the wider world's heroes and iconoclasts was thus approved of by their Viet Minh parents and teachers. So too was their admiration for literary greats like Flaubert and Victor Hugo whom they were taught to think of as social critics whose modernist perspective could be readily appropriated for the purposes of their liberation struggle.[11] Of the shift to Russian and Chinese, they say the

---

[10] 'If you want to be a strong man in this life; If you want your path in life to be ever forward...' From the 1920s, uniformed youth organisations modelled on Baden-Powell's British scout movement were established in France and its overseas colonies. Both Vietnamese nationalists and the Vichy authorities promoted *le scout*; each saw it as embodying an ideal of youth-led revolutionary nationhood. See Marr 1981: 79–82, 97; Larcher-Goscha 2003; Raffin 2005: 92–5, 112–21, 195–210. On scouting songs and other pre-independence musical forms involving the adaptation of Western-style rhythmic and melodic styles, see Gibbs 2000; Raffin 2005: 77–8.

[11] Compare Bousquet 2002: 442–5 and Goscha 2004: 14–15.

reasons were pragmatic, reflecting the DRV's need for Soviet and Chinese support, rather than a belief that knowledge of French was a mark of what Nandy and other theorists have called a colonised mind (Nandy 1983: xi; Marglin 1990: 25–6).

Thus for my friends, the attainment of the knowledge they call modern and scientific – not French, Western or European – is widely seen as complementing rather than supplanting their sense of Vietnameseness. It is something they associate with the warmth of home and family, and with revolutionary modernity. They see nothing incongruous in a revolutionary extolling Paris as a site of learning and 'culturedness'. On the contrary: Paris looms large in many socialist 'imaginaries', its importance as a meeting point for the world's revolutionaries giving it a persona significantly unlike that of other former imperial metropoles. For Hanoi intellectuals it is a place associated with childhood memories of their revolutionary parents' achievements. Many also know it as a jumping-off point for their own travels across the socialist ecumene. Those who did *chuyen gia* ('expert') work in Algeria and sub-Saharan Africa in the 1980s and 90s like to recall their Paris stopovers as occasions when they could gratify long-held dreams of intelligentsia cosmopolitanism by visiting its museums and beauty spots.

These enthusiasms are not seen as an exalting of the foreign over the products of their homeland's life and culture. My friends all know and love the classics of Vietnamese literature and the love songs, patriotic ballads and poetry of the nationalist era, especially the works of the resistance poet Pham Duy, and the revolutionary lyricist Van Cao, composer of the national anthem. They speak of the imparting and acquisition of the cultivated knowledge which they attained in youth in a language of feeling and nurture: 'My father loved those songs. He taught them to us, and the poems. We sing them and I think of him.'[12]

My friends say too that the cosmopolitan knowledge they achieved in childhood was a means of connecting people in the interzones to a wider supranational terrain in which their achievements were recognised and applauded. I show below that there were very particular forms of mapping and depiction by which this was achieved. In so doing, I seek to show that such items as maps and visual images can be much more than tools of official power. In the settings where my informants experienced the forging of those supralocal connections, processes of personal

---

[12] Recent publications on the careers and compositions of the revolutionary composers include Huynh Van Tieng and Bui Duc Tinh 2002 and Nguyen Thuy Kha 2002. See also Hue Tam Ho Tai 2001: 171–2; P. Taylor 2001: 25, 15; and on the work of official war poets such as To Huu, see Ninh 2002: 84–6.

image-making interacted very actively with those arising from official representation practices. Such things as map-making tend to be treated in studies of so-called visuality and spatialisation regimens as projections of possessive or controlling power, coldly rationalising in their inscription of boundaries and ownership claims. This approach is especially pervasive in accounts of colonial settings where map-makers are widely thought of as expunging or denaturing prior conceptions of human space.[13] In proposing the notion of auto-cartography, I have in mind a very different idea of mapping operations, one that can impart intimacy and affective meaning through the use of skills and knowledge which are no less human and affectively personalised for being scientific, rationalising and ultra-modern.

Remembering an occupied land

The supralocal connections referred to here have entailed a focus on two key elements of that wider world's advances: the cultivation of progressive personal morality, and the attainment of a sense of involvement in the achievements of global scientific and technological achievement. The effects of these initiatives were sometimes painful and problematic, but they entailed something that was both more open-ended and more far-reaching than an attempt by cosmopolitan modernisers to colonise the people and spaces of the interzone countryside in the name of an updated socialist version of the French *mission civilisatrice* ('civilising mission').

Dr Tran describes his father's Marxism as humane and cosmopolitan. These are qualities that he associates with his fellow Vietnamese, and with certain peoples in the wider world. He thinks of Russians but not Chinese or Japanese as sharing Vietnamese traits of 'heart' and 'feeling' (*long*). Throughout his childhood, Viet Minh propagandists represented the Japanese as a brutal *'phat-xit'* (fascist) occupation force.[14] He still speaks of Japan as soulless and materialistic, and Maoist socialism as joyless and dehumanising. As I noted above, this view of China, officially a socialist 'friend' nowadays, harks back in part to the Cultural Revolution, still widely recalled as a time of terror for their Chinese intelligentsia

---

[13] E.g. Blunt and Rose 1992; Scott 1998; Harley 2001. For a more nuanced account of the divergent narratives and inscriptional modes that can be discerned in different types of official and local mapping practices, see Orlove 1991; compare Edney 1997 and Winichakul 1994.

[14] Compare Stoler and Strassler 2000: 12. The Viet Minh supported the Allied powers against the Axis in the Second World War.

counterparts, its destruction of books and personal treasures particularly repellant in its repudiation of 'culturedness' and filial feeling.[15]

The things that his parents wore and owned, and their deportment and style, are matters of deep significance for Dr Tran. His pre-war family photographs provide vivid glimpses of the urban life led by those Vietnamese who attended cinemas, read newspapers and illustrated reviews, and embraced the new modes of dress and consumption depicted in the city's shop signs and advertising hoardings. Much of the new vocabulary that attained currency in the 1920s and 30s is still in use today: *ao so-mi*, a phonetic rendering of the French *chemise*, hence the term for a Western-style shirt; *ca-vat*, from *cravate*, for tie; *bo com-le* from *complet*, suit. These were the garments worn by those in clerical work and other forms of salaried employment in the pre-war period, and also by male *lycéens* and their teachers. Such garb is recalled as having been immediately distinguishable from the gown with loose trousers (*ao the*) and turban-like headdress still worn in those days by traditional *thay do* or village schoolmasters.[16]

In pre-war Hanoi, Dr Tran's parents lived in modest circumstances but occasionally took pleasure in acquiring imported goods from the expensive shops around the Opera House. Possessions of this kind – prams, dolls, garments, home furnishings, tennis rackets – are visible in many of my friends' pre-war photos. One man who spent the 1946–54 resistance years in the interzones said that in the year of his birth in the late 1930s, it had been his father's pride to buy two elegant little baby suits for his sons from a shop in the Rue Paul Bert. This was the showcase boulevard running from the Opera House to the café-lined pleasure zone around the Hoan Kiem (Restored Sword) Lake, returned today to its pre-conquest name, Trang Tien (Mint Street).[17]

The faded studio photographs of the little boys in their imported *bo com-le* outfits are family treasures (see Plates 7 and 8). The friend who showed them to me said they evoked for him a gratifying vision of his father as '*capable*', '*connaissant*' (discerning), a man with the confidence and savoir-faire to hold his own in a foreign-owned shop in the Rue Paul

---

[15] It also reflects Vietnam's official shift in alignment from China to the USSR in the late 1970s, a move more usually discussed in terms of its economic and political consequences than its cultural residues at a more intimate level.

[16] *Ao* is the term for any sleeved garment. Words like *so-mi* and *phat-xit* (fascist) are hyphenated to show they derive from European languages. Other terms of similar derivation include suitcase, *cai va-li*, from the French *valise*; *len*, wool, from *laine*, and many more, including chocolate, cigarette and aspirin, as well as the terms for wine, cognac, and other foreign spirits.

[17] Papin 2001: 238.

Bert. It is true that the Viet Minh sought to foster an ideal of revolutionary austerity among its adherents, and campaigned for the consumption of 'home goods' like the Indian *swadeshi* ('of our homeland') products popularised by Gandhi through the mapping out of the new Indian nation as a terrain of novel socialities and moral practices engendered through the circulation of home-produced textiles and other national commodities[18] (see Plate 12). But my friends have made it clear that they do not regard these photos as static cameos of petit bourgeois domesticity. What they wish me to see in them are active moments experienced and recalled as the movement through time of revolutionaries leading lives of purpose and initiative, either obeying or eagerly awaiting the call to insurgent action.

This is a time sense like that implied in those official poster images pointing forward to the nation's future. The people I know treat their family photographs as narrative statements, to be presented as items in a sequence leading on to the moment when urban garb and possessions were willingly dispensed with as their families embraced the new life of the interzones. This is the way they have shown them to me, and to their students and younger kin, our attention being drawn to the ways in which people's revolutionary parents displayed the signs and attributes of cosmopolitans whose possessions and savoir-faire connected them with a wider world which both included and transcended that of the coloniser.

For Dr Tran, these markers include his father's smart appearance. He speaks of his father as wearing and having things with the glamour and cosmopolitanism that urban Vietnamese growing up in the 1930s and 40s often associated with the USA. This was not the America of capitalists and Cold Warriors, but one imagined through cinema and dance band music: youthful and dashing, accoutred with the things Tran likes to recall as the hallmarks of his father's style and elegance: 'toujours un blouson Americain', a smart sports jacket, an American pen – 'stylo Shaeffer, Suzanne!'

What my informants also convey is that such things as the foreign-made baby suits were not the same as the corrupting foreign luxuries that good patriots were enjoined to renounce. Indeed these items bought with a parent's love and care were much like the shared-out forms of sustenance with which a devoted elder or senior comrade saw to the nurture of those in their charge. These objects clearly belonged to that other strand

---

[18] Trivedi 2003; see also Sarkar 1973; Bayly 1986; Tarlo 1996: 62–128. For China's 'national products' movement, see Gerth 2003.

of imagining about Vietnam's revolutionary future in the making as conveyed in the poster images that my friends all know and recognise. This is a vision of educated socialist citizens staking their claim to the fruits of the wider world's scientific and cultural attainments. In doing so, they do not turn their backs on the good, wholesome things of their homeland and do not renounce its sites of affective moral life in taking on the dress and habituations of progressive 'socialist moderns'. What they must understand is that it is consistent with both filial and patriotic duty to acquire informed and selective knowledge of the wider world's tangible and intangible goods and products.[19]

A striking evocation of this is provided in a memoir by Professor Dang Anh Dao, a Hanoi scholar who has studied Victor Hugo's writings in colonial Indochina. Her father was a leading Viet Minh intellectual, Professor Dang Thai Mai (1902–84). He too was a francophone scholar who relocated with his wife and children to the 'liberated territories' at the start of the anti-French war. From his base in Interzone IV, he became a leading Viet Minh cultural policy-maker; his wartime writings called on creative intellectuals to dedicate themselves to the revolutionary nation's needs by producing works consistent with the ideals of socialist realism.[20] One passage in Professor Dao's memoir describes an occasion when she, together with her mother and young sisters, were detained at gunpoint at a Viet Minh checkpoint at the time of the 1945 August Revolution. A search of the car hired to take them to Hanoi from her father's ancestral village had revealed apparent evidence of *Viet gian* (traitor) sympathies. The items in question included a pile of her father's French-language books, a box of ammunition they were taking to the son of friends who had just joined the Viet Minh and a picture of a 'bald

[19] For insightful discussion of Vietnamese intellectuals' views on dress as a key element in contested 'civilisational' (*van minh*) discourse, see Goscha 2004: 22–6. In Buchli's account (2000 esp. Ch. 3) of the importance of material culture to Soviet 'social negotiations', dress and home furnishings came to be thought of as signifying either petit bourgeois or socialist values not in and of themselves, but in the context of their use. One recognised the good socialist by his treatment of a clean suit and 'cosy' domestic setting not as goals in their own right, but as the means to an end: this was the achievement of an advanced cultural level for himself and society at large (56–60). My informants have conveyed a similar message, though with an even stronger emphasis on their lack of attachment to domestic comforts and their willing surrender of hearth and possessions in the revolutionary cause.

[20] See Marr 1981: 41, 280, 393–4; Dang Anh Dao 1999. Mentioning his name in Hanoi usually elicits the response: 'Ah – Professor Mai – he was General Giap's father-in-law': his elder daughter married General Vo Nguyen Giap, the DRV's greatest military hero, key architect of the DRV's victory strategies in the anti-French and anti-US wars. See Ninh 2002: 62, 74.

Western foreigner': this was her father's framed photograph of the Nobel laureate André Gide.[21]

The rich 'transculturations' of the revolutionary *tri thuc* world are also apparent in Professor Dao's account of the family's life in Hanoi in the months between the August Revolution and their relocation to the 'liberated territories' in 1946. Having no city residence of their own, the family were assigned a handsome villa with a garden; its French owner had either died or fled Hanoi during the Japanese occupation (Dang Anh Dao 2002: 163–4). Far from deprecating this temporary home as a decadent bourgeois space, Professor Dao celebrates it as a domain of refinement to be legitimately used and valued in the spirit of the nation's new life. She describes its spaces and furnishings in expressive detail, focusing not on its 'female' inner domains, but on the study her father used as his working room, and in which he was visited by Ho Chi Minh. She recalls this room with particular affection, referring to it as a wonderful place, a 'true Western intellectual's room' (*mot can phong cua tri thuc Tay han hoi*) equipped with all the essentials (*bo sau*) of a learned modern life. These she lovingly enumerates, itemising the room's contents with their transliterated French names – bureau (*buy-ro*), divan (*di-vang*), bookshelf (*tu sach*), upholstered reading chairs (*ghe banh*) – paying tribute to the aplomb with which her father and his contemporaries established themselves in these confidently mastered modern settings.

As a schoolchild in that brief period of Hanoi's 1945–6 revolutionary interlude, she too was an active agent in these appropriations of the city's modern spaces. Despite their commitment to the revolution,

---

[21] Dang Anh Dao 1999: 38. See McHale 2004: 134. Professor Mai is one of many *tri thuc* intellectuals of the Viet Minh resistance era who have been the subject of recent memorial essays in the 'Culture' (*Van Hoa*) section of the Party newspaper *Nhan Dan* (The People). The essay on Professor Mai extols him as a patriotic revolutionary and man of learning, citing his students' affectionate memories of him: his warmth of manner, his elegant appearance and stylish dress, his love of good things – wine, cigarettes smoked through a holder. This invites comparison with the twentieth-century Indonesian revolutionaries who wore their fashionable Western-style garments in a 'mode of translation', not imitating the foreigner but engaging in acts of knowing and selective appropriation (Siegel 1997: 9–10. See also Nordholf 1997, especially Mrázek (1997) on the politics of 'dandified' clothes in colonial. Indonesia, and Frederick (1997) on the revolutionary attire of *pemuda* youth organisations). The *Nhan Dan* newspaper article about Professor Mai also makes much of his exemplary family background. Readers are told that his forebears included members of the early twentieth-century generation of scholar-patriots who travelled to Japan, Siam and China seeking new models for Vietnam's revolutionary enlightenment, as well as participants in the nineteenth- and early twentieth-century regional insurgencies which are now conventionally identified as prefigurings of the 1946–54 resistance war.

parents like hers were reluctant to let their daughters venture out alone. The streets were dangerous, she says; women and girls were at risk from the foreign soldiers encamped around the city, especially the unruly nationalist Chinese whose occupation of key northern provinces was an unwelcome feature of the Allied victory over Japan and its Axis partners (Marr 1997; Brocheux 2007: 106–8). But the sisters were proud recruits to the Viet Minh youth movement, the *Thieu Nien Tien Phong* ('Youth Vanguard').[22] Its rallies were staged among the educational pavilions at the Au Tri Vien amusement park which subsequently became the site of the children's Culture Palace, and the girls were sometimes able to attend these meetings with their rituals of flag-raising (*chao co*) and clenched-fist salutes (*gio nam dam len*) (Reid 2002: 149). Slackers were punished with the duck-walk (*di vit*), which my friends say was still carried out in Hanoi secondary schools in the 1990s. This is a mildly painful indignity requiring culprits to atone for misdeeds by being made to parade before their comrades in an ungainly shuffling squat (Dang Anh Dao 2002: 164). While shaming and unpleasant, these quasi-martial disciplines clearly held the excitement of initiation ordeals endured and even gloried in.[23]

As in the contexts explored above, there was no sense of renouncing family ties when children embraced these allegiances to the party state's new socialities. Yet the punitive hand of authority here was that of an adolescent group leader in a party badge and uniform, conveying unmistakably that even if only in brief moments of separation from a nurturing family home, the young revolutionary could take pride in the experience of those bracingly novel attachments and obligations. These related them to their insurgent homeland and to the wider socialist world's regimens of mobilised youth and soldiery. The implied demand of this new life was that the young citizen must be a willing and fearless traveller, someone ready and able to cross the temporal and spatial frontiers dividing the here and now from the attainable socialist future. This was a future being actively constructed through the disciplines they were enacting on this suitably modern site of appropriated colonial

---

[22] This subsequently became the Communist mass organisation known in other socialist countries as the Young Pioneers; it originated as a patriotic youth movement created in the final months of the 1939–45 war when the Japanese replaced their client Vichyite French administration with a nominally independent Vietnamese premiership under the Emperor Bao Dai; its uniformed adherents played an important role in the Viet Minh seizure of power in Hanoi and other urban centres at the time of the 1945 August Revolution. See Nguyen The Anh 2002b: 64–6.

[23] I have been told that this form of schoolroom discipline was widely used in other socialist societies, including the Soviet Union and the Mongolian People's Republic.

space. And it was a future in which the claims of home and kin would have to coexist with the authority of youth-group leaders and other representatives of the new order. Such visions of progressive social life recognised and even exalted the affective bonds of modern filial and conjugal life, but also connected them with the family-like allegiances of the nation and the wider socialist world (compare Reid 2002: 144–9).[24]

My friends are familiar with a wide range of older and more recent propaganda art, and with the artists who produced them. The depiction of Vietnam as having taken its place in those spaces of triumphant modernity has been a feature of this pictorial propaganda both during and since the anti-French war. It is notable that Vietnam has never had a *swadeshi*-style ideal of 'traditional' or peasant dress as the primary garb of nationalist exemplarship. Both insurgent and in triumph, the nation is portrayed as a composite of collectivities whose distinctiveness is rendered in a visual language evoking modern patriotic and socialist ideals, if not always in strict conformity with Marxist-Leninist class and nationality theory.[25] Among the Vietnamese 'moderns' depicted in government posters showing productive citizens cherishing the 'fruits of the revolution' (*thanh qua cach mang*), one often sees a conventional socialist array of uniformed soldiers and workers in factory garb. Such images also commonly feature nurses and teachers – usually female – together with doctors who are almost always male, as are the scientists holding test tubes or microscopes. In addition, such posters frequently show male figures in suits and ties. Such dress is not French or even Western (*Tay*), people say, but the universal garb of modernity as worn within and beyond the socialist world. This is clearly a world of scientific modernity which the Vietnamese citizen can and should aspire to master (see Plate 24).

Even before the August Revolution, the official Viet Minh news-sheet *Viet Nam Doc Lap* (Independent Vietnam, founded in 1941) carried vivid woodcuts representing the new nation as a land of youthful modern citizens. Inspired by the loving warmth and 'ardent spirit' (*tinh than cao*) of their leader Ho Chi Minh, they embrace the skills and accoutrements

---

[24] This is in striking contrast to Yan's (2003) observations of Chinese family life in which the growth of consumerist attitudes is generating a markedly un-'traditional' privileging of conjugality over conventions of filial duty and deference.

[25] See Taylor P. 2001: 11; N.A. Taylor 2004: 59–62. As I noted earlier, significant numbers of Hanoi women have returned to the wearing of the *ao dai*. This includes schoolgirls and also teachers (though for formal school occasions rather than everyday classroom wear), as well as Party members performing official duties, but Western-style 'modern' dress is far more pervasive in Vietnam than in India (see Tarlo 1996; Miller and Banerjee 2004).

of a productive socialist future. One such image in the June 1945 issue which describes the Axis defeat in Europe presents the five *gioi* (groupings or class strata) of the new socialist order as a row of sturdy young men in characteristic occupational garb standing united beneath the national flag. Its caption is '*Nam gioi: si, nong, cong, thuong, binh*' ([These are] the five classes: the learned, the peasants, workers, traders, soldiers) (see Plate 11). A student friend said he was taught this slogan at primary school as a key statement about the solidarity of the nation's people mobilised under revolutionary leadership.[26]

In the drawing that illustrates this evocation of class unity, only the cheerful peasant with his sickle wears 'traditional' rural dress. Standing with him are a uniformed soldier and hammer-wielding proletarian in Russian-style worker's cap and apron. Two other comrades are shown, one a trader/merchant with a traditional market vendor's balance (*can*). The fifth figure is the man of learning. The caption uses the old-fashioned term *si* denoting a Sino-Confucian scholar, but he too is drawn as a recognisable 'modern' with a Western-style shirt, short 'modern' haircut instead of an old-style scholar's head covering and an outsize modern fountain pen rather than a traditional inkbrush.[27]

One of the students with whom I talked about these *Viet Nam Doc Lap* news-sheet images said he was particularly struck by one of the adjoining cartoons, which juxtaposes a personification of revolutionary ardour

---

[26] The Hanoi Revolution Museum uses this issue of *Viet Nam Doc Lap* as part of its display section on the 1946–54 anti-French war, signalling that the people's resistance struggle was an experience of anti-colonial insurgency in which only the 'feudal' landlord is a class enemy of the mobilised revolutionary nation. *Si, nong, cong* and *thuong* are premodern terms for the ordered ranks of traditional society: scholar, peasant, artisan, merchant (Rato 2004: 326).

[27] I return below to the significance of Viet Minh representations of village traders. This set of cartoons also includes an image of President Ho Chi Minh in a traditional scholar's gown (*ao the*) above a poem exalting him as a venerable silver-haired elder inspiring the nation with his ardent spirit. On satirical and propaganda art in the pre-independence war period, see Nguyen Van Ky 1995 and Pham Thu Thuy 2003; see also McHale's (2004: Ch. 4) discussion of the wartime Vichy administration's visual propaganda strategies including commemoration days and touring cinema shows – Hanoi was an especially active site of competing visual cultures (2004: 132–5). McHale also notes (2004: 134) that while print runs were very small, revolutionary communication techniques had significant impact through such means as the use of inclusively intimate language addressing readers as 'friends'. See also Dang Phong 2002: 430. My informants remember the revolutionary songs they sang with greater clarity than newsheets and other printed propaganda material from the wartime period; a few have mentioned touring magic lantern shows and screenings of newsreels produced by DRV battlefield camera teams, the most famous of which included footage of the great Dien Bien Phu victory in 1954 that ended the anti-French war (Pham Ngoc Truong and Trung Son 1987: 8–12).

with a commonly used territorial image, that of the epic landscape in which the great deeds of patriotic insurgency are enacted. This drawing shows a youthful giant emerging sword in hand from a mountain-top; a caricatured set of enemies flee in disarray.[28] My friend recognised all the villains in the picture from his school history classes: the Japanese and nationalist Chinese occupiers, and the Dai Viet 'puppet' (*bu nhin*), a reference to the non-Communist revolutionary nationalist organisation whose members are still reviled as traitors in league with fascist Japan (*phat-xit Nhat Ban*). No Frenchmen appear in these images. What is being represented here is a world in which colonialism is already obsolete; the new world order in which revolutionary Vietnam is seen taking its rightful place is defined around the newly concluded struggle between the great socialist and fascist powers. All this was familiar to my student friend; the only detail he found surprising was that the artist had drawn the muscular young hero with a shirtless torso. Bared flesh still signals primitive 'otherness' in Vietnam, but this was the period when Vietnam's revolutionary nationalists were becoming increasingly enthusiastic about the novel practices of outdoor sport, the cultivation of a fit physique and the wearing of abbreviated athletic costume by young patriots – both male and female.[29]

Such representations of idealised moderns are also a feature of more recent posters commemorating the 1945 August Revolution as the moment when Vietnam made its formal entry into that world of universal modernity. This is often signalled through portrayals of the nation's citizenry in what even my very young informants recognise as the attire of the nation's constituent collectivities. An August Revolution anniversary poster issued in 1974 carries the caption 'Hold tightly to your gun to protect the fruits of the revolution' (*Nam chac tay sung bao ve thanh qua cach mang*). Among the citizens shown happy and flourishing beneath the protection of a female fighter bearing a rifle is a man in a suit and tie. When I discussed this poster with student friends, one said of the male figure, 'He is one of us – the *Kinh*' (i.e. the Viet or 'national majority'). I asked what viewers would expect his occupation to be, and my friend said, 'a teacher or government official'. In my experience, few if any people would react differently: one sees a man in a suit and tie, and one

---

[28] Viet Minh periodicals were identified as emanating from the new named subdivisions of the socialist proto-state. This issue was captioned 'Voice of the Viet Minh in the 3 mountain areas': this was the northern zone adjoining the Chinese border designated by a composite rendering of the area's three existing provinces: Cao-Bac-Lang.

[29] On socialist 'body culture', see Brownell 1995; and for Vietnam Raffin 2005.

automatically takes these as the markers of an educated modern, implying to most a Viet (*Kinh*).[30]

Among the remaining figures in this August Revolution image, the other key moderns are a boy and girl in student uniform with the Soviet-style red scarves (*khan do*) that are still worn in Hanoi primary schools. There is also a woman in 'ethnic minority' dress, together with a worker, a peasant and a soldier, all equally recognisable in their characteristic garb.[31] Together they embody the nation in its divergent but harmoniously interacting guises and identities. The 'modern' in his sober suit serves the nation and the revolution, as do all the others including the uniformed soldiers. All are garbed for purposeful service: even those attired for the relatively comfortable life of desk, lab or lectern are to be thought of as available at a moment's notice to leave home and do their duty for the nation, either under arms or as 'experts' providing service in the wider socialist world.

Gaze, sight and action in revolutionary spaces

The experience of relinquishing their comfortable urban homes, selling off their furniture, giving away or burning other superfluous possessions, packing bare essentials into baskets and panniers and setting off on cross-country treks to the interzones are all acts which feature in my friends' accounts of their interzone childhoods. Such scenes have been written about by historians, and they feature in many of the narratives my friends have shared with me, including Dr Tran's. He is also one of the people I know for whom shared recollections of the interzones have played an important role in maintaining key relationships during their adult lives. For academics, this includes bonds with students, often the sons and daughters of former classmates and wartime comrades with whom many have cross-cutting ties of marriage and kinship.

---

[30] On Vietnam's official policy towards the 'ethnic minority' peoples (*dan toc*: ethnie or race) who are still widely represented as junior siblings within the national family, thus in need of tutelage from the majority Viet (*Kinh*) citizenry, see Pelley 1998; Proschan 2001; Salemink 2003. As Taylor (1998: 955) explains, the use of *Kinh* (lowlander) distinguishes plains-dwelling Vietnamese-speakers from other regional peoples.

[31] Guarding them all is a female fighter equipped with rifle and bandolier. On the garb of the well-dressed workers and other emblematic figures depicted in Soviet propaganda posters, see Bonnell 1997. For a comparable image of the nation's classes and ethnic populations united in the anti-French cause, see Plate 5. The central figures are a female peasant and male worker; the man on the far left is recognisably of 'ethnic minority' origin, and the figure on the far right equally recognisable by her dress and martial arts staff as a Viet (*Kinh*) woman from the rural south.

In the families I know, Axis Japan is spoken of in ways that both parallel and contrast with what is said about the distinction to be drawn between French civilisation and French colonisers. While older people emphasise the brutalities of the Japanese occupation years, this does not entail a simple oppositional pairing between 'good' French and 'bad' Japanese, as in the discursive pairings of the Dutch and Japanese found by Stoler and Strassler in Indonesians' accounts of the war years (2000: 11–12).[32] Unlike France, wartime Japan is widely thought of as a site of potently militarised modernity, yet it too is recalled as a source of porous and uneven ruling power.

Dr Tran was a schoolboy during the Japanese occupation, a time of which he has horrible memories. He believes that he saw dead or dying victims of the 1944–5 Tonkin famine which Vietnamese of his generation regard as a product of calculated brutality on the part of the Japanese (Bose 1990; Bui Minh Dung 1995). Another painful memory is of the day he saw his father weep, his father who was always a man of impeccable dignity and decorum, showing but only rarely articulating his deep, loving pride in his children.[33] The cause, Dr Tran said, was the indignity of being slapped by a Japanese soldier when their bicycles collided in a Hanoi street. The vileness of face-slapping is a highly charged memory in the lands of what the Japanese called the Asian Co-Prosperity Sphere (*khu thinh vuong chung*), a geographical entity which Viet Minh propagandists portrayed as an arena of oppression and brutality.[34] What is notable here are the multiple layerings and time frames of colonial experience. In the war years, the Japanese were both imperialist enemy and a source of gratifying reversal in the power relations of colonialism, their behaviour recalled as inhuman in its

---

[32] Stoler and Strassler (2000) attribute this to the downplaying of heroic anti-imperialism in present-day official renderings of the Indonesian national narrative. I too am concerned with the significance of silences and evasions, and the points at which people cease to personalise their accounts of such experiences. Especially important for my fieldwork with intellectual families is the fact that 'sanctioned' versions of the national narrative are now rapidly changing, as are the often ambiguous official renderings of their own place as intellectuals in this story.

[33] Dr Tran never speaks of his father as distant or cold, though stern, commanding fathers do figure in other Hanoi people's recollections. I have been told of a man who publicly flogged his adult son, a high achiever with a prestigious public service post, for creating disharmony in the family, and of another who evinces no pleasure in his son's achievements, though they too involve exceptional distinction: this son is often berated for failing in his filial duty, pleading the demands of his high-powered academic career when he absents himself from family rites and festivals.

[34] One of the Viet Minh's 1945 news-sheet cartoons represents the power relations of the Co-Prosperity Sphere with the image of a brutish Japanese soldier impaling Asian victims on a samurai sword.

degrading treatment of Vietnamese, yet welcome in its effects when it was the French whom they saw being abused in their turn.

Dr Tran shed tears when recounting this incident, the affront to his father still shocking to recall.[35] It was terrible, he says, that the soldier paid no heed to his father's sincere but unobsequious apology. They might have exchanged civilities, shaken hands and shared a cigarette, he said: what the soldier did was a denial of humanity, the act of a brute. At this time, he reminded me, his father was already a covert Viet Minh operative, a francophone intellectual engaged in underground activities like the narrator of *Au Coeur de la Ville Captive*. 'My father was a *man*,' Dr Tran says, with emphasis, 'un vrai homme'. 'You understand, Suzanne, that he was armed that day, as always.' Beneath his coat he had his pistol, Party issue. 'But he thought of his duty, and of us, the family, what would become of us if he acted': he meant by shooting the soldier. 'So he held back'; he chose not to act, though he could have done so.

His point was clear. This was the purposive choice of a man under discipline, yet with the strength and self-command to make decisive moves and choices in the light of strong convictions. He was neither an unthinking slave of the Party, nor a brutalised subject of the multiple, leaky colonialisms afflicting his homeland. His tears, shed at home among his kin and not in public, were marks of sensibility and moral feeling (*chan tinh*), neither shameful nor unmanly. Indeed as I show below, the patriot who sheds tears of sensibility is a role model (*neu guong*: mirror or exemplar) for the nation. All schoolchildren learn of the occasions on which President Ho Chi Minh wept before his comrades as a man of both action and 'spirit' (*tinh than*) who shares feelingly in the sorrows of the world. In Dr Tran's account, while under the gaze of power his father controlled what the enemy occupier saw, maintaining his disguise as an innocuous passerby, thereby retaining the initiative as he misdirected the coloniser's gaze, choosing his moment to reveal or not reveal his true identity.

---

[35] He also told me about the satisfaction experienced by Vietnamese who saw Frenchmen being subjected to the same humiliation by the Japanese occupiers in wartime Hanoi. See Hy Van Luong 1992: 81. For Vietnamese of his generation, Hanoi life involved the handling of multiple and intersecting forms of colonialism, the relations between Japanese, Vichy and Free French, Chinese and Vietnamese (including both Viet (*Kinh*) and 'minority' peoples) reflecting a host of different and overlapping entanglements and power relations. The Japanese were both 'imperialist' enemy and a source of satisfying reversal in existing hierarchies at the point when they reduced the French to the state of despised colonial subjects, and were then in turn disarmed and subsequently rearmed by the incoming Allied forces in 1945. See Harper and Bayly 2007: 141–5.

The epic of urban revolution

With the Japanese surrender in 1945 came the entry of both French and nationalist Chinese troops into the northern regions of Indochina, and in 1946 the onset of armed confrontation between the French and the Viet Minh. Early in 1947, like the many other Hanoi people who were joining the flow of Viet Minh adherents into the interzones, Dr Tran's parents were instructed to relocate to Thanh Hoa. But before they left Hanoi, he said, they experienced the epic events of the 1945 August Revolution which Vietnamese schoolchildren are taught to regard as the series of highly disciplined insurrectionary acts by which the Party and people joined forces to take power in their liberated homeland (Marr 1995a).

All the young people I know can provide detailed accounts of that sequence of epic events, especially the proclamation of the new nation's birth on 2 September 1945, now celebrated as Vietnamese Independence Day. Dr Tran said that as a nine-year-old schoolboy, he was present at this climactic moment of the August Revolution, standing among his classmates in what is now known as Ba Dinh Square when the great crowd of half a million Hanoians and incomers from the countryside heard President Ho Chi Minh utter the famous words of his Declaration of Independence address (*Tuyen Ngon Doc Lap*).[36]

Today Ba Dinh Square is a high-security zone used for solemn state occasions, its vast open vistas overshadowed by the massive Soviet-style mausoleum containing Ho Chi Minh's embalmed remains. Like Moscow's Red Square, the area is rigorously policed; it has been widely described as a dead space drained of vitality by these regimens of 'imposed everyday vacancy' (Thomas 2003: 182). It is true that strict decorum is imposed on visitors to the mausoleum and neighbouring monuments, including the remarkable Ho Chi Minh museum which I discuss in Chapter 8. Yet my friends do not speak of the square as a lifeless zone where officialdom commands and scrutinises a regimented citizenry. It is instead a place to which they refer in terms of vivid visual

---

[36] Compare Marr 1995b; Duong Thi Thoa and Sidel 1998; Logan 2000: 133–4; Nguyen The Anh 2002b: 70–2. This urban space adjoining the Governor-General's palace and the former west gate of the ancient Hanoi citadel was known as Place Puginier in honour of a nineteenth-century missionary who founded Indochina's first French-language schools. It is now the heart of the great memorial complex containing the mausoleum of President Ho Chi Minh and was given the name Ba Dinh Square by the DRV provisional government to commemorate a key site of the 1886–7 *Can Vuong* ('Loyalty to the King') movement. This insurgency took place in the region around Thanh Hoa which is now regarded as the formative heartland of Vietnamese patriotic consciousness (Marr 1971:15; Lieberman 1997: 477; Papin 2001: 213n).

memories making the square a composite of living images both personal and patriotic, thus a place peopled, alive and active in ways that both connect with and transcend its official representations and depictions.

Predictably enough, my friends connect their personal images of the square and its history with the powerful pictorial representations with which they have all grown up, especially the celebrated images of the great Independence Day crowd scene in 1945. These images are instantly recognisable to everyone I know. Like the 1976 reunification images described above, the events of Independence Day have been officially portrayed in much-reproduced photographs and artist's renditions. Among them is a massive painting on display in Hanoi's National Museum of Vietnamese History (the Bao Tang Lich Su), housed since 1958 in the palatial premises of one of the great centres of colonial Orientalist scholarship, the former Ecole Française (EFEO) ethnology museum (Sutherland 2005) (see Plates 26 and 27).

School parties view this vast, crowded canvas by the Hanoi artist Van Tho as the final stage in an itinerary which starts with the ground floor displays of prehistoric artefacts, including a hominid to *homo sapiens* 'ascent of man' tableau. Visitors then move on through an evolutionary unfolding of the nation's story much like that described in Donham's account of the museum display created by Ethiopia's former Marxist government to commemorate its seizure of power in 1974. This too was a revolution represented as a story beginning with the prehistoric, in this case the relics of the earliest protohumans found on Ethiopian soil, then progressing from stage to stage in the nation's life as it moved purposefully towards the moment of glorious fulfilment under Communist rule (1999: 14–15).

In the Hanoi museum, the unfolding of the nation's epic life is also shown as embracing the prehistoric, in this case archaeological treasures from the former EFEO museum.The most precious of these are specimens of Indochina's famous Bronze Age Dong Son drums, now officially defined as the earliest archaeological relics of Vietnamese culture.[37] The upstairs displays illustrate proto-revolutionary actions taking place at critical moments and in key locations of the nation's dynastic and colonial past. The culmination of this story is the great moment of liberation in 1945 as depicted in the giant 'Declaration of Independence' (*Tuyen Ngon Doc Lap*) painting. This shows the Ba Dinh Square site as a metropolitan space transformed by the will of the people into a zone of triumphant

---

[37] On the Dong Son drums see Taylor 1991: 9–57; Han 2004. Compare Lu 2005.

revolutionary nationhood. Those who have concealed their true selves as fighters and patriots are to be seen taking command of the city's colonised spaces, stepping forward in their tens of thousands into a brilliantly lit scene of triumph and revolutionary order.

The painting presents a strikingly decorous and disciplined image of the revolution's 'exemplary theatrics'. This is Martha Kaplan's term for colonial India's 1930 Salt March and the other great spectacles of nationalist self-assertion devised by Gandhi as key acts of the Indian freedom struggle, though Kaplan's concern is not with the perceptions or memories of the multitudes whose participation was essential to the efficacy or 'truth force' (*satyagraha*) of these exemplary actions (1995: 94). In the Hanoi museum's Independence Day painting, the massed throng is not shown annihilating the villainies of colonialism and feudal oppression, or performing acts of vengeance against national or class enemies.There are militiamen on the alert with drawn guns guarding the new provisional government, but no shots are fired, no blood is shed and no gestures of strong emotion are shown. The banners held aloft by members of the crowd all bear the slogan *Doc Lap* (Independence), thus conveying a message of triumph and unity rather than aggression or class war.

With their air of sobriety and intelligent awareness as they direct their gaze to the speaker's platform, the symmetrically arrayed multitudes embody the purposiveness of the *foule révolutionnaire* (revolutionary crowd) in a mode of exemplary propriety rather than catharsis or upheaval. It is clearly expected that observers will see this scene as one of many future-making episodes in the unfolding story of the revolution. What the schoolbooks say is that the nation's triumph on 2 September was soon challenged by the returning French forces. Ho Chi Minh and his followers launched an armed insurrection, and after a period of resistance from their redoubt inside Hanoi's Old Quarter, their break-out and retreat to the Viet Bac in December 1946 marked the beginning of the nine-year liberation war. Like my friends' family photos, the painting is thus an episode in an action sequence plotted out in tangibly experienced, determinate clock time, not a representation of an unanchored millennial moment of idealised revolutionary 'theatrics'.

When Dr Tran has told me about his Independence Day memories he speaks with pride, though with the touch of mild self-mockery with which many of my informants savour the lighter details of such experiences. It is not so much that they wish to distance themselves from the official narratives of these events. But they do like to personalise their accounts of living through epic times, and as having done so as thinking actors able to muse reflectively both then and now about their experiences. Their accounts of these events certainly do not suggest that they should be thought of as mere lay figures or exhibited subjects plotted out in their serried ranks to bear mute witness to the power of those directing or orchestrating such spectacles.

During as well as after the August Revolution, the great open-air spaces of the new state's public life were deemed to be places in which children should be both visible and actively engaged in the making of the revolutionary nation. Dr Tran says he was aware that some of the groups arrayed around the square were units and delegations from distant provinces. And he remembers crossing the city in procession with his classmates, then being led in his school uniform to the spot where he and the other children stood waving their little flags in a prominent position near the bunting-draped speaker's platform.[38] Like other Hanoi people I know, as a student he learned by heart much of the speech he said he heard being made that day. Thus, like Mr Raman's daughter in the south Indian district I visited thirty years later, he too was encouraged to connect with that epiphanic moment of the nation's birth by mastering one of its foundational texts. And like Nehru's Freedom at Midnight speech, Ho's address is widely recalled as an act of oratory which citizens should see as having been manifested in the form of a public dialogue between the crowd and the leader who addressed them, a point to which I return below.

As I have noted, museums are spaces with which my intelligentsia informants are very familiar. Many recall childhood museum visits and can speak in detail about the History Museum's Independence Day picture, and also about the famous Vietnamese artists and artworks they learned about at school. Several have relations who are or were professional artists or proficient amateurs, and most made a point of displaying that informed appreciation of the fine arts which is an enduring feature of the *tri thuc* (modern intellectual) ideal of cultivation and civility (see N.A. Taylor 2004). Even quite young people I know are aware that the DRV authorities gave the name Ba Dinh Square to the hallowed site of the declaration speech at the time of the August Revolution, being taught at school that this was to connect the square's importance as a scene of revolutionary action with a more extensive map of Vietnam as an arena of patriotic actions dating back to ancient times. The 1886 uprising to which the name refers is now celebrated as a key early act of

---

[38] The scene has been widely described in personal memoirs and official histories and portrayed in many paintings and published photographs.

resistance to the French conquest of Indochina. The schoolbooks note that this took place in the Thanh Hoa region, the area in which most of my informants spent their interzone childhoods. They note too that this heartland of the revolution is the cradle of their national identity, being the site where archaeologists first found those precious historic relics, the Dong Son drums.[39]

My student informants can also identify the key groups represented in the Independence Day painting, each a representative unit of the new nation, just as in the 'Fruits of the Revolution' poster described above: the ranked files of uniformed schoolboys and khaki-clad Viet Minh fighters; the robed Buddhist monks and 'ethnic minority' people in their distinctive hill garb; the peasants in conical hats; the girl students dressed in white *ao dais* whom I mentioned in Chapter 4.[40] One of my student friends pointed out a cluster of what he called 'feudal' teachers in their distinctive turbans and gowns (*ao the*); these are *thay do*, scholars trained to teach the old-style Sino-Vietnamese curriculum. The implication is that even those of 'traditional' background were knowingly stepping forward into the new world of socialist modernity being brought into being by the DRV authorities under the inspirational leadership of Ho Chi Minh and the Viet Minh high command.

This student also pointed out to me that posters with texts commemorating the August Revolution and showing Ho Chi Minh with a microphone (*mic-ca-ro*) are referring symbolically to the moments in the 2 September speech when the President exchanged utterances with the crowd (see Plate 28). The young are still taught at school that Ho Chi Minh was a thoughtful man, a poet and scholar with a quiet voice, and that far from projecting it as a daunting roar of power from a booming electrified sound system, his first words to the crowd were, 'Compatriots, can you hear me?' (*Toi noi dong bao nghe ro khong?*: lit. 'Am I speaking clearly?'). The phrase is familiar to all, especially the use of *dong bao*, compatriot, which is recalled today as a signal of shared citizenship, very unlike those denoting a ruler's power to command (McHale 2004: 133). The crowd's answering shout of 'Yes!' – '*Vang!*' – was a tribute to the President's unassuming tone and attitude, the

---

[39] Thanh Hoa was also the heartland of an event now commemorated as yet another key moment of Vietnamese patriotic consciousness, the fifteenth-century insurrection against Ming Chinese occupation led by the 'pacification ruler' Le Loi, who proclaimed his sovereignty in a mode suffused with Chinese imperial symbols (Marr 1971:15; Lieberman 1997: 477; Papin 2001:213n.).

[40] White shirts and blue trousers have replaced the *ao dai* as girls' everyday uniforms in Hanoi secondary schools, though they are still worn on formal occasions such as weekly flag-raising days and Teachers' Day on 20 November.

intimacies that united them all as loving sharers in the familial warmth he transmitted as nurturing elder kinsman of all the nation, that is as *Bac* ('Uncle') *Ho*, a key reference point in the familiar narratives of Vietnamese nationhood. My friends have also been taught that the President later elicited a second cry of acclaim from the massed multitudes, and that this constituted a declaration of allegiance by which the new DRV government was granted its legitimacy by the will of the people.

The President's August Revolution speech famously quoted from the American Declaration of Independence and the critical text of France's revolution of 1789, the Declaration of the Rights of Man and the Citizen. With amusement, Dr Tran recalls that he was actually clutching two objects on the great day: not the new DRV national flag with its gold star on a red ground, but the American Stars and Stripes and a photograph of the US President Harry Truman. With hindsight Dr Tran sees himself as having been a real if unintending contributor to this early point in the DRV's life of outward projection into the wider global ecumene. As in other postcolonies, achieving international recognition for the embryonic republic was an important step in the making of a new polity with the capacity to deploy credible 'state effects' both at home and further afield.[41] As conceptualised by the DRV's propagandists, the new Vietnam was in a position to expunge colonial power through armed insurgency and the embrace of new global allegiances. These included new ties to the socialist world. My informants remember the ways in which the interzones' new revolutionary calendar with its novel commemoration festivals drew attention to these wider links and contacts. Even if the young did not altogether grasp who they were singing about on Rosa Luxemburg Day, they knew she was someone from one of the faraway socialist lands where they were told that children like them were learning to applaud their liberation struggle.[42]

Yet through the command of French of its educated 'moderns' and their knowledge of a world far wider than that of many other

---

[41] Scott 1998; Trouillot 2001. At the time, the new regime was still representing the USA as a fraternal power with whom they had stood against fascism and, like the Free French, as sharers in the revolutionary tradition of 1789 that they and other socialist 'friends' were bringing to fruition on the world stage. (See Nguyen The Anh 2002b: 72, and compare Cooper 2005.) Well-known photos of the Independence Day ceremonies show American officers on the speaker's platform with Ho Chi Minh. This moment of self-assertion was timed to coincide with the worldwide diplomatic manoeuvrings which had been set in train by the founding of the United Nations Organisation in San Francisco in June 1945.

[42] Compare McHale 2004: 127.

revolutionaries, notably those inhabiting the much more insular world of Mao's Chinese Communist followers, the DRV was claiming a bigger and more plural worldwide terrain as its natural habitat of modernity and resistance. In this respect, revolutionary Vietnam may have had more in common with Europe's 'fringe' or so-called satellite revolutionary societies like post-1945 East Germany and the Baltic states than with its neighbour and ally the PRC (revolutionary China). Like India, these European socialist 'satellites' were also places where 'socialist moderns' were represented and in some cases represented themselves as living in terrain that they experienced as both tangible in its time sense, and cosmopolitan in its educated people's sense of engagement with wider revolutionary modernities.

So what my friends' narratives also suggest is that even for the children taking part in the events of 2 September, Ba Dinh Square was a site of movement and initiative rather than a static 'exhibitionary space' in which those present were mere objects on display, deprived of voice and agency beneath a panoptic gaze of power (Mitchell 1988). What Dr Tran recalls about the flag and picture is that his teacher had offered all his class a choice of emblems of what the DRV provisional government were still representing as 'friendly' allies with a shared legacy of anti-Axis resistance. Securing their support would be of key importance in the attempt to deny the legitimacy of the French campaign to reclaim Indochina. Dr Tran said he had not liked the face of the Chinese nationalist leader Chiang Kai-shek, whose picture he had initially been offered. Chiang was bald – 'like a monk', he said – and he found this disquieting. So more by default than choice, he had ended up with Truman and the Stars and Stripes.

Clearly a child will not necessarily understand the significance of a great national event as either officialdom or adult kin and other elders might intend. And of course the whole event had been elaborately orchestrated. As in other countries' propaganda representations, the museum picture makes much of the presence of schoolchildren, thereby making didactic points about the birth of the new nation as a youthful and vigorous power with a commitment to educate and uplift its hitherto benighted populace (Bonnell 1997). The schoolboys in their youth movement caps were precisely such a presence in the Ba Dinh picture. In this depiction, as in my friends' accounts, theirs was a form of 'spatial practice' particularly indicative of purpose and awareness rather than regimented disciplinarity.

As I have already noted, my informants have extensive experience of classroom life and the many other ordering disciplines through which young Vietnamese are still imbued with the knowledge and habituations of a modern citizenry. Dr Tran has told me about many unpleasant experiences in his childhood, but his accounts of such things as pupil roll-calls and the collectivising regimens of the new socialist order's youth movements do not represent these as uncongenial or coercive aspects of a life led as the object of coldly 'specularized' and 'spectacularized' forms of modern power (Weiner 1997: 199).

As when friends have taken me through their personal photographs, Dr Tran refers to the Ba Dinh Square spectacle in dynamic terms, referring to his own experiences of the day and using active verbs for things done and seen – marching, waving, choosing, listening. In these accounts, the event is an unfolding of actions both immediate and continuing far into the future, and definitely not as an experience of being 'enframed' in the grand design of officialdom's 'exemplary projects'. Even within the massed crowd there was action and movement, and in his own accounts the day was much more than that single formal event taking place within the confines of Ba Dinh square. He tells the story as a series of moves made and spaces crossed as he travelled with friends and kin from home to school and on to the square, then dispersing to return home again to experience further moments of dramatic change in the life of the nation and, crucially, that of his family.

The scene on 2 September thus registers as part of a longer process of purposeful activity in which the personal and the national connect in arenas of extensive space both traversed and mastered. And while these connections can be inharmonious or even dissonant, my friends do like to relate their own experiences to the big public representations of these events. On the personal side, the Ba Dinh Square ceremony tends to feature above all as a prelude to the time of their removal to the interzones. As I noted above, the people I know speak of their families as having ungrudgingly relinquished almost everything that defined Hanoi life for them: their homes and schools, and the allure and brightness of public spaces, including the cinemas and other sites where city-dwellers experienced modernity in the form of image and spectacle.

As informants often said, there were no electric lights or shop windows in the interzones, no visits to theatres or the cinema until the great day after liberation in 1954 when they returned to Hanoi from the interzones. They knew that they were not to see their lives in these rural relocation sites as benighted or primitive, even though the phrase often used for relocation, *vao rung*, 'going to the forest', implies not just going somewhere (*di*) but entering a different realm or space (*vao*). Yet as educated 'moderns' in the interzones, they were regularly presented with images which encouraged them to project forward as well as outward to a future defined as an array of brightly lit modern vistas, taking note of the representations of socialist modernity which their teachers showed them, drawing pictures at school of the liberated capital city to which they would one day return, and attending photographic and poster exhibitions portraying the nation's fighters, leaders and enlightened populace pointing forward to a happy, modern future.

In many cases the youthful faces they saw in these representations were their own, or those of young people much like them performing in their youth movement chorale troupes or gymnastics units. These sites and experiences are recalled in strongly affective terms, often with an emphasis on the active role of children in both registering and communicating important claims about feeling, nurture and energetic sociality as activating virtues of interzone life. Yet as I show in Chapter 7, there was scope for great tension in these processes. This was especially so when the habitation of personal and national space took divergent forms for parents and their children, raising difficult questions about the defining of intelligentsia families as distinctive moral units within the newly emerging national landscape.

Mapping one's own land

Early in 1947 Dr Tran and his elder brother were smuggled out of Hanoi
by their parents, in response to the Viet Minh high command's call for
Party cadres to relocate and pursue the independence struggle from the
interzones. He has shown me the difficult route they took to Thanh Hoa,
trudging for a week with their possessions in baskets on shoulder poles.
He can still identify the boundaries and crossing points between the
French-controlled zones and the 'liberated territories'. When we have
travelled together, he has taken pains with our bearings and map coor-
dinates. 'Of course we did not have road maps then', he said. Families in
transit made their way from place to place, deciding as best they could
which locals and wayfarers they could safely ask for guidance. In effect
what he was describing was a discovery of homeland, and as in the
writings of Indian nationalists, it was an experience of discovery involving
key moments of contact within these rural spaces. Nowadays the willingness of strangers to assist families like theirs is spoken of as evidence of
the trusting spirit of those patriotic times. As in the case of the story about
the falling out of the old comrades living in adjoining houses, for some
this is clearly a lament about the declining morals of the present day,
though certainly not a claim that it has been maps or 'science' which have
expunged the caring virtues of that wartime world.

  Dr Tran's delineation of that complex war geography with its shifting,
permeable boundary zones – he refers to the interzone borders as '*souples*'
(pliant, flexible) – is a means of demonstrating that these were movements
in mapped space, always purposeful, never random or directionless.[1]

---

[1] The idea of borders and markets as ordered spaces traversed and frequented by patriotic
citizens serving the nation's needs is very much in contrast to the demonising attitudes
documented by ethnographers of Soviet and post-Soviet contexts. (See especially
Humphrey 2002: Ch. 4 esp. 72–3.) As I explain below, the difference in Vietnam was the
colonial context in which the small trader could be readily identified as a patriotic
contributor to the nation's needs whose movements through space were definable as

What mattered was both the intimate scale of local geographies as known by the villagers who helped them, and also the larger scale cartographic knowledge that the educated incomers were bringing with them to the interzones. In his accounts, there is nothing dehumanising or colonial about this sense of being active in the traversing of formally demarcated space. The process I am calling auto-cartography involves precisely the sense conveyed by Dr Tran that the achievement of crossing from the 'occupied' French zones into Viet Minh territory and then returning from the interzones when the war was won were acts of deeply felt significance, their meaning enhanced rather than diminished by the fact that they can chart their movements on a modern map.

It clearly mattered very little that at the time such maps as they encountered in their classrooms or through wartime service came initially from the colonial *service cartographique*. Many people of their education and background saw service in the technical directorates of the new revolutionary proto-state (the Democratic Republic of Vietnam or DRV), and are now hailed for their contributions to the liberation process in fields such as military map-making. Even participation in colonial mapping and techno-economic survey initiatives could be readily conceptualised as acts of service to the nation. The notion of human science as an ideology of colonial dominance is one that my Hanoi friends find uncongenial – 'C'est tout science!' I was told ('It is all science', the Vietnamese term for which – *khoa hoc* – is much used by my informants). The involvement of their parents and other elders in such initiatives is a matter of pride, its effects seen both as a fostering of national consciousness and as a means of exposing and attacking the deprivations engendered by colonial rule. Several of my informants mentioned that as a radical young *lycée* teacher, the DRV's great military strategist Vo Nguyen Giap was assistant to the colonial geographer Pierre Gourou in the village survey work used for Gourou's much-cited 1936 study of the Red River delta economy. The Viet Minh *tri thuc* (modern intellectual) luminary Nguyen Van Huyen is also known to have undertaken studies of Viet (*Kinh*) peasants' subsistence conditions in the pre-independence period, complementing his work on ethnological and cultural topics with investigations of household consumption patterns and other indices of rural living standards. Such work is seen as a productive deployment of

breachings of boundaries that were illegitimate and parochialising rather than protective of endangered localisms (Humphrey 2002: 72). These attitudes changed significantly after the anti-French war, though as has been noted in a number of key studies (e.g. Fforde 1989 and Kerkvliet and Selden 1998), both collectivisation and anti-market initiatives were significantly less far-reaching in socialist Vietnam than in China.

learned skill, not collaboration in the work of a data-hungry colonial state. Indeed the French were not modern and scientific enough, my friends say, leaving it to their Vietnamese subjects to use cartography and the other human sciences to integrate and advance the nation.[2]

Thus the mapping and knowing of homeland space is suffused with affective meanings associated with powerful memories of personal and family life, including the moment of reaching and negotiating one of the all-important crossing points into the interzones. Many such places are still clearly visible as frontier sites. Some are marked by battle-site memorials. Elsewhere, the old frontiers can be traced from the surviving French blockhouses which once comprised the fortified chain of Red River delta defence points known as the de Lattre line.[3]

On the journey from Hanoi to their first interzone village, Dr Tran travelled with his mother. The Viet Minh authorities encouraged villagers to shelter incomers, but much was left up to individuals and their families. One scientist, Professor Duc, said his father found the household with whom they initially lodged through a Hanoi friend, a man from a modestly prosperous land-owning family whose ancestral village was close to his parents' interzone work sites. This friend was a retired *fonctionnaire*, i.e. a former petty official in the colonial administration. He spoke good French, and Professor Duc's father arranged for him to provide language tutoring to the family's school-age children. This coaching was desirable, Professor Duc said, because one could know French for access to the things a modern child should learn to recognise and value, though always selectively: 'pour la science, beaucoup des choses modernes – pas pour aimer les français' (for science, for many modern things, not out of love for the French).

The lessons were said to have been given out of friendship, though there were hints that it might also have been done for the sake of favourable relations with Party people. It was certainly an arrangement which few village families could have made for their children. This was a sign of the very real distinctions between local people's lives and those led by educated Hanoi incomers, even those like Professor Duc and his family whose younger members went to school with village children, and

---

[2] On Gourou, see Bowd and Clayton 2005 and Kleinen 2005; on other scientific initiatives in this period, see Goscha 2003.

[3] This was the brainchild of France's military commander in Indochina from 1950 to 1952, Jean de Lattre de Tassigny. It was actually the first of France's two replications in Vietnam of the disastrous Second World War strategy of the Maginot Line. The second, known as the Navarre line, was conceived by France's commander-in-chief at the time of the defeat at Dien Bien Phu which effectively destroyed French rule in Indochina (Ruscio 1986).

who lodged in peasant houses, dressed and ate as they did, and experienced the same dangers and difficulties, including bombing raids, ill health and food shortages.

As I have mentioned, the typical pattern for relocation was the unaccustomed one of a nuclear family unit residing in an allocated house or in housing shared with strangers, often moving from locality to locality at unpredictable intervals and with long separations from close kin. As my informants also made clear, the decision to relocate gave rise to ramifying networks of fellow interzone migrants who might include adult siblings of both husband and wife, together with their spouses and children, and in many cases close friends from the incomers' *lycée* or university days. There were often marital links between such people, as in the case of the *lycée* teacher and his wife whose decision to leave Hanoi led to a similar move on the part of his wife's two siblings; each was married to one of his former *lycée* classmates. Among those who took me through such family histories was Professor Bui, the former 'expert' mentioned in Chapter 2 who had taught at a Madagascar pedagogical college. He was the son of a Hanoi literary scholar; four of the family's five brothers became senior academics after independence. Their father was a wartime recruit to the Viet Minh, and the household and several other family members 'went to the forest' in the early months of the war. One brother fought under Marshal Giap at Dien Bien Phu, the climactic battle which achieved final victory for the Viet Minh in 1954. Another attended one of the schools for cadres' children in China; like Dr Tran, the rest of the family spent the war years near Thanh Hoa in Interzone IV.

In all cases relocation entailed a sense of life-changing rupture. Of course all Hanoi people had rural roots, a *que* or ancestral village containing agnatic grave sites.[4] Many were from families of relatively recent city incomers. Furthermore, the DRV's official narratives represented the countryside as a revolutionary domain combining the two key virtues of the patriotic Vietnamese: martial zeal and reverence for cultivated learning. I mentioned earlier Ho Chi Minh's wartime aphorism paying tribute to the rural tradition of honouring 'persons of talent', using for this the Confucian term *nhan tai* meaning those who place their erudition at the service of state and people. The message here was that both the modern intellectual and the disciplined child striving to learn and

---

[4] See above, Chapter 2. One's *que* (sometimes translated 'homeland') is widely thought of as a place endowed with potent meaning for city-dwellers through the presence of ancestral graves and memorial tablets, as well as living kinfolk whose household altars may also commemorate one's near or distant kin (Schlecker 2005).

achieve for the good of all were heirs to the scholar-patriots who in past centuries had exemplified patriotic virtue by spurning high office and retreating to the countryside to live righteously as teachers and critical moralists.[5]

This is why I feel it is right to see the Indian rural districts where people like Mr Raman were posted in the 1960s and 70s as closely comparable to the DRV's interzones. They too were vested with much importance in national and subnational narrative of progressive achievement, they too were places of discovery entailing encounters which were widely represented as deepening and energising the patriotic modernisers' sense of service to the nation. This was certainly in keeping with the Viet Minh propaganda messages which treated rural people (*dan que*: villagers or country folk, as opposed to city people: *nguoi thanh pho*) as key participants in the resistance struggle. Yet it was made clear that the countryside and its people had to be subjected to the gaze of sympathetic though critical modernisers. In this there was no room for a sentimentalist's complacency; the rustic way of life was neither incompatible with nor superior to the path of science and enlightenment. Thus while there were things to value and learn from within the peasant world, the village was a place to be transformed by the dutiful service of those who embodied the ways and knowledge of the new socialist order.[6]

Moral trading and revolutionary movement

The sense of being pioneers in a perilous environment came across at many points in people's narratives. 'There were tigers', said one man, showing me round the village near Thanh Hoa where he had lived in the 1950s; 'my father shot them'. This seemed improbable to me, standing not in a wilderness but on a brick-paved street among households engaged in poultry-rearing, fish-farming and the other intensive small-scale enterprises that now typify the post-'renovation'

---

[5] These old-style scholars' merits and legacy were to be understood as belonging to all. This included the unlettered peasantry from the learned men's natal villages where, so the propagandists said, the whole community had honoured the old Confucian degree-holders, revering them in life and preserving their memory for subsequent generations through the memorial steles on which their names and honours were inscribed. This was a practice extolled by Ho Chi Minh and never denounced as a relic of the feudal order (Duiker 2000).

[6] My friends do not use the derogatory term *nha que* which has connotations of 'bumpkin' to refer to the rural people they lived with in the interzones. On the Viet Minh strategy of appealing to traditional village patriotism as a force compatible with the aims of national liberation and the creation of state socialism, see Nguyen The Anh 2002b: 60–2 and Smith 1996: 215.

(*doi moi*) economy. It is true that there were stands of bamboo from which I was told dangerous animals still sometimes preyed on village livestock. All the same, we were in the area that the schoolbooks define as the country's ancient cultural heartland, a terrain also extolled for its richness in landmarks of the country's long history of resistance to foreign invaders (Pelley 2002).

During the anti-French war, this had been one of the Interzone IV localities where village people had been responsive to the DRV authorities' call for the expansion of established artisanship and commercial agriculture as well as the development of new trades and products, not only to meet local subsistence needs in the war zones but to generate revenue for the nascent DRV exchequer (Dang Phong 1999b and 2002).[7] These aims were pursued through a host of novel initiatives including the development of flood-season inland fisheries and the fostering of many old and newer specialities including pottery making, silk-reeling and the manufacture of foodstuffs and plant-based medicaments. The Viet Minh even created customs posts where imposts were paid on items in transit to and from the interzones, as well as those sold in provincial markets within their territories. These markets were of great importance. They were not only exchange and supply points but also arenas for the inculcation of the new socialist comportment regimens with their injunctions against waste and uncleanliness, and their attacks on the sale of foreign luxuries and 'superstitious' items such as gold leaf and the burnable paper votaries used as funeral offerings (*vang ma*).[8]

My friends who spent their childhoods in the interzones have their own narratives of a moralised marketplace. This was a site of marvels from which a long-absent parent would return bearing something rare and wonderful: a sack of 'St Louis' brand sugar, an American pen called a Warever. Far from being manifestations of capitalism's dehumanising commodity logic, these things with their bright packaging and evocative brand names were treasures rendered precious and personal, imparted with love by one's revolutionary parents. They were also key elements in the process I am calling auto-cartography – material embodiments of the trajectories through which individuals and families map their moves across the spaces of the socialist ecumene.

These understandings of the familial and the national as experiences of circulation and the meeting of need help to explain the exaltation of

---

[7] See also Duiker 1996; Gordon 1981; Dang Phong and Beresford 1998: 15–32.
[8] See Hy Van Luong 1998: 297–8; ; Malarney 2002: 61–3; Dang Phong 2002: 204–8.

the petty trader (*thuong*) as a contributor to the revolutionary cause.[9] As I noted in Chapter 6, images of small-scale trade in foodstuffs and other basic necessities feature in a variety of wartime propaganda posters. Some of my friends have been explicit in drawing a parallel between this view of the small-scale trader as a nurturing provider, and the grey-economy trading life led by members of their own families during their overseas sojourns in the post-reunification period and early *doi moi* ('renovation') years from the late 1970s to the early 1990s.

I explore the dilemmas arising from these activities in Chapter 8. In contrast to the more consistently negative portrayal of trading activities in the post-'Geneva' years (i.e. after liberation from French rule, and the partition of Vietnam brokered under the Geneva Peace Accords in 1954), Viet Minh political art in the anti-French war years conveyed surprisingly positive messages about rural trade, though in fact it is not hard to see why this was so. Clearly in Vietnam, especially in the deltaic north with its dynamic village to city artisanal culture, there were strong traditions comparable to those identified by Parry (1989) in the Indian context as a basis for the view of moneyed exchange as morally benign and indeed a prerequisite of ordered sociality, rather than a parasitical activity corrosive of feeling and moral life. Thus even for revolutionary socialists, in the context of anti-colonial resistance the circulation of things needed and valued by all, including wholesome 'national products' emanating from home soil like India's *swadeshi* goods, as well as many modern manufactured items, could be plausibly represented as both heroic and virtuous. Viet Minh artists thus juxtaposed the 'buy native' and 'boycott foreign luxuries' themes with representations of the nation's productive landscape as a terrain of moral action sustained and nurtured by small-scale traders, their panniers or pedlar's bicycles conveying the health-giving products of tilled land and productive villages. Such homely rustic trade was to be understood as arising from the norms of the peasant world within which wellbeing was sustained by the circulation of goods and people through a landscape in which sociability was to be equated with the meeting of need. So long as

[9] This was in direct contrast to the use of this terminology after the anti-French war (especially in the form *tieu thuong*, small trader) when it came to depict something more akin to what Humphrey documents for the Soviet context (2002: 59–65): the trader as parasite, profiting from illicit trading in rationed goods, thereby violating the norms and decencies of a fully established socialist order which, in theory at least, had mastered the art of providing necessities for all through official distribution regimens. On pre-and post-independence attitudes to commerce in Vietnam, see Marr 1981: 121–7; Hy Van Luong 1998: 297–309; Malarney 1998; Kleinen 1999: 126, 140–55; P. Taylor 2001; Pettus 2003: 32–3, 217–18n; Leshkowich 2006.

excesses were held in check, it was legitimate to take modest profits from such provision, all the more so since traders could also be visualised as resistance heroes, concealing documents and smuggling arms in their baskets and bicycle loads (Kleinen 1999: 87).

Yet as in India, where the widely shared cultural construction of *banias* (traditional Hindu, Jain or Parsi merchants) is a stereotype of outsiders holding themselves apart from the wider community and operating rapaciously in a dehumanised marketplace, Vietnam's idea of virtuous trading is not to be mistaken for the parasitism ascribed to the foreign capitalist and his local *bourgeois* collaborators, even when the goods being transported are foreign imports. Although the invention of improvised substitutes was a Viet Minh priority, the DRV authorities did not tell their mobilised citizenry that they should do without the many modern items which could not be produced within the interzones, or were obtainable only in limited quantities from the country's socialist aid providers when the victory of Mao's revolutionary forces opened the vital cross-border supply route linking the 'liberated territories' with southern China.

It was therefore understood that a significant proportion of such things as textbooks, typewriters, bicycle parts, rubber goods, batteries and pharmaceuticals would have to be acquired from the French zones. The petty traders would be their providers. And, my friends recall, such key enlighteners as Party cadres and interzone teachers had the task of conveying to the rural 'masses' that these were important elements of their new revolutionary world. Children in particular were to understand about such things as vitamins and modern medicines. Even if they were unlikely to see or use such items in wartime, they were told that they would one day be a familiar part of their lives. In the meantime, they were to learn their transliterated Vietnamese names and attain familiarity with them in classroom lessons about the ways of the modern world. At the same time, they would retain respect for the native products and practices with which such modern items were compatible.

The wartime slogan 'Fight on the economic front!' (*Dau tranh kinh te voi dich*: lit. 'fight the enemy [through] the economy') conveyed a relevant message about these interactions. Patriotic Vietnamese were supposed to understand that the war was a composite of three domains of struggle, the work of soldiering being sustained and supplemented by the contributions of economic producers and 'brain workers'. It was a message that one friend glossed as a reference to the treatment of the interzone boundaries as open frontiers across which exports and imports could travel to and from the 'occupied' (French-controlled) territories. My friend said that I should understand the meaning of that slogan 'fight them on the economic front' as 'don't embargo them – fight them and trade with them'. I return to this idea of commerce as a form of justifiable interaction across notionally closed moral frontiers in Chapter 8.

Propaganda posters from this period depict rural life not as an enclaved village world, but as a to-ing and fro-ing of homely peasant traders traversing the countryside with foodstuffs and other wares that were welcomed by all. Their activities are to be seen as an unexploitative meeting of need, for which they must move and travel. Thus they too are part of the purposeful mobility which is indispensable to the nation's life and progress. Traditional Vietnamese life had never been static and bound to a natal locality, said the party propagandists. It only seemed so because the French had killed off native craft industries and restricted the free movement of both people and goods. Thus a key Viet Minh claim was that the countryside was not a site of torpor where peasants cherished the insularity conferred by the proverbial village hedge (Hy Van Luong 1992; Kleinen 1999). This image of immobility was widely deployed in French colonial writings much like those pointing to India's 'village republics' as arenas of equally inward-looking peasant conservativism. And like those Indian nationalists who did not subscribe to Gandhi's vision of uncommercialised village self-sufficiency, the Viet Minh message was that rural Vietnamese had no fear of change and movement. On the contrary, the rural 'masses' were extolled as people well endowed with the will and energy to traverse expansive spaces, thus ready and eager to follow the Party's lead in pursuit of both liberation and productive modernity for their native land. These too are themes now being revived for the purposes of the country's post-'renovation' initiatives in overseas commerce and remittance-earning labour exports.

So the homely traders and those for whom they provided were to be seen as embracing the new conventions being introduced to the rural populace by the revolutionaries in their midst. These included new spatial practices, and also a new time-reckoning involving such markers as commemoration days adapted from a variety of socialist models. Among these was Wounded Serviceman's Day, still celebrated annually on 27 July, and depicted in one wartime poster from the late 1940s as a calling-home of those pursuing the productive tasks which take them out into the wider world (Plate 13). It is thus portrayed in terms evocative of other key occasions of Vietnamese 'reunion commensality' (a term borrowed from Stafford 2000: 102–9) especially the Lunar New Year festival, *Tet*, when separated families traditionally strive to reunite. The poster's caption is a verse couplet:

> *Ngay thuong binh tu si.*
> *Ngay thuong binh*
> *Du ai buon dau, ban dau,*
> *27 thang 7 ru nhau tim ve.*

Wherever you roam, wherever you trade/do business (*buon*), return home for Wounded Serviceman's Day.

The poster shows two barefooted fruit vendors arriving home to play their part in this new celebration. Their village is already a space of socialist modernity; the scene includes a smiling child holding a book and an invalided soldier in Viet Minh uniform. There is a sign announcing the commemoration day above the entrance gate. This display of the written word and the book in the child's hand indicate that the village is a place of literate people, hence one where both young and old are contributors to the revolutionary cause. Ho Chi Minh had famously proclaimed diligence in study and the war against 'word blindness' (*mu chu*) to be as important to the nation as the valour of its soldiers.[10]

Such messages could not be fully acted on in village spaces in either 'liberated' or French-occupied territory without the exemplary contributions of 'socialist moderns', both adult and very young. So as the tiger story indicates, much of what my friends recall about their interzone childhoods involves an idea of being called to lead lives of action and exemplarship. 'C'est une vie très dure pour les hanoiens comme nous' (It is [was] a hard life for Hanoi people like us), I was told by a retired academic who spent the war in Thanh Hoa. Recalling bombing raids, the war games her brothers played with village children, and a terrifying occasion when she saw a cluster of village livestock mown down by gunfire from low-flying French aircraft, she too showed me a cherished family photo album containing images of familial life both before and during the war, as well as vivid glimpses of the interzones' new socialities.

The earliest of the pictures were studio portraits of her mother and elder sisters in *ao dai*s, still leading the kind of modestly comfortable pre-war life I have described in earlier chapters. Other images from the early 1940s are of the families' young men and women arm in arm with their *lycée* and Ecole Normale contemporaries, and, in a few exceptional cases,

---

[10] Harrison-Hall 2002: 26, plate 1.10. The name given to the anti-illiteracy campaign evoked an image of teaching as an act of revolutionary war against the social blights of a bygone era: *xoa nan mu chu*, literally 'destroy the evil of word blindness'.

pictures of friends who studied together in pre-war France.[11] Pictures of the same individuals in their relocation villages present a striking contrast, the young men who served as civilian cadres shown in their berets and sporty belted jackets arm in arm with other male comrades. The unmarried girls have had their hair cut short and wear skirts or trousers with open-necked military style blouses; they stand with school friends in a rugged hilly landscape (Plates 14 and 15). In other pictures the same girls accompany their parents – both high-ranking officials – on visits to Viet Minh field hospitals.

There are also many pictures of children in shorts taking part in gymnastic competitions and the musical performances put on by the Young Pioneer chorales to which a number of my older friends belonged (Plates 17 and 18). Many can still sing the songs they learned for these occasions. Among the most famous is the celebrated 'Return to Hanoi' song of which more below, and also '*Song Lo*', the 1948 anthem extolling an early Viet Minh victory against French forces. Both are by Van Cao, the much-loved composer of the national anthem. Other friends recall the 'Youth Song' (*Thanh Nien Ca*), composed in 1950: 'Youth march on! Youth build [new] life! We are the Ho Chi Minh generation!', and the 1948 'Song of the Children's Musical Arts Troupe' (*Bai Hat Doan Thieu Nhi Nghe Thuat*), a composition in which the children sing of their ardent love for 'Uncle Ho' (*Bac Ho*) and their yearning for the loving parents from whom they must part to do their duty as givers and doers for the good of all.

These children's chorale songs evoke scenes of drama and sacrifice in the war effort and, often in the same composition, the beauties of the Vietnamese countryside and the rhythms of its rustic seasonal harmonies. These are conveyed in the elegiac terms still pervading a wide range of literary and popular art forms (see Cao Thi Nhu-Quynh and Schafer 1988). Yet their terms of reference are emphatically

---

[11] There are also wedding pictures. Some are of massive gatherings of all the kin and other guests at the nuptial celebrations, representing the marriage as a great moment in the life of the extended family. Like those I have been shown by other members of intelligentsia families, in this album the wedding photos date from the 1930s and are notable for the fact that they are not big family group photos but instead present the bride and groom on their own, as a couple, in close-up and seated close together. The young husband wears a smart Western-style evening suit. Younger people have told me that the bride's elegant hairstyle, *ao dai* and jewellery are immediately recognisable as the accoutrements of an educated young urbanite of the pre-independence period. Such double portraits identify the couples shown with the aims of the pre-war social reformers who extolled the virtues of 'modern' monogamous marriage and called for the extirpation of polygamy, prostitution and concubinage as relics of an oppressive, 'feudal' past (Malarney 2002).

unparochial, the insistence on awareness of the bonds and 'friend-ships' of the wider socialist world apparent in such works as 'I Love Elder Sister Raymonde' (*Em Yeu Chi Ray-mong*). This composition of 1950 was based on a contemporary news story picked up by the Viet Minh propaganda and information service. Evoking a wider world in which the Viet Minh struggle is known and supported even in the enemy's heartland, it is a song of praise for a young French girl, Raymonde (*Ray-mong* in Vietnamese) hailed as a 'brave soldier for peace' who risked her life in a daring attempt to block the route of a troop train on its way to embarkation for Indochina: 'East, West, full of love; stop the enemy – Elder Sister Raymonde has become our life model (*neu guong*)'.

Dangerous frontiers

Dr Tran attended both primary and secondary schools in villages around Thanh Hoa. He still has his exercise books, stamped with an A on the cover. This identified him as a 'category A' pupil, the child of a DRV cadre who was entitled to such benefits as quota places in the special schools in China. Of course such markers set him and his con-temporaries apart from local villagers, and from the many incomers from 'occupied' areas who were not officials of the new revolutionary proto-state. Yet Dr Tran says that he and his family never felt that they were living in privileged isolation from village life. Here again the experiences of children were critical in the forging of new socialities.

Children's lives in the interzones sites could be so different from those of their elders that their parents could find themselves facing great challenges in their efforts to sustain the bonds of affective awareness through which young people acquired their sense of *tri thuc* (intellectual) family identity. As young people, even those who did not go to China for their schooling often lived apart from their parents for long periods. It was not uncommon for them to be placed as quasi-foster children in peasant households rather than those of other Hanoi incomers. During our village visits, Dr Tran showed me that he could still winnow grain and work a foot-powered rice-pounder. These and other rural skills and work rhythms have stayed with him since childhood.

No-one I know denies the very real differences between these intelligentsia incomers and the peasants among whom they lived. They do bristle though at the suggestion that they were anything like an alien occupation force within their relocation villages. This does not mean taking literally or uncritically everything that my informants say. But I do see what younger people experienced in childhood as calling into question any idea of simple two-sided power relations between the rural populace and the incoming 'socialist moderns' even though they all, children included, unmistakably embodied the new socialist order which the DRV authorities were seeking to bring into being in the interzones.

Dr Tran has a pen-and-ink sketch that he made for a secondary-school art lesson in 1953, giving it the poignant caption 'My House in Hanoi'. The structure he drew is unmistakably urban, in the hybrid architectural style characterising the residences of comparatively prosperous Hanoians in the pre-war period (Papin 2001: 234–5). Though modest in scale it has two storeys, fretted shutters and a frieze of decorative *beaux arts* stucco-work, all very much in contrast to the peasant houses he and other Hanoi incomers lived in throughout their interzone years. These were single-storey mud–brick structures with minimal furnishings, thatched roofs and, of course, no plumbing or electricity. Those I have visited in the Thanh Hoa countryside are set in scrupulously clean, low-walled courtyards amid flowering creepers and shade trees. Some adjoin the dramatic limestone cliff and cave formations which were used as anti-aircraft shelters and camouflaged production sites. Many have been rebuilt in concrete with the proceeds of recent post-*doi moi* commercial ventures; others are much as my friends knew them in the war years.[12]

The people I know say they grew up expecting to return to their urban homes when the war was won, though they were taught that it was wrong and unrevolutionary to anticipate this prematurely. The great Van Cao's 1949 patriotic composition *Tien ve Ha Noi* (On the March Back to Hanoi), now taught to every schoolchild, is widely hailed as the most evocative of the anti-French war's songs of love and yearning. Yet when first performed, it was condemned by the Viet Minh cultural authorities as an expression of faulty sentiment through its elegiac images of the traversing of flower-strewn spaces by a triumphant soldiery returning to their urban homes. What were needed

---

[12] Those I have visited are still sparsely furnished, though nowadays they have electricity, and most households have such key items of the post-*doi moi* consumer revolution as televisions, rice cookers and electric fans; most have motor-scooters as well as bicycles. In common with Hanoi homes they have ancestor altars placed centrally against the wall of the main room, some with a photograph of Ho Chi Minh placed among the memorial photographs and offering items. It has been suggested that such commemorations are becoming uncommon, though I encountered many instances of Ho Chi Minh veneration in the course of field work. At one village wedding I attended in 2006, the bride's family had placed their offering of a cooked pig's head directly under the large picture of Ho Chi Minh ('Uncle' or *Bac Ho*, ancestor to all the nation) that was affixed to the wall above the family photos and other items on their household ancestor altar (compare Malarney 1996b and 2002; Schlecker 2005: 518 and ns. 19–22, pp. 523–4).

in 1949, the censors said, were works exalting the ardour of those with battles still to fight; their images of homeland must be of earth and rivers stained with enemy blood.[13]

Yet while generally long and of uncertain duration, these sojourns in the interzone were thought of as impermanent relocations. I know of only one case of someone from an intelligentsia family who remained in a former interzone village after independence. This was a man who married a girl from a farming family who found she could not bear Hanoi life and separation from her natal kin. So, when he completed his military service after the anti-US war, he settled with her in her family's joint farming household, living in a shared house with her parents and unmarried siblings.

Yet for all their consciousness of being only temporary sojourners in their relocation sites, I have never heard anyone speak even obliquely of the villagers with whom they lived as 'uncivilised' (*chua khai hoa*) or backward (*lac hau*), a term used for 'ethnic minority' peoples but not of one's fellow 'Viet (*Kinh*)'.[14] Nor do they speak of the peasants they knew in the war years as lacking the virtue or patriotic fervour of their parents and other incomers, though they say that both rural people and city-dwellers in the 'occupied' zones were thought of as potential *Viet gian* (traitors).

All the same, my *tri thuc* friends say they knew that even as children they were part of a process that was bringing novel modes of speech and comportment into the 'liberated' areas. And while it was youth in general whom the DRV propagandists represented as exemplary of the nation's new life, intelligentsia children were often in the limelight as the most conspicuous representatives of its new habituations. As I have noted, the building of the DRV proto-state involved a great deal of exhortatory propagandising by means of posters, painted wall slogans and public megaphone readings. In all these media, much emphasis was given to mobilised youth as key agents of the initiatives aimed at interzone civilians. Paramount among these was the mass literacy campaign, in which uniformed schoolchildren had the task of standing at the entry point into interzone villages to test those coming and going on their ability to read patriotic slogans like '*Viet Nam Doc Lap*' (Independence for Vietnam)

---

[13] Pelley 2002; Ninh 2002. My friends have much to say about the power of these songs' evocative words as well as their rhythmic melodies; they are critical of the coldly instrumental quality of some though not all 'official' or 'red' music with its martial messages and conventionalised vocabulary.

[14] Salemink 2003. On the complexities of writers' and artists' attitudes to the wartime peasant world, see Ninh 2002: 48–82 and Rato 2004. See also Tessier 2002: 416.

painted on boards and rice-winnowers. This was an effective means of inducing village people to attend to their lessons: to fail such tests beneath the gaze of chiding twelve-year-olds was an indignity which few adults were willing to endure.[15]

In theory of course the monitoring schoolchildren were village youths, the rural society's first beneficiaries of the new order's enlightenment policies, sharing the fruits of their new schooling with the wider community. But the incomers were special. While they wore village garb and socialised with the village children, they did stand out. The fact that almost all of them had educated womenfolk in their families was a prime marker of this difference. The people I know speak with pride of their female elders' educational attainments. This includes their fluency in French. When people say 'My mother had top marks in French before the war' or 'My elder sister won the *lycée* prize for language', it is clear that they see these as honourable achievements, in keeping with both patriotic and familial duty, the product of agency and initiative rather than the imposition of a coloniser's will on passive or collaborating subjects.

As I have already noted, the people I know associate knowledge of French with moments of pleasure and intimacy which are specific to their memories of the war years and their experiences of both family and classroom sociality within the interzones. Of course these skills are also spoken of instrumentally, though in many cases as hard-won proficiencies which their elders deployed with skill and daring in negotiating the dangers of wartime life. Dr Tran says he remembers his mother's deft handling of the colonial troops, both white and African, manning checkpoints along their difficult cross-country route from Hanoi to the first of their interzone villages.

His mother spoke French in these encounters, Dr Tran says. He enjoys recalling the effect of her correct speech and confident demeanour on the soldiers; the stories of what she did on those occasions have long been told and retold within the family. He says the soldiers never challenged her claim to be a lady of 'loyal' family travelling innocently with her children to her husband's natal village. I asked if his mother had

---

[15] The Viet Minh propaganda service relayed information via news-sheets conveyed by cadres from village to village and read out by megaphone (Dang Phong 2002: 430). Hy Van Luong's informants recall schoolchildren belonging to the mass youth wing of the National Salvation Front (*Cuu Quoc*) being recruited for Viet Minh campaigns against gaming, shamanic worship and other 'evils' of village life (1992: 145). After independence the mass literacy campaign was masterminded by the DRV's Education Minister, Professor Nguyen Van Huyen (Nguyen Kim Nu Hanh 2003). On the ideology of social duty underpinning Soviet literacy campaigns, see Kelly 2001: 268.

identity papers to show at the checkpoints. No, he said; this was before the Viet Minh authorities had developed the sophisticated interzone production units which produced items such as counterfeit traders' passes for their officials. 'She spoke French. That was her passport. The language was her passport' ('La langue est le passeport'), meaning that knowledge of French was sufficient guarantee of her bona fides in the eyes of the naively gallant soldiers. He said they even called her *Madame*, and employed the respectful pronoun *vous* rather than the familiar *tu* which had long been a hotly resented usage of colonial linguistic interactions (Brocheux and Hémery 1995: 188).

When his father negotiated such checkpoints, he dressed as an impecunious village schoolmaster and made his French hesitant and unidiomatic. 'Pour un homme, c'ést dangereux,' said Dr Tran. 'Une femme qui parle français, c'est différent, respectable – c'est le respect pour la civilisation française. Avec la typique gallanterie française, il ne peut faire jamais quelque-chose contre une femme qui parle la langue.' (It was dangerous for men. As for a woman speaking French – for them [the French soldiers], that was different, respected – a matter of respect for French civilisation. With their typical Frenchman's gallantry, they could never think of doing anything against [or: thinking ill of] a woman able to speak the language.)

This notion of correct French as the mark of a 'civilised' person identifying with France and French values, an *évolué* in the colonisers' enduring neo-Darwinian terminology, is reminiscent of the standards by which colonial officials passed judgement on mixed-race and 'native' citizenship candidates.[16] The element of gender difference is striking here. Both sons and daughters like to connect their memories of their fathers' strength and virtue with this idea of the fluent male French-speaker as a figure of power, someone for the French to be frightened of rather than taken for granted as a tamed and compliant collaborator. By the same token, Dr Tran's story about his mother is an account of a francophone woman embodying both strength and respectability, triumphantly duping the foolish Frenchmen and their non-white agents, thus emphatically not someone to confuse with that other key figure of Orientalist gender discourse in colonial Indochina, the bed-servant (*con gai*) whose fluent French is both product and tool of her degrading concubinage (Stoler 2002). What is to be seen here is that important

---

[16] Throughout the empire, these markers included appropriate bodily comportment – notably European-style dress and table manners – as well as linguistic knowledge, and a record of unproblematic political sympathies (Conklin 1998; Pederson 1998; White 2000; Stoler 2002).

other side of the story. Rather than focusing on what the French 'civi-lisers' thought or feared in the attempt to distinguish ordinary 'natives' from *évolués*, the points being made are about the knowing deployment of those same concepts of civilisation and civility to confuse the colo-niser's scrutinising eye and ear.[17]

What is also striking here is the amount of thought my friends have given to the question of language as a vehicle of both resistance and subjection. As I show below, these are issues that many found themselves having to reflect on in the course of the various post-independence shifts in language policy which both advantaged and disadvantaged families like theirs. Dr Tran himself said that there was a certain irony in the appropriation of French-style surveillance and control techniques by the DRV's own literacy campaigners. He also told me about a panoptic strategy devised specifically for Viet Minh soldiers, noting that bodies as well as walls and other objects were pressed into service as display sites for the written word. While on the move, DRV troops were supposed to have small lesson boards chalked with a daily reading exercise slung on strings between their shoulders; each fighter could then spend his day conning the text displayed on the back of the comrade in the rank ahead of him. 'En ce temps-la, on porte les mots, on lit les mots.' (In those days people wore words as well as reading them.)[18]

So far as I can tell, the people I know do not think of this as coercive or dehumanising, but rather as the kind of inspired improvisation under-pinning all their wartime victories. Of course it is acknowledged that support from the Soviet Union and Mao's China was critical in the anti-French war, as was the legendary heroism of the Viet Minh fighters. But my friends also like to celebrate feats of ingenuity and visual misdirection like the strategy devised in an early anti-French war battle, now com-memorated with a massive hill-top memorial. The Viet Minh are said to have used blackened floating grapefruit as imitation mines to dupe French patrol boats into swerving towards a river bank where their troops waited in ambush. 'Si simple!' (So simple!) said Dr Tran of this tactic.

---

[17] Such occlusions and misdirections were devised by insurgents in other anti-colonial contexts. A case in point is the 1956–60 Algerian independence war when women members of the revolutionary FLN movement (*Front de Libération Nationale*) famously subverted French preoccupations with the veiled female body, smuggling weapons out of the *casbah* by donning Western dress and speaking French to the checkpoint soldiers, thereby successfully representing themselves as harmless *évoluées* on their way to the seaside (Fanon 1965: 35–64; Slyomovics 1995: 8–9).

[18] Dang Phong 2002: 425–6; compare Marr 1993: 338.

There is no question for him of seeing the soldiers' feat as the tactic of backward people for whom modern armaments were a mystery. He said the grapefruit mines were like the many other improvised devices which he recalls from his interzone years. He remembers his family saving resealable 'Gibbs' tooth-powder tins – a French brand despite the English-sounding name – much prized by civilians and Viet Minh soldiers as waterproof containers. He also recalls doing his schoolwork by the light of petrol- or kerosene-burning lamps made from scavenged wine bottles and penicillin ampoules with wick-holders made out of coiled wire.[19] Indeed he recalls that the war gave rise to a commodity culture involving a whole host of such items produced both in households and under the supervision of the DRV supply ministry: strips of parachute silk painted by children for use as camouflage sheets; lightweight synthetic sheeting worn as rainproofs by soldiers on the march. These 'self-mades' (*tu tao*) were generally salvage products. Like the famous rubber-tyre sandals worn by Vietnamese fighters in both liberation wars, most were made from materials and objects either originally imported or manufactured in factories inside the French zones, and transported openly or covertly across that dangerous but permeable frontier dividing the occupied areas from the interzones.

Throughout the war and thereafter, children used the term 'atomic' (*nguyen tu*, literally 'nuclear' in Vietnamese) for such items as ballpoint pens, chewing gum, rechargeable batteries, and even synthethic sweeteners and American-style powdered milk. At school in the 1950s, they were taught about the significance of the atomic weapons used to bomb Hiroshima and Nagasaki, as well as the post-war atom tests and the great triumph for the socialist world of the 1957 Sputnik launch. Of the word 'atomic', a friend said, 'It was our word for everything remarkable': 'Toutes les choses qui sont fortes, ultra-modernes, durables, superbes sont les "atomiques"' (Everything strong, ultra-modern, durable, wonderful was 'atomic'). One thing this signalled was that truly supermodern things in the post-1945 world order came not from France but from the new global superpowers, the USA and the USSR. In addition to their lessons about the bomb and its importance to the emerging global struggle between the superpowers, interzone schoolchildren were told that the best of the amazing new 'wonder drugs' (*than duoc*) being marvelled at in every modern country came from the USA, and that the

---

[19] Lights made from salvaged bottles – *den tu tao* – were still widely used even in urban households until quite recently; a young graduate I know says her family was still using them in the early 1990s.

attempt by the French to create an antibiotic comparable to penicillin was dismissed around the world as a failure.[20]

So for my friends, the world beyond the interzone frontiers was not unknown space. They were encouraged to feel connected with its peoples and places in a host of ways, not least by the moral meanings which they attached to the modern goods and knowledge which their elders brought across its boundaries. Important for them too, they say, was the idea of the many goods from faraway places which were transformed and recontextualised by Vietnamese. It was their homeland's great gift to be able to see the world and its resources in ways that both embraced and transcended the aims and uses of their former colonisers and other materially advantaged peoples. This includes their socialist 'friends' in other lands, and in more recent times the peoples of the wider capitalist world, as I show in later chapters.

Dr Tran liked my suggestion that French, long extolled by Francophonie polemicists as humanity's supreme vehicle of reason and revelatory truth-seeking, was appropriated by people like his mother as a device to make Frenchmen see what the insurgents wanted them to see.[21] Using the power of speech, they turned the enemy checkpoints into spaces where the 'specularising' gaze of power was played back against their enemies, blinding as well as deafening them to the truth of what they thought they were establishing through their 'exhibitionary' detection protocols. It was to illustrate this point that Dr Tran introduced me to Mr Quan, a former Viet Minh peasant fighter who told me that as a child growing up in an 'occupied zone' village near Hanoi, he and his six siblings were early beneficiaries of the Viet Minh mass literacy scheme. In the 'occupied territories', this was a means of establishing a covert Viet Minh presence among those whom the French believed to be safely 'loyal'. Mr Quan said that the villagers took much pride in being able to report to the Viet Minh officials with whom they were secretly in contact that they had achieved a pass rate of 100 per cent

---

[20] This was a reference to French sulfonamides (sulfa drugs) with trade names like Dagénan. These precursors of the more powerful antibiotics like pencillin were available in Indochina from the late 1930s and had become popular with the growing population of Vietnamese consumers with access to commercial pharmaceuticals; what the interzone schools were thus teaching was that these 'colonial' medications were inferior to those pioneered by the more scientifically advanced world powers. See Dang Phong 2002: 423–4; Monnais and Tousignant 2006: 145. On the 'localisation' of foreign products in contemporary Vietnam see Fforde 2003.

[21] La Francophonie is France's officially sponsored campaign for worldwide use of French as a means of resisting Anglo-American globalisation (see Agence de la Francophonie 1997).

in the scheme's basic proficiency test.[22] As a schoolchild he had volunteered for the dangerous night-time work of painting patriotic slogans on walls and other open-air surfaces. Their aim, said Mr Quan, was to 'make everyone see': even those who could not read would know from observing the painted words that their liberators were an active presence in their midst.

Dr Tran made much the same point during our visit with students and colleagues to see the blockhouses on the river Day where he demonstrated Viet Minh grenading techniques. On that occasion he also directed our attention to the limestone cliffs on the opposite side of what for much of the war had been a critical frontier line between the 'occupied' and 'liberated' territories. From inside the now ruined blockhouses with their narrow peepholes and firing points, French troops were supposed to maintain surveillance over precisely delineated sections of the surrounding countryside. But this too was a site where my friends wanted to represent the colonisers' attempts to construct their exhibitionary order as a contest in which their own side fought back with their own subtly effective version of panoptic power. This was one of the places where the insurgents exploited the blockhouses' fixed lines of sight by ensuring that the French soldiers staring through their binoculars at the Viet Minh side of the river would see giant letters painted on the chalk-like rockfaces spelling out '*Viet Nam Doc Lap*' (Vietnam – Independence); '*Ho Chi Minh Muon Nam*' (long live Ho Chi Minh); and '*Tu Do Hanh Phuc*' (*tu do*: liberty; *hanh phuc*: blessing or boon, a phrase often used as a good luck expression at weddings, hence 'blessed is liberty'or 'liberty is joy'). This was not only to demoralise the enemy. 'It was for our people too', said Dr Tran. The idea was to ensure that both fighters and local civilians would visualise the French not in a state of all-powerful mastery subjecting land and people to their gaze, but as quasi-prisoners surrounded by enemies, continually forced to read and even inwardly pronounce the key slogans of the resistance war.[23]

Life and friendship in the interzones

As I have shown in other chapters, my friends speak often of the poignancy of their separation and reunion experiences. From the early

---

[22] Compare Hy Van Luong 1992: 153, 173.

[23] I have been told many stories about the ways in which Ho Chi Minh used evasions and disguises to elude the colonial surveillance regimens; there are also many published accounts of his escapes and ingenious deceptions. See e.g. www.hochiminh.org/Pages/1970_Bac_Po.html.

years of his family's sojourn in Thanh Hoa, Dr Tran spent much time apart from his parents. Their official duties often took them far afield, and like other interzone schoolchildren, he too was much taken up with the organised group activities which were central to the new socialities being forged in the 'liberated territories'. I noted above the Party youth movement occasions at which children traversed the interzones to engage in sporting and cultural displays. There were dangers and privations of course, but my friends say they found these exciting and pleasurable experiences. They often involved long night-time treks of 20 kilometres or more, with hundreds or even thousands of people assembling at the big open-air regional convocations at which official speakers reported on their travels to other socialist lands where they said they had found warm-hearted foreign comrades expressing ardent admiration for Vietnam's resistance struggle. It was clearly important for the DRV authorities to be able to co-ordinate these occasions. Like the staging of Independence Day in Hanoi in 1945, they were demonstrations of the new life and purpose of the revolutionary order, enacted for all to see as a continual mapping out of rural terrain through the massing of those taking part in these highly ordered mobility exercises. Once again, the presence of uniformed schoolchildren did much to identify such occasions as spectacles of the new life being engendered and enacted by the nation's citizenry. Those involved were being called upon to see themselves as sharers in the forging of long-distance connections across the spaces of the homeland's inner ecumene, as well as its growing array of ties to such people as those admiring comrades in the wider socialist world.

Here too Dr Tran has a personal perspective to convey. One such trek was memorable for providing an opportunity for his first adolescent flirtation. He has also described a frightening day three years earlier when he was nearly caught in a French bombing raid while out playing with friends. His father searched anxiously for him. He was not hurt, and he describes the moment when they found one another as an exchange of exquisite caring intimacy, expressed by his father not with words or an embrace, but with the most delicate of loving gestures. 'Il a pris ma main' (He took my hand), Dr Tran said 'C'est tout' (That was all), except that his father led him to one of the village's open-air market stalls and gently urged him to choose whatever he most wanted from the vendor's limited display.

Dr Tran moved from this account to another story about feeling and provision, this one expressing the more painful and problematic side of interzone experience for *tri thuc* families. On occasions when his parents were away on official duties, they made arrangements for him to lodge with local people, most commonly a couple on their own with grown up children away on military service. He was unhappy in the first such household, recalling the couple who took him in as cold and unfeeling. He has shown me the limestone cliff near a quarry against which their small house was built, conveniently situated for their regular dashes to the caves which the villagers used as air raid shelters.

Dr Tran conveyed the unhappiness of this time in terms of that much-described key experience of family life in Vietnam: the sharing of household meals. I have often experienced such occasions. My older friends say the conventions are much as they recall them from childhood: the rice in its pot, and the other items – meat being the most costly and valued – placed in dishes intended for common use. Among the many nuances of food sharing to be learned in early childhood is the polite invitation word '*moi*', affirming that one's elders should help themselves before their juniors, though with the expectation that elders will show nurturing care by serving the young with occasional tempting tidbits. As in the Chinese contexts described by Stafford, I have seen too that there can be tricky relational terrain to negotiate when the young are offered food in the households of non-kin (Stafford 1995: 107–8; Pham Van Bich 1999: 25).

What Dr Tran says he remembers from mealtimes in this uncongenial home is the woman's unfeeling gaze, through which he knew he was being wordlessly forbidden to take meat from the common dish. 'It was there, but I did not dare touch it', he said. The couple were traders in bicycle parts, thus modestly prosperous by village standards; there were usually adequate if not abundant quantities of food. He says they made him feel an unwelcome outsider, a person of no account. As he tells the story, while under their roof he was subject to the couple's power to bestow or withhold the expressive words and gestures by which Vietnamese create and sustain sociality, both within and beyond the familial arena. Although the child of Hanoi intelligentsia officials, in that household he was far from being privileged or deferred to, in no sense a sharer in the power of an urban elite acting as bringers of compelling new modernity regimens to the interzones' peasant villagers.

After some months, Dr Tran was rescued from this household by a classmate who has remained a lifelong friend. Knowing that Tran was unhappy, this other fourteen-year-old, Trieu, appealed to his parents to offer him a home with them. They agreed, and when Dr Tran's father next came to Thanh Hoa he inspected the new arrangement and gave it his sanction. This second family were poor peasants, their means far more meagre than the other household's. But his friend's kin were warm and welcoming, and generously shared what little they had, their staples locally grown and eked out with seasonal items such as tiny shrimps gathered from flooded wet-season rice fields. This is the rural fare Dr Tran still relishes and regularly serves to friends. It was in this family's luxuriant garden plot with its fruit trees and chicken run, and in the company of Mr Trieu, that Dr Tran showed me his old class-room compositions and school reports. With his arm round his friend's shoulders, Dr Tran told me that the other woman and her husband had used the neutral pronoun *chau* to address him, this being the way in which people speak of and to a junior who is neither kin to them, nor the child of intimate friends. Mr Trieu's parents, he said, had employed the familial pronoun *con*, the equivalent of calling him 'my son'. This he greatly valued. Equally important to him was that his own parents reciprocated in kind, addressing his friend warmly as *con*, thus including him within the familial bonds of their own household, their word choice identifying him as son-like in relation to them, and brother-like in relation to him.

So although a child of intelligentsia parents, Dr Tran clearly lived much more of a peasant life in wartime than his elders ever did. He said that in the first household there had been many chores to perform which he had found onerous and unpleasant; it was in relation to the second family that he spoke of his daily tasks – winnowing and rice-pounding – as skills learned and still with him. Yet in both settings, he was clearly living a life of remarkable change and diversity, both materially and affectively. Its components included his experiences of school and youth movement activities, together with peasant family life and life with his parents. It was this mix of divergent experiences that distinguished his childhood from those of his parents and other elders. Such separations from the world of close kin in terms of physical location and the nature of their everyday life experiences was even more pronounced in the case of the children who went to China. What was said both by and about these people is that their schoolmates and often their teachers became co-sharers in enduring bonds of friendship and professional support in later life, often with people whom their own parents and other close kin did not know at all.

This is not to say, however, that people like Dr Tran felt estranged from their natal families through having acquired these attachments. Indeed for Hanoi people who grew up in the interzones, it is clear that bonds of family have remained extremely powerful and emotionally charged. This I found to be the case even among those whose wartime and post-war experiences led them to embrace values and aspirations which were notably at odds with those of their intelligentsia parents. A case I have in mind is that of a Hanoi intellectual's daughter who became a committed Maoist while at school in China. She greatly distressed her parents after the war by refusing to attend university, taking up employment as what she called a 'real worker'. Yet in later years she rethought her repudiation of *tri thuc* values: in retirement she took the lead in compiling a family memorial volume paying tribute to the career achievements of her distinguished father.

Dr Tran said he thought it entirely proper that his parents should make a point of scrutinising the household to which he had moved. Yet it is striking that as a fourteen-year-old, he had felt himself entitled to take such an initiative. As Dr Tran tells the story, he had not meant to be rebellious or unfilial. Yet the implication of what he said was that his parents had been presented with a situation in which their son had created his own new social and affective networks, leaving it to them to make sense of what had been done, and to reaffirm their authority to judge and sanction these acts. This then was a moment when we can see some of the challenges entailed for intelligentsia incomers in seeking to lead the new revolutionary life of the interzones, while still attempting to instil in their children the sense of distinctiveness underpinning their sense of *tri thuc* family identity. It is a problem such families continued to face as war service and overseas work and study sojourns confronted them with the challenge of sustaining these affective bonds over both time and distance in the post-independence period.

Of course it is not surprising that Dr Tran's parents found his move acceptable. Mr Trieu's father and mother had been among the first successful participants in the village's mass literacy classes. And Trieu was a bright student who later became a Party member and a figure of consequence in the province. Yet this was an attachment of a kind very unlike those the two households would have forged in the prewar era. Of course as has been observed in accounts of other socialist contexts, such friendships could be advantageous on both sides (Fitzpatrick 1999: 110). For an official of peasant background, contact with the intelligentsia world can still be gratifying, there being even today significant lustre to be gained through association with the polish and cultivation of the Hanoi *tri thuc* milieu. And of course in times of danger like those of the anti-bourgeois campaigns of the 1950s, friendship with a well-placed Party member could be of considerable advantage on the intellectual's side.

I do not mean to portray any of these relations as coldly instrumental or lacking in 'heart' and affective warmth for those involved. The point I do wish to make is that it was the initiatives of fourteen-year-olds that had engendered this new connection between the two families. So this was a case of interzone life having far-reaching effects on Hanoi 'moderns' and their rural counterparts, but with children acting as critical agents of these transformations, and with the experience of emotion, provision and the forging of familiality being central to their enactment.

These changes certainly did not sound any kind of death knell for the distinctiveness of intelligentsia family life. It is clear, however, that the boundaries of the *tri thuc* family world were and are anything but closed or impermeable. It is evident too that the various kinds of relationships which could most effectively bridge the gap between the Hanoi incomers' milieu and those encountered in these fluid interzone environments were not those officially defined or promoted as ideals for the new socialist order, but rather those emanating from the more intimate and personal dimensions of individual and family life.

As I have shown, Vietnam's revolutionary propagandists have long used a language of intimate familial emotion to exalt the claims of nationhood and socialist solidarity. Strategies of much the same kind are deployed in other contexts, as Stafford shows in his account of the Taiwanese school textbooks which represent the ideal of service to the nation as an expression of filial love and duty (1995:112–21). But for all the importance of familial and affective idioms in the 'naturalising' of nationalist claims and goals, what has not been widely recognised is the extent to which evocations of feeling and intimacy have been deployed in official expressions of the socialist ecumene's internationalising ideals. Even today, the family of the Vietnamese nation and its socialist friends and allies are still widely represented much as in that news-sheet propaganda image of the five young heroes standing shoulder to shoulder, personifying the five *gioi* or classes acting in heartfelt concord as makers of the revolutionary order. Equally pervasive are the warm familial images of '*Bac Ho*', President Ho Chi Minh as loving elder kinsman to the nation and the wider socialist world which I discuss in greater detail in later chapters (see Plates 11 and 22).

A striking element of these representations is that they are so often juxtaposed to a pervasive imagery of epic landscapes and expanses of global terrain heroically traversed by selfless patriots for the good of the nation and the wider world. Yet as my friends have made clear, there were inevitably many slippages and contestations in the process of transmitting and enacting these ideals. It will be recalled that one of the five young heroes in the wartime propaganda picture was immediately recognisable as an educated 'modern' like the many Hanoi people I know who had to learn the new skills of revolutionary sociality in those challenging years. Even as young children, they and their elders were part of a process assigning special and often very onerous tasks to those whose 'culturedness' could be of service to state and nation. This meant that like the Indian 'moderns' described in Chapter 5, they had to lead lives of high mobility and to find ways of coping with the fact that their presence as incomers in the unfamiliar spaces of the DRV's inner socialist ecumene could sometimes be regarded with coldness or incomprehension. Like my Indian IAS friend Mr Raman, they too could find that their exemplification of progressive familial virtues was some-how suspect, associated by those who observed and interacted with them as a means of making gains for themselves and their kin at the expense of those unendowed with the same cultural capital.

These dilemmas did not disappear when the anti-French war ended. Indeed with liberation in 1954 came a need to project the nation's moral life onto a far larger and more expansive global canvas than that of the interzones and adjacent terrain at home and in China, which had been the focus of my informants' childhood relocation experiences. As the DRV sought to distance itself from the colonial past, and to establish its identity as a co-participant in worldwide socialist life, the interactions and solidarities of the Cold War were taking shape in ways that pro-foundly affected my Hanoi intelligentsia friends. What was now required of them was to act as mediators in the processes of aid, skill and goods exchanges which did so much to lubricate the tricky relations between international socialist 'friends' and allies.

What I suggest in the next chapter is that what such people have experienced is the plight of the various kinds of gift-givers described by anthropologists in a wide variety of settings and cultural contexts. I have in mind here the dilemmas of those whose imparting of goods, care or service may make unwelcome moral claims on those transacted with. I see this as something especially problematic in socialist contexts. As I show in relation to my friends' experiences as globe-trotting aid provi-ders and development 'experts' (*chuyen gia*), those with the power to bestow or elicit the gifts of cultural or scientific modernity may appear to be advantaged in ways that can look very much at odds with the logic of a revolutionary order in which all inequalities have been expunged, including those between fellow citizens, and also those relating to the co-equal 'friendly' nations of the wider socialist world.

8   At home and beyond in the new socialist era

'Socialist moderns' in a marketised world

As I noted earlier, during as well as after the years of giant Cold War development projects and superpower proxy wars, many of Hanoi's intelligentsia 'moderns' became transnational travellers of a very particular kind: multilingual, professionally trained, self-consciously modern, and adept in the deployment of externally generated acquisitions in many tangible and intangible forms. I have noted too that their experiences of study and salaried employment took them to a remarkable array of places in the years after the anti-French war including the USSR and Eastern Europe, as well as China, Cambodia and Iraq, and many countries in north and sub-Saharan Africa. They and thousands of other Vietnamese were thus part of the great flow of students, teachers, technicians, scientists, officials, military advisers, manual workers and combatants whose continual circulation at home and abroad became a defining feature of twentieth-century socialist modernity in all its varied forms.

I thus return here to a key issue raised earlier in my discussion of India's 'Nehruvians'. This is the extent to which socialism's distinctive enactments of modernity have derived their particularity from the making of claims about moral community, beneficent provision and shared affective life within the arenas of what I have been calling the global socialist ecumene. What I explore in this chapter are the distinctive features of this socialist world system as it was experienced by Hanoi's globe-trotting 'socialist moderns' in the post-liberation years. I focus particularly on the language of gift-giving as a central element in personal and official accounts of these activities. I am also concerned with something too often overlooked in studies of global modernity, this being the transformative effects of colonialism and decolonisation as processes intertwined with the making and unmaking of socialism in the shaping of that modernity.

Of critical importance for the Hanoi 'moderns' whose members have served as experts (*chuyen gia*) in other countries was the constitution during the Cold War years of a vast set of interconnections involving Vietnam and the former French- and Portuguese-ruled regions of north and sub-Saharan Africa. These links have not died away with the embrace of neo-liberal economic reforms in the formerly socialist or quasi-socialist 'postcolonies'. Indeed since the early 1990s, these connections have taken on new life in the form of Vietnam's post-*doi moi* ('renovation') search for markets and investment partners in a highly diverse array of overseas sites and settings. These include both China, whose own embrace of the market has been both a challenge and a stimulus to Vietnam's marketisation initiatives, and a host of capitalist states including Malaysia, Singapore and Thailand. Having become a full member of ASEAN (the Association of Southeast Asian Nations) in 1995, the first socialist state to do so, it is to these ASEAN neighbours that Vietnam has been directing much of its all-important labour and commodity export drives in recent years.[1]

Of great importance too are the trade agreements forged since the 1990s with African countries which Vietnamese diplomats call 'old friends' and partners in enduring 'traditional friendships' (*quan he huu nghi truyen thong*).[2] These accords have secured lucrative markets for Vietnam's low-priced rice, pharmaceuticals and consumer goods in a growing array of African economies. I return below to the issue of how this entry into capitalist relations with Vietnam's old socialist 'friends' has been represented in renderings of the national narrative which once again place the country's intellectuals at the centre of a complex moral story about benefaction, familiality and socialist exemplarship.

Paramount among these 'old friends' are the African states to which Cuba, East Germany and other socialist providers sent their own technicians and military advisers during the Cold War years. The presence of these globetrotting foreign 'experts' was a central feature of the many aid projects through which the Eastern and Western blocs vied for prestige and influence in the Third World. What has not been widely recognised

---

[1] ASEAN was founded in 1967 as a basis for regional co-operation between the five founding member states (Indonesia, Malaysia, Singapore, Thailand and the Philippines), all of which considered the repression of internal Communist-led insurgencies to be their most pressing political priority (Narine 1998).

[2] In addition to information provided by informants, I draw here on official sources including articles published since 2003 in the online edition of the official Foreign Ministry newspaper *Quoc Te* ('Foreign Affairs', renamed in 2006 *The Gioi & Viet Nam* (The World and Viet Nam Report), e.g. 'Viet Nam – Chau Phi: Ben nhau tren moi buoc duong phat trien (Vietnam – Africa: Side by side together on every development path). There are other accompanying items with titles such as 'Vietnam and Africa: Old Friends, New Markets'. See also Turley and Selden 1993; Thayer 1995; Fforde and de Vylder 1996; Kolko 1997; Hy Van Luong 2003; Grossheim and Houben 2001.

is that having been a major recipient of Soviet and Chinese 'expertise' in the initial post-independence period, Vietnam became a major supplier of such expertise to other socialist 'postcolonies' both during and after the final stages of the Cold War.

For Vietnam, the mechanism for these moves was the signing of far-reaching co-operation pacts (*hop dong*) under which thousands of Vietnamese engineers, medics and other technical specialists were despatched to such countries as Algeria, Mozambique, Angola, Madagascar, Guinea and Congo-Brazzaville. There were posts for humanities graduates too, like my friend Dr Toan who grew up near Thanh Hoa in Interzone IV and, having mastered Portuguese as well as Chinese and Russian, taught for three years in Angola's Portuguese-medium pedagogical colleges during the 1980s.[3] The first of these aid and remittance ventures were initiated during the period when the Vietnamese government was grappling with the massive economic problems arising from the thirty-year US trade embargo (1964–94) and the costly Cambodia and China wars of 1977–9 by becoming a large-scale exporter of labour. Manual workers were the backbone of this system, but intellectuals became another of the country's key exportable assets. Under agreements signed by Vietnam's Labour Ministry, from the early 1980s those 'friendly' leftist states which had been supportive of Vietnam during the anti-US war were provided with thousands of university-level science teachers, engineers, agronomists and medics, with the experts' salaries and other costs paid for by the host government.

These specialist 'experts' (*chuyen gia*) are not to be confused with the much greater numbers of Vietnamese who were known as 'export labourers' (*xuat khau lao dong*). These manual workers were sent under a separate set of co-operation pacts to earn remittances for the national

---

[3] The majority of these initial 'expert' agreements were made with leftist African states which had retained French as the language of government and higher education. All belonged to the international Francophonie Community. As I noted in Chapter 7, this is the African-dominated (though French-sponsored) network of francophone or quasi-francophone ex-colonies based in Paris: Vietnam joined La Francophonie, its first non-socialist international organisation, the same year it implemented *doi moi* (partial marketisation). (Bousquet 2002: 421–2). Dr Toan's father had been a Hanoi *lycée* student in the 1930s; like most of his close relations he joined the Viet Minh and spent the war years in the interzones. Dr Toan was old enough to have taught in an interzone secondary school during the anti-French war. In Angola he taught in three different teacher training institutes; he is one of several former 'experts' I know who were recruited for service in Africa in those still-pervasive seats of modernist 'development' thinking, which taught and often still teach in a tradition inherited from that of the nineteenth-century European Ecoles Normales. His brother, an engineer, studied in China and India and in the mid-1980s had a *chuyen gia* post teaching engineering in Congo-Brazzaville.

exchequer in the USSR and other labour-hungry COMECON states during the Cold War years. They too were part of the giant flows of labour which once traversed the socialist world, joining the hosts of north Koreans, Cubans and Chinese who were an equally conspicuous presence in such countries as Czechoslovakia and the DDR (former East Germany). The DDR alone took over 100,000 such Vietnamese factory workers.[4]

I have also met members of Hanoi intellectual families who worked in the Soviet and Eastern European factory towns as shop floor supervisors and interpreters for the Vietnamese labourers. These managerial jobs were often taken by women.[5] As I explain below, this was also the case among the 'experts' who went to Africa, many of whom have remained in such places as Luanda and Brazzaville, the majority running small businesses in the provisioning and grooming trades. But wherever one goes in Hanoi there are people who say, 'Oh yes, I worked in Brno'[6] – or in the steelworks in Eisenhüttenstadt, or in a machine shop in Rostock, or in the catering trade in Warsaw or Bucharest. Everyone knows too about the 'Dresdeners' who made fortunes from illicit commercial operations in those years, and the thousands of Vietnamese ex-students and workers still living in the old rust-belt towns of the former COMECON states, now often targetted by racist gangs and ultra-nationalist groups as 'illegals' living on the margins of the law.

These 'expert' agreements are still hailed in Vietnam as proud achievements of socialist humanitarianism.[7] But they too have been sources of much-needed remittances, both for the state and for the individuals taking part. What is striking about the 'expert' schemes is that they served to transform members of one former colonial society's intelligentsia into agents of developmentalism in other 'postcolonies'. This made the country's intellectuals key agents of its projection outward into the life of the wider socialist ecumene. The embracing of that distinctive translocality is much spoken of as a necessity for all sharers in

---

[4] Hardy 2000; Raendchen 2000.

[5] Rosenthal reports (2002: 118) that the managers were almost all male in the state-owned Vietnamese factory where she did her fieldwork.

[6] Brno is the Czech Republic's second largest city; like other central European towns, it is still home to many expatriate Vietnamese.

[7] 'To the Algerian people, the two words "Viet Nam" bring wonder' (Voi nguoi dan Algeria, hai tieng "Viet Nam" that huyen dieu'), *Quoc Te* online 2003 Special Supplement 'Vietnam-Africa', available at www.mofa.gov.vn/quocte/africa03/ALGERIA. Similar co-operation agreement which involved the drafting of Vietnamese irrigation experts for specialist work in Iraq in 1990 was aborted at the start of the first Gulf War in January 1991.

that wider world of socialist 'friendships' (*quan he huu nghi*) as extolled by national leaders speaking of their states and peoples as interacting in a spirit of benevolence and dedication to common moral goals. Throughout the years of its two resistance wars, the DRV ('North Vietnam') was tied to China and the USSR through bonds which were ostensibly fraternal yet often deeply fraught. So as for other smaller socialist powers, it was important for the country's spokesmen to be able to represent the socialist ecumene as comprising a much wider array of cross-cutting mutualities than those between individual socialist states and any single Communist superpower. The work of 'experts' as aid-bringers to that array of other leftist 'friendship' partners therefore played a critical role in establishing Vietnam's credentials as a major architect of that wider socialist world, rather than a mere client of the bigger, richer Communist states.

Both in official accounts and my informants' personal narratives, *chuyen gia* work is spoken of as an act of disinterested benevolence, a gift of tutelage and enlightenment given freely and without expectation of return to the peoples of 'needy' and 'undeveloped' countries. The term for such gifts in Vietnamese is *tang* (or *qua tang*), this being a general word for things given which is used in compound words denoting charitable contribution (*tang vat*) and awards or prizes (*tang pham*).[8] Yet the situation of the Hanoi 'experts' was challenging and often painful. Those who have done such work know that they have sometimes been derided and envied, even though officially they are selfless givers imbued with the distinctive qualities of which President Ho Chi Minh was the perfect exemplar. These are the qualities of 'feeling' (*chan tinh*) and 'heart'. The term for this is *long*, which can mean both true sentiment and the bodily seat of sensibility, i.e. the heart or 'guts', as in other Asian contexts.[9] It is one's qualities of 'heart' from which come the inspiration and moral commitment to endure the privations and sacrifices entailed in bringing the gifts of socialist modernity to distant, needy lands.

---

[8] The word for items given by juniors to seniors and superiors is *bieu*. This is the word for respectful offerings made as a gesture of deference to senior relations or such people as workplace superiors. One could also use *dang*: this is a semi-archaic term for presents given in situations of very great deference, especially by subjects to their rulers: a loving birthday gift made to President Ho Chi Minh would be described as *dang*.

[9] See Marr 2000: 771. Compare Parish 1991: 316–20. Someone offering a gift as part of the process of asking a favour might refer to the item as *qua que*. Use of the term *que*, which means ancestral village or simply rustic or rural, implies 'just a little something', i.e. a thing from one's own garden or homeplace without material value, a token of one's sentiment and good feeling for someone, for which the term would be *tinh cam* (Rydstrøm 2003: 51–2).

Yet this uttering of public praise for the former *chuyen gia* experts is a recent development in Hanoi life. As I explain below, the reasons why this form of service has had such an uncertain place in the national narrative relate to the other key dimension of 'expert' service overseas. This is its critical importance to the 'experts' as a means of providing materially for their families through participation in a world of long-distance 'grey-economy' trading operations. These are difficult matters for my informants, raising complex questions about the extent to which their elders' experiences of a moralised marketplace in wartime could provide a legitimating model for their new lives in the post-war socialist ecumene. To understand these experiences, it is necessary to see that former colonial subjects may come to live lives of very great diversity, negotiating encounters which go far beyond the 'hybridised' self–other relationships of coloniser and colonised. It is necessary too to take note of the affective side of these exchanges, and in particular the power of familial emotion, and the assertion of moral claims about love, nurture and mutuality as presences in both official and personal accounts of these interactions.

Throughout the post-liberation period and continuing through to the present era of *doi moi* ('renovation') and 'market socialism', the distinction between giving and receiving as understood by those who have taken part in the wide-ranging 'friendship' relations of the socialist world system has been a prevailing theme in many areas of Vietnamese life. This includes both official and personal discussions of the work done by Hanoi academics, scientists and technical specialists as remittance-earners and socialist civilisers in Africa's formerly French- and Portuguese-ruled 'postcolonies'.

Thus post-independence Vietnam's need for educated people with the skills and knowledge to deal with foreigners from a host of problematic places, including the richer and more powerful socialist states as well as countries very much further afield, has presented many challenges to my informants, and to the country at large. These dilemmas relate in particular to the purposes for which both states and individuals may be called upon to engage with one another through the deployment of cultural capital, especially when that capital involves linguistic and other knowledge deriving from 'élitist' sources, and in particular from the colonial past.[10]

---

[10] For an account of the often problematic valuations assigned to the acquired cultural capital of Viet Kieu (overseas Vietnamese, i.e. former refugees and other expatriates) recruited as business professionals in the post-'renovation' period, see Carruthers 2002; and compare Ong 1999.

My key concern here is with the ways in which acts of acquisition, exchange and provisioning in these farflung transnational settings have been described and reflected on in individual and public narratives of the socialist world system's ramifying 'friendship' relations. In exploring these narratives I draw on anthropologists' understandings of gift-giving and exchange relations, especially the key distinction made in studies of the kind of gift-giving that has been recognised by ethnographers of *guanxi* (social relations/connection practices) in China. This includes giving that is directed upwards and confers honour on the recipient, and also the type more widely portrayed in anthropology involving gifts that flow downwards, pressurising recipients by demeaning them unless or until they can reciprocate appropriately.[11]

Receiving development aid is demeaning in precisely these terms, as it defines the taker as too poor ever to give in reciprocation. Hence the importance of the gifts of modernity which Vietnam has been able to impart to its African 'friendship' partners, these standing in sharp contrast to the 'interested', corrupting practices of the capitalist world, as in capitalist states' giving of development aid to poor 'Third World' countries. For Vietnamese and other socialists, these aid donors' gifts are not bestowed in token of true 'friendship' and beneficent mutuality. I therefore focus in particular on the ways in which a language of emotion and feeling and the invocation of an ideal of revolutionary neo-tradition have pervaded both personal and official attempts to represent those Vietnamese who were involved in these socialist 'friendship' relations as beneficent providers rather than humble receivers of the empowering tokens of socialist modernity.[12]

There are questions here too about the distinctions made in both official and personal accounts between those who perform commercial transactions for meritorious national purposes, and those for whom the benefits of such exchanges translate into the immoral trading of cultural assets for personal enrichment or familial advantage. This in turn raises the dangerous question of whether as a country made officially classless under socialism, Vietnam's colonial past had equipped certain people – those of formerly francophone intelligentsia background – to do better than others in gaining access to the good things on offer in the new

---

[11] On *guanxi*, see Smart 1993; Yang 1994; Kipnis 1996; Yan 1996b. Gold identifies emotional qualities including empathy, delicacy and finesse as important components in successful *guanxi* relations (1985: 660–1).

[12] The idea of socialist and revolutionary traditions and neo-traditions is explored from a variety of perspectives in my own and other contributors' chapters in West and Raman (forthcoming).

socialist world system: superior schooling, overseas study sojourns, desirable accommodation, prestigious career moves.

Returning from the interzones

At an early stage in my Hanoi fieldwork, I asked a number of my friends to tell me what they recalled about leaving the interzones at the end of the anti-French liberation war. Once again, Dr Tran spoke of his father, and as on other occasions his story focused on the giving and receiving of nurture and feeling. The context of this *fin-de-guerre* experience was another of those connecting the intimacies of home and family life with the wider arenas in which sophisticated knowledge and habituations were to be attained and mastered. 'I was at school one day. We knew the war had ended. Our teacher had told us about Dien Bien Phu [the great battle in 1954 which ended the anti-French war with an overwhelming victory for the Viet Minh]. It was raining. I had not seen my father for many weeks, and he came to my school. He had a bicycle.' This was rare: few civilians other than senior officials had their own transport in those days. Off they went, he said, in the rain, the two of them sharing the bike. 'It was a long ride. But we did not stop. I was so happy. We were going to Ninh Binh.'

This was the great moment for Tran: for the first time in nine years he was able to cross the former interzone frontier. His father was taking him to the nearest town in what had been French-controlled territory. This was where he saw electric lights and paved streets for the first time since leaving Hanoi in 1946. Both of them were muddy from their ride, he said. But to his delight, there was a treat in store: lunch at a Chinese-run restaurant. 'Pour nous, en ce temps-la, la cuisine chinoise, les préparations chinoises: on pense riche, gras, pour les occasions festives et exceptionnelles'. (For us in those days, Chinese cookery, Chinese dishes, we thought of them as rich, fatty, for happy, special occasions.) There had been nothing like this in the interzones, he said, describing the mannerly but commanding way in which his father conducted himself, knowing just what to order and how to override the proprietor's initial disdain at their dishevelled appearance.

As on other occasions I was struck by Dr Tran's pride in his father's social competence, his savoir-faire recalled as a quality befitting a revolutionary with challenging tasks to perform on behalf of kin and homeland. It is significant too that Dr Tran remembers the restaurant owner as a Sino-Vietnamese. Of the fifty-four officially designated *dan toc* (ethnies or peoples of the national family), until recently the Hoa or Chinese-descended Vietnamese were assigned a problematic place in the national narrative. This is still a matter of great sensitivity, as it relates to a history of Soviet-style ethnic stereotyping defining the Hoa as descendants of relatively recent incomers who had not been part of the great story of enduring resistance to foreign invaders dating back to ancient times.[13] These stereotypes represented the Hoa as a people predisposed to seditious political allegiances. They were also supposed to be inherently given to the kind of predatory parasitical capitalism which the DRV propaganda messages said was the practice of foreigners and their local collaborators, but not of the Vietnamese petty traders whose circulation of modest necessities was beneficent and unexploitative. Even Sino/Hoa food was different, something appropriate for a moment of special indulgence, but decidedly unlike the sparing and delicate staples of the 'ethnic majority' Viet (*Kinh*) kitchen.

Clearly, then, there was something of an edge in that account of Dr Tran's father putting the *restaurateur* in his place. As a supply specialist, his father's key mission for the DRV was to obtain strategic items from a variety of providers, including the notoriously corrupt nationalist Chinese whose unruly soldiery I mentioned earlier. Of course the establishment of the Chinese People's Republic in 1949 accelerated the processes of remapping through which the Viet Minh had proclaimed the authenticity of Vietnam's new existence as a socialist proto-state, its geography and diplomatic life defined by its people's own initiatives, rather than those of their colonisers. Yet despite China's new identity as a socialist 'friend' and provider, deep anxieties remained about the extent to which Vietnam could establish itself as something other than a humble suppliant and unreciprocating taker of largesse from 'Elder Sister China' (*Chi Hai Trung Quoc*) in the form of resources, military aid and even sites of schooling for its new socialist intelligentsia.

China is always Vietnam's elder sister in slogans and other invocations of socialist familiality, while until the end of Soviet Communism in 1989, the USSR was always 'Elder Brother' (*Anh Ca Lien Xo*). These questions about the inequalities of socialist exchange relations are still matters of great concern, if anything even more so now that the former aid routes have been given over to the massive export trades currently flooding Vietnam's northern markets with the cheap electronic items

---

[13] Chang 1982; Keyes 2002; compare Hirsch 2005. The Hoa were even debarred from military service until 1986 (Keyes 2002: 1192). The memory of repeated victories over Chinese invasion forces in past centuries has been a critical reference point in the shaping of Vietnamese nationalist ideologies since at least the early twentieth century. See Henley 1995.

and other Chinese-made consumer goods which have become the core of a new imbalance in the nominally equal relations of the two socialist 'sisters'.[14]

A few weeks after Dr Tran's cycle ride to Ninh Binh, the whole family made the journey back to Hanoi, stopping for a time at the bigger town of Nam Dinh on the way. We visited the same town together so I could meet one of his former interzone teachers, a vigorous 85-year old who was still fluently francophone and warmly welcoming on a cold December night. It was there that Dr Tran saw his first cinema film, the 1949 Hollywood epic *Samson and Delilah*. 'That was after Geneva', he said, meaning the 1954 international accords which partitioned Vietnam at the 17th Parallel, this being the first critical step in the sequence of events leading to the 1961–75 war between the DRV and the US-backed RVN (Republic of South Vietnam) regime.

Dien Bien Phu and 'Geneva' are important time markers in my informants' accounts of returning 'from the forest'.[15] To evoke the great victory at Dien Bien Phu is to conjure up images of a triumph enacted on home soil by the nation and its leaders. Citizens are still regularly enjoined to live their lives in the selfless spirit of Dien Bien Phu. Such messages are not received uncritically, but the battle is regularly brought into conversation as a matter of interest and family pride: '*Chi* [Miss/ Sister] Susan, you must meet my father's elder brother; he was at Dien Bien Phu.' 'This is my father's friend Mr Hung; he was with General Giap in the battle. He was wounded there.'

At school, my friends were told that Dien Bien Phu was a great world event, and that like the DRV's citizen soldiers, they too were under the gaze of others for whom the battle was a landmark and inspiration. Those who have worked overseas have mentioned encounters with people who spoke of Dien Bien Phu as an achievement admired by all the world. 'They had feeling (*long*) for us', said a retired nurse who had been an 'expert' in Algeria. I had asked whether she made friends during her posting; she replied by mentioning local people who had said such things to her as 'We know about Dien Bien Phu; we admire what you did; you fought the French like us'.

---

[14] Vietnam is still primarily an exporter of agricultural produce and semi-skilled labour to China, and the high-profit industrial products which it receives in exchange provide a painful demonstration of 'Elder Sister''s apparently more effective growth strategies. See Womack 1994 and 2006; Beresford and Dang Phong 2000: Ch. 10.

[15] The other defining event by which people date personal experience is the 'liberation' of the south, and specifically the occupation of Saigon by People's Liberation forces in April 1975. See Bayly 2004a: 332–3.

At a personal level, Dien Bien Phu carries associations of the war's end, and the much-reproduced images of Hanoi on liberation day: the last French soldiers departing, the incoming DRV troops welcomed by jubilant crowds.[16] My older friends speak of 'after Dien Bien Phu' as a time of decisive movement, of people setting out for their long-unseen homes in a land made whole again, the 'occupied' territories united with the former interzones. Of course that moment of wholeness was soon expunged. In Vietnam, the cease-fire accord signed at Geneva is still recalled as a shameful dismemberment brokered by foreigners in a distant land. So this was a partition experience engendering voiced and unvoiced subjectivities comparable to those of other divided states, especially the traumatising 'critical events' of India's partition in 1947. Indian women who were forced into marriage or concubinage as partition 'abductees' have been widely represented as troubling embodiments of a fallen nation's dishonour. Their closest equivalent are Vietnamese women who had liaisons with enemy soldiers in the two liberation wars. When these involved black soldiers in French or American uniform, the consequences for the women and their families were particularly grim and stigmatising.[17]

'After Geneva' thus evokes that darker side of the *après-guerre*, its losses and separations, its families divided by divergent political allegiances, or

---

[16] My friends took much interest in the vivid images of the city's liberation (*Ngay Tiep Quan* or 'Takeover Day') produced by the veteran photographer Nguyen Duy Kien. These and other selections from the work of this pioneering Hanoi *tri thuc* photojournalist were published with the co-operation of his widow, a *lycée*-educated Hanoi teacher, in a memorial tribute volume released in 2006 (Duong Trung Quoc 2006: 95–8).

[17] As I noted in Chapter 2, I am aware that the 1954 division of Vietnam at the 17th Parallel was not intended as a permanent partition involving the creation of two separate states. Nevertheless, in the intensity of its personal consequences and powerfully expressed official narrativisations, it does invite comparison with the cases of Palestine, Germany, Korea and Cyprus. See Borneman 1995; Svasek 2002; Swedenberg 2003; Navaro-Yashin 2005 and 2007; Greenberg 2005; for India, see Das 1995; Butalia 1998; Menon and Bhasin 1998. There are striking contrasts as well as parallels with the case of south Asian 'abductees' in the DRV's decision to repatriate former colonial soldiers from Morocco who had remained in Vietnam after 1954. Some had been captured by the Viet Minh; others claimed to be defectors who had joined the DRV forces in a spirit of anti-imperialist solidarity. Many had local wives or partners and children; they too were 'repatriated', often unwillingly, such people clearly being hard to assimilate into the national family, even when their children had become achieving participants in the DRV's post-war modernisation projects. See Delanoë (2002), an oral history in which the daughter of one such 'repatriated' family describes the anguish she felt when her father destroyed her Vietnamese books and school prize certificates. He feared that if spotted, these treasures with their state emblems featuring the hammer and sickle would brand them all as subversives in the eyes of the fiercely anti-Communist Moroccan authorities.

tainted by accusations of *Viet gian* (traitor) or 'bad class' antecedents. My informants speak of 'Geneva' as a moment of hope deferred, an evocation of the distress of those who found old friends and comrades joining the great migration to the south, or even fleeing abroad to resettle in France or other foreign lands. Families throughout Vietnam were painfully divided by this process. Yet as I noted in relation to the 1976 mother–son reunion picture, the commanding public imagery of this division is of families parted not by malign or unpatriotic acts, but by the virtuous deeds of soldiers and other heroes, the nation a family united by its heartfelt yearning for the great redeeming moment of reunification.[18]

The other great theme of people's post-liberation memories is of continuing mobility through socialist space. No-one I know led a sedentary, home-based life in the years following 'Geneva'. Those initial frontier crossings and homeward journeys involved poignant reunions and home-comings. Yet for many, these were a prelude to further movements and separations, including long periods of military service in the wars against the USA, Cambodia and China. Others had long sojourns in the rural relocation sites to which their universities or ministry research units were evacuated during the anti-US war. These too were experiences involving discovery of a rural heartland, and the shaping on home soil of something much like the domesticated socialist ecumene forged by India's IAS (Indian Administrative Service) modernisers. But the challenges involved in being a giver and receiver of modernising cultural capital were even greater for those of my informants who became recruits to that great international army of 'experts' (*chuyen gia*) who plied the far-flung spaces of the post-war socialist world system.[19]

[18] As in the Indian subcontinent, it appears that imaginings of Korea's division in 1945 have had a very different thrust. Here too the sufferings of women are emphasised, but according to Jager (1996) the focus has been on idealised wives and mothers for whom healing may one day come through the joy of families and homeland made one again. Korea even has a romantic neo-Confucian literary canon containing works comparable to Vietnam's *Tale of Kieu*. These too, Jager shows, are stories of the cruel fate befalling wronged female protagonists who endure separation from home and kin. Such works have recently been made the focus of daring new readings in which dissident members of South Korea's intelligentsia have explored the dangerous issue of a possible reconciliation with their own society's lost 'other', Communist-ruled North Korea. On familial loss themes in Chinese representations of the long-standing PRC goal of reunification with Taiwan, see Stafford 2000: 28–9.

[19] Among the early intelligentsia participants in the plying of those worldwide socialist spaces were members of cultural delegations sent to exhibit films produced by the DRV's newly established cinema studios at competitions in such places as Moscow, Jakarta and Karlovy Vary (Carlsbad) in Czechoslovakia. In the 1950s much pride was taken in awards won at these festivals for documentaries celebrating the country's epic

Mr Can was the first of these Hanoi globetrotters who spoke to me at length about his *chuyen gia* experiences. I met him through a friend whose father, a Hanoi academic, had known him when they had worked together in the 1950s. He was in his early nineties when I met him in 2002 in his tiny, book-filled flat. He too spoke fluent French and was tirelessly articulate over many long hours of conversation, dressing with care and elegance during our chilly winter discussion sessions. During the anti-French war, he had served as a Viet Minh political officer. He came from a village near Ha Dong in the Red River delta; his family had been too poor to aspire to a *lycée* education for their gifted son. So as a young man in the 1930s, he became an auto-didact, polishing his French from a much-thumbed copy of the *Dictionnaire Larousse*.

At eighteen, Mr Can became resident tutor to a rich family; he wryly recalls that their son never thanked him for ensuring his success in the *lycée* entrance examinations. By the late 1930s, he had taken a route followed by many people of similar background: from village tutor to petty *fonctionnaire* in Hanoi, then recruitment as a teacher by the semi-secret network of Communist-run literacy classes for urban workers, and then into the Party itself. This led to wartime service in the Viet Minh's military mass literacy initiative; his parents and all his siblings also 'went to the forest'. After liberation he remained in government service. His knowledge of French qualified him to be sent in 1965 to serve as cultural attaché in Guinea, one of the key African socialist countries with which Vietnam was establishing diplomatic and strategic links in the early stages of the USA–Vietnam war. He was the man who told me the story of the memorable moment when '*Bac Ho*', President Ho Chi Minh, vested him with the mission of serving the nation in faraway Conakry.[20]

It was of course the abolition of French in teaching and government that gave Mr Can's language skills their value as cultural capital for the new revolutionary nation. In the early post-liberation years, the deployment of French-speakers for such purposes as overseas delegation and diplomatic work took place on the kind of ad hoc and individualised basis which Mr Can experienced. A major change occurred in the wake of

acts of developmental achievement in fields such as education and drought relief (Pham Ngoc Truong and Trung Son 1987: 14–15).

[20] This was a period when the DRV was becoming increasingly involved in networks of both covert and open diplomatic interaction with some of the key states of the Non-Aligned Movement, and with others whose governments had positioned their countries outside the two Cold War power blocs. Guinea embraced state socialism following independence in 1958 and became an early supporter of the DRV.

reunification, when recruitment of French-speakers became a matter of official policy. Central to the experiences of many Hanoi intellectuals is the fact that in the 1980s and early 90s, this entailed a systematic revival of French language teaching. Its purpose was to underpin the remittance-earning 'expert' schemes through which Vietnam was able to show the wider socialist world that its citizens were fully equipped to bring the gifts of scientific and technical modernity to hitherto 'undeveloped' lands.

Taking enlightened possession

Mr Can's accounts of the post-liberation period focus on moments when he felt himself to be a key actor in the securing of that new modernity within the DRV. This is apparent in the experiences he described when I asked about his memories of the period immediately after Dien Bien Phu in 1954. All were encounters involving the claiming of spaces which the French had proclaimed as critical arenas of their much-vaunted *mission civilisatrice*. This 'civilising mission' has been widely seen as an exercise in one-sided cultural gift-giving of a kind definitive of the demeaningly unequal exchange relations of colonialism.[21] It is therefore notable that Mr Can tells his end of the war story as an account of a dedicated 'modern' ensuring that the nation's cultural capital is placed in the hands of those to whom it rightfully belonged.

A week after the announcement of the Dien Bien Phu victory, Mr Can said he was assigned a series of handover duties along a route taking him from the frontier of Interzone IV to the northern port city of Haiphong. He recalls that there were other cadres dealing with such sites as police stations, banks and government offices. His task was to take official possession of libraries, schools, and sports grounds. 'Pour moi: les écoles, le sport, les choses de culture – on dit ca, et je comprends bien: pour les jeunes, pour tout le monde.' (For me [my job]: the schools, sport, cultural things. I was told, and I understood very well: for the young people, for all our people.)

Locks, keys and the throwing open of barred and shuttered spaces featured in his account. But these were not stories of Bastilles forced open, or the unseating of oppressive disciplinary modernisms. On the contrary: they are proudly positive accounts of a liberated land coming into its own. An episode he recounted repeatedly, savouring the details and adding new embellishments, turned on his arrival in a village near

---

[21] Comaroff 1998; Mani 1998; Clancy Smith and Gouda 1998; Cumming 2005; Conklin 1997.

Hanoi to take possession of its modest *bibliothèque populaire*. This was not a Vietnamese equivalent of the Indian manuscript libraries and seats of traditional Sanskrit learning (*pathsalas*) often targetted at times of intercommunal tension.[22] Its holdings were 'modern': books and newspapers in French and *quoc ngu* (romanised Vietnamese).[23]

Mr Can said he found the building in the custody of a frightened young French officer and a Vietnamese caretaker. The caretaker had the keys and tried to hand them over. 'J'ai dit: non, Monsieur – donnez-les lui.' (I said no, Monsieur [to the caretaker]; give them to him – [meaning the Frenchman].) What this achieved, he explained, was to ensure that as the nation's representative he took possession directly from the hand of the defeated enemy.

This was an encounter in which the possibility of humanising warmth and sociality was strictly curtailed: rigid, unsmiling formality towards the Frenchman; respectful warmth towards the elderly custodian. He said he addressed only one terse sentence to the young officer, proud that he could do so in accurate French: 'Vous m'avez renvoyé notre clef.' (You have returned our key to me.) It is thus a story of wrongs righted, bullies humbled and misapproprated power cast down by a sternly righteous victor. There was no violence; it was a moment of power made all the more effective for being exercised with discipline and restraint, in defiance of the French authorities' stereotypes of the Viet Minh as uncivilised fanatics, burners of books and desecrators of churches. As Mr Can tells the story, he was the one taking the initiative as the embodiment of a sovereign people now come of age. He was the figure of power; the nameless Frenchman a humbled boy. And by

---

[22] As in the case of the burning in 2002 of Pune's Bhandarkar Oriental Research Institute by a regional anti-Brahman organisation with an ideology much like south India's Dravidian chauvinist organisations; their claim had been that its Sanskrit and Pali manuscripts had been used by an American scholar who had defamed their culture hero, the seventeenth-century ruler Shivaji.

[23] The library and its attached reading room were typical of those the French authorities had established in many parts of the empire in the 1940s, seeking to show that under the pro-Axis wartime Vichy administration, France had become an enlightened coloniser, committed to its subjects' cultural advancement. On the Vichy colonial administration's blend of neo-traditionalism and modernist cultural policies, see Raffin 2005. While these libraries were thought of as places of basic information and education for 'the masses', precisely as outlined in the New Life/New Culture schemes (Dang Phong 2002; Malarney 2002), it is notable that many places of 'traditional' importance have played a key role in official accounts of the revolution. Many of these have been represented as sites of remembered resistance; other treasures of the nation's cultural heritage, including Hanoi's One-Pillar pagoda and the imperial palace at Hue, have been given prominence in the country's decolonisation story as historic national monuments maliciously despoiled by the defeated French.

ensuring that there was no conversational exchange between them, he stopped the moment of appropriation from becoming an act of gift-giving, whether of the kind described by anthropologists as establishing a largesse-giver's lordly superiority, or in the form that confirms relations of mutuality and 'heart-felt' beneficence between giver and receiver. Either would have demeaned both him and the nation. Having established that the keys were the nation's to take and not the Frenchman's to give, there could then be a true 'gift of the heart', made in a spirit of loving mutuality. This was the transfer of the library to the nation by Mr Can, a francophone cadre using his knowledge and skill for the benefit of his fellow citizens.

There are keys in Mr Can's other stories too, notably one about a comrade taking possession of the keys to Hanoi's Ecole Normale from its departing French director. This too was one of the nation's treasures; it was right to feel joy and pride in having secured rightful possession of the tools of reason and science on its behalf. For Mr Can, as for my friend Dr Tran, these are matters of the heart as well as the intellect. None of my friends express any doubts about the value of such places as libraries, museums and universities, whether founded under French rule or more recently, or have suggested that their knowledge systems are too foreign to be used and valued in Vietnam. The view they share is that Vietnamese have the will and insight to be selective in their appropriation of these universals, and to do so without losing confidence in their own forms of thought and knowledge, recognising that such things as their traditional medical lore are products of borrowings and adaptations from a host of external sources, including China (Thompson 2003). What is wrong and illegitimate in their view have been the claims made by Frenchmen, and even by some fellow socialists, that there are forms of learning and scientific achievement which are exclusively theirs to possess or impart.

For my ex-*chuyen gia* friends the issue of sharing and contributing on the world stage is of great significance. When Vietnamese took possession of the country's French-built libraries, schools and hospitals, all that they embodied in the form of beneficial and empowering knowledge became cultural capital to be shared with the wider world. Through these acts of mastery, state and people were equipped to become socialist gift-givers to those in need in all the places to which they went as aid-bringers and technical experts. On this point the affective significance of such cultural capital has come across very strongly in my friends' accounts, the socialist ecumene being an arena constructed as much through affective interactions and meanings of the heart as through the instrumental operations which underpinned them.

Yet the post-'Geneva' years were testing times for my informants. No-one I know was accompanied by wives and children when they took an overseas posting, and for everyone the long separations were painful to endure. Unlike those who served overseas from the 1980s onwards, Mr Can had no home leave during his stay and did not see his family until his five-year posting came to an end. There were other anxieties too in the post-liberation years. Few of my friends have spoken at length about the 1950s Land Reform campaigns, though as I have already noted, a few people have told me about the ordeals and insecurities of those times. But their comments about less dramatic everyday things do convey something of the flavour of that revolutionary 'egalitarian moment' (Low 1996).

One friend said that when she was a child in the 1980s, her *lycée*-educated grandmother had expressed mixed feelings to her about the new linguistic conventions which came into use from the 1950s onwards. These included moves which are spoken of as sound and beneficial, with people noting for example that President Ho Chi Minh had called on those in authority to use simple, accessible expressions in their speech and writing. Pruning out archaicisms and helping to make Vietnamese an effective tool of modern teaching and public communication was a good and worthy task, people say, and one in which Hanoians of their own intelligentsia background had taken a leading role.

Yet it was not easy, my friend Ms Huong said, for women of her grandmother's age and background to accustom themselves to the personal aspects of these changes, especially the shifts in address terms which came into use in the 1950s. The new pronoun etiquette was far from being a thoroughgoing Chinese-style proletarianisation of the language, and people were not expected to do without the relational hierarchy terms which still structure everyday speech and writing. But what was unsettling and difficult was that the ideal prescribed for interactions outside the home and family circle struck at the refinements that typified the speech of intelligentsia families. The established usage *Ba*, meaning a woman senior to one's parents and used much like *Madame* in French, ceased to be acceptable as the proper address for a married woman by her juniors. My friend said that for her grandmother, it had been a struggle not to show distress when non-kin called her *Chi* (elder sister) rather than *Ba*.[24]

---

[24] Mastery of good Vietnamese was a post-liberation educational priority, though when the Vietnamese literary classics were taught in the schools, students were taught to make a clear distinction between the flowery, refined vocabulary that was appropriate for poetic use, and the more direct, modern, conversational usages that people were expected to

These and other novelties were part of the great transformation of behavioural norms which had begun in the interzones and was now projecting the whole country into its new life as a sharer in the conventions and solidarities of the wider socialist world.[25] The presence in Vietnam of foreign 'friends' from other lands was a key part of that new life. People mention these Russians and other incomers as a source of compelling interest, especially for the young, though in recalling this they describe attitudes that were far from naively wondering or deferential. In post-liberation Hanoi, people of foreign appearance glimpsed on the streets or on public platforms were assumed to be either 'Soviets' (*Lien Xo*) or Chinese (*Trung Quoc*). As children in the 1970s and 80s many Hanoians knew a comic schoolyard verse about these foreign 'friends'. In its nonsense couplets, 'Mr Soviet' and 'Mrs China' (the pronouns used being those for elders older than one's parents) do everyday things – including modern things like eating icecream and wearing Western shoes – in an upside-down manner with comically indelicate overtones. 'They never knew', said the friend who recited it for me, referring to the passing foreign experts blissfully unaware of the gazing schoolchildren giggling at its verses:

> *Ong Lien Xo*
> *Ong di guoc*
> Mr Soviet
> He is wearing sandals

> *Ba Trung Quoc*
> *Ba di giay*
> Mrs China
> She is wearing a pair of shoes

> *Ong nhay day*
> *Ba da bong*
> He is playing with a skipping rope
> She is playing football

> *Ong di tam*
> *Ba dung xem*
> He is taking a shower
> She is watching

> *Ong an kem*
> *Ba uong nuoc*

employ in everyday contexts. On pronoun etiquette, see Hy Van Luong 1988 and 1990; speakers take a third party's referential perspective towards the person addressed (Malarney 2002: 34; Rydstrøm 2003: 60–7).

[25] For Vietnam, see Malarney 2002; for other socialist contexts, see Humphrey 2002.

He is eating icecream
She is drinking water.

But what people have also made clear, sometimes explicitly though more often by inference and allusion, is that while the socialist ecumene is supposed to be a world of harmoniously interacting equals, there were difficult nuances to master for those most exposed to scrutiny in its cosmopolitan arenas. In particular, there were real dangers for those of *tri thuc* intelligentsia background who evinced too much urbane, supralocal knowledge, especially when they showed too plainly how much more congenial they found the credential-revering Soviet version of socialist modernity than its levelling, Maoist counterpart. The great difficulty from the period of liberation in the 1950s to the early *doi moi* 'marketisation' era was that Vietnam needed the support of both socialist superpowers. Especially during the anti-US war, the DRV had to steer a middle course between the two, while trying to avoid taking on the humiliating *persona* of a poor suppliant or client, forever beholden to bigger, richer benefactors.

People of the urban intelligentsia world were vulnerable as well as important to this process. The *tri thuc* 'moderns' were of undeniable value as source and conduit for the special kinds of productive cultural capital which Vietnam was seeking to deploy both at home and overseas. Yet they were also possessors of things and knowledge that could look dangerously out of step with that delicate balancing act between the country's two great socialist providers.

My intelligentsia friends say they all knew that many of the new features of post-liberation life were derived from Chinese models, and that in the early years of the DRV even their currency and official documents were printed in China. But they also like to point out that the conventions of Chinese socialist life were not embraced unquestioningly, and that in this as in so much else, Vietnamese were selective and discerning. Those of my friends who are old enough can still sing the Chinese Party anthems which they learned at school or as youth group chorale members. 'No-one knew what they meant', one man said; they were learned phonetically, neither imbibed as doctrine nor cherished like the Vietnamese songs and poems which they cite and quote.

People also like to represent themselves as having made their own sense of the new political vocabulary that came into use in this period, and which even very young people know to be of Chinese derivation. As Hy Van Luong has shown, in the DRV the Vietnamese version of that most characteristic of socialist appellations, *dong chi* (comrade, from Chinese *tongzhi*) rapidly became a term of deference used by citizens in addressing party officials and other authority figures.[26] My friends have confirmed that they too do not think of *dong chi* as an equaliser overriding the everyday conventions of elder–younger/junior–senior terminology. A student friend said, 'I know they use it that way in China'; in Vietnam, it would be out of place in anything but formal situations such as end-of-year meetings in schools and workplaces and major national occasions.

I asked about teachers: they are never 'comrade' either, always *co* (a relational term best translated as Aunty or Miss) for women and *thay* (Master) for men. A woman academic in her fifties told me that nowadays *dong chi* has mildly comical connotations for her. She said a woman might use it as a jocular way to address her husband, agreeing with my suggestion that this would be like the teasing use of 'master' or 'my lord' by a British or American wife. An older acquaintance recalled press coverage of the death of a senior official in the early 1980s, well before 'renovation' (*doi moi*). He had found it distasteful that in her funeral speech, the dead man's widow – also a Party member – had referred to her deceased husband as *dong chi*. This had been heartless, he said, *vo tinh*. It was a time when human feeling should have overridden the claims of state and Party. Even a high-ranking public figure should be lovingly referred to by the appropriate relational term at such a moment: wives and husbands are normally *em* and *anh* to one another.[27]

In this as in much else that my friends said about the post-liberation period, there was a continuing concern with the pressure they have felt to engage both critically and creditably with these comportment regimens. And for those of intelligentsia background, there was the anxiety of knowing that their behaviour might be judged by others as driven by narrowly familial sentiment, hence improperly attuned to the affective claims and standards of the new socialist order.

It was in the schoolroom that such lessons could be most painfully learned. Few of my older friends have told me anything other than nostalgically upbeat stories about their interzone schooldays. But for younger people who had their schooling in post-liberation Hanoi, the morality of the socialist schoolroom could be dauntingly severe. In the DRV, the brightly lit modern schoolroom was widely represented as a critical arena for the forging of the new nation. Thus while the family too was at least potentially a seat of progressive values and experiences, the

---

[26] See Hy Van Luong 1988: 248; 1992: 185. For China, see Gold 1985: 671.

[27] This has familial connotations of a same-generation pairing which in this case identifies the girl or woman as the junior.

young needed the experience of life in the wider world – in schools and youth groups, and then in military service and possibly work and travel overseas – to ensure that they were not constrained and narrowed by identification with self and family. There were many slogans exhorting the young to study diligently, and to realise as they did so that their academic successes were a duty fulfilled for the collective good, not for their own or their families' gratification or advantage.[28]

Of course, academic achievement was strongly associated with filial bonds and duties. For children from intelligentsia families, there were clear expectations of disciplined work habits and attainment of credentials comparable to or even surpassing those of one's parents and distinguished forebears. Yet home values could sit uneasily with those imparted at school. My friend Ms Dao, whose scientist mother had studied in Moscow in the 1960s, told me about an unhappy day when she had been sent to her city centre infant school dressed in a way that made her stand out all too noticeably from her classmates. This was in the late 1970s when life in commodity-starved post-reunification Hanoi was particularly bleak, and official strictures against waste, display and 'individualist' self-indulgence both persistent and forceful. Her mother had tied her plaits with a brightly coloured bow made from glossy fabric brought home by a friend from an overseas study trip. She was also wearing a somewhat more elaborate home-made dress and sandals than those usually worn by Hanoi children.

Ms Dao said the teacher encouraged the other children to laugh at her, and told them to call her a bourgeoise (*trung luu*). She went home in tears. Although she had not understood the rude name she had been called, the story hit hard at home and has been retained as a family memory ever since. Even in the 1970s, a generation after the brief but bitter experiences of Chinese-style land reform persecutions, 'bad' or 'bourgeois' class background could debar an individual from many advantages including overseas study opportunities, and membership of the Party.[29] So even as a schoolroom taunt, the bourgeois label was hurtful and alarming. It implied a powerful challenge to the claim of intelligentsia families to be active sharers in the moral life of the nation and the wider socialist world, performing acts of familial care and nurture

---

[28] In areas where Provisional Committees claiming allegiance to Ho Chi Minh seized power following the 1945 August Revolution, Hy Van Luong's informants recall schoolchildren belonging to the mass youth organisation of the National Salvation Front (*Cuu Quoc*) being vested with key tasks in Viet Minh campaigns to eradicate gaming, shamanic worship and other 'evils' of village life (1992: 145).

[29] Hy Van Luong 1990; Papin 2001: 307–10; Malarney 2002.

as an exemplification for all, rather than as an accumulative strategy for the benefit of their kin and class allies.

So in the DRV as in China, intellectuals and their relations were vulnerable in the post-liberation years. While they were not subjected to sustained persecution on the scale of the Cultural Revolution, everyone knew that those labelled 'bourgeois' in the workplace could experience blocked promotions, demotion or dismissal. Student life brought these lessons home at an even earlier age. 'It was difficult for us', said one friend. She was referring to her university days in the 1980s, when she and her friends from intelligentsia families had been required to show mastery of the 1957 Le Duan speech disparaging intellectuals as deficient in the strength and will which characterised the 'masses', therefore prone to misdirect their qualities of heart and feeling towards narrowly 'familistic' ends.

What is also striking about Ms Dao's infant-school story is that she said her mother had intended to dress her in the style she identified with the bright-faced Soviet children she recalled seeing in their school uniforms in Moscow. They had pictures at home of such children, cut out of Russian magazines saved from her mother's Moscow student days. She had used their illustrations of Soviet children as a model. Ms Dao recalled the fascination of such publications, especially those encountered at the Culture Palace, their colour photography a compelling novelty in those days.

The problem, Ms Dao said, was not so much that she and her family appeared to possess luxuries that were beyond the means of others. In her childhood, many people owned items that were known to be far costlier than anything her family possessed. The quilted children's winterwear that so many factory workers brought home from their overseas labour stints was regarded approvingly if enviously by other Hanoians. And certainly no schoolchild should be shabby or unkempt. The DRV's citizens were regularly addressed on the topic of the health and grooming of the young (Malarney 2002; compare Rydstrøm 2003). All good modern families should send their children to school properly garbed, fit and fed, and well prepared for a life of public scrutiny within as well as beyond the socialist classroom. And while waste and vanity were certainly not condoned in those grim privation years, that vision of the fit and well-conducted child was an approving echo of what had been said by so many of the wider world's prophets of modernity about youth as the model and embodiment of human progress. It was a vision that also recalled a host of more specifically Vietnamese ideas about filial life and duty, with an emphasis on physical fitness, cleanliness and hygiene, as well as propriety and devotion to community, homeland and Party.

Adults too should take pains over the management of their appearance. To do less would have been unbefitting a socialist modern, and unworthy of the duties owed to kin and ancestors: it would be shameful for one's family to be seen by others as disordered or feckless. One's complexion mattered particularly. As a young married woman in the pre-independence period, Ms Dao's formidable grandmother had used face powder and other cosmetics of the kind worn by Chinese and Japanese 'new women', as had many of her *lycée*-educated contemporaries (Lee 1999: 93–5; Edwards 2000; Sato 2003). Traditionalists disapproved, but to Hanoi 'moderns' this was progressive rather than frivolous or 'feudal', bespeaking mastery of the techniques used by educated women in Tokyo and pre-revolutionary Shanghai to maintain the brightness of skin that was then as now a marker of health and wellbeing.

Ms Dao's mother has never worn cosmetics. Even if such things had been obtainable in post-liberation Hanoi, they would have been a real impropriety, all too redolent of that other Vietnam, the former RVN. Despite the official expressions of joy attending the 1976 reunification, southern ways and mores were regarded with much suspicion in the years that followed.[30] Even in the 1990s, Saigon in particular was still widely associated in the north with the flauntings of prostituted women corrupted by American money, American and Japanese consumer goods, and American immorality. All the same, Ms Dao said her mother taught her to take pains with her skin and grooming, even though she conformed to the self-consciously proletarian style favoured in the post-war era, dressing in a far more utilitarian manner than the stylish elders depicted in the family photo album.[31]

---

[30] All the more so since many northerners could recall the daring Hanoi youths in the wartime years who had affronted their elders by kitting themselves out in cautious imitations of Western-style bellbottoms and pop star haircuts. See K. Taylor's account of post-war campaigns against 'neo-colonial poisons' emanating from the south's urban consumerist lifestyles. (2001: Ch. 1)

[31] The Hanoi women I know protect their skin from the sun with hats, cotton face masks (*khau trang*) and arm-length gloves. Some use face-whitening creams and other manufactured cosmetics and toiletries, though often in combination with traditional herbal preparations. (See Fforde 2003: 53–5. Vietnamese are beginning to see commercial potential in these substances. I know a young business school graduate who believes there may be an international export market for the country's traditional skin and hair care products.) As Malarney shows (2002: 34), the 1950s Land Reform campaigners' violent attacks on rural élites led to the rapid abandonment of practices associated with 'feudal' privilege, including the wearing of garments associated with 'tradition' and class distinction. It was 'modern' rather than 'Western' to eschew the *ao dai* and corresponding respectable man's dress of turban, tunic and trousers (*ao thung*), and old-style shoes with upturned toes. Olive fatigues and sandals, the garb of the

So the real trouble for Ms Dao and her family was that in signalling enthusiasm for things Soviet, they were reminding others of her family's special cosmopolitanism, its experience of things and places to which few had access. Here of course there is a parallel with other socialist societies, especially Mao's China. The claim that a Hanoi intellectual's children are the undeserving beneficiaries of their elders' inherited social capital can be an anti-'élitist' smear, hence a way of differentiating between the virtues and simplicities of one's own people, the uncorrupted stay-at-home populace, and the unrepresentative minority, people of privilege. Although they may have impeccable revolutionary credentials, sophisticates who speak foreign languages and have knowledge of the wider world can be inherently suspect, even – indeed sometimes especially – when their work and study sojourns take them to other socialist countries. So even when China became temporarily an enemy state rather than a 'friend' at the time of the 1977–9 wars with China and Cambodia, Maoist-inspired ideas about the unearned privileges of intellectual élites were still current in Hanoi. Even a trivial style choice could suddenly take on a worrying public or political dimension, especially if one could be identified as an over-sophisticated lover of élitist Russian forms of socialist cosmopolitanism.[32]

I have encountered similar attitudes in other contexts: that is, an indication that in the post-independence years there was something questionable about evincing too much admiration for the accoutrements and lifestyles of other socialist societies, especially the richer European COMECON states. It was one thing for Vietnam to be a virtuous provider to needy backward nations, or even a recipient of valuable remittances from such friendly sources, or of training from the Soviets and their neighbours. But to embrace too heartily the modern tastes of foreigners – even fellow socialists – was to risk conveying that Vietnam was itself a site of uplift and tutelage, and not the maker of its own independently conceived and distinctive socialist modernities.

Yet as I show below, it was those same tastes and cultural competences which equipped my Hanoi friends to become precisely what was needed to try to dispel that humiliating image of a land too poor and backward to be anything but a recipient of other people's humbling acts

returning soldier, became a safely classless dress choice for rural people and are still common in the north Vietnamese countryside. Compare Unger 1998: 88, n. 14.

[32] Compare Humphrey 2004. For young Hanoi women now in their twenties and thirties, a common given name is Nga, which means Russia or Russian: this is always a girl's name and is always thought of as a name given to daughters by intelligentsia couples to evoke their happy student days in Moscow or other Soviet cities in the pre-*doi moi* era.

of provision and beneficence. I therefore turn now to the ways in which the 'experts' who served in Africa deployed those sensitive forms of cultural capital. They did so in two ways. One entailed their role in making official 'gifts of the heart' confirming Vietnam's standing as a senior and elder in the socialist ecumene. The other, paradoxically, required them to become proficient in the ways of capitalists as a means of serving the needs of their kin and, more latterly, those of their rapidly 'marketising' socialist homeland.

Serving and earning in Africa

Mr Can has told me that long after 'Geneva', he harboured a dream of one day enacting in Saigon (now Ho Chi Minh City) a scene just like the ones he recalled from his Viet Minh cultural handover duties in 1954. It saddened him, he said, that he never experienced that particular joy when the southern capital experienced liberation (*giai phong*) in April 1975.[33] As I noted above, having settled into post-'Geneva' life in Hanoi, he became one of the first of the thousands of Vietnamese recruited for specialist overseas 'expert' (*chuyen gia*) work in 'friendly' African post-colonies. He speaks with pride of his service in Guinea, despite its high personal costs, as do the other former experts and their families.

Among them is Ms Dao's mother Professor Le, whose four-year stint teaching college-level chemistry in Algeria first came up as an unelaborated throwaway as she described her father's career. Together with her daughter and younger siblings, she has had much to tell me about the public spirit her father evinced throughout his life. He was a man of science, they said, his intellectual achievements wholly in keeping with the family's distinguished tradition of learning, all the more so since he had dedicated his skills and knowledge to the service of the nation. In the course of one of our early meetings Professor Le mentioned a high-level mission to Algeria via Paris in the 1960s. I expressed interest; she said

---

[33] I have written elsewhere (Bayly 2004a) about Dr Tran's accounts of post-liberation Saigon, including his descriptions of friendships established with local intellectuals, and the discriminating attitude he says he and his friends took towards the profusion of abandoned American military supplies and luxury goods being purchased (not looted, he insists) by the incoming northerners. His 'liberation' stories focus on the pleasure he took in being able to acquire such things as a roll of colour film, the first he ever had for use with his cherished Russian 'Lomo' camera, and his purchase of a Tchaikovsky record and a Vietnamese translation of *Dr Zhivago*, a book still banned in the north in those days. All were items obtained from the impromptu street markets described by P. Taylor (2001: 33–4); predictably enough, these are not accounts of disoriented 'consumer-liberators' whose confidence in their socialist affiliations was painfully undermined by the city's commodified opulence (2001: 34–5).

'Oh yes; I went to Algeria too – that was in 1982.' I realised that I was on sensitive ground, though did not then know why.

According to official published sources, several thousand Vietnamese with training in scientific and technical fields worked in a dozen or more African countries in the 1980s and early 90s, with Algeria, Congo, Madagascar and Angola taking the largest numbers. On the face of it, this 'expert' work was in the best tradition of the socialist ecumene, unimpeachable as an enactment of nation-to-nation 'friendship' and the improving power of state-managed science.[34] In addition to Professor Le my chemist friend, and Dr Toan who taught 'scientific pedagogy' in Angola, the former *chuyen gia* specialists I have met include irrigation engineers, agronomists and medics in specialities such as radiology and cardiac care. Much pride is taken in the fact that Vietnam, though still struggling with the daunting economic legacy of the war years and the collapse of aid flows from China and the Soviet Union, could supply 'needy' host countries with trained practitioners in all these sophisticated modern fields.

Great significance is also attached to the eagerness of other countries to receive Vietnamese specialists whose skills involved a fusion of established international science with distinctively Vietnamese forms of skill and knowledge. Water management technology is one such area of expertise. Another is a uniquely Vietnamese updating of 'oriental' healing art. This is electric acupuncture (*cham cuu dien*), a therapeutic art said by one of its trained practitioners, Mrs Chau, to have been much appreciated by the patients she treated during her thirty-month sojourn in Algiers.[35] The complex circuits of the global socialist ecumene first brought this Vietnamese skill to the attention of Algeria's medical authorities by way of the Soviet Union: in the early 1950s Soviet doctors had become interested in acupuncture through contacts with medical specialists from both China and the DRV. Before going to Algeria, Mrs Chau had been a qualified nurse (*y ta*) at Hanoi's state-run hospital for 'oriental' or 'traditional' medicine, the Benh Vien Y Hoc Co Truyen Ha Noi. (Thompson 2003: 137). Her initial posting as a *chuyen gia* worker in 1982 was for two years; it was a great day, she said, when her hospital

---

[34] The published figures I have seen for Vietnamese involved in overseas 'friendship' schemes do not include military advisers and combatants.

[35] On the development of electric acupuncture in China, which was part of a 1950s initiative to create a scientific synthesis between Western medicine and traditional Chinese healing systems, see Crozier 1965: 16 and n. 75. See also Tran Thi Lien 2002: 300.

superiors in Algiers invited her to extend her stay for a further six months in recognition of her skill and dedication.

In fact, being an overseas 'expert' in the 1980s and early 90s is something I have heard Hanoi people discuss in one of two ways. One involves personal narratives of pains, gains and losses, as I show below. But former *chuyen gia* specialists also echo the old official language, speaking of their experiences as acts of care and nurture, both for Vietnam and for the countries in which they worked. The states that paid for their services were supplying Vietnam with hard currency and other inputs at a time when their homeland had urgent needs yet was still equipped to act as a provider in far 'needier' lands.[36]

Thus both officially and in personal narratives, when referring to such acts as the sending of aid and development specialists to other countries, this mode of communication featured a dual language, the idiom of the gift interpenetrating with that of the moralised socialist marketplace. Those involved thus place much emphasis on a vocabulary of mutuality and warm-heartedness, of doing the business of international contacts in terms of imparting, sharing and succouring. The key claim is to have performed such acts without calculation of profit and loss. Where gains are made, they are legitimated by something akin to the moral logic that had exalted the wartime petty trader (*thuong*) as a contributor to the revolutionary cause, a provider of necessities embodying the love and care of those who nurtured both kin and fellow socialist citizens. It is these qualities of 'heart' and affect which are said to differentiate bilateral relations of benevolence and mutuality from those involving 'profit' or 'interest' (*loi ich*).

This language of diplomatic affect should not be dismissed as empty conventionisation deployed as a device to mask the realities of Cold War power politics. For socialist countries, these quasi-anthropomorphic representations of states as altruistic, feeling actors on the international stage can be seen as projections of the Party-state's claims that its actions and judgements embody the heartfelt sentiments of 'the people'. Much as 'the people' were to be seen as righteous arbiters of morality and justice on home soil, it was their will and sensibilities that were held to underpin the generosity and fellow feeling being shown when their leaders identified the provision of development and military aid as acts

---

[36] Ministry statistics are provided in *Quoc Te*'s 'Vietnam-Africa' supplement. The scheme is still active; there were said to be Vietnamese experts working in twenty African countries as of 2000. In the period from 1992 to 2001 the 'experts' are said to have contributed 30 billion *dong* to the state budget and to have received 80 billion *dong* in personal earnings (www.mofa.gov.vn:8080/tbqt/africa03).

of 'co-operation' and 'friendship' between the peoples of interacting states.

I have written elsewhere about the remarkable Ho Chi Minh memorial museum in Hanoi and its colossal display of gifts presented to the former President by world leaders and their admiring 'peoples'. This is a narrativisation of objects and their meaningful lives that turns such diplomatic courtesy offerings as tea-sets, gold watches and 'traditional' craftware into a socialist counterpart of the world-ordering tributary homage flows focused in past centuries on the persons of Sino-Confucian emperors, as described in Marshal Sahlins's celebrated essay 'Cosmologies of Capitalism' (1988).[37] What I propose for Vietnam's version of these gift-giving flows is a kind of cosmology of socialism, in its own way as world-ordering and universalising as the regimens of those pre-modern Sinic statecraft conventions. It too involved an uneven movement of goods, a trafficking in things wanted and appreciated in some places but not in others. This is cosmology to be seen not as 'structure', but rather as 'traffic', with stops, starts, hesitations and flows.

The profusion of goods and products flowing into Vietnam as gifts to the nation's leader proclaimed Ho Chi Minh's standing as an eternal and cherished elder to all the world, thus the focus of the most moral of enduring, affective ties. These are the ties of pupil to teacher and junior to nurturing elder kin. Both are still regularly given form in Vietnam through the conventions of honorific upward gift-giving. What Ho Chi Minh embodies in this and the many other settings in which he has been hailed and praised both at home and abroad are a whole host of claims about the gifts of revolutionary exemplarship which Vietnam has conferred on the wider world. In this arena of socialist interaction, there need not be equivalence in the items thus exchanged. The gifts given by Vietnam, say its spokesmen and admirers, include its victories in

---

[37] Bayly in West and Raman forthcoming. Compare Giebel 2004: 177–9. In Ssorin-Chaikov's (2006) and Ssorin-Chaikov and Sosnina's (2006) pioneering account of gift-giving to Stalin and his successors, a key insight is the representation of all the world as a temporally complex and plural gift economy centred on the person of the Soviet leader. Finn's treatment of affective gift-giving in the context of imperial political and domestic relations also makes key points about the capacity of gifting practices to collapse and transform space and time (Finn 2006: 205). In the Ho Chi Minh museum, items that came originally from capitalist countries would appear to have gained a new, decommodified identity through their incorporation into the moral space of this socialist gift stream. I am indebted to James Laidlaw for suggesting the idea of cosmologies as a basis for interpreting socialist gift practices, and to Caroline Humphrey and Nikolai Ssorin-Chaikov for their insightful thoughts on other important elements of the ideas explored here.

righteous wars; these inspired the world and taught other struggling nations to resist oppressors. Vietnam has also been a giver of the expertise and knowledge brought to those who reaped the benefits of its experts' skills. When other countries, most of them very poor, have paid for the work of its teachers and technical specialists, these too are transactions within a moralised marketplace in which exchanges occur in familial and unexploitative terms.

So there was nothing demeaning for either the givers or receivers of this aid. Vietnam too was a poor country, but this was because of the costly wars it had fought in defence of its homeland, and as a defender of revolutionary modernity on behalf of all the world's progressive peoples and nations. It was therefore neither problematic nor shameful to receive the payments which African countries were offering in return for the Vietnamese experts' services. The former *chuyen gia* speak of themselves as humanitarian providers and bringers of advancement to 'backward' (*lac hau*) African nations, expressing pride in having done work that reflects credit on themselves, their families and their homeland. They speak of themselves as enlighteners and providers (*nguoi cung cap*), unlike Western experts and aid workers whose countries are routinely represented as professing humanitarian aims but undertaking such giving merely to acquire strategic clients, captive markets and cheap labour.

Yet just as there was an in-built tension in the relations between Vietnam and its 'elder sibling' allies and providers, so too for the role and self-identity of the *chuyen gia* experts themselves. Those who took these postings also did so to acquire and to earn, and to do so by means and for ends which are full of emotional and moral ambivalence for those who have discussed their experiences with me. This too entailed provisioning activities, though of a kind that would once have been thought of as falling into a difficult and morally uncertain frontier zone between the familial and the narrowly 'familistic'. Certainly this aspect of people's narratives makes their accounts of *chuyen gia* work far more than a simple story of uncritical complicity in a monolithic project of 'developmental modernity'.

Accessing the 'expert' schemes

As my informants describe it, Hanoi was a bleak place in the immediate post-reunification period. Most of the great landmarks and monuments – the Temple of Literature, the Old Quarter, the Thanh Long Citadel's famous flag tower – had survived the anti-French and anti-US wars, but the streets were cheerless and dark. Most of the cafés had closed. I was told that there was a single establishment, a city-centre restaurant, with an illuminated neon sign spelling out its name: people used to go out to view it at night as a diversion. Households were sparsely furnished, electricity in the home still a rarity; medicines and other basic commodities scarce and strictly rationed. Everyone recalls the complexities of the rationing and coupon regimens, including the elaborate points scheme governing entitlements to basic household requirements. If the shop had one, those with priority to buy a bed were young couples getting married; there were extra entitlement points for the parents or children of serving soldiers.[38]

People effortlessly recall the entitlement figures for periods dating back twenty years or more. Those now in their twenties know the details of their parents' coupon classifications, even for the years before they were born. To be 'E' category as young marrieds in the late 1960s meant an entitlement of half a kilo of meat per week and 10 kilos of rice, said one young woman who had heard accounts of the system since early childhood; her parents were teachers. 'I earned the equivalent of $10 a month in 1985–6', said a retired professor in his early sixties, writing out from memory a table of the monthly cloth, sugar and rice ration for the different categories of household. As I noted earlier, entitlements were calculated in terms of the household head's occupational classification: those classed as 'intellectuals' (*si*) had significantly smaller food and cloth rations than peasant and worker families (*nong* and *cong*), though more than those classed as traders (*thuong*).[39]

A Hanoi social scientist and long-standing Party member from a high-achieving intelligentsia family said he still recalls the tension he felt on returning home from the long monthly business of queuing for his household's grain ration. Sometimes there was no rice, only unpalatable staples like *bo bo* (sorghum), in better times used only for animal feed and requiring hours of boiling to make it edible. If there had been rice in

[38] In 2006, many such features of the 1975–86 command economy system were commemorated in a remarkable exhibition at Hanoi's Museum of Ethnology entitled *Thoi Bao Cap* (The Subsidised Economy Period), with visitors commenting in detail on their memories of those difficult privation years. See Dang Phong 1999a: 96–70; Turley 1993. For other socialist contexts, compare Humphrey 2002 and Verdery 1991b. On the bleakness of pre-*doi moi* Hanoi as represented by the artist Bui Xuan Phai, an intimate of the clandestine café world of Hanoi's 'underground intellectual élite' of the 1960s and 1970s, see N. Taylor 2001: 121–5.

[39] My friend used the old 'five class' formula which I described in Chapter 6. These were 'scientific' calculations assuming greater calorific need on the part of those involved in manual as opposed to 'brain' labour. Certain other groups, notably pregnant and lactating women, were entitled to larger rations on grounds of special nutritional need: an intimate physical examination was required of women seeking to qualify for these entitlements.

the state store, everyone would gather as the sack was opened. On a good day the scent was sweet, but all too often they smelled the sourness of badly stored rice allowed to grow damp and mouldy. Professor Cuong was a young father; it was painful to be thus revealed as a deficient provider.

I learned more about those difficult times from Professor Le and her immediate family. At the time when they faced the difficult decision of whether to seek a *chuyen gia* posting, the household included Professor Le and her husband, their two young children, and her widowed mother. Our conversations have taken place very much in the presence of Professor Le's late father, whose bust and photographs are grouped around the main ground-floor altar of their house in Hanoi. He was eminent, francophone, renowned for his learning and had a Viet Minh background. His library and papers are kept in the upstairs rooms, where more distant ancestors are memorialised.

Professor Le's husband had a senior post in a research institute; she too had an academic salary, and both have Soviet doctorates. But in the early 1980s their combined monthly salaries were insufficient to cover more than two weeks of the household's food needs. Professor Le remembers her mother, painfully ill, yearning for the taste of fresh grapes – far too expensive for everyday purchase. She remembers the extravagance of buying precisely ten grapes, all she could afford.

Those in a position to do so made quasi-illicit swap arrangements, exchanging rationed cloth and other commodities that were more readily available in Hanoi for foodstuffs grown in their ancestral villages (*que*). Professor Le's family obtained essentials in this way. Ms Dao remembers her father making the long cycle ride to the countryside, and the potatoes, rice, dried fish and peanuts he would bring back from these forays. Normally no cash changed hands; these swap transactions were useful preparation for the far more complex forms of trade which so many people engaged in during their overseas study and 'expert' sojourns.

For intelligentsia families, there was one other key subsistence strategy in post-reunification Hanoi. This is still a painful topic. What was involved was the taking on of domestic outwork of a kind that would once have been unthinkable for people of their education and background, although they had all experienced many dangers and deprivations in the war years. But this work entailed forms of manual labour that were gruelling and only minimally remunerative, performed at home and in secrecy. It was not that their activities were illegal. In the 1970s and 80s, the putting out of finishing work by state factories producing such things as army uniforms was a recognised feature of the production economy.[40] When such units had met their initial targets they were encouraged to produce further output, thereby generating extra income for managers and the regular workforce, as well as placing more goods in circulation and creating a flow of available exports to other socialist countries.

It was accepted that this extra production would be achieved through the use of domestic outworkers. Everything was done by word of mouth. Those seeking such work used contacts secured through family or close friends. Professor Le's sister was in the army and thus able to put such work in her family's way. They were told that items like the jerseys onto which they stitched cuffs and collars were for export through army channels to the USSR. Those who were of school age remember their daily share of these routines: snipping threads on the garments their parents were assembling; knotting scraps of knitting wool to sell by weight in the market; spreading the glue used to assemble paper sacks which their parents sold to market traders as bulk product containers. This was a popular job for the children; they liked playing with the brush and glue pot. For 100 kilogram-sized sugar sacks, the rate was 1 *xu*, a hundredth of a *dong*.[41]

It would have been terrible for others to see that one's kin and household were doing such work, the terms for which were *lam them* (extra work) and *nhan gia cong* (take piece-work). People say they felt they were letting down distinguished ancestral tradition by falling into need. The better-paid tasks were those such as assembling soldiers' uniform hats and sandals, securing the insignia and plastic laces with needles heated on a charcoal fire. These were the jobs that were liable to burn or mark the skin. This was deeply distressing: shameful if one allowed it to happen to one's own body, bad too for children to see when it involved their elders.

Ms Dao remembers the burns on her father's fingers, and her mother wearing gloves to stop her hands being stained by the charcoal she shaped into cakes for household cooking fuel; they used these at home and sometimes sold them to market traders. Such activities were discussed with kin and close friends only, but the people I know say they are

[40] The 1975–86 *bao cap* (subsidy) period, with its cautious forays into licensed enterprise radiating outward from the public sector production units, is remembered now as an era of partial liberalisation and thus a prelude to full *doi moi* (marketisation). See Marr and White 1988; Fforde 1989: Ch. 12; Porter 1993; Thayer 1994; Kerkvliet 1995: 398–40; Abuza 2001; Dang Phong 2002; Rosenthal 2002: 121.

[41] 10 *xu* = 1 *hao*, 10 *hao* = 1 *dong*. The *hao* and *xu* (derived from Fr. *sou*) are no longer issued.

sure that everyone in their position in those bad privation years engaged in *lam them* work. There was a common saying at the time: *'chan trong, chan ngoai*: one foot inside, one foot outside', meaning something like 'I'm based in the state sector but get things I need from outside.' So such families struggled to conceal what they were doing to eke out their state salaries, determined to appear impeccably dressed every day, sleep-deprived but never late for work, sending their children off to school immaculately turned out and well prepared for their lessons.

When the big push to recruit overseas 'experts' began, the schemes became a lifeline. 'We were going down', I was told, 'then we could live again'. This is what makes being an 'expert' so sensitive. As experts they earned personally, rather than for the selfless ends of their own and other progressing and progressive nations. And they did so by cultivating skills and aptitudes that could prove difficult to reconcile with the attributes of a cultivated socialist modern.[42] They also had to accept that skewing of traditional gender roles which I have already mentioned in relation to the distinctive mobility of *tri thuc* life. Wives invariably earned less than their husbands. So when 'expert' employment opportunities arose, it made financial sense for husbands to stay behind. They took over the running of the household, as well as working with their older children and other kin to sustain the Hanoi end of the all-important illicit trading operations in which virtually everyone was engaged in those years, discussing both 'business' (*buon*) and the children's health and doings with their absent wives in letters like the ones which Professor Le's family have shared with me.

Even the securing of a *chuyen gia* post was a demanding exercise, requiring a high level of initiative and insider knowledge. Here too, people made use of friendships and family networks. In the early years especially, it was up to individuals to find out about possible openings. There were slogans with generalised exhortations to serve the nation by 'going [out] as an expert' (*di chuyen gia*), but no public advertising of terms or recruitment criteria. Even in the 1990s, most of what people wanted to find out about the scheme could only be gleaned in the same way they informed themselves about domestic outwork, that is by word of mouth.

The procedures were complex; there were numerous clearances and certifications to be obtained. The host countries all had stringent language requirements. The language could be either French or Portuguese, as the lusophone socialist states – Angola and Mozambique – were also

---

[42] For China, compare Davis 1992.

eager to recruit Vietnamese experts. Older intellectuals who had been educated in French rather than Russian found new ways to deploy old cultural capital by running remunerative crash-course French classes for the would-be experts. Professor Le's childhood French was not good enough. She paid for the gruelling regimen of night-time French classes by teaching Russian to Hanoi students who were still eager to study in the USSR.

The language tests were administered by the foreign embassies, but everything else was in the hands of Vietnamese officials. Seekers of *chuyen gia* posts had to show that they had suitable qualifications and professional experience. One also needed a clean political record: for these schemes too, as in the case of those seeking study places and factory work in the COMECON states, preference went to the close kin of 'war martyrs' and other priority candidates such as former soldiers 'downsized' from the military after the 1977–9 China and Cambodia wars.

Mr Vuong was in this category; in the early 1980s he worked as a van driver in an East German engineering works, and his experiences provide an instructive comparison to those of the 'experts'. His children are the first graduates on either side of the family, though some of his close relations are senior military men, including an uncle who fought at Dien Bien Phu. Their small house is comfortable rather than palatial, unlike the homes of the super-rich former 'Dresdeners'.[43] During his stay in the DDR his wife remained in Hanoi working as a machinist in a state factory. The long separation was painful, though Mr Vuong said he enjoyed the works outings to cathedral towns and workers' health spas. His homecoming was a long-awaited joy; his earnings provided the seed money for the small provisioning business they now own, as well as paying for after-school crammer classes for the children. They still have the certificate of exemplary service he received from his work unit in the former East German socialist showcase town of Eisenhüttenstadt, together with photos of the children wearing the glossy rubber boots and hooded snowsuit outfits he brought home for them. They too speak of the chance to work overseas as a lifeline, with a transforming effect on their family's life and prospects, of particular significance for the children.

Factory workers were recruited *en bloc* through their work units; those seeking 'expert' postings had to obtain their own permits and clearances. An official might 'mislay' a vital document, or claim that the validity of one's degree certificates was in doubt. The colloquial term for these

---

[43] In Hanoi one of the city-centre areas with a concentration of showy houses built by rich ex-factory workers is known as 'Dresden village'.

dealings was 'making arrangements', *chay chot*, a phrase which can mean soliciting, seeking or taking steps. In effect, this was an allocation system much as described by Verdery for the socialist systems of Eastern Europe, even though in this case the scarce goods being distributed were services and 'favours': for example, persuading officials to use their contacts and connections to provide a posting to a desirable location. Professor Le had to settle for a teaching post in a poorly resourced technical institute in Guelma, a small town in north-eastern Algeria, envious of her friends working in larger places with other Vietnamese experts for company. So the principles were much like those reported by ethnographers of other socialist distribution economies (Verdery 1991b; compare Humphrey 2002). Indeed my friends say that when they eventually began their work stints in quasi-socialist countries like Algeria, they found themselves well prepared for the handling of subornable state-store assistants and ration-system gatekeepers: the niceties of *chay chot* 'arranging' proved to be one of the great commonalities of the socialist world system.

For those seeking entry to the 'expert' schemes, there was often need for investment in 'gifts', usually in kind rather than cash. One had to be able to judge if and when this should be done, how costly the items should be and of what type. There was the problem of sourcing such things, and the need to learn the delicate art of presenting them. Much as in the cases documented by anthropologists of *guanxi* networking in China, one had to avoid displaying both the arrogance of the insultingly open bribe-giver, and the obsequiousness of the abject suppliant.[44] Learning the right demeanour and language to employ with official 'gatekeepers' was especially problematic for women, Professor Le said; she hated this part of the process. The tone and language needed to be suitably adjusted to the official's age, seniority and sex, as well as the difficulty of the particular service to be provided. And if problems arose, one had to discuss within the household and with other kin the difficult question of whether to press on, investing more and more of the family's scarce resources in what might prove a fruitless quest.

Having passed her French proficiency exam at the Algerian embassy in Hanoi, my friend Mrs Chau, the acupuncture specialist, recalls receiving the issue of ration coupons entitling her to obtain the state-store clothes and other items with which the overseas experts were

---

[44] Smart 1993. For socialist Russia, compare Humphrey 2001 and Fitzpatrick 1999: 63–5 on the need to display appropriate signs of 'feeling' in *blat* ('favours') exchanges. The Vietnamese equivalent of the term *guanxi* is *quan he* (relations, connections), or, more colloquially, *co di co lai* (lit. 'go forward – go back', a usage conveying the reciprocities of such networking and gift-exchange practices).

supposed to be equipped. For men the standard issue was a suitcase plus two pairs of shoes (Western-style: *giay*, not sandals: *dep*), together with two shirts (*ao so-mi*) and two suits (*bo com-le*). There could be no question of Vietnam's educated 'moderns' disembarking at a foreign airport carrying sacks and bundles, or dressed in anything other than the modern garb of an international traveller. This was not battledress or 'native' attire. Vietnamese men did not emulate Ho Chi Minh's quasi-military apparel when going abroad, even though olive uniform-style shirts and trousers became everyday workwear in the countryside after independence. Nor have Vietnamese women turned the *ao dai* into a globetrotter's everyday wear analagous to the sari or *kurta pajama* widely worn by professional women in India.[45]

For women, Mrs Chau said, the issue for experts was two outfits of daywear with either skirt or trousers, plus two pairs of Western-style shoes and a suitcase (*va-li*). But in these times of shortages and erratic production regimens, the kitting-out process was often far from straightforward, and again it was women who had the greatest difficulties. Mrs Linh, another former 'traditional medicine' nurse who worked in Algeria from 1982 to 1985, recalls the frustration of finding that her clothing issue contained men's rather than women's shoes. Rubber sandals were still the norm for both men and women at this time, and Western-style women's garments were always in shorter supply than men's. One had to be both perservering and ingenious: people contrived elaborate swap arrangements involving multiple exchange partners and a whole range of different commodities being sourced and bartered: Mrs Linh managed to offload her men's *giay*, and after several more swaps obtained two pairs of oversized but wearable women's shoes.

It was not the official salaries that made the 'expert' schemes attractive: officially, they were all in post to earn for the state. Professor Le's personal entitlement was a fraction of the sum officially paid for her teaching. She is certain that the *thoa thuan* ('acceptance of terms') document she signed did not mention the sum to be paid by the Algerian government for her services. She learned later that what she received through the nearest Vietnamese consulate was only 15 per cent of her Algerian salary; the rest

---

[45] Tarlo 1996; Miller and Banerjee 2004. Hanoi women I know who go abroad as graduate students, delegation members and professional trainees have begun to adopt as a kind of modified national dress for such travel a style which is also popular with their Chinese counterparts: a tailored jacket and skirt made from good-quality local silk and decorated with the embroidered motifs that make such garments favoured fashion purchases by foreign tourists.

went straight to the ministry that had placed her. Because people had no documents specifying their salaries and entitlements, they consulted members of their families and contacted other ex-*chuyen gia* to work out the details for me. All the ex-*chuyen gia* I know eventually discovered the disparity between their official salaries and the amount they actually received.[46]

That 15 per cent which Professor Le received was significantly more than her Hanoi salary, but it was through trade that the 'experts' made their real gains from *chuyen gia* work. Indeed they are much talked about in Hanoi as a small but energetic regiment of grey-economy entrepreneurs within the much larger army of 'export labourers' (*xuat khau lao dong*) employed in the Eastern bloc countries, with all the powerful moral ambiguities which that entails (Hardy 2000). The background to the trading done by the *chuyen gia* experts in African countries was the infinitely larger-scale economy of illicit transnational trading in which very large numbers of Vietnamese began to engage in the post-reunification period. Beginning in 1975, a highly profitable new world of multidirectional consumer goods trading began to open up between Vietnam and the Soviet and Eastern European socialist economies. At the Vietnam end, these developments rapidly became bound up with the massive changes affecting social and economic life across the entire socialist world. Central to Vietnam's initial involvement in this process was the treasure trove of consumer durables from the 'liberated' South to which significant numbers of military people and other northerners had newfound access. Vietnamese academics are now writing sophisticated accounts of the transformations that overtook the socialist world system in this period, with a focus on Vietnam's involvement in this process, fuelled initially by the North's encounters with the bonanza of discarded American and Japanese consumer products left behind at the end of the anti-US war (See e.g. Beresford and Dang Phong 2000: 72–96).

People I know express a variety of emotions – wonderment, distress, self-congratulation – in discussing the widely held view among educated

---

[46] No-one retained a written contract with details of salary figures or other entitlements; this was a practice associated with capitalism's exploitative labour arrangements. Compare Rofel's account (1999: 274) of the documentation regimens affecting Chinese factory workers. Professor Le verified the figures provided here by consulting the letters she exchanged with her family during her stay, and by checking with other ex-*chuyen gia*. Conditions improved markedly in the 1990s: another friend, the Hanoi-born son of a francophone teacher, taught mathematics at an Algerian university from 1990 to 1994: he and his fellow experts received documents – in French – issued annually by the Algerian Education Ministry confirming their job titles, salaries and other terms of employment.

Hanoians view that the ability to acquire and trade in these items gave them a direct role in the downfall of Soviet socialism.[47] There is no doubt that many people have an exaggerated idea of the importance of Vietnamese consumer goods trafficking to these complex events. Yet I do know Hanoi people who see this illicit private trading as a contributing factor in the massive Soviet economic crisis of the 1980s, linking it to the loss of political confidence which played a key role in the country's collapse. What they have in mind is that from the mid-1970s, many Vietnamese officials and guest-workers had access to goods that were in great demand throughout the USSR and in Eastern Europe (Patsiorkovsky, Fugita and O'Brien 1995; Konstantinov, Kressel and Thuen 1998: 732; Lemon 1998: 35; Dang Phong and Beresford 2000: 90–3). People explain that Vietnamese students and factory workers would go to Russia or Poland with Japanese cassette players or Seiko watches in their suitcases. Such spoils from the 'liberated' south could be obtained in a variety of ways, and once the would-be seller reached Moscow or Poznan, it was not hard to find a local factory manager or state-store assistant who would gladly buy these dazzling, desirable items for roubles. In return, they would siphon off scarce state-produced goods to sell to their Vietnamese trading partners. At the end of their stays, the Vietnamese then took their purchases back to goods-hungry Hanoi, where there was still a market in the 1980s for East German fur coats and clunky Russian household goods.

If they were not already familiar with these operations, the experts too had to master the kinds of transnational trading techniques that people learned to deploy as students, workers or delegation members in Eastern Europe. In the years after reunification these travellers were active in bringing consumerism to North Vietnam, first with a limited flow of high-value goods like Japanese motor-scooters, and then an unstoppable flood of both luxuries and humbler consumer products. Sizeable fortunes were made, mostly by the factory workers; these are the people Hanoians have in mind when they use the term 'Dresdeners'. The people I know speak of their own and other people's 'grey economy' trading in the pre-'renovation' era as a process involving a great deal of collaborative networking among close friends and family members; women often took a prominent role in these transactions, but such commerce does not seem to be widely thought of as a specifically female activity (compare Hy Van Luong 1998 and P. Taylor 2004: 15–16).

---

[47] Compare Yurchak's account (2003) of Soviet intelligentsia perceptions of the 1989 collapse.

In dusty Guelma, Professor Le lived in a foreigners' compound, ever conscious of the instructions she had received about minimising her contacts with Algerians, especially men. Some of the male 'experts' I know describe much happier interactions with their students and local work colleagues, especially those based in larger cities where French was more widely known. Those who worked in Algeria in the early 1990s when the country was experiencing rapidly escalating conflict between government forces and militant Islamist groups were in an altogether different situation. There were rumours of violence directed against foreigners, and those in teaching posts were perplexed by the signs of tension among their students, especially when young women began to disappear from the classroom, under pressure, they were told, from radical Islamisers.

For Professor Le, the concerns were very different, but no less pressing. If her students found her unintelligible, there was the threat of non-renewal or the sack. They were not really francophone and spoke to each other in what she calls 'their own language'. She meant Tamazight, the language of the Kabylia region's local Berber population. They also staged strikes, a thing hitherto unknown to her; she was relieved when she realised that this was not a protest about her teaching, though still uncertain about whether their grievances were to do with their grim campus living conditions or something more dangerous and political. Worried, lonely and frustrated – her swear words were in Russian, she says, as she struggled with her French lecture scripts – what made all the difference were her Russian-speaking colleagues, especially two Poles with whom she discussed books and music, and visited local archaeological sites.

Guelma was then at the heart of the large-scale public agitations which have come to be known as the 'Berber Spring'. Professor Le knew no Arabic or Tamazight and had little sense of what was happening around her, though she recalls the occasional teasing remark from her students: 'Madame: you Communists have no religion, so why don't you become a Muslim like us?' She did not connect this with the local political situation, recalling it instead as a reference to a story her students had heard about a son or daughter of a prominent French Communist who was said to have caused an uproar in the socialist world by converting to Islam. Clearly it is possible to be transnational and to live a life of what I am calling socialist world citizenry, to be present in other people's revolutionary or insurgent times, and yet to make little or no connection with them. Much the same was true for other experts, as in the case of Mr Tu, who taught electronics (*dien tu*) from 1983 to 1985 in the former Foreign Legion headquarters town of Sidi Bel Abbes near Oran. Mr Tu knew nothing of this, although it more than any other place in Algeria has a particularly rich history of entanglement with the colonial life of Indochina.[48]

It was thanks to her Polish friends, Professor Le says, that she was able to carry on living a proper intellectual's life in Guelma. This was crucial, because at the same time, and through her friends the Poles, she was able to trade. Indeed there were only two sources of intimacy and emotional satisfaction for Professor Le in those years in Algeria. One was the Polish couple. With them, she could lead in Guelma, and through Russian, the universalising, cultivated life of a 'socialist modern'. This was a life consistent with her own sense of personal fulfilment, and with her sense of obligation to a family tradition combining both pre- and post-independence forms of attainment and intellectual refinement. Such experiences should not be seen as a means of establishing hierarchical separations or 'distinctions' in Bourdieu's terms. Indeed it is here particularly that one sees the capacity for discriminating tastes and knowledge to build relations between 'socialist moderns', both within and across the disparate spaces of that fluid and open-ended socialist world system.

Professor Le's other source of warmth and satisfaction was her family in Hanoi, as can be seen from the carefully preserved letters to and from home. These discuss a host of domestic concerns but are also a detailed record of the family's entrepreneurial life. Her son became a skilful researcher of market opportunities in Hanoi, building on contacts both within the family and with close friends from his parents' student days; the Polish couple were crucial at the Guelma end. The critical first step was an improbable consignment of Vietnamese-made Japanese-style

---

[48] Founded as a military encampment by the invading French forces in 1843, the town had a long tradition of entanglement in the ramifying networks of soldiering, high politics and individual experience which cross-cut the French colonial system and created many unexpected links and bonds between its individual colonial territories. From the middle of the nineteenth century, it was one of the early showcases of French modernist colonial urbanism with a geometrical street plan, schools and technical institutes, broad tree-lined avenues and massive walls and gates (demolished after independence) (Rabinow 1989; www.piednoirs-aujourdhui.com). It was also famous in France as the headquarters of the French Foreign Legion whose troops played a major role in the conquest of Tonkin in the 1880s, as well as furnishing over half of the forces who were defeated at Dien Bien Phu at the end of the 1946–54 anti-French war. The martyr-revering military culture that grew up around the Legion's epic history turned Sidi Bel Abbes into a repository of relics from many far-flung conflicts. These included the *pavillon chinois*, a wooden structure seized in Tonkin (the northern region of present-day Vietnam) in 1884, and transported as a battle spoil to Sidi Bel Abbes. It was burnt by departing Legionnaires in 1962, to prevent it from falling into the hands of victorious Algerian nationalists when the French vacated the town at Algerian independence.

nylon kimonos (*ki-mo-no* in Vietnamese). The semi-official rules for overseas workers said that one's luggage could contain no more than ten duplicate items of something that was intended for overseas sale; individuals could send themselves another twenty items by post. Female garments were ideal: portable, and suitable for handling by a woman on her own. But then came the day when Professor Le found herself with thirty kimonos representing her whole disposable income, and in a state of high anxiety about how to market them.

The Poles were her saviours; they had a car and took the consignment to big-city Annaba. Twenty-four hours later, Professor Le's kimonos were high-fashion beach-wear for the area's Eastern European workforce, and the local expatriates were clamouring for more. Professor Le sold most of them at double what they had cost in Hanoi. The last few were bought by a local middleman, and shortly thereafter, she glimpsed something remarkable through the window of a neighbouring flat. A group of Algerian women were wearing her kimonos – a transnational first in Guelma. More ventures followed; when she had amassed the necessary savings, the culmination was investment in a shipment of second-hand Japanese motorbikes, which were resold successfully in Hanoi.

For Professor Le, none of this was 'business'. 'If I'd been interested, I'd be rich now. I'd have done what other people did.' She meant the factory labourers: 'I'd have invested it all in the property market. But I didn't.' Like Mr Vuong, she spent the money on evening crammer classes for her children, and those of her sister and brother. This then was not entrepreneurship for its own sake, or as a continuing way of life. I met this distinction repeatedly – 'that's where it all went', someone else said, of her overseas expert earnings: 'my son's piano', and there it was: a Russian-made 'Belarus' prominently positioned in another small Hanoi living room.

This vision of families preserved and provided for through the deployment of skill, care and nurture is now a central element in Vietnam's official account of the country's new life in the age of post-*doi moi* marketisation and international trading initiatives. And having been an important if sometimes ambivalently regarded force in the country's earlier moments of outreach into the wider socialist ecumene, intellectuals are once again a critical focus in these expressions of needs met and national interests achieved. This is still a challenging and unpredictable experience, and it is to these issues of contemporary Hanoi life that I turn in the book's final chapter.

9   Conclusion

Ecumenes and cosmopolitanisms

This study began with an account of people, places and ideas intersecting in the disparate spaces of what I have been calling the global socialist ecumene. My thinking about this borrows from Pollock's idea of 'vernacular cosmopolitanism' (1998) and Engseng Ho's account of 'local cosmopolitans' speaking a common moral language structured around credentialised Islamic learning and transregional genealogical knowledge.[1] Building on both, I have used the concept in two distinct though related ways to contextualise the experiences of the Vietnamese and Indian intelligentsia families whose striking mobility and commitment to self-consciously modern ideals of personal and national attainment have been the book's chief concerns. I have also benefitted from Cooper's bracing challenge to amorphous, ahistorical and agentless conceptions of globalisation and diasporic connectivity that lack engagement with the concerns that have been central to this book: 'units of affinity and mobilization, the kinds of subjective attachments people form and the collectivities that are capable of action' (Cooper 2005: 108).

The notion of ecumene employed here thus differs significantly from its use by contemporary globalisation theorists to describe the economic and cultural conditions of 'late capitalism'. These processes of directionless transnational interaction have been widely represented as producing a 'world of movement and mixture' (Hannerz 1987: 551, cited in Foster 1991: 236) in which formerly fixed and bounded identifications of nation, place or community become fragmented, vernacularised or 'creolised' (Appadurai 1996). The danger here is one of reducing translocality to a rooted, static 'before' and a radically different 'now' or 'after' in which the world's key cultural processes have become unanchored and deterritorialised. I believe that Engseng Ho's local cosmopolitan concept in concert

---

[1] Ho 2002; 2004; see also Humphrey 2004.

with Pollock's idea of an ancient Sanskrit ecumene or 'cosmopolis' offers something more illuminating.

What local cosmopolitanism suggests is a basis for seeing socialism's intelligentsia moderns as active moral agents in a transnational world where they and their kin have made gains as well as losses through the deployment of distinctive forms of intellectual and cultural capital. Pollock's account of the ecumene or cosmopolis as a cultural formation not resting on territorial conquest or mass migration, but taking shape around shared practices of cultural circulation, a 'periphery without centre, community without unity' (1998: 13), captures much of the distinctiveness and dynamism of the arenas in which my informants have moved and interacted.

Of course Vietnamese intelligentsia people like Mr Can and Professor Le were anything but footloose, independent globetrotters in that wider world. Unlike the Indian socialist moderns who could often make career and travel choices with a freedom undreamt of by their Vietnamese counterparts, my Hanoi friends were subject to a very high degree of control and regimentation in such matters. They have made it clear that the plying of the socialist ecumene's distant spaces was often far from happy or unproblematic, and that the family-like solidarities and 'friendships' they were called on to forge on behalf of the nation could be full of pitfalls.

Women especially were often subject to imputations of impropriety in their dealings with male African, European and even Vietnamese superiors and work colleagues. As I noted in Chapter 4, socialist cosmopolitanism has thus had very strict limits, a cosmopolitan's mobility being all too easily thought of as rootlessness and a basis for licence and laxity (Boym 1995: 153–6; Humphrey 2004). Indeed in a 'postcolony', these are associations calling to mind bad memories of foreigners despoiling the nation by debauching its women (and often its boys). Such views carried over very strongly into the sensitive issue of sexual liaisons with non-Vietnamese either at home or abroad. It is this which is hinted at in the ribald jokes about promiscuous 'Natashas' encountered in overseas work sojourns, and even in the children's rhymes my informants recited about the ways and morés of foreign 'friendship' visitors. In the heyday of the overseas study and expert schemes, even a Russian or Pole of impeccable 'culturedness' was unthinkable as a marriage partner for a Vietnamese from the Hanoi *tri thuc* intelligentsia world.

Even so, mobility has been much hailed as a quality rendering the intelligentsia moderns exemplary of the confident, outward-looking way of life that was widely exalted as a goal for all in an advancing socialist society. Yet leaving aside the extensive literature on deportation, forced rustication and the gulags, even the sophisticated 'revisionist' accounts of socialism which have done so much to illuminate the lived experience of socialist citizenship have quite understandably tended to challenge out-moded totalitarianism perspectives by exploring contexts in which such citizens led comparatively rooted and localised lives.[2]

The problem is that this can lead to a view of the socialist world as a set of rigidly enclaved spaces deprived of any dynamic of human mobility or circulation. This of course is a problematic view, implying that it took the bringing down of the Cold War's walls and watchtowers to teach former socialists how to lead a 'natural' life as tourists, consumers and translocal labour migrants. In the form of triumphalist 'end of history'/ 'downfall of totalitarianism' narratives, such renderings of the post-socialist story are strikingly close in spirit to the accounts of colonisation produced by Western Orientalists who portrayed themselves as enligh-teners battling against the supposed aversion of Algerians and other subject peoples to the 'civilising' circulation of people, ideas and money (Bayly 2002).[3] It is also a view that homogenises socialist societies in a way that I have sought to avoid by treating the world of socialism as a very broad spectrum encompassing Third World or postcolonial soci-alisms as well as the revolutionary socialist superpowers.

The static enclave view certainly fails to recognise the extent to which significant numbers of citizens both within and beyond the 'postcolonies' knew the socialist world as one in which the processes of meeting and movement in faraway spaces were compelling reference points, to be understood as definitive of modernity and progressive moral life for one's kin and compatriots. The idea of cosmopolis is thus especially apt in evoking that world's professed purposefulness, its language of com-munity and affective sensibility, and its expressions of refined discrim-ination in evaluating the different products and projects of former colonisers and self-professed external emancipators. Surely much of that oppositional moral energy is missed if we see the translocalities of the twentieth-century world as arising exclusively from the effects of capit-alist commodity flows and communication technologies.

Taken together, the two ideas thus provide support for the book's central premise, which is that studies of the globalised world should

---

[2] An important exception is Borneman 1995.

[3] Indeed the conditions of post-socialist life have been represented as 'colonial' by commentators pointing to the alleged backwardness ascribed to societies once proclaiming themselves to be triumphant models of socialist modernity. See Slezkine 2000.

take account of the powerful sense of translocal community created within and beyond the so-called postcolonies by past and more recent versions of socialism. This allows for an understanding of translocality that avoids a narrow focus on homogenised notions of either colonialism or capitalist globalisation as the engines of novelty and transformation in contemporary cultural life. It also helps to ensure an enriched and pluralised understanding of both the colonial/postcolonial and the socialist/post-socialist. In an ecumene, particularities are not lost, and those who meet and mingle in its common spaces need not renounce their distinctiveness in favour of an all-embracing uniformity of ideals or comportment.[4]

I have therefore sought to make this book both ethnographic and comparative, building on my research in India and Vietnam, two very different Asian 'postcolonies' with contrasting experiences of empire and its legacies. This has not been comparison in the tradition of the structuralist or neo-evolutionist and other 'grand theory' comparative projects of the past. It has emphatically not been rooted in a framework of outmoded oppositional comparison between modern, rational, dynamic West and a crudely 'othered' traditional, modernising or evolving 'Rest'. On the contrary, I share with other recent advocates of anthropological comparison a belief in approaches that are 'time-conscious' (Moore 2005: 1), ethnographically rich and comprehensively contextualised (Gingrich and Fox 2002). I believe too that comparison offers an important means of bringing divergent disciplinary perspectives into dialogue, which is why I have tried to combine historical and anthropological perspectives in exploring the family and career lives of intelligentsia moderns within and beyond their postcolonial homelands.

In the book's initial chapters I employed the concept of ecumene to refer to the intersections and commonalities which brought together the people I have been calling socialist moderns in Vietnam's wartime 'liberated territories' (the *lien khu* or interzones), and much further afield in such places as the schools and hospitals of southern China, Algeria and Guinea. These socialist moderns include my Russian- and French-speaking Hanoi friend Professor Le, and also the Polish colleagues who became her friends in Algeria in the early 1980s. They were the couple

---

[4] The term ecumene is of course widely used for expansive communities of religious communality, as in the case of idealisations of both Christendom and the Muslim idea of *umma*, and for the classical notions of Chinese, Greek and other commonalities to which one brings distinctiveness as well as many forms of shared identification. There is a comparison here with the notion of a familial or household form of cosmopolitanism, an issue to which I return below.

with whom she shared a love of Pushkin, a strong sense of both the virtues and precariousness of an intelligentsia family heritage, and a Soviet training in the scientific disciplines which formed the basis of their work as 'experts' and socialist civilisers. When my Hanoi friends have recalled such interactions, they have represented them as productive encounters of a kind wholly appropriate to a life of socialist world citizenry as lived by those with the skills and knowledge to advantage their kin, their compatriots and the world at large with the fruits of their cosmopolitan experiences.

So this was a notion of the socialist ecumene as comprising the very big, expansive spaces plied both in the past and more recently by children as well as adults. Many are people who have spent their lives crossing and recrossing the urban and rural landscapes from which local accounts of socialist life in the making have been projected onto much bigger vistas of nation-to-nation solidarities and friendship ties. The Hanoi intellectuals I know are not uncritical or passively accepting of this idealised world system's official imaginings. But they do tend to profess a strong sense of the significance of those translocal spaces, and of their own role as knowledgeable cosmopolitans whose Vietnameseness has been complemented and enhanced by their mastery of that wider world's socialities and comportment regimens.

As described by my informants and also documented in their remarkable photographs and other family memorabilia, this plying of expansive socialist spaces has been experienced in many different ways. These include older people's dangerous wartime treks to the 'liberated' interzones and thence, for some, to the special cadres' schools in China. In later years, there were their educational and work sojourns in Cambodia and the COMECON states, and their stays in the African countries in which so many of Hanoi's *tri thuc* intellectual moderns served as aid workers and technical experts (*chuyen gia*).

What I came to recognise in the course of my fieldwork was the importance of shared family narratives of these experiences. I have referred to these as exercises in collective reflection and articulation for which I employed the term critical memory to evoke the creative and moral significance of this process for those engaging in its verbal and affective exchanges.[5] I fully recognise that its operation involves many evasions and silences about matters too sensitive to be openly alluded to, though I have been aware too that for Hanoi intelligentsia families

---

[5] Fabian 2001. Works which have contributed to my thinking on these issues include Tonkin 1992; Gilsenan 1996; Butalia 1998; Skultans 1998 and Lambek 1996.

such occasions provide a means of subtly challenging other narratives containing unwelcome or even threatening representations of their past and current lives.

As 'interpretive reconstructions' (Antze and Lambek 1996: vii) shaped by narrative conventions deriving from many sources and intellectual traditions, such narratives call for a responsive, participatory mode of exposition. And, as a researcher from a 'famous' (*noi tieng*) overseas university, I too was made an active sharer in this process. This involved being assigned something of the role of the younger family members who are expected to take an eager interest in the imparting and pooling of anecdotes and information about their elders' and forebears' attainments, and to contextualise what they hear and learn as affective knowledge to be spoken of and experienced in an idiom of heartfelt love and feeling (*chan tinh*). In so doing, it is possible even for the very young and those without overseas experiences of their own to gain a sense of personal participation in that world of cosmopolitan achievement, thereby helping to sustain and expand the stock of factual and emotional knowledge which I found to be so widely valued in the Hanoi intelligentsia world.

For many, these narrative processes are a source of profound personal gratification. They are also a critical resource in their interactions with others, including those involving the kinds of knowledge exchanges and affective interactions which have been of great help in providing for their educational and career needs, especially at times when families like theirs were at risk of looking unduly privileged or even being labelled 'bourgeois' by socialist officialdom.

I found too that there were other important means of achieving this sense of involvement in global socialist space, including the pictorial representations and propaganda songs evoking overseas socialist 'friends' and allies which people recall so vividly from their interzone childhoods. There was also the consumption of modern rarities brought or sourced from distant places. Ironically, both before and after independence many of these came from the capitalist West. Yet as my friends recall them today, these foreign wares could be assimilated and naturalised within such places as the revolutionary wartime interzones, when imparted by loving elders with sophisticated knowledge of the wider world, and a modern revolutionary's capacity to perform acts of selective appropriation from that wider world's material and intellectual trappings. As artefacts of memory which translate particularly well between the realms of personal and official history-making, such items have the capacity to act as critical instruments of the process I have referred to as auto-cartography. What I had in mind here is the infusing of officially marked and mapped terrain with meanings that humanise and moralise the experience of panoptic operations and visuality regimens. This bears very much on the concern with family life and the processes of provision and gift-giving which has been the other central theme of the book. I return below to the topic of the cosmopolitan intellectual family and the distinctiveness of its moral and affective interactions.

First, though, it should be noted that in this initial use of the concept of a socialist ecumene, I had in mind moral and temporal topographies on a scale both larger and more complex in scope than the official alliances linking the socialist superpowers and their so-called satellites through ties of strategic and economic clientage. In theory at least, this wider vision of a socialist world system resting on professed ties of nurturing care and gift exchange accords far more closely to the ideal of socialism as a familial relation of community at the level of both persons and societies, one that embraces all the world's socialist and quasi-socialist 'postcolonies' together with the officially Communist societies of Europe and Asia.

What is thus allowed for is the possibility of enduring 'friendships' of the kind which from the late 1970s made Vietnam a provider of 'expert' skill and knowledge to African postcolonies espousing socialist or quasi-socialist ideals and a high regard for Vietnam's revolutionary exemplarship. This, of course, has been a much more attractive idea of socialism than one defining one's people and homeland as eternally unreciprocating takers of aid and tutelage from the big socialist superpowers, thereby denying them recognition as active makers of the world's great emancipatory projects. Such projects do not belong exclusively to the pre-'renovation' (*doi moi*) period when even non-Communist postcolonies like India professed themselves to be ardent sharers in the spirit of Vietnam's revolution and resistance struggles.

Indeed, inspired by the anthropologist Harry West's notion of neo-tradition as an enduring feature of 'late' or post-socialist experience in many parts of the world, I have been struck by the adoption of an idiom of socialist neo-tradition in official representations of Vietnam's present-day pursuit of overseas trade and investment opportunities.[6] What has been said since the early 2000s in official media accounts of these initiatives is that Vietnam's quest for export markets in a host of newly 'liberalising' African economies is not a pursuit of narrow economic gain or 'interest' (*loi ich*). On the contrary, say the ministries' media

---

[6] West and Raman forthcoming; and see Bayly forthcoming.

spokesmen, these efforts are wholly consistent with the country's heritage as a socialist provider and maker of 'traditional friendships' (*quan he huu nghi truyen thong*) through the imparting of aid and tutelage to the continent's 'needy' postcolonies.

This reportage points to the work of the former *chuyen gia* experts as providers of skill and knowledge whose efforts enabled Vietnam to bring the gifts of developmental modernity to these distant regions of the worldwide socialist ecumene. Indeed the media spokesmen say quite specifically that these were acts of beneficent mutuality which directly prefigured today's proliferating commercial export deals with both new and established African 'friends'. The same spirit is still said to animate these relations. This is a spirit of socialist familiality exemplified jointly by the 'experts' and by the inspiring figure of *Bac Ho*, President Ho Chi Minh as loving elder and revolutionary exemplar to all the world, and thus to be sharply distinguished from the amoral ethos of the valueless, unfamilial and impersonal capitalist marketplace.

I have therefore sought to show that much light may be shed on the so-called postcolonies' experiences of global socialist life through the use of anthropologists' insights into the complex processes of exchange, reciprocity and gift-giving. Of the two forms of provision most commonly described in the literature on gift provision, one involves 'upward' giving as from juniors to honoured seniors, while the other takes the form of 'downward' provision as from superiors to humble clients and dependents. Anthropologists have most commonly identified only one of these two gifting modes in the settings where they have explored the moral and instrumental complexities of interpersonal exchange relations. But in the life of a postcolony within the socialist ecumene, both modes have been of critical importance, and the two together have provided a kind of structuring logic to the often very difficult affective life lived by those who have plied the great spaces of the socialist world system.

My argument about Vietnam has therefore been that its ramifying overseas friendship relations have entailed consistent attempts to assert to its own citizens and the world at large that Vietnam has been much more than a recipient of support and material benefits from richer and more powerful socialist providers. These claims that the country has never been anything other than an exemplary senior in this world of socialist familiality are, if anything, even more strongly asserted in today's era of 'late' or post-socialist marketisation than in the past. The key basis for such assertions is the celebration of Vietnam's 'tradition' (*truyen thong*) of gift-giving to other lands within the socialist ecumene in the form of the 'downward' munificence of superiors to juniors.

These are most commonly portrayed as gifts of revolutionary exemplarship rather than material aid or military support. All peoples, say the
media narratives, especially those from the poorer and more deprived
regions of the postcolonial world, admire and learn from Vietnam's
educational attainments and other modernising feats, and from its
victories against French and American imperialism. All the world is also
said to recognise its munificence as an imparter of skills and tutelage to
'needier' postcolonies.

While there are clearly many ways to understand the socialist world
system both during and since its Cold War heyday, there is much to be
learned by seeing it as a dynamic though often painfully fraught moral
economy in which the distinction between being a giver and a receiver of
the tokens of socialist modernity has been a matter of great significance
and sensitivity. What I have argued about Vietnam's participation in the
life of the worldwide socialist ecumene is that it is all too easy for
countries receiving flows of support and 'friendship' benefits from the
bigger socialist providers to be thought of in precisely this way, that is as
backward and lowly juniors in an eternal relation of inferiority to its elder
'sister' and 'brother' aid providers, i.e. China and the USSR. It was
therefore by showing both its own and other peoples that Vietnam has
long acted as a giver of aid and uplift to 'needy' Africans that this
ignominious situation could be given a very different slant. Instead of a
two-way relation of morally superior giver and humbly beholden suppliant, Vietnam's entry into that much bigger socialist ecumene which
included such countries as Algeria and Mozambique made the nation a
giver and provider in its own right, as in a domestic familial context
where the young and dependent can look forward to the stage in life
when they too will have juniors who defer to them as providers of an
elder's care and nurture.

This is what made the intelligentsia moderns so important in the
post-independence period. Their skills and knowledge were the critical
currency of this 'downward' provisioning economy. In addition to their
technical credentials, they had mastery of languages which had been
transformed from colonial to revolutionary communication modes by
the usages of the worldwide socialist system. Together, these equipped
them to earn much-needed remittances for the national exchequer. And
the uplifting image of their refinement and 'culturedness' forging bonds
of socialist friendship in such places as Conakry and Luanda created a
convincing context for the claim that these earnings were the legitimate
fruits of a moralised marketplace, indeed that the true purpose of their
presence in foreign lands was provision rather than profit, and that this
was a matter of 'expressive' rather than demeaningly 'instrumental' or

interested gift-giving.[7] All this was far from painless or uncontested, there being always a basis for the condemnation of these pursuits as alien to the traditions of both socialist and national heritage. So on this very large global scale, the extensive sphere of worldwide interactions which I have referred to as a socialist ecumene has been both an arena of instrumental exchange relations, and one in which complex moral dilemmas could be worked out, though often at great cost to those called on to embody the spirit and ethos of these socialist gift relations.

Following on from this, I have also proposed the idea of a more localised though still very large sphere or cosmopolis of official and personal enactments. For this I have used the term inner socialist ecumene. The focus here has been India's intelligentsia moderns as a key case of cultivated cosmopolitans whose career and family lives took shape within their own homeland's expansive developmental spaces and reformist moral projects. And while the book's chief concern has been with the first of those two cosmopolitanisms, I believe that the notion of an inner socialist ecumene throws much light on the ways in which socialist ideals and idioms have been embraced and colloquialised across much of the former colonial world. What can be seen in India then is an instance of socialist or quasi-socialist ideas of developmental modernism generating moral narratives about the homeland's needs and the selfless virtues of those who defined and met them. These narratives have been couched in terms much like those of the wider socialist world's ideas of enlightenment brought to farflung locales both at home and abroad through the initiatives of its mobile intelligentsia service specialists.

It will be recalled that at the time when Professor Le was teaching chemistry in Guelma and learning the risky skills of long-distance shuttle and suitcase trading in collaboration with her Polish lecturer friends, Algeria's leftist government professed a keen commitment to ideals of progressive developmentalism of a kind still widely propounded in the former colonial states. In this same period, India too was a non-Communist postcolony where in the years of my early fieldwork, the Nehruvian ideals of so-called soft socialism were still commonly couched in much the same language of moralising developmental modernism by 'local cosmopolitans' such as my administrator friend Mr Raman. What I suggested in my discussion of these anglophone Indians' career patterns and family lives is that they too were knowledgeable participants in the moral and practical interactions of that worldwide socialist arena.

[7] I build here on Yan 1996a.

I also sought to show that the Indian intelligentsia moderns I knew in the 1970s and 80s were much like my Vietnamese informants in their use of a language of sensibility and affective insight to narrativise the moral world in which they moved as self-conscious and often beleaguered embodiments of its familial and scientific norms. Like Stoler, who has made a strong case for issues of sentiment to be included in the understanding of colonialism's 'affective states' (2004), I regard the moral terrain of emotion as having been widely overlooked in accounts of the modernist social projects of both the colonial and the postcolonial world. What I also proposed in my discussion of the Indian 'inner ecumene' was that for anglophone moderns like Mr Raman, this world and its affective reference points did not take shape around a narrowly 'postcolonial' definition of self and other. Either directly or indirectly, they too made contact with a multitude of people and things evoking the other states and peoples – including the DRV – with whom India had forged ties of alliance and friendship.[8]

In contrast to these very extensive, transcontinental forms of a cosmopolitan's life and thought, my other use of the socialist ecumene concept pointed to the ways in which the provinces and districts of the Indian Union came to comprise for people like Mr Raman and his contemporaries an expansive inner space with many of the same community-like translocal features. What they had been taught in their IAS (Indian Administrative Service) training was that this vision of a homogenised, progressive 'super-India' was wholly compatible with the nation's great heritage of 'native' spiritual and religious traditions. Both these teachings and those who sought to act on them have had many critics and debunkers. In the view of their enemies, they had what have come to be referred to as 'colonised minds', their thinking inherently alien to the particularities of culture and history which the Nehruvian modernist ideal was intended to transcend and harmonise within its bigger universalising cosmopolis.

Of course in its twentieth-century heyday, the socialist world system was much more than a space of didactic moral imagination or a transitory meeting ground for expatriate experts, technicians and development workers. But I found much to learn from my friends' narratives of family

---

[8] My approach is also reflective of Gupta's (1999) call for recognition of those twentieth-century 'imaginings' which envisaged a modernist future on a scale much wider than those of either ethnic or civic nationality or subnationality. What Gupta cites are the European Union and the Non-Aligned Movement led by Nehru's India, Sukarno's Indonesia and other leftist Third World nation-states in the 1950s and 60s as important arenas for the 'imagining' of transnational identities (see also Ong 1999 and Duara 1997).

and career life in the multiple arenas of this globetrotting intelligentsia world. Indeed it is important to recognise that the distinctively mobile lives of these scientific moderns played a critical role in the processes of vernacularisation which implanted variants of socialist life and thought in so many places both within and beyond the former white-ruled empires. I have therefore argued that the global socialist ecumene has been a space deriving much of its shape and dynamism from the initiatives of multi-lingual 'local cosmopolitans' from the so-called postcolonies. This point has underpinned the book's focus on Indian and Vietnamese intelli-gentsia families.

It is true that in most if not all forms of socialism, white-collared 'brain workers' are ascribed a major role in the imparting of ideological essentials. They are also commonly called on to exemplify the norms of 'culturedness' that are deemed essential for the life and health of a socialist nation. Yet in Vietnam as in India, academics and technically trained professionals are neither 'élite' nor 'subaltern' in any simple sense. Indeed the ambiguity of their situation both now and in the past gives added interest to the project of engaging with their accounts of amassing and handling their distinctive stocks of cultural capital, espe-cially at times of rapid change in the valuations assigned to their knowledge and credentials.

These are matters that bear directly on the operations of state power as well as the intimacies of personal and domestic experience. In past decades, the key concern in many studies of social transformation in former colonial societies was the driving force of popular movements from 'below'. Yet it should be clear that the forging of new life in the socialist or quasi-socialist postcolonies has also been bound up with the changing relations between the agencies of state power and the tasks of representation and articulation performed by intelligentsias. Those who have lived and worked as 'brain workers' in these societies are anomalous people, always close to the processes by which the ruling discourses of class and status are generated within the socialist world, yet often unable to benefit directly from their association with this potentially dangerous form of productive cultural power.

Indeed as people definable in terms that are not quite those of a class or a self-contained virtuoso status group, they have often found them-selves occupying an uneasy position within the analytical schemes used throughout the socialist world to differentiate between the moral worth of peasants and workers on the one hand, and problematic bourgeois class elements on the other. In effect, even though they are not in any simple sense an economic or social class, the educated cosmopolitans have found it hard to escape from being thought of within Vietnam as the residue of a bourgeoisie whose privileged condition was created by the economic and cultural processes of colonial rule. This is much like the more general idea that a former colonial society's educated people comprise a self-serving bourgeois élite, a view owing much to the Gramscian version of late Marxist class analysis that is still an important reference point for many anthropologists.[9]

This Gramscian analysis of class societies tends to treat intellectuals as instruments of oppressive power, their role being to produce the hegemonic discourses through which class dominance is sustained and normalised. Of course socialists exalt the new revolutionary society as one in which class opposition dies away and all productive groups learn to act in harmony under the tutelage of state and Party. This is what was shown in the early Viet Minh propaganda picture of the exemplary young heroes representing the solidarity of the insurgent nation, the intellectual with his pen and modern garb standing shoulder to shoulder with the soldier, worker and peasant. It will be recalled too that with these four key makers of the nation's new life stood that important fifth element of its new revolutionary order, the virtuous petty trader, seen in many representations from this period as a provisioner rather than an exploiter of need.

One would not expect to find such a person represented as heroic and moral in a comparable Chinese or Russian propaganda image. But of course at the time of the 1946–54 anti-French war, Vietnam's revolutionaries expressed themselves in strongly anti-colonial terms. So the hawker dealing in locally sourced necessities could easily be seen as a figure close in spirit to the purveyor of 'home produce' (*swadeshi* goods) in colonial India (Sarkar 1973; Bayly 1986; Trivedi 2003). Furthermore, there is a sense in which the modern *tri thuc* intellectual is that virtuous trader's alter ego. Vietnam's petty purveyors are providers of items needed by all. Their foodstuffs, country-made medicaments and other wholesome wares are strictly local, products of home soil and the homeland's unique artisanal skills. The cultivated modern intellectual is a provider too, though what he or she imparts are skills and knowledge from the wider world of science, medicine and the creative arts. In theory at least, these are universals which can be stripped of racist colonial baggage and imbued with powerful moral meanings connected

---

[9] Critical engagements with the use of Gramscian conceptual perspectives in anthropology include Linger 1993; Kaplan and Kelly 1994; and Crehan 2002. Some studies have broadened the notion of subalternity so greatly that it might include postcolonial intelligentsias as well, but I regard this as stretching the concept so far as to drain it of analytical value.

with the care, nurture and feeling (*chan tinh*) of familial and patriotic life. So they are forms of cultural capital which are just as moral and conducive to collective wellbeing as the stock of essentials purveyed by the virtuous trader.

Indeed it is the intellectual who can tell other citizens that the former coloniser was not at all what he claimed, that his penicillin substitute was defective, and his version of modernity deficient even in comparison to that of other powers within the capitalist world, and especially in comparison to the modernity of the American capitalist superpower. So once suitably adapted, what the intellectual has at his command is equally indispensable to the new social order as visualised by a postcolony's revolutionaries. Its intellectuals can therefore claim to be another group of providers rather than possessors of élite tastes and cultural dispositions which must be rectified or expunged in favour of the truer knowledge of the masses. Indeed in Vietnam, as in other former French colonies, knowledge originally derived from colonial schooling can be represented as a product of universal revolutionary tradition. So the multilingual sons and daughters of Vietnamese revolutionaries can profess a love of Mallarmé and Victor Hugo and a reverence for the achievements of the medical pioneers Pasteur and Yersin without shame or stigma, all the more so since the kind of schooling that such people received after independence extended their intellectual repertoire to include Pushkin, Borodin and the patriotic Vietnamese 'moderns' as well as the *Tale of Kieu* and other pre-revolutionary Vietnamese classics.

But of course neither the internal nor the wider global versions of that socialist ecumene were spaces of placid harmony. In reality, under socialism in Vietnam as elsewhere, both intelligentsias and commercial people have lived in a dangerously liminal realm of that imagined revolutionary community, their members always under threat of being identified as holdovers from the pre-socialist past, their advantages all too easily condemned as the ignoble fruits of colonial collaboration. And intellectuals who take ministerial posts or accept other forms of high office know that they may well be vilified as seekers of advantage who have done something discreditable by making gains from what they know.

This danger is all the greater because among Hanoi people, and I believe in Vietnam more generally, intelligentsia identity has been so much a matter of family tradition as well as individual attainment. And both as individuals and family units, intelligentsia moderns have not simply been a kind of inverse counterpart of the trader/purveyor. In many cases the two categories have overlapped and interpenetrated, with women in particular being the critical agents of this mixing of productive pursuits.

This of course relates directly to the other key issue with which the book has been concerned, that of family life and familial tradition as enduring yet highly dynamic points of reference in my informants' experiences of 'socialist modern' life. I found this sense of family to be closely interwoven with the allegiances and connections which people forged through schooling, work and military service in the many arenas in which they moved and interacted. I have therefore sought to show that we can see important processes at work in my informants' narrativisations of that distinctive sense of family. What I have tried to convey in relation to anthropologists' long-standing interest in the domestic and the familial, and in particular our field's more recent concern with the production and active experience of affective and embodied 'relatedness', is the extent to which the family unit matters as a moral, ritual and affective focus in the contexts in which I have worked.

Of course to a considerable degree this reflects the extensive official moralising about family life to which the citizens of all modernising socialist and quasi-socialist states are continually exposed (for Vietnam, see Pettus 2003). Yet these concerns with the familial as a project and active moral arena are far more than reflections of or engagements with these official norms and discourses. The critical point here is that while many official and academic representations homogenise bonds of blood and conjugal relatedness into a single category of 'the family', or in some cases 'the Vietnamese (or Indian, or modern) family', I was struck throughout the time of my fieldwork by the importance which people attach to the notion of different types or kinds of families, each with their own distinctive qualities and endowments.

I have therefore sought to emphasise the processes through which the moral life of one particular type of family, the 'modern intellectual family' or *gia dinh tri thuc*, together with its closely comparable Indian counterparts, has been forged, sustained and experienced. These are processes of affect as well as intellect. A notable feature of their enactment is the extent to which they make a sense of history experienced through the imparting and archiving of memory a critical feature of intelligentsia family life.

As I have sought to show through my exploration of childhood narratives, achieving children and also women are as critical as adult male actors in these dynamic if often painful processes. In the pre- and post-liberation periods, Vietnamese women did 'business' (*buon*) while their educated menfolk learned and taught. This division of labour was a pervasive feature of intelligentsia family life both before independence and in the difficult years of post-reunification overseas expert service. In my informants' family narratives, the amassing of money for these purposes has been spoken of as an honourable act of care and nurture, close in spirit to the bravado and fortitude of their remarkable female elders who braved enemy checkpoints and learned to pilot aircraft in the heroic days of the country's resistance wars.

Yet such earning did leave the intelligentsia moderns open to something much like the accusations of misuse or sale of skill that dogged India's 'Nehruvian' cosmopolitans. They too were endowed with apparent advantages which made them vulnerable to attacks like those of the regional ethno-nationalists who in effect claimed to be habitués of their own superior version of a supralocal socialist ecumene. Tamil/Dravidian culture was world culture, said the organisers of events such as the World Tamil Congresses of the 1970s and 80s. Their charge against anglophone cosmopolitans like Mr Raman was that they were rootless opportunists without the moral anchoring which is the hallmark of an ecumene's global citizens. They thus proclaimed in their war against the so-called Nehruvians a kind of parallel universalising mission couched in terms much like theirs, rather than an anti-modern 'traditionalist's' production of locality.

In Vietnam too, intellectuals may face the charge that they do not serve the 'common man'. Indeed even when acclaimed for their skill and virtue, they are a problematic group for a socialist state. By definition intelligentsias are people with knowledge that others do not possess. On this basis they have what the state needs and wants, this being the capacity to evaluate, and to show the wider world the progressive, achieving face of a modern socialist 'postcolony'. Of course the possession of discriminating knowledge entails the capacity to live a refined and cultivated life which sets one apart from others. This can sometimes be suspect in Vietnam but never to the extent seen in China. Indeed the real danger is that such people are equipped with the potential to criticise the state's aims and actions; this makes them a source of anxiety, to be watched and monitored even when they are praised and rewarded.

I have certainly not intended to disregard the great diversity of the world's past and current socialist systems, or to overlook their coercive and often brutalising manifestations. And as I noted earlier on, the people I worked with do not necessarily identify themselves as socialists and certainly do not all possess an uncritical allegiance to Marxist analytical thought. What they do share are personal and career experiences that involve travelling both literally and conceptually beyond their homelands' borders to the many places in which socialist traditions and 'neo-traditions' have long held sway. When they have done so, they have been applauded as well as vilified for their skill in amassing and deploying forms of cultural capital that have had a very particular kind of value in the wider world.

It is in this regard that issues of familial life and its practices of care and nurture come into sharp relief in the contexts with which I have been concerned. In most if not all the places where socialist or quasi-socialist ideals of developmental modernism have been embraced and propagated, the socialist world citizens' ties to kin and other family-like affective collectivities have both defined and challenged the moral projects which they are expected to exemplify. It has been widely observed that the political imaginings of revolutionaries have often been structured by narratives of familial relations. A case in point is L. Hunt's (1992) account of French revolutionary thought as a many-faceted expression of Freud's 'family romance', this being the myth of a primordial patricide leading to the triumph of a liberty-loving, republican 'band of brothers'. The anthropologist F. Vergès has built on this to propose for the case of France's former Indian Ocean colony of Réunion, now an overseas metropolitan dependency, the idea of a 'colonial family romance' (1999). Her argument is that the poisoned legacy of empire was the reshaping of that same emancipatory ideal into an inexpungible sense of family, co-produced in imaginative interactions between locals and the metropolitan French. This was conceived as a familial bond between gift-giving metropolitan white elders and childlike 'native' juniors, with the islanders remaining eternally indebted for the gift of tutelage and liberation bestowed on them by the nurturing motherland/fatherland (*mère-patrie*) (Vergès 1999: 5–7).

For intelligentsia moderns in India as well as Vietnam, I believe that we need a conception of the familial with even more nuances. If it is right to see the lives of separation and displacement which so many of them have led as entailing something in the nature of a 'socialist family romance', it has been one in which the family as an open-ended moral project has taken shape around a host of competing moral narratives deriving from many variants of socialist and colonial experience. Some of these narratives exalt the family in general as well as the distinctive life of the modern intellectual family as models for the generous life of provision and high-principled culturedness to which all civilised states and citizenries should aspire in the world of the modern socialist ecumene. Other versions marginalise or even vilify one or both of these, or portray the revolution's triumph as a purging of all that makes for 'feudal' relations of hierarchy and oppression either within families or between those of good and bad class origins.

In India, the anglophone academics, professionals and upper-level administrators who compare most closely with my Hanoi intelligentsia informants have found that their distinctive sense of family has sometimes come dangerously adrift from the visions of conjugality and enlightened parenthood through which Indian citizens are encouraged to visualise the national family's virtues and resistance struggles. These are still widely associated with the well-known biographical and autobiographical accounts of familial life as led by Nehru and Gandhi, though other high-profile figures have exemplified similar or contrasting familial narratives for the nation and its constituent subregions.[10]

In Vietnam, too, the life of the nation has been widely represented as that of a dynamic, outward-looking super-family. But it is one in which the elderless revolutionary 'band of brothers' is replaced by a Vietnamese-style hierarchy of age grades and generational differences given order and life by the eternal, loving eldership of *Bac Ho*.[11] As beneficent, far-seeing elder to all, Ho Chi Minh's bountiful compassion is beyond time, indestructible and eternally animating of the selfless mutuality which Vietnam tells the world it has brought to its life of service and 'friendship' in the socialist ecumene.

This vision of *Bac Ho*'s 'shining love' (Pham Van Dong 1990: iii) and tenderly refined, expressive nature has been an important reference point for my informants, whose personal and family narratives build on though also subtly depart from these widely known official narratives of Vietnamese national life. So I do not mean to suggest an uncritical, cult-like adulation of the kind widely documented in relation to Stalin and Mao, and the other socialist authority figures still vested with officially sentimentalised idol status, the key example here being North Korea's 'Dear Leader' Kim Jong-il. But I have been greatly struck by my informants' regular references to sayings and anecdotes about Ho's enactments of love and feeling when they have thought aloud about the transformations of the pre and post-*doi moi* ('renovation') eras.

---

[10] Including that of 'Netaji' Subhas Chandra Bose, who like Ho Chi Minh is widely represented as having abstained from marriage and conventional family life so as to serve the higher familial needs of the nation (Gordon 1990: 82). This is a sensitive issue in India. In 2005 there was a public outcry over a dramatisation of Bose's life made by a leading Bengali cinema director, with a suit filed in the Calcutta High Court by litigants demanding censorship of scenes showing a wartime romance and marriage between 'Netaji' and his Viennese secretary-companion.

[11] He is also widely known as *Cu*, the term of loving reverence for a very senior relation, as well as 'beloved' *Bac Ho kinh yeu. Kinh yeu* is the respectful and uncarnal love directed by juniors to cherished seniors; *yeu* on its own is for spouses or lovers, and also a parent's love for their children. It is striking that like Nehru and Gandhi in India, but unlike Stalin and Mao, *Bac Ho* has not lost his central place in these Vietnamese familial narratives.

Young people now in their twenties recall being taught at school that Ho wept with joy on first reading Lenin, and that he shed tears at other moments of epic significance for the nation and the socialist world, including the closed-door Party Congress session announcing the great moment of Cold War transformation when Khrushchev made his famous 1956 speech denouncing Stalin.[12] When my friends have mentioned these expressions of 'true feeling', the connections they have made are very often to moments of change and choice in the moral and expressive lives of their families, and to those of the family-like collectivities which have been an equally dynamic source of connectedness and interaction in the Hanoi *tri thuc* world.

This should not be mistaken for a tame recapitulation of officially generated narratives about the authority of state and Party to define modes of feeling and action in a revolutionary society (compare Malarney 2002). It would appear that Ho Chi Minh can become a repository of these family-centred visions of the world and its moral life precisely because there are figures like his successor Le Duan who are still known as sources of those enduringly hostile views of intellectuals as people prone to 'indiscipline' in thought and action. In Ho Chi Minh there is of course a link which all my informants can make with the heroic generation of their parents and other elders, including the interzone teachers of whom they also speak as imparters of love and care. These glamorous, youthful freedom fighters of the Viet Minh resistance era feature in their narratives as francophone moderns setting a tradition of revolutionary attainment to which their descendants can look with pride, and with a sense of filial obligation fulfilled when they equip themselves and their younger kin with the skills and knowledge appropriate to today's version of the civilising socialist ecumene.

So in Ho there is an idealised but compelling model for all the qualities extolled as key markers of the Hanoi intellectual: refinement of feeling, deep patriotism and compassion for others, productively deployed linguistic and verbal skill, appreciation for the sights and cultivated pleasures of the wider cosmopolitan world. Critical too is the ascribing to him of an enlightened modern patriot's capacity to embrace and motivate change. This includes the capacity of the families of such moderns to change their shape and form in very substantial ways, while still enduring through time as active moral units.

---

[12] Such moments of tearful emotion are recorded at many points in writings by and about Ho Chi Minh, as in the 1960 essay which my younger friends all read at school, 'The Path which Led Me to Leninism' (www.marxists.org/reference/archive/ho-chi-minh/works/1960/04/x01.htm). See also Brocheux 2007: 19.

Vasavakul has shown that the Party leadership invoked *Bac Ho's* posthumous legitimating authority for the momentous move to 'internationalism' at the time of the great crisis of world socialism in 1989. In effect this involved having Ho Chi Minh speak in death as an all-seeing guide to the nation's future through the assertion that the new policy was in keeping with a hitherto unpublished portion of the iconic document known as his 'Last Will and Testament' (1995: 277). Now too, my friends point to his presence as a kind of moral compass, both for the nation and for families like theirs facing testing decisions about whether their talented young should seek employment in Hanoi's burgeoning international business world.

I have seen such matters discussed in Hanoi homes very much in the presence of the distinguished *tri thuc* forebears who remain a strong and active point of reference in their descendants' lives. The sense of their presence is nourished in a number of ways, not only through the careful tending of family ancestor altars, but through the narrative exchanges and other enactments of what I have called critical memory (compare Kwon 2006). In these moments of shared decision-making, *Bac Ho* is often mentioned as an exemplary agent of their families' past moments of choice and change. The expectation here is that the young will still lead lives in the spirit of that loving exemplarship, however differently their educations and career trajectories take shape in the future. It is widely if not enthusiastically accepted that this is a future in which the key models of progress and 'development' will come from the West, or from closer to home among the country's array of new and older Asian 'friends'. These include China, that eternally troubling socialist friend and familial elder, together with the countries like Singapore and Malaysia to which a new generation of export labourers is now being despatched, and even Japan, once reviled in both official and personal narratives as a land of unfeeling fascist colonisers – 'Very cold: like I used to think of the English', said an older friend. Looking at a poster depicting Ho Chi Minh standing above a landscape of green trees and a distant shoreline, a student friend in his early twenties said, 'We hear now that we shouldn't keep on thinking about that the way we learned it at school – the land and seas of Vietnam are very rich; we should use the wealth of nature; that is how to advance. Now we hear that maybe we should change that. We should tell the children what they say in Japan: the country does not have many natural resources – just our brains, so we have to study hard and that will make us advance.'[13]

---

[13] See Beresford 1995.

I certainly do not mean to suggest that the past and present lives of intelligentsia moderns in these arenas of ever-shifting overseas friendship ties are the only source of insight into the legacies of either colonialism or socialism in the complex societies I have discussed here. I do feel, however, that the Hanoi *tri thuc* world and its Indian equivalents offer compelling case studies of the negotiation of those disparate legacies on the part of people whom it is right to see as active moral agents engaging reflectively and dynamically with the multiple pasts and presents which they have forged and shared.

Bibliography

Abuza, Zachary (2001). *Renovating Politics in Contemporary Vietnam*. Boulder and London: Lynne Rienner.

Agence de la Francophonie (ACCT) (1997). *Quelle Francophonie pour le XXIe siècle?* Paris: Karthala.

Ahmad, Aijaz (1992). *In Theory: Nations, Classes, Literatures*. London and New York: Verso.

(1995). 'The politics of literary postcoloniality'. *Race and Class* 36, 3: 1–20.

Alter, J.S. (2004). 'Indian clubs and colonialism: Hindu masculinity and muscular Christianity'. *Comparative Studies in Society and History* 46, 3: 497–534.

Amin, Sonia Nishat (1996). *The World of Muslim Women in Colonial Bengal 1876–1939*. Leiden: Brill.

Antze, P. and M. Lambek (eds.) (1996). *Tense Past. Cultural Essays in Trauma and Memory*. London and New York: Routledge.

Appadurai, Arjun (1985). 'Gratitude as a social mode in South India'. *Ethos* 13, 4: 236–45.

(1996). *Modernity at Large: Cultural Dimensions of Globalization*. Minneapolis, MN: University of Minnesota Press.

Arnold, David (2004). 'The self and the cell: Indian prison narratives as life histories', in David Arnold and Stuart Blackburn (eds.), *Telling Lives in India: Biography, Autobiography and Life History*. Bloomington: Indiana University Press, pp. 29–53.

Arnold, David and Stuart Blackburn (eds.) (2004). *Telling Lives in India: Biography, Autobiography and Life History*. Bloomington: Indiana University Press.

Attwell, David (1999). 'Reprisals of modernity in black South African "mission" writing'. *Journal of Southern African Studies* 25, 2: 267–85.

Baber, Zaheer (1998). 'Communal conflict and the nostalgic imagination in India'. *Journal of Contemporary Asia* 28, 1: 27–44.

Bahloul, J. (1996). *The Architecture of Memory: A Jewish–Muslim Household in Colonial Algeria, 1937–1962*. Cambridge: Cambridge University Press.

Banfield, E.C. (1958). *The Moral Basis of a Backward Society*. New York: Free Press.

Barlow, Tani (1991). '*Zhishifenzi* [Chinese intellectuals] and power'. *Dialectical Anthropology*, 16, 3–4: 209–32.

241

Barnett, Marguerite Ross (1976). *The Politics of Cultural Nationalism in South India*. Princeton: Princeton University Press.

Bauman, Z. (1987) *Legislators and Interpreters: On Modernity, Post-Modernity and Intellectuals*. Ithaca, NY: Cornell University Press.

Bauman, R. and C. Briggs (2003). *Voices of Modernity: Language Ideologies and the Politics of Inequality*. Cambridge: Cambridge University Press.

Baxi, Upendra and Bhikhu Parekh (eds.) (1995). *Crisis and Change in Contemporary India*. New Delhi: Sage Publications.

Bayly, C.A. (1983) *Rulers, Townsmen and Bazaars: North Indian Society in the Age of British Expansion 1770–1870*. Cambridge: Cambridge University Press.

  (1986). 'The origins of swadeshi (home industry): cloth and Indian society, 1700–1930,' in Arjun Appadurai (ed.), *The Social Life of Things: Commodities in Cultural Perspective*. Cambridge: Cambridge University Press, pp. 285–81.

Bayly, C.A. and Tim Harper (2007). *Forgotten Wars: The End of Britain's Asian Empire*. London: Allen Lane.

Bayly, Susan (1999). *Caste, Society and Politics in India from the Eighteenth Century to the Modern Age*. Cambridge: Cambridge University Press.

  (2000). 'French anthropology and the Durkheimians in colonial Indochina'. *Modern Asian Studies* 34, 3: 581–622.

  (2002). 'Racial readings of empire: Britain, France and colonial modernity in the Mediterranean and Asia', in L. Fawaz and C. Bayly (eds.), *Modernity and Culture from the Mediterranean to the Indian Ocean*. New York: Columbia University Press, pp. 285–313.

  (2004a). 'Vietnamese intellectuals in revolutionary and postcolonial times'. *Critique of Anthropology* 24, 3: 320–44.

  (2004b). 'Conceptualising from within', in H. Whitehouse and J. Laidlaw (eds.), *Ritual and Memory: Towards a Comparative Anthropology of Religion*. London and Oxford: Altamira Press, pp. 111–34.

  (2004c). 'Imagining "Greater India": French and Indian visions of colonialism in the Indic mode'. *Modern Asian Studies* 38, 3: 703–44.

  (forthcoming). 'Vietnamese narratives of tradition, exchange and friendship in the worlds of the global socialist ecumene', in Harry West and Paru Raman (eds.), *Enduring Socialism: Explorations of Revolution, Transformation and Restoration*. Oxford: Berghahn Books.

Beatty, Andrew (2005). 'Emotions in the field: what are we talking about?' *Journal of the Royal Anthropological Institute* 11, 1: 17–37.

Benei, V. (2005). 'Of languages, passions and interests: education, regionalism and globalization in Maharashta, 1800–2000', in J. Assayag and C. Fuller (eds.), *Globalizing India: Locality, Nation and the World*. London: Anthem Press, pp. 141–62.

Beresford, Melanie (1995). 'Economy and the environment', in Benedict J. Tria Kerkvliet (ed.), *Dilemmas of Development: Vietnam Update 1994*. Political and Social Change Monograph no. 22. Canberra: Australian National University, pp. 69–88.

Beresford, Melanie and Dang Phong (2000). *Economic Transition in Vietnam: Trade and Aid in the Demise of a Centrally Planned Economy*. Cheltenham and Northampton, MA: Edward Elgar.

Bernal, Martin (1981). 'The Nghe-Tinh Soviet movement 1930–1931', *Past and Present* 92: 148–68.

Bernstein, G.L. (2005). 'Social networks among daughters', in G.L. Bernstein, A. Gordon and K.W. Nakai (eds.), *Public Spheres, Private Lives in Modern Japan, 1600–1950*. Cambridge, MA and London: Harvard University Press, pp.293–317.

Béteille, André (1991). 'The reproduction of inequality: occupation, caste and family'. *Contributions to Indian Sociology* 25, 1: 3–28.

Betts, Paul (2000). 'The twilight of the idols: East German memory and material culture'. *Journal of Modern History* 72, 3: 731–65.

Blunt, Alison and Gillian Rose (1992). 'Women's colonial and postcolonial geographies', in Blunt and Rose (eds.), *Writing Women and Space: Colonial and Postcolonial Geographies*. New York and London, pp.1–28.

Bonnell, Victoria (1997). *Iconography of Power: Soviet Political Posters under Lenin and Stalin*. Berkeley, Los Angeles and London: University of California Press.

Bonnin, M. and Y. Chevrier (1991). 'The intellectual and the state: social dynamics of intellectual autonomy during the post-Mao era'. *China Quarterly* 127: 569–93.

Borneman, John (1995). *Belonging in the Two Berlins: Kin, State, Nation*. Cambridge and New York: Cambridge University Press.

Borocz, J. and C. Southworth (1996). 'Decomposing the intellectuals' class power: conversion of cultural capital to income, Hungary, 1986'. *Social Forces* 74, 3: 797–822.

Bose, Sugata (1990). 'Starvation amidst plenty: the making of famine in Bengal, Honan and Tonkin, 1942–45'. *Modern Asian Studies* 24, 4: 699–727.

(2003). 'Post-colonial histories of South Asia: some reflections'. *Journal of Contemporary History* 38, 1: 133–46.

(2006). *A Hundred Horizons: The Indian Ocean in the Age of Global Empire*. New Delhi: Permanent Black.

Bose, Sugata and Ayesha Jalal (1998). *Modern South Asia: History, Culture, Political Economy*. London and New York: Routledge.

Bose, S.C. and S.K. Bose (1997). *An Indian Pilgrim: Subhas Chandra Bose: An Unfinished Autobiography*. ed. Sisir K. Bose and Sugata Bose. New Delhi: Oxford University Press.

Boudarel, G. (1991). 'Intellectual dissidence in the 1950s: the Nhan Van-Giai Pham Affair'. *Viet Nam Forum* 13: 154–74.

Bourdieu, Pierre (1984) *Distinction: A Social Critique of the Judgement of Taste*, trans. Richard Nice. Cambridge, MA: Harvard University Press.

Bousquet, G.L. (2002). 'Facing globalization: Vietnam and the Francophone community', in G. Bousquet and P. Brocheux (eds.), *Viêt-Nam Exposé: French Scholarship on Twentieth-Century Vietnamese Society*. Ann Arbor: University of Michigan Press, pp.421–55.

Bousquet, G.L. and P. Brocheux (eds.) (2002). *Viêt-Nam Exposé: French Scholarship on Twentieth-Century Vietnamese Society*. Ann Arbor: University of Michigan Press.

Bowd, Gavin and Daniel Clayton (2005). 'Tropicality, Orientalism and French colonialism in Indochina: the work of Pierre Gourou, 1927–1982', *French Historical Studies* 28, 2: 297–327.

Boyer, D. and C. Lomnitz (2005). 'Intellectuals and nationalism: anthropological engagements'. *Annual Review of Anthropology* 34: 105–20.

Boym, Svetlana (1995). 'From the Russian soul to post-Communist nostalgia'. *Representations* 49: 133–66.

Bradley, M.P. (2000). *Imagining Vietnam and America. The Making of Postcolonial Vietnam, 1919–1950.* Chapel Hill and London: University of North Carolina Press.

(2004). 'Becoming *Van Minh*: civilizational discourse and visions of the self in twentieth-century Vietnam'. *Journal of World History* 15, 1: 65–84, at www.historycooperative.org/journals/jwh/15.1/bradley.html.

Brass, P. (1990). *The Politics of India since Independence.* Cambridge: Cambridge University Press.

Brass, T. (1995). *New Farmers' Movements in India.* London: Frank Cass.

Brenner, S. (1998). *The Domestication of Desire. Women, Wealth and Modernity in Java.* Princeton, NJ: Princeton University Press.

Broaded, C.M. (1983). 'Higher education policy changes and stratification in China'. *China Quarterly* 93: 125–37.

Brocheux, Pierre (2002). 'The economy of war as a prelude to a "socialist economy": the case of the Vietnamese resistance against the French, 1945–1954', in G.L Bousquet and P. Brocheux (eds.), *Viêt-Nam Exposé: French Scholarship on Twentieth-Century Vietnamese Society.* Ann Arbor: University of Michigan Press, pp.313–30.

(2007). *Ho Chi Minh: A Biography,* trans. Claire Duiker. Cambridge and New York: Cambridge University Press.

Brocheux, Pierre and Daniel Hémery (1995). *Indochine: la Colonisation Ambiguë 1858–1954.* Paris: Éditions la Découverte.

Brownell, Susan (1995). *Training the Body for China: Sports in the Moral Order of the People's Republic.* Chicago: University of Chicago Press.

Bruun, Ole (1993). *Business and Bureaucracy in a Chinese City: An Ethnography of Private Business Households in Contemporary China.* Berkeley: Institute of East Asian Studies.

Buchli, Victor (2000). *An Archaeology of Socialism.* Oxford and New York: Berg.

Bui Minh Dung (1995). 'Japan's role in the Vietnamese starvation of 1944–1945'. *Modern Asian Studies* 29, 3: 573–618.

Burgess, T. (2002). 'Cinema, bell bottoms, and miniskirts: struggles over youth and citizenship in revolutionary Zanzibar'. *International Journal of African Historical Studies* 35, 2/3: 287–313.

Burke, T. (1996). *Lifebuoy Men, Lux Women: Commodification, Consumption and Cleanliness in Modern Zimbabwe.* Durham and London: Duke University Press.

Burton, A. (1997). 'House/daughter/nation: interiority, architecture, and historical imagination in Janaki Majumdar's "Family History"'. *Journal of Asian Studies* 56, 4: 921–46.

Butalia, U. (1998). *The Other Side of Silence: Voices from the Partition of India.* New Delhi: Penguin.

Cao, Cong (1999). 'Social origins of the Chinese scientific elite'. *China Quarterly* 160: 992–1018.

Cao Thi Nhu-Quynh and John C. Schafer (1988). 'From verse narrative to novel: the development of prose fiction in Vietnam'. *Journal of Asian Studies* 47, 4: 756–77.

Caplan, P. (1997). *African Voices, African Lives: Personal Narratives from a Swahili Village*. London and New York: Routledge.

Carruthers, Ashley (2002). 'The accumulation of national belonging in transnational fields: ways of being at home in Vietnam'. *Identities: Global Studies in Culture and Power* 9: 423–44.

Carsten, Janet (2000). '"Knowing where you've come from": ruptures and continuites of time and kinship in narratives of adoption reunions'. *Journal of the Royal Anthropological Institute* 6, 4: 687–703.

Césaire, Aimé (1970 [1955]). *Discours sur le colonialisme*. Paris: Présence Africaine.

Chakrabarty, Dipesh (1994). 'The difference-deferral of a colonial modernity: public debates on domesticity in British India', in D. Arnold and D. Hardiman (eds.), *Subaltern Studies VIII*. New Delhi: Oxford University Press, pp. 50–88.

  (2002). *Habitations of Modernity: Essays in the Wake of Subaltern Studies*. Chicago: University of Chicago Press.

Chan, Kwok-Bun (2002). 'Both sides now: culture contact, hybridisation and cosmopolitanism', in Steven Vertovec and Robin Cohen (eds.), *Conceiving Cosmopolitanism. Theory, Context and Practice*. Oxford: Oxford University Press, pp. 191–208.

Chan, Anita, Benedict J. Tria Kerkvliet and Jonathan Unger (eds.) (1999) *Transforming Asian Socialism: China and Vietnam Compared*. Canberra: Allen and Unwin.

Chandra, Sudhir (1992). *The Oppressive Present: Literature and Social Consciousness in Colonial India*. Oxford: Oxford University Press.

Chang, Pao-min (1982). 'The Sino-Vietnamese dispute over the ethnic Chinese'. *China Quarterly* 90: 195–230.

Chatterjee, Partha (1990) 'The nationalist resolution of the women's question', in Kumkum Sangari and Sudesh Vaid (eds.), *Essays in Indian Colonial History*, New Brunswick, NJ: Rutgers University Press, pp. 233–53.

  (1994). *The Nation and its Fragments: Colonial and Postcolonial Histories*. Princeton: Princeton University.

Cheal, D. (1991). *Family and the State of Theory*. Toronto: University of Toronto Press.

Chen, Jian (1993). 'China and the first Indo-China War, 1950–54'. *China Quarterly* 133: 85–110.

Cheng, Yinghong (2004). 'Beyond Moscow-centric interpretation: an examination of the China connection in Eastern Europe and North Vietnam during the era of de-Stalinization'. *Journal of World History* 15, 4: 487–518.

Clancy-Smith, Julia and Frances Gouda (eds.) (1998). *Domesticating the Empire: Race, Gender and Family Life in French and Dutch Colonialism*. Charlottesville and London: University Press of Virginia.

Cole, Jennifer (2001). *Forget Colonialism? Sacrifice and the Art of Memory in Madagascar*. Berkeley and Los Angeles: University of California Press.

Collier, J.F. (1997). *From Duty to Desire: Remaking Families in a Spanish Village*. Princeton, NJ: Princeton University Press.

Comaroff, J. (1998). 'Reflections on the colonial state, in South Africa and elsewhere: factions, fragments, facts and fictions'. *Social Identities* 4, 3: 321–61.

Conklin, Alice L. (1997). *A Mission to Civilize: The Republican Idea of Empire in France and West Africa, 1895–1930*. Stanford: Stanford University Press.

(1998). 'Redefining "Frenchness": citizenship, race regeneration and imperial motherhood in France and West Africa, 1914–40', in Julia Clancy-Smith and Frances Gouda (eds.), *Domesticating the Empire, Race, Gender and Family Life in French and Dutch colonialism*. Charlottesville: University of Virginia Press, pp.65–83.

Cooke, Nola (1995). 'The composition of the nineteenth-century political elite of pre-colonial Nguyen Vietnam (1802–1883)'. *Modern Asian Studies* 29, 4: 741–64.

Cooper, Frederick (2005). *Colonialism in Question: Theory, Knowledge, History*. Berkeley: University of California Press.

Craig, D. (2002). *Familiar Medicine: Everyday Health Knowledge and Practice in Today's Vietnam*. Honolulu: University of Hawai'i Press.

Crehan, Kate (2002). *Gramsci, Culture and Anthropology*. Berkeley: University of California Press.

Croll, E. (1994). *From Heaven to Earth: Images and Experiences of Development in China*. London: Routledge.

Crozier, Ralph C. (1965). 'Traditional medicine in Communist China: science, Communism and cultural nationalism', *China Quarterly* 23: 1–27.

Cumming, Gordon (2005). 'Transposing the "republican" model? A critical appraisal of France's historic mission in Africa'. *Journal of Contemporary African Studies* 23, 2: 233–52.

Cutler, N. (1983). 'The fish-eyed goddess meets the movie star: an eyewitness account of the fifth International Tamil Conference'. *Pacific Affairs* 56, 2: 270–87.

Dang Anh Dao. (1999). *Tam Xuan Hoi Uc* [Sweetbriar Diaries] Hanoi: NXB Phu Nu.

(2002). 'Ky niem mua thu [Autumn Memories]', in Nhieu Tac Gia (ed.) [Many authors], *Nho Dang Thai Mai* [In Memory of Dang Thai Mai], Hanoi: NXB Hoi Nha Van, pp.161–8.

Dang Phong (1999a). 'Itinéraire économique du Vietnam: événements et éléments d'orientation'. *Etudes Vietnamiennes* 133, 3: 91–106.

(1999b). 'Vietnamese economy in the period 1945–1954'. *Vietnam's Socio-Economic Development* 18: 41–55.

(2002) *Lich Su Kinh Te Viet Nam, 1945–2000 Tap 1:1945–1954*. [Economic History of Vietnam 1945–2000 Vol. I: 1945–1954]. Hanoi: NXB Khoa Hoc Xa Hoi.

Dang Phong and Melanie Beresford (1998). *Authority Relations and Economic Decision Making in Vietnam*. Copenhagen: NIAS Publications.

Das, Suranjan (2001). *The Nehru Years in Indian Politics*. Edinburgh Papers in South Asian Studies No. 16. Centre for South Asian Studies, School of Social and Political Studies, University of Edinburgh.

Das, Veena (1995). *Critical Events: An Anthropological Perspective on Contemporary India*. Delhi: Oxford University Press.

Davidson, J. H. C. S. (1986). '"Collaborateur" versus "Abstentioniste" ("Tuong" versus "Tri"): a political polemic in poetic dialogue during the French acquisition of southern Viet-Nam'. *Bulletin of the School of Oriental and African Studies, University of London* 49 (2): 321–63.

Davis, D. (1992). '"Skidding": downward mobility among children of the Maoist middle class'. *Modern China* 18, 4: 410–37.

Delanoë, Nelcya (2002). *Poussières d'Empire: trois couleurs, un drapeau, un empire*. Paris: Presses Universitaires de France.

De Munck, V. C. (1996). 'Love and marriage in a Sri Lankan Muslim community: toward a reevaluation of Dravidian marriage practices'. *American Ethnologist* 23, 4: 698–716.

de Vylder, Stefan and Adam Fforde (1996). *From Plan to Market: The Economic Transition in Vietnam*. Boulder: Westview.

Diamant, N. (2000). *Revolutionising the Family. Politics, Love and Divorce in Urban and Rural China 1949–68*. Berkeley and London: University of California Press.

Dikötter, F. (1998). 'Race culture: recent perspectives on the history of eugenics'. *American Historical Review* 103, 2: 467–78.

Dirlik, Arif (1994). 'The postcolonial aura: Third World criticism in the age of global capitalism'. *Critical Inquiry* 20, 2: 328–56.

  (1997). 'Narrativizing revolution: the Guangzhou uprising (11–13 December 1927) in workers' perspective'. *Modern China* 23, 4: 363–97.

Donham, D. (1999). *Marxist Modern: An Ethnographic History of the Ethiopian Revolution*. Berkeley: University of California Press.

Donner, Henrike (2005). 'Children are capital, grandchildren are interest: changing educational strategies and parenting in Calcutta's middle-class families', in J. Assayag and C. J. Fuller (eds.), *Globalizing India: Perspectives from Below*. London: Anthem Press, pp. 119–40.

Drummond, Lisa B. W. (2001). 'Street scenes: practices of public and private space in urban Vietnam'. *Urban Studies* 37, 12: 2377–91.

Duara, P. (1995). *Rescuing History from the Nation: Questioning Narratives of Modern China*. Chicago, London: University of Chicago Press.

  (1997) 'Transnationalism and the predicament of sovereignty: China, 1900–1945'. *American Historical Review* 102, 4: 1030–51.

Duiker, W. J. (1996). *The Communist Road to Power in Vietnam*. Boulder: Westview.

  (2000). *Ho Chi Minh*. New York: Hyperion.

Duncan, Ian (1999). 'Dalits and politics in rural North India: the Bahujan Samaj Party in Uttar Pradesh'. *Journal of Peasant Studies* 27, 1: 35–60.

Duong Thi Thoa (Le Thi) and Mark Sidel (1998). 'Changing my life: how I came to the Vietnamese revolution'. *Signs*. 23, 4: 1017–29.

Duong Trung Quoc (ed.) (2006). *Nguyen Duy Kien: Nhung Ky Uc Con Lai* [Enduring Memories of Nguyen Duy Kien]. Hanoi: NXB Lao Dong Xa Hoi.

Edney, Matthew (1997). *Mapping an Empire: The Geographical Construction of British India, 1765–1843*. Chicago: University of Chicago Press.

Edwards, Louise. (2000). 'Policing the modern woman in Republican China'. *Modern China* 26, (2): 115–47.

Endres, K.W. (2001). 'Local dynamics of renegotiating ritual space in Northern Vietnam: the case of the dinh'. *SOJOURN: Journal of Social Issues in Southeast Asia* 16, 1: 70–101.

Esbenshade, R.S. (1995). 'Remembering to forget: memory, history, national identity in postwar east-central Europe'. *Representations* 49: 72–96.

Esherick, Joseph W. (1998). 'Revolution in a feudal fortress: Yangjiagou, Mizhi County, Shaanxi, 1937–1948', *Modern China* 24, 4: 339–77.

Fabian, J. (2001). *Anthropology with an Attitude: Critical Essays*. Stanford, CA: Stanford University Press.

Fall, B. (1960). *Le Viet-Minh: la République Démocratique du Viet-Nam, 1945–1960*. Paris: Armand Colin.

Falzon, Mark-Anthony (2004). *Cosmopolitan Connections: The Sindi Diaspora, 1860–2000*. Leiden, Boston: Brill.

Fanon, Franz (1965). *A Dying Colonialism*. New York: Grove Press.

(1992[1952]). *Peau noire, masques blancs*. Paris: Seuil.

Farquhar, J. (1996). 'Market magic: getting rich and getting personal in medicine after Mao'. *American Ethnologist* 23, 2: 239–57.

Fay, P.W. (1993). *The Forgotten Army: India's Armed Struggle for Independence 1942–1945*. Ann Arbor: University of Michigan Press.

Ferguson, J. (1990). *The Anti-Politics Machine: 'Development', Depoliticization and Bureaucratic Power in Lesotho*. Cambridge: Cambridge University Press.

(1992). 'The country and the city on the Copperbelt'. *Cultural Anthropology* 7, 1: 80–92.

Feuchtwang, Stephan (2002). 'Remnants of revolution in China', in C.M. Hann (ed.), *Postsocialism. Ideals, Ideologies and Practices in Eurasia*. London and New York: Routledge, pp. 196–214.

(2006). 'Images of sub-humanity and their realization'. *Critique of Anthropology* 26, 3: 259–78.

Fforde, A. (1989). *The Agrarian Question in North Vietnam, 1974–1979: A Study of Cooperator Resistance to State Policy*. Armonk, NY: M.E. Sharpe.

(2003). 'Vietnam – culture and economy: dyed-in-the-wool tigers?', in L.B.W. Drummond and M. Thomas (eds.), *Consuming Urban Culture in Contemporary Vietnam*. London and New York: Routledge Curzon, pp. 35–59.

Finn, Margot (2006). 'Colonial gifts: family politics and the exchange of goods in British India, c. 1780–1820'. *Modern Asian Studies* 40, 1: 203–31.

Finnane, A. (1996). 'What should Chinese women wear?: A national problem'. *Modern China* 22, 2: 99–131.

Fitzpatrick, S. (1992). *The Cultural Front: Power and Culture in Revolutionary Russia*. Ithaca and London: Cornell University Press.

(1999). *Everyday Stalinism. Ordinary Life in Extraordinary Times: Soviet Russia in the 1930s*. Oxford: Oxford University Press.

Forrester, D. (1976). 'Factions and filmstars: Tamil Nadu politics since 1971'. *Asian Survey* 16, 3: 283–96.

Foster, Robert J. (1991). 'Making national cultures in the global ecumene'. *Annual Review of Anthropology* 20: 235–60.

Frank, Katherine (2002). *Indira: The Life of Indira Nehru Gandhi*. Boston, New York: Houghton Mifflin.

Frederick, William H. (1997). 'The appearance of revolution: cloth, uniform and the "pemuda style" in East Java, 1945–1949', in H.S. Nordholt (ed.), *Outward Appearances: Dressing State and Society in Indonesia*. Leiden, Netherlands: KITLV Press, pp. 117–50.

Frieson, Kate (2000). 'Sentimental education: *Les sages femmes* and colonial Cambodia'. *Journal of Colonialism and Colonial History* 1, 1.

Gainsborough, Martin (2002). 'Political change in Vietnam: in search of the middle-class challenge to the state'. *Asian Survey* 42, 5: 694–707.

Gandhi, M.K. (1940). *An Autobiography. Or, The Story of My Experiments with Truth*, trans. Mahadev Desai. Ahmedabad: Navajivan Publishing House.

Gerth, K. (2003). *China Made: Consumer Culture and the Creation of the Nation*. Cambridge, MA: Harvard University Press.

Gibbs, Jason (2000). 'Spoken theater, *La Scène Tonkinoise*, and the first modern Vietnamese songs'. *Asian Music* 31, 2: 1–33.

Giebel, C. (2004). *Imagined Ancestries of Vietnamese Communism: Ton Duc Thang and the Politics of History and Memory*. Seattle: University of Washington Press.

Gilsenan, Michael (1996). *Lords of the Lebanese Marches: Violence and Narrative in an Arab Society*. London and New York: I.B. Tauris.

Gingrich, André and Richard G. Fox (eds.) (2002). *Anthropology, by Comparison*. London and New York: Routledge.

Gold, T.B. (1985). 'After comradeship: personal relations in China since the Cultural Revolution'. *China Quarterly* 104: 657–75.

Goldman, Merle (1999). 'Politically engaged individuals in the 1990s'. *China Quarterly* 159, special issue: *The People's Republic of China after 50 years*: 700–11.

Goldman, Merle, with Timothy Cheek and Carol Lee Hamrin (1987). *China's Intellectuals and the State: In Search of a New Relationship*. Cambridge: Harvard University Press.

Gordon, A. (1981). 'North Vietnam's collectivisation campaigns: class struggle, production and the "middle peasant" problem'. *Journal of Contemporary Asia* 11, 1: 19–43.

Gordon, L.A. (1990). *Brothers Against the Raj: A Biography of Indian Nationalists Sarat and Subhas Chandra Bose*. New York: Columbia University Press.

Goscha, C.E. (2000). 'The borders of Vietnam's early wartime trade with southern China: a contemporary perspective'. *Asian Survey* 40, 6: 987–1018.

(2003) 'Building force: Asian origins of 20th century military science in Vietnam 1905–54'. *Journal of Southeast Asian Studies* 34, 3: 535–60.

(2004a). 'Vietnam and the world outside: the case of Vietnamese Communist advisers in Laos (1948–62)'. *South East Asia Research* 12, 2: 141–85.

(2004b). 'The modern barbarian: Nguyen Van Vinh and the complexity of colonial modernity in Vietnam'. *European Journal of East Asian Studies* 3, 1: 135–69.

(2006). 'Courting diplomatic disaster? The difficult integration of Vietnam into the internationalist Communist movement (1945–1950)'. *Journal of Vietnamese Studies* 1, 1/2: 59–103.

Goscha, C.E. and Benôit de Tréglodé (2004). *Naissance d'un Etat-Parti: Le Vietnam depuis 1945/The Birth of a Party-State: Vietnam Since 1945*. Paris: Les Indes Savantes.

Gourou, P. (1936). *Les Payans du Delta Tonkinois: Etude de géographie humaine*. Paris: Les Editions d'Art et d'Histoire.

Greenberg, J.D. (2005). 'Generations of memory: remembering partition in India/Pakistan and Israel/Palestine'. *Comparative Studies of South Asia, Africa and the Middle East* 25, 1: 89–110.

Greenhalgh, S. (1994). 'De-orientalizing the Chinese family firm'. *American Ethnologist* 21, 4: 746–75.

Grossheim, M. and J.H. Vincent (eds.) (2001). *Vietnam, Regional Integration and the Asian Financial Crisis: Vietnamese and European Perspectives*. Passau: Passau Contributions to Southeast Asian Studies.

Gu, Edward X. (1999). 'Cultural intellectuals and the politics of the cultural public space in Communist China (1979–1989): a case study of three intellectual groups'. *Journal of Asian Studies* 58, 2: 389–431.

Gupta, Akhil (1999). 'The song of the Nonaligned world: transnational identities and the reinscription of space in late capitalism', in Steven Vertovec and Robin Cohen (eds.), *Migration, Diasporas and Transnationalism*. Northampton MA: Edgar Elgar.

Ha, M.P. (2003). 'From "Nos ancêtres, les Gaulois" to "leur culture ancestrale": symbolic violence and the politics of colonial schooling in Indochina'. *French Colonial History* 3: 101–17.

Halfin, Igal (1997). 'The rape of the intelligentsia: a proletarian foundational myth'. *Russian Review* 56 1: 90–109.

Hamabata, Matthews Masayuki (1991). *Crested Kimono. Power and Love in the Japanese Business Family*. Ithaca and London: Cornell University Press.

Han, Xiaorong (2004). 'Who invented the bronze drum? Nationalism, politics, and a Sino-Vietnamese archaeological debate of the 1970s and 1980s'. *Asian Perspectives* 43, 1: 7–33.

Hancock, M. (1995). 'Hindu culture for an Indian nation: gender, politics, and elite identity in urban south India'. *American Ethnologist* 22, 4: 907–26.

Hannerz, Ulf (1987). 'The world in creolization'. *Africa: Journal of the International African Institute* 57, 4: 546–59.

Hansen, Thomas Blum (1999). *The Saffron Wave: Democracy and Hindu Nationalism in Modern India*. Princeton: Princeton University Press.

Hardgrave, Robert L. (1965). *The Dravidian Movement*. Bombay: Popular Prakashan.

Hardy, Andrew (2000). 'Des valeurs de l'amitié: esquisse ethnographique des travailleurs vietnamiens dans les pays socialistes de l'Europe'. *Revue Européenne des Migrations Internationales* 16, 1: 235–46.

(2003). *Red Hills: Migrants and the State in the Highlands of Vietnam*. Copenhagen: Nordic Institute of Asian Studies Press.

Harley, J.B. (2001). *The New Nature of Maps: Essays in the History of Cartography*. Baltimore: John Hopkins University Press.

Harris, John (2002). 'Whatever happened to cultural nationalism in Tamil Nadu? A reading of current events and the recent literature on Tamil politics'. *Commonwealth and Comparative Politics* 40, 3: 97–117.

Harrison-Hall, Jessica (2002). *Vietnam Behind the Lines: Images from the War, 1965–1975*. London: British Museum Press.

Hasan, Mushirul (2005). *A Moral Reckoning: Muslim Intellectuals in Nineteenth-Century Delhi*. Oxford: Oxford University Press.

Henley, D. (1995). 'Ethnogeographic integration and exclusion in anticolonial nationalism: Indonesia and Indochina'. *Comparative Studies in Society and History* 37, 2: 286–324.

Herrick, T. (2005). '"A book which is no longer discussed today": Tran Duc Thao, Jacques Derrida, and Maurice Merleau-Ponty'. *Journal of the History of Ideas* 66, 1: 113–31.

Hills, C. and Silverman, D.C. (1993). 'Nationalism and feminism in late colonial India: the Rani of Jhansi Regiment, 1943–1945'. *Modern Asian Studies* 27, 4: 741–60.

Hirsch, F. (2005). *Empire of Nations: Ethnographic Knowledge and the Making of the Soviet Union*. Ithaca: Cornell University Press.

Hirschman, C. and Vu Manh Loi (1996). 'Family and household structure in Vietnam: some glimpses from a recent survey'. *Pacific Affairs* 69, 2: 229–49.

Ho, Engseng (2002). 'Names beyond nations: the making of local cosmopolitans'. *Études Rurales* 163/164: 215–32.

(2004). 'Empire through diasporic eyes: a view from the other boat'. *Comparative Studies in Society and History* 46, 2: 210–46.

(2006). *The Graves of Tarim: Genealogy and Mobility Across the Indian Ocean*. Berkeley: University of California.

Hodges, Sarah (2005). 'Revolutionary family life and the Self-Respect Movement in Tamil South India, 1926–49'. *Contributions to Indian Sociology* 39, 2: 251–77.

Holm, David (1991). *Art and Ideology in Revolutionary China*. Oxford: Clarendon.

Holy, L. (1994). 'Metaphors of the natural and the artificial in Czech political discourse'. *Man* 29, 4: 809–29.

Hua, Shiping (1994). 'One servant, two masters: the dilemma of Chinese establishment intellectuals'. *Modern China* 20, 1: 92–121.

Humphrey, C. (1994). 'Remembering an "enemy": the Bogd Khaan in twentieth-century Mongolia', in R.Watson (ed.), *Memory, History, and Opposition under State Socialism*. Santa Fe: School of American Research Press, pp.21–44.

(2001). 'Rethinking bribery in contemporary Russia', in Stephen Lovell, Alena Ledeneva and Andrei Rogachevskii (eds.), *Bribery and Blat in Russia: Negotiating Reciprocity from the Middle Ages to the 1990s*. London: Macmillan, pp.216–41.

(2002). *The Unmaking of Soviet Life: Everyday Economies after Socialism*. Ithaca: Cornell University Press.

(2004). 'Cosmopolitanism and *kosmopolitizm* in the political life of Soviet citizens'. *Focaal – European Journal of Anthropology* 44: 138–52.

Hunt, Lynn (1992). *The Family Romance of the French Revolution*. Berkeley: University of California Press.

Huu Ngoc (2002). 'A colonial textbook on the Vietnamese language'. *Vietnamese Studies* 145, 3: 5–16.

Huynh Van Tieng and Bui Duc Tinh (2002). *Hoang Mai Luu va Cac Ca Khuc Trong Phong Trao Am Nhac Cach Mang* [Hoang Mai Luu and his songs during the revolutionary music movement]. Hanoi: NXB Tre.

Hy Van Luong (1988). 'Discursive practices and power structure: person-referring forms and sociopolitical struggles in colonial Vietnam'. *American Ethnologist* 15, 2: 239–53.

(1989) 'Vietnamese kinship: structural principles and the socialist transformation in Northern Vietnam'. *Journal of Asian Studies* 48, 4: 741–56.

(1990). *Discursive Practices and Linguistic Meanings: The Vietnamese System of Person Reference*. Amsterdam and Philadelphia: John Benjamins.

(1998). 'Engendered entrepreneurship: ideologies and political-economic transformation in a northern Vietnamese centre of ceramics production', in R.W. Hefner (ed.), *Market Cultures: Society and Morality in the New Asian Capitalisms*. Boulder and Oxford: Westview Press, pp. 290–314.

(1992). *Revolution in the Village: Tradition and Transformation in North Vietnam: 1925–1988*. Honolulu: University of Hawai'i Press.

Hy Van Luong (ed.) (2003). *Postwar Vietnam: Dynamics of a Transforming Society*. Oxford and Singapore: Bowman and Littlefield.

The Indian Civil Service Manual (Madras) (1931). Madras: Government Press.

Irschick, Eugene F. (1969). *Politics and Social Conflict in South India: The Non-Brahman Movement and Tamil Separatism, 1916–1929*. Berkeley and Los Angeles: University of California Press.

Jaffrelot, C. (2002). *India's Silent Revolution: The Rise of the Lower Castes in North Indian Politics*. Delhi: Permanent Black.

Jager, S.M. (1996). 'Women, resistance and the divided nation: the romantic rhetoric of Korean reunification'. *Journal of Asian Studies* 55, 1: 3–21.

Jalal, Ayesha (1995). 'Conjuring Pakistan history as official imagining'. *International Journal of Middle East Studies* 27, 1: 73–89.

James, Wendy (1997). 'The names of fear: memory, history, and the ethnography of feeling among Uduk refugees'. *Journal of the Royal Anthropological Institute* 3, 1: 115–31.

Jellema, K. (2005). 'Making good on debt: the remoralisation of wealth in post-revolutionary Vietnam'. *Asia Pacific Journal of Anthropology* 6, 3: 231–48.

Jennings, E.T. (2001). *Vichy in the Tropics. Pétain's National Revolution in Madagascar, Guadeloupe and Indochina, 1940–44*. Stanford, CA: Stanford University Press.

Judd, Ellen (1983). 'Revolutionary drama and song in the Jiangxi Soviet'. *Modern China* 9, 1: 127–60.

(1985). 'Prelude to the "Yan'an talks": problems in transforming a literary intelligentsia'. *Modern China* 11, 3: 377–408.

Kaplan, M. (1995). 'Panopticon in Poona: an essay on Foucault and colonialism'. *Cultural Anthropology* 10, 1: 85–98.

Kaplan, M. and John D. Kelly (1994). 'Rethinking resistance: dialogics of "disaffection" in colonial Fiji'. *American Ethnologist* 21, 1: 123–51.

Karabel, J. (1996). 'Towards a theory of intellectuals and politics'. *Theory and Society* 25, 2: 205–33.

Karlekar, Malavika (1993) *Voices from Within: Early Personal Narratives of Bengali Women*. Delhi: Oxford University Press.

Kautsky, Karl (1903). 'Intellectuals and workers'. *Die Neue Zeit* 22, 4, at www. marxists.org/archive/kautsky/1903/xx/int-work.htm.

Kelly, Catriona (2001). *Refining Russia: Advice Literature, Polite Culture, and Gender from Catherine to Yeltsin*. Oxford: Oxford University Press.

Kelly, Gail Paradise (2000). *French Colonial Education. Essays on Vietnam and West Africa*, ed. David H. Kelly. New York: AMS Press.

Kelly, J.D. (1989). 'Fear of culture: British regulation of Indian marriage in post-indenture Fiji'. *Ethnohistory* 36, 4: 372–91.

Kerkvliet, Benedict J. Tria (1995). 'Village-state relations in Vietnam: the effect of everyday politics on decollectivization'. *Journal of Asian Studies* 54, 2: 396–418.

Kerkvliet, Benedict J. Tria and Mark Selden (1998). 'Agrarian transformations in China and Vietnam'. *China Journal* 40: 37–58.

Keyes, C. (2002). 'Presidential address. "The peoples of Asia": science and politics in the classification of ethnic groups in Thailand, China and Vietnam'. *Journal of Asian Studies* 61, 4: 1163–203.

Khare, R.S. (1971). 'Home and office: some trends of modernization among the Kanya-Kubja Brahmans'. *Comparative Studies in Society and History* 13, 2: 196–216.

Khilnani, S. (1997). *The Idea of India*. London: Hamish Hamilton.

Kim, Sung Chull (2002). 'Dynamism of politics and status of intellectuals in North Korea'. *Development and Society* 31, 1: 79–106.

Kipnis, A.B. (1996). 'The language of gifts: managing *guanxi* in a north China village'. *Modern China* 22, 3: 285–314.

Kleinen, John (1999). *Facing the Future, Reviving the Past: A Study of Social Change in a Northern Vietnamese Village*. Singapore: Institute of Southeast Asian Studies.

(2005). 'Tropicality and Topicality. Pierre Gourou and the genealogy of French colonial scholarship on rural Vietnam'. *Singapore Journal of Tropical Geography* 26, 3: 339–58.

Kleinman, Arthur and Joan Kleinman (1994). 'How bodies remember: social memory and bodily experience of criticism, resistance, and delegitimation following China's Cultural Revolution'. *New Literary History* 25, 3: 707–23.

Kolko, Gabriel (1997). *Vietnam: Anatomy of a Peace*. London: Routledge.

Konstantinov, Yulian; Gideon M. Kressel, and Trond Thuen (1998). 'Outclassed by former outcasts: petty trading in Varna'. *American Ethnologist* 25, 4: 729–45.

Koriat, Asher, and Morris Goldsmith (1996). 'Memory metaphors and the real-life/laboratory controversy: correspondence versus storehouse conceptions of memory'. *Behavioural and Brain Sciences* 19: 67–228.

Kraus, R.C. (1981). *Class Conflict in Chinese Socialism*. New York: Columbia University Press.

Kuisel, Richard F. (1993). *Seducing the French: The Dilemma of Americanization*. Berkeley and Los Angeles: University of California Press.

Kürti, L. (1990). 'People vs the State: political rituals in contemporary Hungary'. *Anthropology Today* 6, 2: 5–8.

Kwon, Heonik (2006). *After the Massacre: Commemoration and Consolation in Ha My and My Lai*. Berkeley, Los Angeles and London: University of California Press.

(2007). 'The dollarization of Vietnamese ghost money'. *Journal of the Royal Anthropological Institute* (n.s.) 13, 1: 73–90.

Kwong, J. (1994). 'Ideological crisis among China's youths: values and official ideology'. *British Journal of Sociology* 45, 2: 247–64.

Lambek, M. (1996). 'The past imperfect: remembering as moral practice', in P. Antze and M. Lambek (eds.), *Tense Past. Cultural Essays in Trauma and Memory*. London and New York: Routledge, pp. 235–54.

Lamont, M. and Lareau, A. (1988). 'Cultural capital: allusions, gaps and glissandos in recent theoretical developments'. *Sociological Theory* 6, 2: 153–68.

Lampland, M. (1991). 'Pigs, party secretaries, and private lives in Hungary'. *American Ethnologist* 18, 3: 459–79.

Larcher-Goscha, Agathe (2003). 'Sport, colonialisme et identités nationales: premières approches du 'corps à corps colonial' en Indochine (1918–1945)', in Nicolas Bancel, D. Denis and Y. Fates (eds.), *De l'Indochine à l'Algérie. La jeunesse en mouvements des deux côtés du miroir colonial 1940–1962*. Paris: Editions la Découverte, pp. 15–30.

Larson, P.M. (1997). 'Capacities and modes of thinking: intellectual engagements and subaltern hegemony in the early history of Malagasy Christianity'. *American Historical Review* 102, 4: 969–1002.

Le Cao Dai (2006). *C'était au Tay Nguyen: Journal de guerre d'un chirugien nord-vietnamien 1965–1973*. Hanoi: The Gioi.

Le Duan (1964). *Some Questions Concerning the International Tasks of our Party: Speech at the Third Plenum of the Ninth Central Committee of the Viet Nam Workers' Party*. Peking: Foreign Languages Press, at www.vietnam.ttu.edu/.

(1965). *On the Socialist Revolution in Vietnam*. Vol. I. Hanoi: Foreign Languages Publishing House, at www.marxists.org/reference/archive/le_duan/works/.

(1977). *Selected Writings*. Hanoi: Foreign Languages Publishing House.

Lee, Hong Yung (1975). 'The radical students in Kwangtung during the Cultural Revolution'. *China Quarterly* 64: 645–83.

Lee, Leo Ou-fan (1999). *Shanghai Modern: The Flowering of a New Urban Culture in China, 1930–1945*. Cambridge, MA: Harvard University Press.

(2000). 'The cultural construction of modernity in urban Shanghai', in W. Yeh (ed.), *Becoming Chinese: Passages to Modernity and Beyond*. Berkeley, Los Angeles and London: University of California Press, pp. 32–61.

Lemon, Alaina (1998). '"Your eyes are green like dollars": counterfeit cash, national substance, and currency apartheid in 1990s Russia'. *Cultural Anthropology* 13, 1: 22–55.

Leroy, J. (1955). *Un homme dans la rizière*. Paris: Editions de Paris.

Leshkowich, A.M. (2003). 'The ao dai goes global: how international influences and female entrepreneurs have shaped Vietnam's "national costume"', in S. Niessen, A.M. Leshkowich and C. Jones (eds.), *Re-Orienting Fashion: The Globalization of Asian Dress*. Oxford and New York: Berg Publishers.

(2006). 'Woman, Buddhist, entrepreneur: gender, moral values and class anxiety in late socialist Vietnam'. *Journal of Vietnamese Studies* 1, 1/2: 277–313.

Lessard, M.R. (2003). '"We know...the duties we must fulfill": modern "mothers and fathers" of the Vietnamese nation'. *French Colonial History* 3: 119–42.

Le Thi (1999). *The Role of the Family in the Formation of Vietnamese Personality*. Hanoi: The Gioi.

Li, T.M. (1998). 'Working separately but eating together: personhood, property, and power in conjugal relations'. *American Ethnologist* 25, 4: 675–94.

Lieberman, Victor (1997). 'Transcending East–West dichotomies: state and culture formation in six ostensibly disparate areas'. *Modern Asian Studies* 31, 3: 463–546.

Liechty, M. (2003). *Suitably Modern: Making Middle-Class Culture in a New Consumer Society*. Princeton, NJ: Princeton University Press.

Linger, Daniel T. (1993). 'The hegemony of discontent'. *American Ethnologist* 20, 1: 3–24.

Litzinger, R.A. (1998). 'Memory work: reconstituting the ethnic in post-Mao China'. *Cultural Anthropology* 13, 2: 224–55.

(2002). 'Theorizing postsocialism: reflections on the politics of marginality in contemporary China'. *South Atlantic Quarterly* 101, 1: 33–55.

Liu, Xin (2000). *In One's Own Shadow: An Ethnographic Account of the Condition of Post-Reform Rural China*. Berkeley: University of California Press.

Logan, William S. (1995). 'Russians on the Red River: the Soviet impact on Hanoi's townscape, 1955–90'. *Europe–Asia Studies* 47, 3: 443–68.

(2000) *Hanoi. Biography of a City*. Singapore: Select.

Low, D.A. (1996). *The Egalitarian Moment: Asia and Africa, 1950–80*. Cambridge: Cambridge University Press.

Lu, Xing-Hua (2005). 'Political representation within the libidinal economy of a pictorial space: a political-semiotic reading of three propaganda posters of the Chinese Cultural Revolution'. *Semiotica* 157, 1–4: 213–32.

Lucas, C. (1988). 'The crowd and politics between "ancien regime" and revolution in France'. *Journal of Modern History*. 60, 3: 421–57.

Ludden, David (1985). *Peasant History in South India*. Princeton: Princeton University Press.

(1992). 'India's development regime', in Nicholas Dirks (ed.), *Colonialism and Culture*. Ann Arbor: University of Michigan Press, pp. 247–87.

Luong Xuan Doan (ed.) (2006). *Vu Giang Huong. Tac Pham Hoi Hoa va Do Hoa* [Vu Giang Huong: Paintings and Graphics]. Hanoi: NXB My Thuat.

Macfarlane, Alan (1986). *Marriage and Love in England. Modes of Reproduction 1300–1840*. Oxford: Basil Blackwell.

Madan, T.N. (1987). 'Secularism in its place'. *Journal of Asian Studies* 46, 4: 747–59.

Malarney, S.K. (1996a). 'The emerging cult of Ho Chi Minh? A report on religious innovation in contemporary northern Viet Nam'. *Asian Cultural Studies* 22, 3: 121–31.

(1996b). 'The limits of state functionalism and the recontruction of funerary ritual in contemporary northern Vietnam'. *American Ethnologist* 23, 3: 540–60.

(1997). 'Culture, virtue and political transformation in contemporary northern Vietnam'. *Journal of Asian Studies* 56, 4: 899–920.

(1998). 'State stigma, family prestige and the development of commerce in the Red River delta of Vietnam', in R.W. Hefner (ed.), *Market Cultures: Society and Morality in the New Asian Capitalisms*. Boulder and Oxford: Westview Press, pp.268–89.

(2002). *Culture, Ritual and Revolution in Vietnam*. Honolulu: University of Hawai'i Press.

Malkki, L. (1992). 'National geographic: the rooting of peoples and the territorialization of national identity among scholars and refugees'. *Cultural Anthropology* 7, 1: 24–44.

Mani, Lata (1998). *Contentious Traditions: The Debate on Sati in Colonial India*. Berkeley: University of California Press.

Mannoni, Octave (1950) *Psychologie de la Colonisation*. Paris: Editions Universitaires.

Marcus, George E. and P.D. Hall (1992). *Lives in Trust: The Fortunes of Dynastic Families in Late Twentieth-Century America*. Boulder: Westview Press.

Marglin, Stephen Alan (1990). 'Towards the decolonization of the mind', in Frédérique Apffel-Marglin and Stephen Alan Marglin (eds.), *Dominating Knowledge. Development, Culture and Resistance*. Oxford: Clarendon Press, pp.1–28.

Marr, D. (1971). *Vietnamese Anticolonialism, 1885–1925*. Berkeley: University of California Press.

(1993). 'Education, research and information circulation in contemporary Vietnam', in William S. Turley and Mark Seldon (eds.), *Reinventing Vietnamese Socialism: Doi Moi in Comparative Perspective*. Boulder: Westview Press, pp.337–8.

(1981). *Vietnamese Tradition on Trial, 1920–1945*. Berkeley: University of California Press.

(1995a). *Vietnam 1945: The Quest for Power*. Berkeley: University of California Press.

(1995b). 'Ho Chi Minh's independence declaration', in K.W. Taylor and J.K. Whitmore (eds.), *Essays into Vietnamese Pasts*. Ithaca, NY: Cornell University Press, pp.221–31.

(2000). 'Concepts of "individual" and "self" in twentieth-century Vietnam'. *Modern Asian Studies* 34, 4: 769–96.

(2003). 'A passion for modernity: intellectuals and the media', in Hy Van Luong (ed.), *Postwar Vietnam: Dynamics of a Transforming Society*. Singapore: Institute of Southeast Asian Studies, pp.257–95.

Marr, David G. and Christine P. White (eds.) (1998). *Postwar Vietnam: Dilemmas in Socialist Development*. Ithaca: Cornell University Press.

Marsden, M. (2005). *Living Islam: Muslim Religious Experience in Pakistan's North-West Frontier.* Cambridge: Cambridge University Press.

Martin, R. (1975). 'The socialization of children in China and on Taiwan: an analysis of elementary school textbooks'. *China Quarterly* 62: 242–62.

McConnell, Scott (1989). *Leftward Journey: The Education of Vietnamese Students in France 1919–1939.* New Brunswick: Transaction Publishers.

McElwee, Pamela D. (2005). '"There is nothing that is difficult": history and hardship on and after the Ho Chi Minh Trail in North Vietnam'. *Asia Pacific Journal of Anthropology* 6, 3: 197–214.

McHale, S. (2002). 'Vietnamese Marxism, dissent, and the politics of postcolonial memory: Tran Duc Thao, 1946–1993'. *Journal of Asian Studies* 61, 1: 7–31.

   (2004). *Print and Power: Confucianism, Communism and Buddhism in the Making of Modern Vietnam.* Honolulu: University of Hawai'i Press.

McIntyre, K. (1996). 'Geography as destiny: cities, villages and Khmer Rouge Orientalism'. *Comparative Studies in Society and History.* 38, 4: 730–58.

Memmi, Albert (1957). *Portrait du colonisé précedé du portrait du colonisateur.* Paris: Buchet-Chastel.

Menon, Ritu and Kamla Bhasin (1998). *Borders and Boundaries: Women in India's Partition.* Brunswick, NJ: Rutgers University Press.

Meyerhoff, M. (2002). 'A vanishing act: Tonkinese migrant labour in Vanuatu in the early 20th century'. *Journal of Pacific History* 37, 1: 45–56.

Miller, Daniel and Mukulika Banerjee (2004). *The Sari.* Oxford: Berg.

Mills, M.B. (1997). 'Contesting the margins of modernity: women, migration and consumption in Thailand'. *American Ethnologist* 24, 1: 37–61.

Mitchell, Timothy (1988). *Colonising Egypt.* Berkeley: University of California Press.

Mitra, Subrata Kumar (1991). 'Desecularising the state: religion and politics in India after Independence'. *Comparative Studies in Society and History.* 33, 4: 755–77.

Mitter, Rana (2004). *A Bitter Revolution. China's Struggle with the Modern World.* Oxford: Oxford University Press.

Moïse, E. (1983) *Land Reform in China and North Vietnam: Consolidating The Revolution at the Village Level.* Chapel Hill: University of North Carolina Press.

Monnais, Laurence and Noémi Tousignant (2006). 'The colonial life of pharmaceuticals: accessibility to healthcare, consumption of medicines, and medical pluralism in French Vietnam, 1905–1945'. *Journal of Vietnamese Studies* 1, 1/2: 131–66.

Moore, Sally Falk (2005). 'Comparisons: possible and impossible'. *Annual Review of Anthropology* 34: 1–11.

Nanda, Meera (2003). *Prophets Facing Backward: Postmodern Critiques of Science and Hindu Nationalism in India.* New Brunswick, NJ, and London: Rutgers University Press.

Nandy, Ashis (1988). 'The politics of secularism and the recovery of religious tolerance'. *Alternatives* 13, 2: 177–94.

Narine, Shaun (1998). 'ASEAN and the management of regional security'. *Pacific Affairs* 71, 2: 195–214.

Navaro-Yashin, Yael (2005). 'Confinement and the imagination: sovereignty and subjectivity in a quasi-state', in Thomas Blom Hansen and Finn Stepputtat (eds.), *Sovereign Bodies: Citizens, Migrants and States in the Post-colonial World*. Princeton, NJ: Princeton University Press, pp. 103–19.

  (2007). 'Make-believe papers, legal forms and the counterfeit. Affective interactions between people and documents in Britain and Cyprus': *Anthropological Theory* 7, 1: 79–98.

Nehru, J. (1956). *The Discovery of India*. London: Asia Publishing House.

Nguyen Bac (2004). *Au coeur de la ville captive: souvenirs d'un agent du Viet-Minh infiltré à Hanoi*, trans. Philippe Papin. Paris: Arléa.

Nguyen Khac (2004). *Renowned Vietnamese Intellectuals prior to the 20th century*. Hanoi: The Gioi.

Nguyen Kim Nu Hanh (2003). *Tiep Buoc Chan Cha. Hoi Ky ve Giao Su Nguyen Van Huyen* [Following in our father's footsteps. Nguyen Van Huyen in his children's memory]. Hanoi: The Gioi.

Nguyen The Anh (1998). 'Japanese food policies and the 1945 Great Famine in Indochina', in Paul H. Kratoska (ed.), *Food Supplies and the Japanese Occupation in South-East Asia*. Houndmills: Macmillan, pp. 208–26.

  (2002a). 'From Indra to Maitreya: Buddhist influence in Vietnamese political thought'. *Journal of Southeast Asian Studies* 33, 2: 225–41.

  (2002b). 'Formulation of the national discourse in 1940–41 Vietnam'. *Journal of International and Area Studies* 9, 1: 57–75.

Nguyen Thi Dinh (1976). *No Other Road to Take: Memoir of Mrs Nguyen Thi Dinh* (trans. Mai Elliot). Ithaca, NY: Cornell University Press.

Nguyen Thuy Kha (ed.) (2002). *Hat Mai Khuc Quan Hanh. Tong Tap Cac Bai Hat Ve Nguoi Linh* [Sing Forever – Soldiers' Marching Songs. A Collection of Soldiers' Songs]. Hanoi: NXB Thanh Nien.

Nguyen Van Huyen. (1994). *La civilisation ancienne du Vietnam*. Hanoi: The Gioi.

Nguyen Van Ky (1995). *La société Vietnamienne face à la modernité. Le Tonkin de la fin du XIXè siècle à la Seconde Guerre Mondiale*. Paris: L'Harmattan.

Nhu Phong (1962). 'Intellectuals, writers and artists'. *China Quarterly* 9: 47–69.

Ninh, Kim Ngoc Bao (2002). *A World Transformed: The Politics of Culture in Revolutionary Vietnam, 1945–1965*. Ann Arbor: University of Michigan Press.

Nordholt, H.S. (ed.) (1997). *Outward Appearances. Dressing State and Society in Indonesia*. Leiden, Netherlands: KITLV Press.

O'Hanlon, Rosalind (1985). *Caste, Conflict and Ideology: Mahatma Jotirao Phule and Low Caste Protest in Nineteenth-Century Western India*. Cambridge: Cambridge University Press.

Ohnuki-Tierney, Emiko (1994). 'Brain death and organ transplantation: cultural bases of medical technology'. *Current Anthropology* 35, 3: 233–54.

Ong, A. (1990). 'State versus Islam: Malay families, women's bodies, and the body politic in Malaysia'. *American Ethnologist* 17, 2: 258–76.

  (1991). 'The gender and labor politics of postmodernity'. *Annual Review of Anthropology* 20: 279–309.

(1999). *Flexible Citizenship: The Cultural Logics of Transnationality* Durham, NC: Duke University Press.

Orlove, Benjamin S. (1991). 'Mapping reeds and reading maps: the politics of representation in Lake Titicaca'. *American Ethnologist* 18, 1: 3–38.

Orlove, B. (ed.) (1997). *The Allure of the Foreign: Imported Goods in Postcolonial Latin America.* Ann Arbor: University of Michigan Press.

Oxfeld, Ellen (1992). 'Individualism, holism, and the market mentality: notes on the recollections of a Chinese entrepreneur'. *Cultural Anthropology* 7, 3: 267–300.

Pandey, G. (2002). 'The long life of rumour'. *Alternatives: Global, Local and Political* 27, 2: 165–93.

Pandian, M.S.S. (2007). *Brahmin and Non-Brahmin: Genealogies of the Tamil Political Present.* New Delhi: Permanent Black.

Pantham, Thomas (1997). 'Indian secularism and its critics: some reflections'. *Review of Politics* 59, 3: 528–40.

Papanek, H. and Schwede, L. (1988). 'Women are good with money: earning and managing in an Indonesian city', in D. Dwyer and J. Bruce (eds.), *A Home Divided: Women and Income in the Third World.* Stanford: Stanford University Press, pp. 71–98.

Papin, P. (2001). *Histoire de Hanoi.* Paris: Fayard.

Parish, S. (1991). 'The sacred mind: Newar cultural representations of mental life and the production of moral consciousness'. *Ethos* 19, 3: 313–51.

Parry, Jonathan (1989). 'On the moral perils of exchange', in M. Bloch and J. Parry (eds.). *Money and the Morality of Exchange.* Cambridge: Cambridge University Press, pp. 64–93.

(2001). 'Ankalu's errant wife: sex, marriage and industry in contemporary Chhattisgarh'. *Modern Asian Studies* 35, 4: 783–820.

(2003). 'Nehru's dream and the village "waiting room": long-distance labour migrants to a central Indian steel town'. *Contributions to Indian Sociology* 37, 1/2: 217–49.

Passerini, L. (ed.) (2005). *Memory and Totalitarianism.* London and New Brunswick: Transaction Publishers.

Patsiorkovsky, Valeri; Stephen S. Fugita and David J. O'Brien (1995). 'Asians in small business in the Russian Far East: a historical overview and comparison with Asians on the American West Coast'. *International Migration Review* 29, 2: 566–75.

Pedersen, Jean Elisabeth (1998). 'Special customs: paternity suits and citizenship in France and the colonies, 1870–1912', in Julia Clancy-Smith and Frances Gouda (eds.), *Domesticating the Empire: Race, Gender and Family Life in French and Dutch Colonialism.* Charlottesville: University of Virginia Press, pp. 43–64.

Peel, J.D.Y. (1995). 'For who hath despised the day of small things? Missionary narratives and historical anthropology'. *Comparative Studies in Society and History* 37, 3: 581–607.

Pelley, P.M. (1998). '"Barbarians and younger brothers": the remaking of race in postcolonial Vietnam'. *Journal of South East Asian Studies* 29, 2: 374–91.

(2002). *Postcolonial Vietnam: New Histories of the National Past.* Durham, NC: Duke University Press.

Pels, R. (1995). 'Knowledge politics and anti-politics: toward a critical appraisal of Bourdieu's concept of intellectual autonomy'. *Theory and Society* 24, 1: 79–104.

Perera, Nihil (2002). 'Indigenising the colonial city: late nineteenth-century Colombo and its landscape', *Urban Studies* 39, 9: 1703–21.

Pettus, Ashley (2003). *Between Sacrifice and Desire: National Identity and the Governing of Femininity in Vietnam.* London and New York: Routledge.

Pham Ngoc Truong and Trung Son (1987). *The Vietnamese Documentary Film.* Hanoi: Foreign Languages Publishing House.

Pham Thu Thuy (2003). 'Speaking pictures: *Biem hoa* or satirical cartoons on government corruption', in L.Drummond and M.Thomas (eds.), *Consuming Urban Culture in Contemporary Vietnam.* London: Routledge, pp.89–109.

Pham Van Bich (1999). *The Vietnamese Family in Change: The Case of the Red River Delta.* Richmond: Curzon.

Pham Van Dong (1990). *President Ho Chi Minh: A Man, a Nation, an Age and a Cause.* Hanoi: Foreign Languages Publishing House, at www.nhandan.com. vn./english/news/120505/history.

Phan Dai Doan and Nguyen Quang Nuoc (2002). 'The relationship between village, family clan and traditional family in the Red River Delta'. *Vietnamese Studies* n.s. 3: 36–52.

Pieke, F.N. (1995). 'Bureaucracy, friends, and money: the growth of capital socialism in China'. *Comparative Studies in Society and History* 37, 3: 494–518.

Pike, Douglas (1978). *History of Vietnamese Communism, 1925–1976.* Stanford: Hoover Institution Press.

Pinney, C. (1995). 'Moral topophilia: the significance of landscape in Indian oleographs', in Eric Hirsch and Michael O'Hanlon (eds.), *The Anthropology of Landscape: Perspectives on Place and Space.* Oxford: Clarendon Press, pp.78–113.

Pollock, Sheldon (1998). 'The cosmopolitan vernacular'. *Journal of Asian Studies* 57, 1: 6–37.

Porter, Gareth (1994). *Vietnam: The Politics of Bureaucratic Socialism.* Ithaca: Cornell University Press.

Potter, S.H. (1988). 'The cultural construction of emotion in rural Chinese social life'. *Ethos* 16, 2: 181–208.

Potter, Sulamith Heins and Jack M. Potter (1990). *China's Peasants: The Anthropology of a Revolution.* Cambridge: Cambridge University Press.

Prakash, Gyan (1996). 'Who's afraid of postcoloniality?' *Social Text* 49: 187–203.

Prendergast, David (2005). *From Elder to Ancestor: Old Age, Death and Inheritance in Modern Korea.* Folkestone: Global Oriental.

Price, Pamela G. (1989). 'Kingly models in Indian political behaviour: culture as a medium of history'. *Asian Survey* 29, 6: 559–72.

(1996). 'Revolution and rank in Tamil nationalism'. *Journal of Asian Studies* 55, 2: 359–83.

Proschan, F. (2001). 'Peoples of the gourd: imagined ethnicities in highland southeast Asia'. *Journal of Asian Studies* 60, 4: 999–1032.

Rabinow, P. (1989). *French Modern: Norms and Forms of the Social Environment.* Cambridge, MA and London: MIT Press.

(1996). *Essays on the Anthropology of Reason.* Princeton, NJ and Chichester, UK: Princeton University Press.

Raendchen, O. (2000). *Vietnamesen in der DDR: Ein Rückblick.* Berlin: SEACOM Studien zur südostasienkunde.

Raffin, Anne (2005). *Youth Mobilization in Vichy Indochina and its Legacies, 1940–1970.* Lanham, Boulder and New York: Lexington Books.

Rahman, Md. Mahbubar and Willem van Schendel (2003). '"I am *not* a refugee": rethinking partition migration'. *Modern Asian Studies* 37, 3: 551–84.

Ramaswamy, S. (1993). 'En/gendering language: the poetics of Tamil identity'. *Comparative Studies in Society and History* 35, 4: 683–725.

(1997). *Passions of the Tongue: Language Devotion in Tamil India, 1891–1970.* Berkeley and London: University of California Press.

Rato, Montira (2004). 'Class, nation and text: the representation of peasants in Vietnamese literature', in Philip Taylor (ed.), *Social Inequality in Vietnam and the Challenges to Reform.* Singapore: Institute of Southeast Asian Studies, pp.325–50.

Raychaudhuri, T. (2000). 'Love in a colonial climate: marriage, sex and romance in nineteenth-century Bengal'. *Modern Asian Studies* 3, 2: 349–78.

Reid, S.E. (2002). 'Khrushchev's children's paradise: the Pioneer Palace, Moscow, 1958–62', in David Crowley and S.E. Reid (eds.), *Socialist Spaces: Sites of Everyday Life in the Eastern Bloc.* Oxford and New York: Berg, pp.141–80.

Riegel, Klaus Georg (2002). 'Divided commitment: East German socialist intellectuals and their attitudes towards the reunification with West Germany'. *Development and Society* 31, 1: 53–78.

Ries, Nancy (1997). *Russian Talk: Culture and Conversation During Perestroika.* Ithaca: Cornell University Press.

Riley, N.E. (1994). 'Interwoven lives: parents, marriage, and *guanxi* in China'. *Journal of Marriage and the Family* 56, 4: 791–803.

Rodgers, S. (1995). *Telling Lives, Telling History: Autobiography and Historical Imagination in Modern Indonesia.* Berekeley and London: University of California Press.

Rofel, Lisa (1999). *Other Modernities: Gendered Yearnings in China After Socialism.* Berkeley and Los Angeles: University of California Press.

Rosenthal, Mila (2002). 'Facing a new revolution in Vietnam: state textile workers in the post-reform economy', in D.S. Gills and N. Piper (eds.), *Women and Work in Globalising Asia.* London and New York: Routledge, pp. 112–30.

Roth, K. (1990). 'Socialist life-cycle rituals in Bulgaria'. *Anthropology Today.* 6, 5: 8–10.

Ruane, Kevin (1998). *War and Revolution in Vietnam, 1930–75.* London: UCL Press.

Rudolph, L. (1997). 'Self as other: Amar Singh's diary as reflexive "native" ethnography'. *Modern Asian Studies* 31, 1: 143–75.

Rudolph, L.I. and S.H. Rudolph (1987). *In Pursuit of Lakshmi: The Political Economy of the Indian State*. Delhi: Orient Longman.

Rudolph, Suzanne Hoeber and Lloyd Rudolph (eds.), with Mohan Singh Kanota (2000). *Reversing the Gaze: Amar Singh's Diary: A Colonial Subject's Narrative of Imperial India*. Delhi and New York: Oxford University Press.

Ruscio, Alain (1986). *Dien Bien Phu: La fin d'une illusion*. Paris: L'Harmattan.

Rydstrøm, H. (2003). *Embodying Morality: Growing Up in Rural Northern Vietnam*. Honolulu: University of Hawai'i Press.

Salemink, Oscar (2003). *The Ethnography of Vietnam's Central Highlanders: A Historical Contextualization, 1850–1990*. London and New York: Routledge Curzon.

Sarkar, S. (1973). *The Swadeshi Movement in Bengal: 1903–1908*. New Delhi: People's Publishing House.

(2002). *Beyond Nationalist Frames: Relocating Postmodernism, Hindutva, History*. New Delhi: Permanent Black.

Sato, Barbara (2003). *The New Japanese Woman: Modernity, Media, and Women in Interwar Japan*. Durham, NC: Duke University Press.

Schlecker, M. (2002). 'A problem of trust: educatedness and cultivatedness in Hanoi'. Unpublished Ph.D. dissertation, Cambridge University.

(2005). 'Going back a long way: "Home place", thrift and temporal orientations in Northern Vietnam'. *Journal of the Royal Anathropological Institute* 11, 3: 509–26.

Schwarcz, V. (1986). 'Behind a partially-open door: Chinese intellectuals and the post-Mao reform process'. *Pacific Affairs*. 59, 4: 577–604.

(1994). 'Strangers no more: personal memory in the interstices of public commemoration', in Rubie Watson (ed.), *Memory, History, and Opposition under State Socialism*. Santa Fe: SAR Press, pp.45–64.

Schwenkel, C. (2006). 'Recombinant history: transnational practices of memory and knowledge production in contemporary Vietnam'. *Cultural Anthropology* 21, 1: 3–30.

Scott, James (1998). *Seeing Like a State: How Certain Schemes to Improve the Human Condition Have Failed*. New Haven: Yale University Press.

Selim, M. (2003). *Pouvoirs et marché au Vietnam. Les morts et l'Etat*, vol. II. Paris: L'Harmattan.

Sen, Amartya (1993). 'The threats to secular India'. *Social Scientist* 21, 3–4: 5–23.

(2005). *The Argumentative Indian: Writings on Indian History, Culture and Identity*. London: Penguin.

Seymour, S. (1999). *Women, Family, and Child Care in India: A World in Transition*. Cambridge: Cambridge University Press.

Shabad, T. (1958). 'Economic developments in North Vietnam'. *Pacific Affairs* 31, 1: 36–53.

Sharp, L.A. (2002). *The Sacrificed Generation: Youth, History and the Colonized Mind in Madagascar*. Berkeley and Los Angeles: University of California Press.

Shih, S. (1996). 'Gender, race and semicolonialism: Liu Na'ou's urban Shanghai landscape'. *Journal of Asian Studies* 55, 4: 934–56.

Siegel, J. T. (1997). *Fetish, Recognition, Revolution*. Princeton, NJ and Chichester, UK: Princeton University Press.

Simic, Andrei (1983). 'Machismo and cryptomatriarchy: power, affect, and authority in the contemporary Yugoslav family'. *Ethos* 11, 1/2: 66–86.

Skultans, V. (1997). 'Theorizing Latvian lives: the quest for identity'. *Journal of the Royal Anthropological Institute* (ns) 3, 4: 761–80.

(1998). *The Testimony of Lives: Narrative and Memory in Post-Soviet Latvia*. London and New York: Routledge.

Slezkine, Y. (2000). 'Commentary: imperialism as the highest stage of socialism'. *Russian Review* 59, 2: 227–34.

Slyomovics, S. (1995). '"Hassiba Ben Bouali, if you could see our Algeria": women and public space in Algeria'. *Middle East Report* 192: 8–13.

Smart, A. (1993). 'Gifts, bribes and *guanxi*: a reconsideration of Bourdieu's social capital'. *Cultural Anthropology* 8, 3: 388–408.

Smith, C. D. (1980). 'The intellectual and modernization – definitions and reconsiderations: the Egyptian experience'. *Comparative Studies in Society and History* 22, 4: 513–33.

Smith, J. H. (1998). 'Njama's supper: the consumption and use of literary potency by Mau Mau insurgents in colonial Kenya'. *Comparative Studies in Society and History* 40, 3: 524–48.

Smith, R. B. (1972). 'The Vietnamese élite of French Cochinchina, 1943'. *Modern Asian Studies* 6, 4: 459–82.

(1978). 'The work of the provisional government of Vietnam, August– December 1945'. *Modern Asian Studies* 12, 4: 571–609.

(1996). 'Vietnam from the 1890s to the 1990s: continuity and change in the longer perspective'. *South East Asia Research* 4, 2: 197–224.

Somers, Margaret R. (1994). 'The narrative constitution of identity: a relational and network approach'. *Theory and Society* 23, 5: 605–49.

Spitta, S. (1995). *Between Two Waters. Narratives of Transculturation in Latin America*. Houston: Rice University Press.

Spivak, G. C. (1985). 'Three women's texts and a critique of imperialism'. *Critical Inquiry* 12, 1: 243–61.

(1988). 'Can the subaltern speak?' in C. Nelson and L. Grossberg (eds.), *Marxism and the Interpretation of Culture*. Urbana and Chicago: University of Illinois Press, pp. 271–313.

Spodek, Howard (1974). 'Rulers, merchants and other groups in the city-states of Saurashtra, India, around 1800'. *Comparative Studies in Society and History* 16, 4: 448–70.

Srivastava, S. (1998). *Constructing Post-Colonial India: National Character and the Doon School*. London and New York: Routledge.

Ssorin-Chaikov, N. (2003). *The Social Life of the State in Subarctic Siberia*. Stanford: Stanford University Press.

(2006). 'On heterochrony: birthday gifts to Stalin, 1949'. *Journal of the Royal Anthropological Institute* (ns) 12, 2: 355–75.

Ssorin-Chaikov, N. and Olga Sosnina (2006). 'The archaeology of power / the anatomy of love', in Ssorin-Chaikov and Sosnina, (eds.), *Gifts to Soviet Leaders*. Moscow: Pinakotheke and the Kremlin Museum, pp. 12–37.

Stafford, C. (1992). 'Good sons and virtuous mothers: kinship and Chinese nationalism in Taiwan'. *Man* 27, 2: 363–78.

(1995). *The Roads of Chinese Childhood. Learning and Identification in Angang.* Cambridge: Cambridge University Press.

(2000). *Separation and Reunion in Modern China.* Cambridge: Cambridge University Press.

Stoler, A.L. (2002). *Carnal Knowledge and Imperial Power: Race and the Intimate in Colonial Rule.* Berkeley: University of California Press.

(2004). 'Affective states', in David Nugent and Joan Vincent, (eds.), *A Companion to the Anthropology of Politics.* Oxford: Blackwell, pp. 4–20.

(forthcoming). *Along the Archival Grain: Thinking through Colonial Ontologies.* Princeton, N.J.: Princeton University Press.

Stoler, A.L. and K. Strassler (2000). 'Casting for the colonial: memory work in "New Order" Java'. *Comparative Studies in Society and History* 42, 1: 4–48.

Sullivan, Michael (1999). 'Art in China since 1949'. *China Quarterly* 159: 712–22.

Sutherland, Claire (2005), 'Represssion and resistance? French colonialism as seen through Vietnamese museums'. *Museum and Society* 3, 3: 153–66.

Sutton, Donald S. (1995). 'Consuming counterrevolution: the ritual and culture of cannibalism in Wuxuan, Guangxi, China, May to July 1968', *Comparative Studies in Society and History* 31, 1: 136–72.

Svasek, Maruska (2000). 'Borders and emotions: hope and fear in the Bohemian-Bavarian frontier zone'. *Ethnologia Europaea* 30, 2: 111–26.

(2003). 'Property, power, and emotions', in D. Torsello and M. Pappova (eds.), *Social Networks in Movement. Time, Interaction, and Inter-ethnic Spaces in Central Eastern Europe.* Samorin: Lilium Aurum, pp. 229–54.

Swedenberg, Ted (2003). *Memories of Revolt: The 1936–1939 Rebellion and the Palestinian National Past.* Fayetteville: University of Arkansaw Press.

Szelenyi, I. (1982). 'The intelligentsia in the class structure of state-socialist societies'. *American Journal of Sociology* 88, Supplement: *Marxist Inquiries: Studies of Labor, Class and States*: S287–S326.

Szelenyi, I. and S. Szelenyi (1995). 'Circulation or reproduction of elites during the postcommunist transformation of Eastern Europe'. *Theory and Society* 24, 5: 615–38.

Tai, Hue Tam Ho (1992). *Radicalism and the Origins of the Vietnamese Revolution.* Cambridge, MA: Harvard.

(2001). 'Faces of remembrance and forgetting', in Hue Tam Ho Tai (ed.). *The Country of Memory.* Berkeley: University of California, pp. 167–95.

Tarlo, Emma (1996). *Clothing Matters: Dress and Identity in India.* London: Hurst and Co.

(2003). *Unsettling Memories: Narratives of India's Emergency.* Delhi: Permanent Black.

Taylor, K. (1991). *The Birth of Vietnam.* Berkeley and London: University of California Press.

(1998). 'Surface orientations in Vietnam: beyond histories of the nation and region', *Journal of Asian Studies* 57, 4: 949–78.

Taylor, N.A. (1997). 'The politics of painting in colonial Vietnam 1925–1945', *Crossroads: An Interdisciplinary Journal of Southeast Asian Studies* 11, 2: 1–33.

(2001). 'Framing the national spirit: viewing and reviewing painting under the revolution', in Hue Tam Ho Tai (ed.), *The Country of Memory*. Berkeley: University of California, pp. 109–34.

(2004). *Painters in Hanoi: An Ethnography of Vietnamese Art*. Honolulu: University of Hawaii Press.

Taylor, Philip (2001). *Fragments of the Present: Searching for Modernity in Vietnam's South*. Honolulu: University of Hawai'i Press.

(2004). 'Spirits, iconoclasts and the borders of the market in urban Vietnam'. *Humanities Research* 11, 1: 8–23.

Tessier, Olivier (2002). 'Commuting from the village to the city: analyzing patterns of migration of the people of the northern village of Hay to Hanoi', in G. Bousquet and P. Brocheux (eds.), *Viêt-Nam Exposé: French Scholarship on Twentieth-Century Vietnamese Society*. Ann Arbor: University of Michigan Press. pp. 387–420.

Thayer, Carlyle (1994a). *The Vietnam People's Army Under Doi Moi*. Singapore: Institute of Southeast Asian Studies.

(1994b). 'Sino-Vietnamese relations: the interplay of ideology and national interest'. *Asian Survey* 34, 6: 513–28.

(1995). *Beyond Indochina: Indochina's Transition from Socialist Central Planning to Market-Oriented Economics and its Integration into South-East Asia*. London: Oxford University Press.

Thomas, M. (2001). 'Public spaces/public disgraces: crowds and the state in contemporary Vietnam'. *Sojourn* 16, 2: 306–30.

(2003). 'Spatiality and political change in urban Vietnam'. in L. Drummond and M. Thomas (eds.), *Consuming Urban Culture in Contemporary Vietnam*. London: Routledge, pp. 170–88.

Thompson, C. M. (2003). 'Medicine, nationalism and revolution in Vietnam: the roots of a medical collaboration to 1945', *East Asian Science, Technology and Medicine* 21: 114–48.

Thurston, Robert W. (1991). 'The Soviet family during the Great Terror, 1935–1941'. *Soviet Studies* 43 3: 553–74.

To Ngoc Thanh (2004). *Nho To Ngoc Van* [In memory of To Ngoc Van]. Hanoi: NXB My Thuat.

To Ngoc Thanh (ed.) (2006). *To Ngoc Van (1906–1954)*. Hanoi: NXB My Thuat.

Tonkin, Elizabeth (1992). *Narrating our Pasts: The Social Construction of Oral History*. Cambridge: Cambridge University Press.

Tönnesson, S. (2001). 'Le Duan and the Break with China'. *Cold War International History Project Bulletin* Issue 12–13, at wwics.si.edu/topics/pubs/ACF37.pdf.

Tran May-Van (1999). 'Japan through Vietnamese eyes (1905–1945)'. *Journal of Southeast Asian Studies*, 30 1: 126–46.

Tran Thi Lien (2002). 'Henriette Bui: the narrative of Vietnam's first woman doctor', in G. Bousquet and P. Brocheux (eds.), *Viêt-Nam Exposé: French Scholarship on Twentieth-Century Vietnamese Society*. Ann Arbor: University of Michigan Press, pp. 278–309.

Tran Tu [Nguyen Duc Tu Chi]. (1996). *Nguoi Muong o Hoa Binh* [The Muong People of Hoa Binh]. Hanoi: Hoi Khoa Hoc Lich Su Viet Nam.

Tran Tu Binh (1985). *The Red Earth. A Vietnamese Memoir of Life on a Colonial Rubber Plantation*, trans J. Sprangens, Jr. Athens, OH: Ohio University Centre for International Studies.

Tran Van Dinh (ed.) (1976). *This Nation and Socialism Are One: Selected Writings of Le Duan.* Chicago: Vanguard Books.

Trawick, M. (1990). *Notes on Love in a Tamil Family.* Berkeley and Oxford: University of California Press.

Trinh Van Thao (1990). *Vietnam: Du Confucianisme au Communisme.* Paris: L'Harmattan.

(1995). *L'école française en Indochine.* Paris: Editions Karthala.

(2002). 'The 1925 generation of Vietnamese intellectuals and their role in the struggle for independence', in G. Bousquet and P. Brocheux (eds.), *Viêt-Nam Exposé: French Scholarship on Twentieth-Century Vietnamese Society.* Ann Arbor: University of Michigan Press, pp. 251–77.

Trivedi, L.N. (2003). 'Visually mapping the "nation": swadeshi politics in nationalist India, 1920–30'. *Journal of Asian Studies* 62, 1: pp. 11–41.

Trouillot, Michel-Rolph (2001). 'The anthropology of the state in the age of globalization: close encounters of the deceptive kind'. *Current Anthropology* 42, 1: 125–38.

Truong Buu Lam (2000). *Colonialism Experienced: Vietnamese Writings on Colonialism, 1900–1931.* Ann Arbor: University of Michigan Press.

Turley, W.S. (1972). 'Women in the Communist Revolution in Vietnam'. *Asian Survey* 12, 9: 793–805.

(1975). 'Urbanization in war: Hanoi, 1946–1973'. *Pacific Affairs* 48 3: 370–97.

(1993). 'Party, state and people: political structure and economic prospects', in William Turley and Mark Selden, (eds.), *Reinventing Vietnamese Socialism.* Boulder: Westview Press, pp. 257–76.

Turner, Robert F. (ed.) (1975). *Vietnamese Communism: Its Origins and Development.* Stanford: Hoover Institution Press.

Turner, Sarah and Phuong An Nguyen (2005). 'Young entrepreneurs, social capital and *doi moi* in Hanoi, Vietnam' *Urban Studies* 42, 10: 1693–1710.

U, Eddy (2003). 'The making of *Zhishifenzi*: the critical impact of the registration of unemployed intellectuals in the early PRC'. *China Quarterly*, 173: 100–21.

Unger, J. (1998). 'Cultural Revolution conflict in the villages'. *China Quarterly* 153: 82–106.

Varma, P.K. (1998). *The Great Indian Middle Class.* New Delhi: Viking.

Varshney, Ashutosh (1998). *Democracy, Development and the Countryside: Urban–Rural Stuggles in India.* Cambridge: Cambridge University Press.

Vasavakul, Thaveeporn (1995). 'Vietnam: the changing models of legitimation', in Muthiah Alagappa (ed.), *Political Legitimacy in Southeast Asia: The Quest for Moral Authority.* Stanford: Stanford University Press, pp. 257–92.

Verdery, K. (1991a). *National Ideology Under Socialism: Identity and Cultural Politics in Ceausescu's Romania.* Berkeley and Los Angeles: University of California Press.

(1991b). 'Theorizing socialism: a prologue to the transition'. *American Ethnologist* 18, 3: 419–39.

(1996). *What Was Socialism and What Comes Next?* Princeton: Princeton University Press.

Vergès, Françoise (1999). *Monsters and Revolutionaries. Colonial Family Romance and Métissage.* Durham N.C.: Duke University Press.

Viswanathan, Gauri (1989). *Masks of Conquest: Literary Study and British Rule in India.* New York: Columbia University Press.

Vu An Chuong (ed.) (1994). *To Ngoc Van.* Hanoi: NXB Van Hoa.

Vu Can (1971). 'Cam Binh, the studious village'. *Vietnamese Studies* 30: 79–110.

Waibel. M. (2004). 'The ancient quarter of Hanoi: a reflection of urban transition processes'. *ASIEN: German Journal for Politics, Economy and Culture* 92, S30–S48.

Walsh, J.E. (1997). 'What women learned when men gave them advice: rewriting patriarchy in late-nineteenth-century Bengal'. *Journal of Asian Studies.* 56, 3: 641–77.

Ward, H.F. (1998). 'Worth its weight: gold, women and value in north-west India'. Unpublished Ph.D. dissertation, University of Cambridge.

Watson, J.L. (1984). *Class and Social Stratification in Post-Revolution China.* Cambridge: Cambridge University Press.

Watson, R.S. (1994). 'Making secret histories', in Rubie Watson (ed.), *Memory, History, and Opposition under State Socialism.* Santa Fe: SAR Press, pp. 1–20.

Watt, Carey A. (2005). *Serving the Nation: Cultures of Service, Association, and Citizenship in Colonial India.* New Delhi: Oxford University Press.

Weiner, J. (1997). 'Televisualist anthropology: representation, aesthetics, politics'. *Current Anthropology* 38, 2: 197–235.

Werbner, P. (1990). 'Economic rationality and hierarchical gift economies: value and ranking among British Pakistanis'. *Man* 25, 2: 266–85.

Werbner, R. (1991). *Tears of the Dead: The Social Biography of an African Family.* Edinburgh: Edinburgh University Press.

Werner, J. (2004). 'State subject-making and womanhoods in the Red River delta of Vietnam'. *Asian Studies Review* 28 2: 115–31.

West, H. (2001). 'Sorcery of construction and socialist modernization: ways of understanding power in postcolonial Mozambique'. *American Ethnologist* 28, 1: 119–50.

West, Harry and Paru Raman (eds.) (forthcoming) *Enduring Socialism: Explorations of Revolution, Transformation and Restoration.* Oxford: Berghahn Books.

White, A. (2000). 'Social change in provincial Russia: the intelligentsia in a *raion* centre'. *Europe–Asia Studies* 52, 4: 677–94.

White, D.L. (1991). 'From crisis to community definition: the dynamics of eighteenth-century Parsi philanthropy'. *Modern Asian Studies* 25, 2: 303–20.

White, Owen (2000). *Children of the French Empire.* Oxford: Clarendon.

Whyte M.K. (1996). 'The Chinese family and economic development: obstacle or engine?' *Economic Development and Culural Change* 45: 1–30.

Wilcox, Wynn (2006). 'Women, westernisation and the origins of modern Vietnamese theatre'. *Journal of Southeast Asian Studies* 37, 2: 205–24.

Winichakul, T. (1994). *Siam Mapped: A History of the Geo-Body of a Nation.* Honolulu: University of Hawai'i Press.

Winichakul, T. (2000). 'The quest for "*siwilai*": a geographical discourse of civilizational thinking in the late nineteenth and early twentieth-century Siam'. *Journal of Asian Studies* 59, 3: 528–49.

Womack, B. (1994). 'Sino-Vietnamese border trade: the edge of normalization'. *Asian Survey* 34, 6: 495–512.

(2006). *China and Vietnam: The Politics of Asymmetry.* Cambridge: Cambridge University Press.

Woodside, Alexander (1971a). 'The development of social organizations in Vietnamese cities in the late colonial period'. *Pacific Affairs* 44, 1: 39–64.

(1971b). 'Ideology and integration in post-colonial Vietnamese nationalism'. *Pacific Affairs* 44, 4: 487–510.

(1983). 'The triumphs and failures of mass education in Vietnam'. *Pacific Affairs* 56, 3: 401–27.

(1998). 'Exalting the latecomer state: intellectuals and the state during the Chinese and Vietnamese reforms'. *China Journal* 40: 9–36.

Worby, E. (2000). '"Discipline without oppression": sequence, timing and marginality in southern Rhodesia's post-war development regime'. *Journal of African History* 41, 1: 101–25.

Wright, Gwendolyn (1991). *The Politics of Design in French Colonial Urbanism.* London and Chicago: University of Chicago Press.

Yan, Yunxiang (1996a). *The Flow of Gifts. Reciprocity and Social Networks in a Chinese Village.* Stanford: Stanford University Press.

(1996b). 'The culture of *guanxi* in a north China village', *China Journal* 35: 1–25.

(2003). *Private Life under Socialism: Love, Intimacy and Family Change in a Chinese Village 1949–1999.* Stanford: Stanford University Press.

Yang, Mayfair Mei-hui (1988). 'The modernity of power in the Chinese socialist order'. *Cultural Anthropology* 3, 4: 408–27.

(1994). *Gifts, Favors and Banquets: The Art of Social Relationships in China.* Ithaca and London: Cornell University Press.

Young, R.J.C. (2001). *Postcolonialism: An Historical Introduction.* Oxford: Blackwell Publishers.

Young, S.B. (1979). 'Vietnamese Marxism: transition in elite ideology'. *Asian Survey* 19, 8: 770–9.

Yurchak, Alexei (2003). 'Soviet hegemony of form: everything was forever, until it was no more'. *Comparative Studies in Society and History* 45, 3: 480–510.

Zachariah, B. (2005). *Developing India: An Intellectual and Social History, c. 1930–50.* New Delhi: Oxford University Press.

Zachernuk, P.S. (2000). *Colonial Subjects: An African Intelligentsia and Atlantic Ideas.* Charlottesville: University of Virginia Press.

Zhou, Xueguang and Liren Hou (1999). 'Children of the Cultural Revolution: the state and the life course in the People's Republic of China'. *American Sociological Review* 64, 1: 12–36.

Zhu, Lisheng (2000). 'The problem of the intelligentsia and radicalism in higher education under Stalin and Mao'. *Europe–Asia Studies* 52, 8: 1489–513.

Zinoman, Peter (2001a). *The Colonial Bastille: A History of Imprisonment in Vietnam 1862–1940.* Berkeley and Los Angeles: University of California Press.

(2001b). 'Reading revolutionary prison memoirs', in Hue-Tam Ho Tai (ed.), *The Country of Memory: Remaking the Past in Late Socialist Vietnam.* Berkeley, Los Angeles and London: University of California Press, pp. 21–45.

(2002). 'Introduction', in Zinoman and Vu Trong Phung, *Dumb Luck: A Novel by Vu Trong Phung,* trans. Peter Zinoman and Nguyen Nguyet Cam. Ann Arbor: University of Michigan Press, pp. 1–30.

Zur, Judith (1999). 'Remembering and forgetting: Guatemalan war widows' forbidden memories', in Kim Lacy Rogers and Selma Leydesdorff, with Graham Dawson (eds.), *Trauma and Life Stories: International Perspectives.* London and New York: Routledge, pp. 45–59.

Index

acupuncture, 204, 204 n. 35, 213–14
address, forms of, 28 n. 9, 56, 81, 94,
    94 n. 32, 128, 168, 175, 183, 195,
    197–8
affect, 9, 13, 24–5, 38, 51, 52, 59–60, 91,
    205
affective ties, 24–5, 38, 59–63, 91, 138,
    164, 194, 206–7, 225, 230
    of conjugality, 24, 38, 101–3, 138,
    138 n. 24, 198, 237
    of family, 20, 24–5, 32, 38, 41–2, 52, 55,
    59–61, 70–1, 81, 91–2, 175–7, 184,
    234
    of friendship, 41, 47, 57, 81, 175
    of military service, 41, 60–1, 62
    of revolutionary geography, 51, 122–3,
    131–2, 152, 155
    of schooling, 25, 41, 141, 175
Africa, 9, 17, 33, 45, 47, 131, 180, 185,
    203–4, 205 n. 36, 207, 227
    see also individual countries
Algeria, 49, 131, 169 n. 17, 181, 182 n. 7,
    188, 203–5, 213, 214, 215 n. 46,
    217–18, 218 n. 48, 223, 228, 229
Algiers, 20, 204, 205
American Declaration of Independence, 149
American products and cultural values,
    11–15, 134, 170–1, 201, 201 n. 30,
    203 n. 33
ancestor veneration, 2, 17, 20, 26 n. 4, 61,
    64, 91–2, 165 n. 12, 239
ancestral places, 48, 104, 106, 106 n. 18,
    135, 155, 156, 156 n. 4, 183 n. 9, 209
    see also que
Anderson, Perry, 74 n. 1
Angola, 18, 181, 181 n. 3, 204, 211
Antananarivo, 50
anthropology, 27 n. 6, 28, 33, 54, 94 n. 33,
    185, 223, 227, 234
antibiotics, 77, 170–1, 171 n. 20, 233
ao dai (Vietnamese women's tunic and
    trouser outfit), 2, 67, 87, 138 n. 25,
    148, 148 n. 40, 162, 163 n. 11,
    201 n. 31, 214
    see also dress
ao the (traditional Vietnamese scholar's
    gown), 133, 139 n. 27, 148
artists, xi–xii, 32 n. 17, 36, 37 n. 28,
    125 n. 3, 126 n. 6, 127 n. 8, 138, 145,
    147, 159, 208 n. 39
ASEAN (Association of Southeast Asian
    Nations), 180, 180 n. 1
Asian Co-Prosperity Sphere, 142,
    142 n. 34
Asoka, Emperor 11
atomic weapons, 170
Attwell, David, 16, 13
Au Coeur de la Ville Captive (Nguyen Bac:
    Giua thanh pho bi chien; In the Heart of
    the Captive City), 49, 50, 143
auto-cartography, 122, 131–2, 153–7, 158,
    225–6
Azad Hind (Free India) movement, 106,
    107

Ba Dinh Square, Hanoi, 84 n. 18, 144–7,
    144 n. 36, 150–1
Ba Dinh uprising, 144 n. 36, 147–8
Bac Ho ('Uncle Ho'), see Ho Chi Minh
Bahloul, J., 55
ban tho (ancestor altar), 26 n. 4, 92
    see also ancestor veneration
banias (traders, Indian), 160
    see also traders
Bao Dai, Emperor, 137 n. 22
Beatty, Andrew, 57 n. 10
Beethoven, Ludwig van 69
Bengal famine (1943), 106
Bengalis, 100, 101, 104, 106–7
'Berber Spring', 217
Berbers, 217
bhadralok ('genteel folk', Bengal), 100
Bhagavad Gita, 11

274   Index